D0518354

# A PRIMER FOR STAR-GAZERS

# A PRIMER FOR STAR-GAZERS

Henry M. Neely

*WITH STAR MAPS AND LINE DRAWINGS BY THE AUTHOR*



GRAMERCY PUBLISHING COMPANY
NEW YORK

This 1989 edition is published by Gramercy Publishing Company, distributed by Crown Publishers, Inc., 225 Park Avenue South, New York, New York 10003, by arrangement with Harper & Row, Publishers, Inc.

Printed and Bound in the United States of America

Library of Congress Cataloging-in-Publication Data

Neely, Henry M. (Henry Milton), 1877-1963.
A primer for star-gazers.

Reprint. Originally published: New York : Harper & Row, [1970].
Includes index.
1. Astronomy—Observers' manuals. I. Title.
QB63.N42 1989 523.8′903 88-34769
ISBN 0-517-67130-1
h g f e d c b a

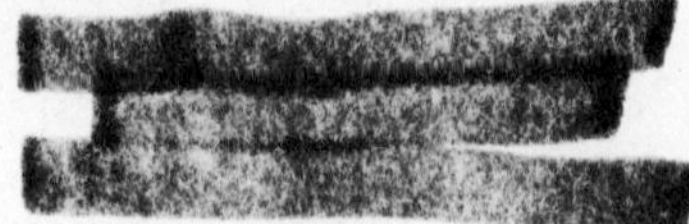

*This book is an effort to rescue the ancient love of simple star-gazing from the avalanche of mathematics and physics under which modern astronomy threatens to bury it.*

## AUTHORITIES USED IN THIS BOOK

For the benefit of any professionals who may happen to see a copy of this Primer, it may be well to list the principal authorities used in its compilation.

In the charts and pictures of the various groups all star positions (refigured for precession to 1950) are derived from the Yale *Catalogue of Bright Stars* by Schlesinger and Jenkins. Stellar magnitudes as given in that catalogue have also been used.

Star distances mentioned in the text are figured from the Yale parallaxes.

Pronunciations are given in my own phonetic spelling of the diacritical marks used in the authorized list of pronunciations adopted by the American Astronomical Society, plus a supplementary list by George A. Davis, Jr., one of the members of the committee, published in *Popular Astronomy*.

The orientation of all charts of the groups for various times has been checked for altitude and azimuth by means of the tables in H. O. 214.

# CONTENTS

## *GROUPS FOR ADVANCED STAR-GAZERS*

# PHOTOGRAPHS

## FOREWORD

EXPERTS who regard their star-gazing as a serious science will dismiss this book as suitable only for children in a kindergarten.

That will be an attitude to which I can have no objection. The book has been planned and written in the firm conviction that the average novice is appalled at the thought of attempting to understand the immensity of the stellar universe and that the kindergarten stage of his experiences should be kept strictly on the kindergarten level.

In fact, the most difficult part of writing the book was in rigidly limiting its material to that conception. This does not imply that it is a book only for children; it simply recognizes the fact that we all feel like children when we first attempt to find our way among the myriad stars.

Possibly it would be well to outline the "composite" reader for whom it is intended. This reader—

(a) knows nothing whatever about the stars.

(b) feels that the whole subject is too scientific and mathematical for him.

(c) has no intention of making a real study of it.

(d) would simply like to be able to recognize the principal stars and constellations

BUT

(e) refuses to wade through a lot of Greek letters, geometrical diagrams and trigonometrical equations just to be able to point out the Big Dipper and Polaris to the boy next door.

Star-gazing is fun.

Star-gazing is an extremely entertaining pastime and there is nothing difficult about it.

It is no more difficult than a cross-word puzzle and not

nearly so complicated as the job of learning to be a good hand at a game of bridge.

So this book has been prepared for those who want a pastime and it will leave the scientific aspects to those whose natural gifts make them receptive to the scientific approach.

## INTRODUCTION TO THE NEW EDITION

Wherever you are on this earth of ours—north or south, city or country, on the high seas or atop a mountain—there are times when you are able to see a star-studded sky. Clouds may obscure the stars much of the time, or the glow of the lights of civilization may reflect from low-hanging mist and smog, but occasionally the stars break through.

At those rare times when the sky is completely dark, the stars sparkle like jewels. There is a grandeur about them. And one feels an affinity for them, because the stars belong to everyone. No matter how humble his station, nor how limited his learning, regardless of age—all people can gaze into the nighttime sky and dream the dreams of which greatness is made.

Henry Neely knew this. He had a feeling for people; he radiated warmth, and when he spoke a rapport was established immediately. Coupled with his understanding of people was an enthusiasm for astronomy, for the stars and the subtleties of the sky. When Henry spoke to you about the stars, chances were a thousand to one that you would forever after be different—the stars would mean more than they had ever before, and you would know that you had been talking with a persuasive, kindly man.

Early in his teaching-lecturing experience Henry Neely became aware of the desire of his students to know the stars better, a desire that was often thwarted by their inability to find their way around the sky. To facilitate sky-watching, to provide a usable procedure for finding principal stars and constellations, Mr. Neely devised and constructed the star charts which comprise the major part of this guidebook. By using these charts and following the simple instructions, the novice, with a little practice, can identify positively the main stars of the sky he is observing whether it be summer or winter, early or late. There is pleasure in looking at the stars. That pleasure is immeasurably enhanced when one can name the star, or group of stars, he is looking at.

If you do not wish to start a new, exciting interest in your life, don't start this book. Mr. Neely knew how to charm people by word of mouth, and he knew how to write with equal charm and clarity. Once involved, you will become a star watcher.

We wish you good seeing.

Franklyn M. Branley
American Museum—Hayden Planetarium

# A PRIMER FOR STAR-GAZERS

# I

# A PARABLE FOR BEGINNERS

SUPPOSE we begin our talks about the stars by talking about young Johnny Jones.

Johnny's family moved to a big city from a little village upstate. Everything in the city was so much bigger than anything Johnny had ever seen before that he was in a constant state of bewilderment.

When he went for the first time to the huge city school, this bewilderment increased to dismay.

Johnny and his father stood across the street looking at the crowded schoolyard. To Johnny's small-village eyes, it seemed as though there were literally millions of boys and girls in that yard—all milling about aimlessly—a formless mass of humans, one scarcely to be distinguished from another.

Johnny's heart sank.

"Gee!" he said, "I'll never get to know anybody in a crowd like that. There's just no use trying. There are too many of them."

"Now listen, Johnny," said his father kindly. "Let me give you a little advice right from the start. If you follow it, you won't have any trouble at all.

"First of all, forget that crowd of boys and girls. Don't think of them as a crowd at all.

"Go over there and go into your classroom. During the morning, look about you. You'll soon find two or three boys who look as though they might be friendly. Pay no attention to the rest.

"Then, at morning recess, you'll find a chance to talk to one of them. You'll find out his name and what sports he likes and where he lives—things like that. You'll probably find that you have interests in common—baseball, hockey, football.

"But don't try to be too friendly too soon. Take your time.

"Maybe you'll feel a bit lost and lonely for a few days but that will not last long.

"Gradually you'll make friends—first one, then another. Almost before you know it, you'll be on familiar terms with every boy and girl in the school who seems to be worth knowing.

"Stick to the ones you like and forget about the others.

"And don't worry too much about remembering their names all at once. In a crowded school like this, you'll find all nationalities—Poles, Russians, Italians, Irish, Balkans—all kinds of names that will be strange to you.

"They won't make sense at first but, after awhile, you'll find that you can recall them without the slightest trouble.

"Why, last year, I remember, you knew the name of every man on the Notre Dame football team and you won't find any stranger names here than that.

"Now go on over there and remember the most important thing of all. Don't be in a hurry; take your time."

So that's how young Johnny Jones started.

And today all those girls and boys are so familiar to him that he sometimes wonders why he was dismayed on that first day.

Now that little story is a parable or a fable, of course. But I think it has a definite place in a star book for beginners.

When you look up at the sky at night and see its teeming crowd of stars, remember Johnny Jones as he looked despairingly across the street at that crowded schoolyard on that first morning.

If you will put yourself in Johnny's place and let me play the part of the father, I'd like to give you exactly the same advice that Johnny's father gave to him.

Forget the thousands of stars in the sky. Most of them will never be of importance to you anyhow.

## A PARABLE FOR BEGINNERS

This book will introduce you to the most interesting and conspicuous ones and will show you how easy it is to find them and to know them—if you will only take your time to it and not try to do it all at once.

There are only fifty-five stars in the whole sky sufficiently important to be listed for navigators and I doubt if there are many men at sea or in the air who know forty of them. Yet those men are expert navigators.

This navigational use of the stars will continue to be a valuable asset for many years to come. In spite of all the scientific aids that have been developed to do the navigating by robot science, the ancient stars will still be a "must" for navigator or pilot.

Machines will get out of order and scientific instruments are notoriously temperamental, but the old stars will still be there, mute but reassuring evidences of an eternal celestial machine that never gets out of order and that scorns the temperamental vagaries of man-made devices.

And, in cases of emergency, the man who can point up into the night sky and say with certainty: "That star up there in the east is Vega and that one over there in the south is Antares" will be the man who will save the ship or bring the plane to a safe landing.

In these pages, we are going to ignore the textbook approach to the stars and, for the time being, we will forget there is such a word as "study."

Here you will find virtually nothing about the mechanics of the solar system nor the physics of the galaxies nor the dynamics of the unfathomable reaches of infinite space.

Here you will simply be invited to learn the fascination of the stars and to acquire the ability to go out under the sky at night and wave an easy and familiar "hello!" to your own particular favorites.

If, however, you will follow the book through a year of the Calendar for Star-Gazers, you will know every navigational star that can be seen from the United States and furthermore (and most valuable) you will learn to place them by means of compact and definite groupings that make simple pictures that you will not forget.

Notice that parenthesis "and most valuable."

Let me explain that by assuming an emergency.

The navigator is uncertain of his position. For two or three days, the skies have been hidden by thick clouds.

Then, one night, there comes a sudden break in the clouds—not a large one, but big enough for a little circlet of stars—or a square or a triangle or a cross—to show through.

Instantly he knows what that little figure is. He does not have to see the whole constellation; he does not even have to know it if he does see it.

He knows that little group is the Northern Crown, or the Northern Cross, or the Great Square or the Teapot—unscientific names, perhaps, but *he knows them.*

And in each, he knows the navigational stars. Therefore he can find out where he is.

That is the basis on which this book has been planned.

It deals principally with the plainly marked and easily recognized pictures that some of the groups of stars make in the sky—most of them, traditional figures; some formed in the fancy of the author.

The book deliberately ignores much that your professor would insist on including. But everything that has been omitted has been omitted because it is difficult to find or understand in the novice stages of star-gazing.

I have ignored the textbook approach because I feel thar that approach is suitable only to those readers who definitely enter star study as an educational activity, to be taken seriously and systematically.

But the textbook does not capture the imagination of the person who is not naturally a student. It fails to present the stars *as fun.*

II

# THE "FIXED" STARS

TO THOSE of us who are veteran star-gazers, the expression "the fixed stars" seems perfectly clear in its meaning. Yet there are few expressions that have caused more misunderstanding among people who know nothing about the subject.

It is a constant surprise to hear intelligent men and women say, "I didn't know the stars moved. I thought they were fixed."

Now these same people can explain quite readily why the sun seems to rise in the east, climb the eastern sky during the forenoon and descend westward in the afternoon to set below the western horizon in the evening.

They know that this is not a real motion of the sun at all. They know that the earth is constantly spinning like a top on its axis (or axle, if you prefer) carrying us around from west to east but that we are entirely unconscious of this movement and, consequently, as the earth carries us around "under" the sun, we get the illusion that it is the sun that is doing the moving from east to west.

The amazing thing is that, knowing this, these people do not apply the same process of reasoning to the stars.

An astonishing number of persons are under the impression that, if a certain star is seen just touching the dome of the courthouse at nine o'clock tonight, it will be in that same place at midnight or at four o'clock in the morning or at any other time of night on any night of the year.

That is what they understand by the expression "fixed star"—that it is fixed in that same spot above the dome of the courthouse for all time.

Now, if the courthouse were also "fixed," this would be true. But the spinning earth is whirling you and me and those same people—and the courthouse—around every second so that the net result is this: the star is fixed but the courthouse is leaving it and you and I are leaving it, all whirling from west to east but unconscious of the fact that we are moving, seeing only that the star is getting farther and farther from the courthouse every hour, apparently going from east to west, just as the sun does, and not acting like a "fixed" star at all.

The misunderstanding comes because we have never thought to ask, "Fixed with relation to what?"

The answer is that the star seems fixed with relation to the other stars—and that includes our sun, for the sun is only one star in the swarm of several billion other stars that we call our "galaxy."

The seven stars of the Big Dipper, for instance, seem fixed with reference to each other and, as seen from the earth, they will continue to outline the form of the Big Dipper for many centuries to come.

And the Big Dipper itself will still have its Pointers pointing to the North Star no matter whether we see the Dipper in the northeast or the northwest or above or below the North Star.

Its apparent change of position nightly and from month to month is due to the fact that our horizon, containing you and me and the courthouse, is whirling with us, tilting all the way around until it has done a complete somersault in space.

If you try to turn a somersault in the air, keeping your eyes open, you will get the impression that earth and sky are whirling around you. Yet you know that they are "fixed." When you stand still, they do not seem to move.

That is how the stars are fixed.

If the earth stood still, they would not appear to move either.

Many thousands of years ago, before the dawn of recorded history, man began to observe the stars and to learn something about them. He became a star-gazer.

Guarding his herd or his flock by night, the wandering nomad could watch a group of stars as it rose above the easterly horizon in the evening, circled slowly and majestically across the sky during the night, and set beneath the western horizon in the glow of morning twilight.

That, in itself, would scarcely excite his curiosity, because the sun did the same thing by day.

But, as month after month passed by, the stars showed a further change which must have been puzzling to him.

One by one, certain groups of stars which were low over his western horizon in the early evening disappeared entirely from the night sky, their places taken by groups which had previously been higher at sunset, and all the groups in all the sky seemed constantly moving over westward while new groups made their appearance on the eastern horizon as darkness fell.

In a few months, this progressive westward movement had taken away all the old stars and had filled the sky with an entirely new set of groups and these too gradually moved westward from their original twilight positions and still others came up over the eastern horizon at sunset.

After many generations of such star-watching, some unnamed primitive scientist must have discovered that there was a great regularity in these changing aspects of the night sky.

He may have noticed, perhaps, that the brilliant group of stars which we now call Orion was at its highest point in the sky at midnight about the time the sun was farthest south and the weather was coldest—in what we now call mid-December.

At midnight three months later—in March—this same Orion was no longer overhead but was low in the west, setting below the horizon, and there was an entirely different group overhead where Orion had been before.

In other words, Orion seemed to have drifted steadily toward the west.

In April, this westward drift was emphasized by the fact that Orion had gone entirely from the sky at midnight. It had disappeared below the western horizon two hours before midnight and a new set of stars had come up over the eastern horizon and a different set was overhead.

Early in May, this steady westward drift took Orion out of the night sky entirely. The group set before darkness made any of the stars visible.

Thus primitive star-hunters came to know Orion as a winter constellation and it was not long before they classified all of their favorite groups as spring stars or summer stars or winter stars. All shared this same westward drift that brought them up into the night sky in the east in their season, gradually moved them a little westward each evening and finally took them out of the night sky entirely, to bring them back to their same positions a year later.

This westward drift, it must be understood, was a motion *in addition* to the daily rising, circling and setting. To turn back once again to that star over the dome of the courthouse, it meant that the star reached the dome earlier tonight than it did last night—in fact it will be at the tip of the dome about four minutes earlier each night until this steady change will bring it to the dome of the courthouse in daylight and we will not see it at all.

This constant westward drift in addition to the daily circling makes the use of conventional star maps a forbidding puzzle to the novice star-gazer. He finds that he has to study and understand the elements of astronomy before he can locate stars by means of such maps and, for some reason or other, the average person seems to feel that astronomy is a labyrinthine maze of mystical mathematics entirely beyond his mundane ken.

In this book, I am accepting that attitude of mind without concurring in its viewpoint. It would be easy enough for me to present here a simple geometrical diagram explaining this westward drift of the stars. The diagram would show that the daily rising, circling and setting of stars is due solely to the spinning of the earth on its axis like a top.

The westward drift is due to the fact that the earth does not simply stand in the same spot and spin but is constantly rushing eastward in a huge orbit around the sun, carrying us steadily toward and under the stars to the east and away from the stars that we are leaving in the west, until we make a complete circle around the sun, which brings us back to our original position in one year and the whole performance starts over again.

That simple geometrical diagram would make the whole thing clear to anyone with mathematical inclinations, but you and I started this book with the agreement that you are allergic to geometry and all forms of mathematics and we will stick to that agreement.

But you can have no idea how strong the temptation is right now to print that diagram.

## III

## THE NORTHERN SKY

LET us once more go back in time and visit our primitive star-gazer. Long before there was any such thing as science, he learned that all of the stars seemed to be steadily drifting westward—a drift that apparently carried them all the way around the earth and brought them back to their original places in the course of a year.

Long observation showed him that groups which rose far to the southward were in the early evening sky for only a few weeks. Those that rose more to the northward were seen for longer periods, and the number of nights on which a group could be seen increased progressively the farther to the northward the group was in the sky.

Finally, as he went northward in his studies, he found that there were several groups that never disappeared from his night sky; they never went below the northern horizon and therefore never rose or set. Instead, they marched in eternal circles around a central point in the sky.

As this point never seemed to have any motion at all, he chose it as a fixed and dependable reference point from which he could describe the directions of all other points.

He called it "north."

Gradually primitive man built up an imaginary picture of the sky. He visioned it as the inside of a huge, star-studded sphere, constantly turning around his immovable flat earth, which he thought to be at the center of the space enclosed by the otherwise empty sphere.

This sphere obviously had that stationary point in the northern sky as one of the pivots about which it turned and it was equally obvious to him that there must be another pivot in the southern sky, just as far below the southern horizon as the northern pivot was above his northern horizon. Therefore the southern pivot was never visible to him.

The axis (or axle) around which the sky-sphere revolved was apparently tilted so that it ran from that north point high in the sky, obliquely down through his position on earth and on down under the flat earth to that perpetually invisible point below his southern horizon.

That seemed to explain why the far southern stars were in his evening sky only a few weeks; they were so near that southern pivot that they came up above his horizon only when they were in the small arcs at the tops of their circles.

It explained why the stars halfway between the two pivots were in his sky for half a year.

And it explained why the stars near the northern pivot of the sky sphere were visible somewhere toward the north every night of the year. They were so near to the elevated northern pivot that the circles they made around it were not wide enough to carry them below the northern horizon.

Now this would be true only for an observer in northern latitudes on the earth. To anyone in the southern hemisphere, the opposite is true; the southern pivot is high in the sky and the northern pivot is never visible.

This seeming paradox is easily explained, though the puzzle could not be solved by man so long as he believed his earth was flat and immovable. It requires a mental picture of a spherical earth to see why it is true.

If you and I stand exactly on the earth's equator, we will see both pivots (or celestial poles, as they are called) exactly on our horizon north and south. While we are on the equator, our north horizon cuts through the North Pole and our south horizon through the South Pole. There is no "bulge" or curve of the earth's sphere to hide them from us.

Now let us go northward. As a nonscientific picture, we can assume that this means that we are going to go "down hill," following the curve of the earth's surface. We are going to leave a "bulge" behind us that will hide the south pivot and, as we progress farther and farther "down" the northern slope, we are going to be able to see farther and farther "under" the North Celestial Pole, which is, for naked-eye purposes, clearly marked by the North Star or Polaris. In other words, as we go north, Polaris will seem to rise higher and higher in our northern sky and more and more of the stars around him will be too high at all points in their circling ever to go below the horizon.

I wish now that I had not promised not to print geometrical diagrams. The one I have in mind would show that, in our northward walk, when we reached 30 degrees north latitude (New Orleans), Polaris would be 30 degrees high above the horizon; when we reached 40 degrees latitude (Philadelphia), Polaris would be 40 degrees high. In other words, the diagram would show that the height of the North Celestial Pole above the horizon is always the same as the latitude of the observer.

That is why we in the United States and Canada from 30 degrees to 50 degrees north latitude see many stars in the northern sky that keep eternally circling about that fairly high celestial pole or sky-pivot and never go below the horizon.

I know of no more dramatic evidence of these circles than the photograph on the opposite page.

This picture was made at the great Yerkes Observatory but any amateur with a good camera and lens and fast panchromatic film can make one—though probably not so good—which will show the same motion of the brightest stars.

In this instance, the Yerkes photographer set up his camera aimed due north and tilted up so that the North Star (Polaris) was approximately in the center of the plate.

With focus at infinity and a wide lens, he then opened the shutter and exposed the film for *exactly one hour.* During that time, the brighter stars left him a permanent record of their trails.

The fact that the camera was not moved is proved by the dim silhouettes of the trees in the two lower corners.

The picture clearly shows one thing that our primitive star-gazer observed—that some of these stars never can set and that others, a little farther from the center, will dip below the horizon only briefly.

You can follow the complete circles all the way down to the horizon and it is obvious that any star within the circle

*Photo Yerkes Observatory*

STAR TRAILS AROUND THE POLE. A one-hour exposure shows the circles made in the northern sky.

with this radius will be perpetually visible. The short arcs in the two lower corners show that these stars, farther from the center and beyond the limits of this circle, *will* dip below the horizon but soon emerge again.

The farther a star is from the center, the longer it will be below the horizon and the farther toward the south will be its point of rising and setting.

The direction of motion of all these stars, by the way, is *counter*-clockwise. Whenever you face north, all stars seem to move counter-clockwise. When you reverse yourself and face south, the stars seem to move clockwise.

Here, then, we have evidence that there is a point in the northern sky which is at the exact center of all the star circles and which obviously does not move. The star Polaris (the North Star) is so near to this point that the naked eye cannot detect its motion so we need not apologize if we refer to Polaris as the North Celestial Pole when we are dealing with noninstrumental observing.

To the navigator in the northern hemisphere, this polar point is the most important point in the sky. If he wants to find his latitude (distance north of the equator) he can use his sextant to measure the altitude, or height above the horizon, of Polaris, make minor corrections to allow for its slight distance from the polar point and the result is his latitude in terms of degrees.

Reversed, this principle can also be of use to the novice star-gazer who does not know how high to look to find Polaris.

Look at a map to find your latitude (the horizontal lines) and Polaris will be that many degrees above your northern horizon. If you clench your fist and hold it out at arm's length, it will cover just about 10 degrees so you have a rough and ready sextant for computing the place of Polaris in the sky.

## IV

## MAPPING THE NORTHERN SKY

A "URANOGRAPHER" is someone who specializes in making maps or pictures of the heavens, just as a geographer specializes in maps or pictures of the earth. The "urano" comes from a Greek word meaning sky; the "geo" comes from the name of the goddess Ge, goddess of the earth. "Grapher" comes from the word meaning drawing or writing.

We can try an interesting little experiment in uranography by turning back and studying that dramatic one-hour photograph of the northern sky. The uranographer would take that picture and, by making dots or star symbols at either the start or the finish of each arc, would make an excellent map of the northern sky as it was at either the start or the end of the hour, depending on which he chose.

Let us pretend for a moment that you and I are primitive uranographers and that we have become interested in this northern sky because it contains quite a number of fairly bright stars that seem to suggest definite patterns and these stars can be seen somewhere in the north every clear night.

I am sure that you yourself, when you were younger, have lain out in the lush grass on a warm summer's day and gazed lazily at the fleecy clouds drifting across the sky. Perhaps you found one cloud that looked like an elephant and you pointed it out to the kid lying beside you (and I hope she is beside you now).

Then she saw one that looked like a camel and you found another that looked like a snake or a dragon. That was when the world was young—to you and her.

Our primitive star-gazer found in the stars much of what you found in the clouds. Certain groups of them, as they became familiar to him, suggested the creatures or the heroes of his tribal myths or the beasts he had seen or had heard about from the wandering tellers of tales.

But the infinite and mysterious sky seemed to a superstitious primitive something far different from the familiar earth; it was dark and eerie and superhuman and anything pictured in the awesome stars had to be endowed with attributes far beyond the attributes of little humans and their little surroundings.

So we will pretend that we are such a primitive uranographer and that we have become particularly interested in just one quadrant of this northern sky.

First of all, we would draw little star figures to represent the brightest stars, ignoring the dim ones that do not seem important. Our first picture would look like Fig. 1 on the opposite page.

As we studied the stars in this picture, we would notice (remember—we are superstitious primitives) that a wandering stream of those stars formed a fairly reasonable suggestion of the terrible dragons we had been taught to fear.

So we would outline those stars with the figure of a dragon and then our picture would look like Figure 2. We would point this figure out to everyone we met and they in turn would point it out to everyone they met and in time everybody would point to that stream of stars and refer to it as the Dragon and later the Romans would give it the Latin word meaning dragon—Draco.

So we would imagine other figures from our primitive folktales around other groups of stars.

Centuries later, perhaps, men would find our map or hear about our ideas. They would accept some of our mythical conceptions but reject others and substitute their own.

On this north sky quadrant, they would find two groups of stars that suggested household implements that were unknown in our day and, connecting these stars with lines, they would call these groups the Big Dipper and the Little Dipper.

All over the sky, there are groups of stars that have suggested similar picturemaking to men all over the world. Individual stars still bear the mutilated vestiges of the names

Fig. 1

Fig. 2

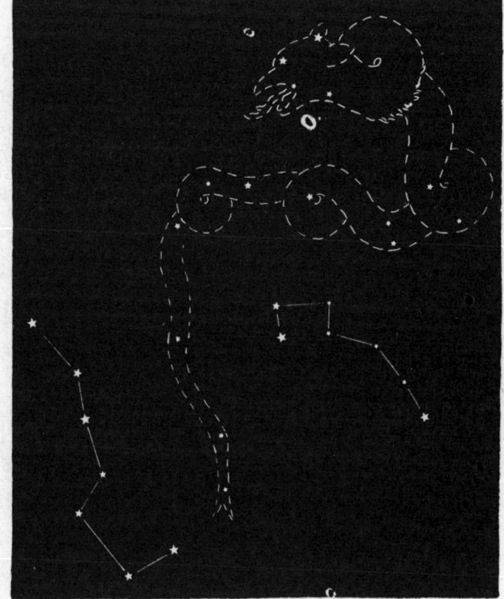

Fig. 3

the ancient Persians and Arabians and other peoples first gave to them, those names originally denoting the part of the man or beast or mythical figure that the star marked in their conceptions.

But the early Greeks and Romans, adopting much from Egypt and Persia and Arabia, began to formulate the night skies into some semblance of the uranography of today. Many of the most ancient conceptions were retained and given Latin names, while other groups of stars were assigned to the gods and goddesses and creatures of land and sea that figured in the Roman and Greek mythology.

Some of those old pictures are quite easily recognized by the star-gazer of today. Draco, the Dragon, is one of them. Others, however, seem to us very confusing and unconvincing. Our own forefathers picked out little groups here and there and assigned to them identifying figures that make them much easier for us to find. Thus we have the Northern Cross, the Northern Crown, the Sickle and the Teapot.

In the Big Dipper, we have seven bright stars which give us quite a convincing tin dipper with its handle bent downward. Or we can easily join the British in seeing it as a plough, with the bent handle representing the curved plough handles and the Dipper's bowl representing the ploughshare and the furrow wheel and the frame.

It is probably safe to say that most star-gazers (and this includes navigators) regard the Big Dipper as the most important group of stars in the sky. For anyone in the latitude of New York or northward, the figure never goes below the horizon. It is one of the most conspicuous formations in the heavens and therefore one of the easiest for the novice to find; it is by means of the Big Dipper that he learns to locate Polaris, the North Star, and so to be certain of his compass directions so long as Polaris is not obscured by clouds.

This simple identification of the otherwise not too conspicuous Polaris is made possible by the two bright stars that mark the outer edge of the bowl of the Big Dipper. These two stars are known as the Pointers, because they *always* point to Polaris, no matter what part of its daily circle the Dipper may have reached at the time we want to find it.

It is as though the northern sky were a great wheel, with Polaris in the hub and the Pointers both attached to the same spoke of the wheel. No matter how the wheel revolves, the spoke, with these two stars, always points to the hub in which we find Polaris.

It is because of this important function of the Big Dipper and the Pointers that the Calendar for Star-Gazers which you will find on later pages in this book always starts each section by referring you to the north sky circle, Chart 1, and telling you how to turn it to find the Big Dipper and Polaris for that particular time. Once you locate the Big Dipper and Polaris, you feel that you have a familiar home port in the night sky to which you can return and reorient yourself if you get lost in voyaging among the unfamiliar parts of the heavens.

The Little Dipper is not so easily traced out in the sky unless the night is clear and dark. It requires very little moonlight or street lighting to dim out the four faintest stars, though Polaris and the star Kochab (pronounced ko-kab) at the end of the bowl will always be seen. The star near Kochab, marking the outer edge of the Little Dipper's bowl, is also fairly bright and will usually be seen. Kochab and that neighboring star are known as the Guardians of the Pole.

And now let me revert once more to that little parable of Johnny Jones and his first day in the big-city school. If this is your first day in this big star-school, let me advise you to choose the Big Dipper and the Little Dipper (or, at least, the North Star, Polaris) as your first friends. They will introduce you to all the other boys and girls in the school.

If you are a far-southerner, you should also become immediately acquainted with the unmistakable W or M of the group called Cassiopeia, shown in the north sky circle and, in detail, on Chart 2, because for you the useful Big Dipper will sometimes be too low to give you directions to Polaris and you will have to depend on Cassiopeia for that purpose.

With this brief summary, then, we are ready to examine the plan on which this primer is constructed, to find out how to use it and to see how its simple pictures and directions make it unnecessary for you to study astronomy or geometry or the other branches of science needed for using the conventional kind of star maps that have discouraged so many people who otherwise might like to go star-gazing if somebody would only take the trouble to reduce it to simple A.B.C.'s.

V

## HOW TO USE THIS BOOK

IF I could go outdoors with you, turn you to face the horizon in some exact direction and, pointing a certain distance up, say—

"See that bright star up there—the brightest one you can see without turning your head."

—you would immediately see it. Then if I said—

"Now just a little lower than that star and a bit to the left, there are five stars—not nearly as bright but still quite plain. They form a cross. You can see three of them almost parallel with the horizon and two others, one above and one below the middle star."

—you would study the sky a minute or two and then the form of the cross would become evident to you.

Then I would probably tell you some of the amazing facts about two or three of those stars of Cygnus, or the Northern Cross, and perhaps the ancient story of how the group got its name and you would begin to feel some of the fascination that grips a confirmed star-gazer. Before long, you would be a sworn member of the brotherhood with a chronic crick in the neck from constantly gazing upward.

Unfortunately for me, I cannot be with you in person tonight but the simple plan on which this book is constructed will serve the same purpose.

*Once you understand this plan, you (and I vision you as an absolute novice) can go outdoors at any hour of any clear night in the year and point directly at and identify any group of stars then visible in the sky, even though you may never have seen them before.*

In a previous chapter, we discussed the constant westward drift of all stars in addition to their daily rising over the eastward horizon, circling up and over the sky and setting under the westward horizon.

As these stars cross the sky, they seem to swing around and many of the figures look entirely different when rising from the way they look when they are setting.

The group just mentioned—Cygnus, the Swan (also called the Northern Cross)—is an excellent illustration of this turn-about which has been a stumbling block for so many novices first struggling with the intricacies of conventional star maps.

This book does away with all those intricacies and presents actual pictures of the various groups for any time, in their exact location and turned just as they will be turned at that time.

I began this chapter by assuming that you and I had gone outdoors to look at some stars and that I had chosen this Swan or Northern Cross for your introduction to star-gazing. The first thing I did was to have you face the horizon in a certain direction.

That is the first thing this primer does and it asks you to use an ordinary pocket compass to point out the correct direction to face. That correct compass direction is given with every picture in this book.

After the correct facing, there were two more points I had to make clear before you could see the Cross for yourself:

1. How high above the horizon the group was and

2. Whether the line of three stars was horizontal, vertical or oblique.

Let us consider the first one first—how high.

There are three points in the sky that can be found instinctively by anyone. They are: the horizon, the overhead point and the point midway between these two—halfway up the sky.

One of these three heights is stipulated for every picture in this primer.

If the group is near the horizon, the picture will include a conventionalized landscape from which you can instinctively judge how high it is.

If the group is well up the sky, high enough for you to lose sight of the horizon when you are looking at the stars, there will be a point marked on the picture or stipulated in the instructions and this point will be halfway up the sky. When you face in the correct compass direction and raise the picture so that that point is halfway up the sky, *the book will cover the stars you are hunting* and all you need do is glance around the edge of the book and you will be looking at them.

The same principle is followed when the stars climb higher than halfway up. You will then find directions for raising the book until a stipulated point in the picture is overhead. Again, when you look past the book, you will be looking at the stars you are hunting.

Lastly, we must solve the problem of whether a line of stars will be horizontal, vertical or oblique at any particular time.

Here again we use universal instinct as our guide.

There are two lines that are instinctive with everyone—the horizontal and the vertical. When a picture includes a landscape, that will take care of the horizontal, for the horizon will eliminate all question of how the stars will look at that time.

When the stars are so high that we lose sight of the horizon, we depend on that other instinctive line—the vertical. In every such picture, you will find one or more lines marked AA, BB, CC, etc. The instructions with the pictures will tell you, for various times, just how you are to face by compass, which one of those lines is to be turned to vertical and just which point in the picture is to be raised halfway up the sky or to be held overhead.

*In every case, when the instructions are correctly followed, the book will be covering the stars you are hunting and the picture will show them just as they will appear in the sky.*

Let us take this same group of Cygnus and picture it as a flying Swan as the ancients did. Then let us follow it across the sky, turning to the charts for Cygnus numbered 35 to 39.

First we have Chart 35 which includes the landscape so that it is quite evident that the Swan is, at that time, flying horizontally and we know just where to look for him and the position in which we will find him. For early evening star-gazers this will be during the first half of June and you will see it so specified in the Calendar for Star-Gazers and in the Cygnus Hour-and-Date Diagram.

There are, however, two lines—AA and BB—in this first picture. The instructions with the picture will tell you that, before the first half of June, the Swan will not yet be as high as shown over the landscape and those lines will be the horizons at earlier periods or times.

The picture in Chart 36 shows the Swan when it is too high for you to see the horizon as a reference point for horizontal and you will then call upon your instinct for the vertical.

There are three lines in this picture—AA, BB, and CC.

The Calendar for Star-Gazers and the Cygnus Hour-and-Date Diagram will tell you for any time when this picture is to be used, which line to turn to vertical. The instructions with the picture tell you the correct compass direction to face and what point in the picture is to be raised to halfway up the sky when the specified line is vertical.

Chart 37 is the picture we use when Cygnus and his neighbors are crossing the sky overhead. Here we have four lines, and one of them will always be specified in the Calendar for Star-Gazers and the Hour-and-Date Diagram. The instructions with the picture will tell you exactly how to hold the book.

We can now begin to see how the Swan is turning as it mounts the sky.

When it rose, it was horizontal, headed south. Now, overhead, it has definitely begun to turn and is headed southwest.

Coming down from the overhead position, still so high that the horizon is not yet in our field of view, we again use our instinct for the vertical.

Chart 38 gives us three lines, each to be turned to the vertical according to instructions in the Calendar and the

Hour-and-Date Diagram, and the description with the picture will tell us the correct compass facing and what point in the picture will be halfway up the sky at that time.

Finally, in Chart 39, we find Cygnus as he is preparing to set, and here, most dramatically, we see the importance to the novice of knowing exactly how to turn the book at any particular time. The Swan rose (Chart 35) flying horizontally and headed south. He is now setting, plunging straight down at the horizon as though he were a pelican diving for a fish in the sea.

Perhaps you will not object if a veteran star-gazer gives you a few hints, on the assumption that you are a novice and not quite sure whether you are going to like this star business or not.

First (and most important) . . . take your time.

If you identify only one group in your first evening of hunting, be satisfied. That group will introduce you to another the next night and, with each success, you will acquire increasing facility in locating and identifying everything in the sky pictures.

If you find difficulty in locating some of the less clearly identifiable groups, don't begin to turn this way and that to look all over the heavens for them. You'll get lost that way.

If you have the right picture and if you are following the directions given, every star in the picture can be seen *without turning your head*—simply by shifting your eyes.

Once you are sure you have the right picture, and the correct point on the horizon, stick to the small part of the sky shown in the picture until you find the group or until you begin to be annoyed by your failure.

In the latter case, don't be discouraged. Leave that group alone for the time being and go on to others. As your familiarity with the sky increases, they will all come to you and it may comfort you to know that we have all gone through exactly that same experience.

In almost every picture, you will find one star obviously

larger than the others. Then you will find the next largest—and so on.

The relative sizes of the stars in the pictures give an accurate measure of the relative brightness of the stars in the sky represented by them.

At first you will find it a little difficult to determine which of a group of fairly equal stars is the brightest. Gradually, however, you will become accustomed to estimating the differences and, as you acquire this ability, you will find it most useful in fixing identities.

As a rule, then, find the brightest star given in a picture and use that one as a reference point in locating the others.

**Never use a white light when you are hunting stars.**

White light deadens the sensitivity of the eyes, even with short exposure.

Put red cloth or red cellophane over the lens of your flashlight or paint it with red fingernail polish and make it thick enough to give only a dim light—just enough to enable you to decipher the pictures and read the captions.

Over a year ago, when I could find nothing red to use on a new flashlight, I took the paper label from a can of tomatoes, cut a disc out of the red picture of the tomato, unscrewed the lens from the flashlight, inserted the paper disc and screwed the lens back in place.

It has been so satisfactory that I have not changed it since.

Don't attempt to hunt for stars all around the horizon until you have become thoroughly acquainted with the five principal groups in the north sky. This is particularly important regarding the Big Dipper and Polaris, the North Star. If you could hang a plumb line from Polaris, the point on the horizon touched by the plumb bob would always be true north, so far as you can judge by the naked eye, and would be mathematically true north twice in every twenty-four hours . . . when Polaris is directly above and directly under the North Celestial Pole. But, without being mathematical, your naked-eye direction fixed by Polaris at any time will be more nearly accurate than any compass is likely to be.

I have seen many advertisements of pocket compasses "guaranteed" to be "accurate." That is impossible, if it means guaranteeing that the needle will always point to true north.

The only accuracy that such a compass can have is to show you the direction of the lines of the strongest magnetic forces at that particular spot and at that particular time.

This shows the "variation" of all magnetic compasses over a curving stretch of the North Atlantic seaboard. The card points to true north. The needle is westward by ten degrees. Many places in the United States have much more violent variation than this.

But, as a start, you can accept the compass needle as reasonably north. Face as it points. Open this book to the picture of the north sky circle, Chart 1. Turn the picture according to the instructions in the Calendar or in the Hour-and-Date Diagram and, as your very first experiment in star-gazing, locate the Big Dipper. From the Pointers of the Big Dipper, you will identify the star Polaris, the famous North Star, and your compass troubles will be over.

Simply turn the compass card around until the N on the card points to the spot on the horizon directly under Polaris and, from then on, use the compass *card* for your directions and ignore the needle entirely.

## VI

## A WORD ABOUT PLANETS

THERE is one feature of the night sky that always puzzles the beginner in star-gazing.

That is the constantly recurring presence of bright planets among the stars.

The planets look exactly like stars. To the naked eye, there is no difference. Yet the planets are not shown on his star map. Why?

Here is one somewhat technical explanation that cannot be avoided, even in a book which is intended to be entirely nontechnical. So you and I might as well face the problem right here.

Every novice will at once ask the inevitable question, "What is the difference between a planet and a star?"

The simplest nontechnical answer, which is not too inaccurate, is that the object which we call a star is a great globe of incandescent gases, situated at a distance so far from us as to be beyond practical comprehension, generating a temperature far beyond our mundane experience, emitting light in such quantity and of such brilliance that we can conceive of it only as a mathematical expression.

Our own sun is a star—and not a particularly big or brilliant one. If we could get into an atomic space-ship and shoot ourselves far out into space, our sun would appear to be just one of thousands of stars in the sky.

And if, as we went out into space, we could keep watching the sun and its vicinity, we would soon see for ourselves the answer to one of our questions.

As we receded farther and farther, we would see, circling around the sun, a numerous "family" of globes of various sizes. Nearest to the sun, and usually hidden in his brilliance, we would see one of the smallest of the globes. That would be the planet Mercury. Circling at a greater distance would be one not very different in size from the earth. That would be the planet Venus.

Then, still farther from the sun, our own earth would be seen, spinning like a top on its own axis and, at the same time, speeding in almost a circle around the sun while, in turn, the little moon kept circling around the earth.

Beyond the earth, we would see Mars, beyond Mars a thousand or more tiny specks which we call asteroids, beyond them the great Jupiter, mighty Saturn, Neptune, Uranus and finally the far-distant Pluto. All of these objects would be seen speeding in elliptical paths around the sun.

We would very soon realize three significant things:

1. All of these globes, which we call planets, belong to the sun and are held bound to the sun by the power of gravitation so that they are eternally destined to swing in endless elliptical paths around the sun and will never be freed to dash out on an independent adventure into space.

2. Our own earth is really one of these planets.

3. *No planet shines by its own light.* The only way we can see a planet is by the sunlight which it reflects to us.

As we continued outward into space in our atomic ship, we would soon be conscious of the fact that our earthly conceptions of time and distance would have to be discarded, because they are too infinitesimal to be of use in measuring the inconceivable reaches of space among the stars.

At first, while we were still fairly near the sun and its planetary children, this would not be so noticeable.

We would find, for instance, that the earth, in its circling around the sun, remained at an average of about 93,000,000 miles from the sun. That is, of course, a tremendous distance as measured by earthly standards. But it is not inconceivable.

This yardstick, however, would become less and less practical for use in the measurements of distances as we sped farther away.

So we might adopt, as our yardstick, the distance from the

sun to little Pluto, the most remote of the planets, so far as we now know. This distance, we would find, averages about four *billion* miles (4,000,000,000). I have put the numbers in parentheses because the British do not call this four billion; they call it four thousand million and they would insist on three more zeros to justify the word billion.

Here, we would conclude, is a yardstick big enough to be used anywhere. Four billion is a lot of miles. It is still conceivable but it requires a good deal of imagination.

We would continue speeding out into space, looking for the next object beyond Pluto.

There would not be any for a long time. In fact, before we saw the next object, all the planets would have faded into invisibility, and the sun itself, instead of looking like a great ball of fire, would have contracted to a mere point of light in the sky. And the whole circle of Pluto's orbit, with its four-billion-mile radius, would have so shrunk by perspective as to be encompassed in that little point.

So we would find a trifling yardstick like a mere four billion miles is of no use to us now that we are out among the stars. How, then, can we measure?

There is one way that we might use for our computations. If we knew the speed of our atomic ship per minute and knew how many minutes we had traveled, we could figure our distance. So let's see if the captain of our ship is keeping a log that will help us.

"Captain," we ask, "how fast is this atomic ship going?"

"With the speed of light," he replies.

"And what is the speed of light?"

"Oh, about 11,000,000 miles a minute."

It will take us some time to get any real comprehension of such a speed. In fact, we cannot really comprehend it. All we can do is take a pencil and enter it as an item in our notebook:

"Speed—11,000,000 miles a minute."

Then we turn to the captain again.

"How long did it take us to go to the earth from the sun?" we ask.

"About 8¼ minutes."

That does not seem to be long enough to help much in our problem. We try again.

"How long did it take us to go from the sun to Pluto?"

"A little over 6 hours."

"But," we protest, "we have been going through space at 11,000,000 miles a minute for nearly a month and we haven't seen anything since we left Pluto that first day. How soon are we going to see something?"

"Well," drawls the captain, "If we were going south toward Centaurus, we'd come to the nearest star about 4⅓ *years* after we left the sun. But we ain't headin' that way. We're goin' north."

"Toward Polaris?"

"Yep."

"How soon will we get there?"

"Well," he says contemplatively, "if Polaris'd only hold still, we could do it in 680 years. Trouble is, Polaris is runnin' to meet us at about 54,000 miles an hour. Makes it a little hard to figure."

We jot this information down in our notebook and start to compute the number of miles involved in our trip to Polaris:

"Speed—11,000,000 miles a minute.

"Multiply by 60, equals miles per hour.

"Multiply by 24, equals miles per day.

"Multiply by 365¼, equals miles per year.

"Multiply by 680, equals miles from sun to Polaris."

We look at the dismaying figures a moment and decide not to do it. There isn't a page in our notebook large enough for it. We turn to the captain again.

"This trip to Polaris must be about the longest trip there is, isn't it?"

He laughs.

"Shucks, no," he says. "Polaris is just a sort of suburb. They tell me they've located a swarm of whole star systems down around Virgo that take 300,000,000 years to git to."

"Three hundred million years!" we exclaim. "But that's impossible."

"Huh!" he grunts. "You don't know our traffic department. Soon's we get ships that'll carry more fuel, there's a feller in the traffic department is plannin' a line to some big star cities he's found that'll take longer than that t' get to."

"How long?"

" 'Tisn't exactly figured out yet but it looks like a trip of about 1,600,000,000 years."

"Traveling at 11,000,000 miles a minute?"

"Yep," he says. "That's the speed of light. That's the schedule in our traffic department."

You have undoubtedly noticed how the apparent speed of an airplane varies with its distance from you.

A plane going 200 miles an hour will whizz across your line of sight and be gone in a minute if it is only a few hundred yards away.

But that same plane, going at that same 200 miles an hour, will seem to be scarcely moving if it is so far away as to be merely a speck over the horizon.

Apply this same principle to the planets and the stars and to our trip in the atomic ship.

All of the stars are hurtling through space (like Polaris in our story) at appalling speeds but they are so far away that, to the naked eye, they appear to have no motion whatever.

We call them the "fixed" stars.

But the planets, as our trip proved to us, are practically next-door neighbors, measured by star distances.

A planet, circling between us and the remote and seemingly immobile stars, will soon betray its motion. We may see it against the distant background of the Taurus stars tonight and, a month from tonight, may find it projected against the distant background of the stars of Gemini. A little later, we may not see it at all because it will have gone so far in its circling around the sun as to be below our horizon when nighttime comes.

Again applying the example of the airplane, the more distant the planet is from us, the more slowly it will seem to be moving.

Thus Mars, when it is closest to us in its orbit, seems to move faster than the more distant Jupiter, Jupiter faster than the still more distant Saturn, and so on.

That is why planets cannot be put in star maps except such maps as are to be used during a certain period and during that period only.

Being at different distances and circling at different angular speeds, the planets are constantly being reshuffled in our night skies. Sometimes we may get a few nights when, at sunset, with the naked eye, we can see all of the five nearest planets—Mercury, Venus, Mars, Jupiter, Saturn—at once; again, we may see none of them.

There is only one regularity about the planets and that is that they are always found in a limited belt, or zone, around the sky and never outside this zone.

The zone is called the Zodiac.

With many of the pictures in this book, you will find that the caption warns you that certain groups of stars shown in the pictures or referred to in connection with them are in the Zodiac.

You may then be quite sure that, if you find a bright "star" in the group in the sky not included in the group in the picture, that "star" is a planet.

Your daily newspaper, in its weather report section, will probably list the "evening stars" and the "morning stars" for that period. That expression is an odd survival from antiquity because an evening star or a morning star is never a star at all; it is *always* a planet.

But the best way to keep yourself informed about the planets and to learn exactly where you will find them every month or to learn when to look for any of the constantly recurring appearances of objects of interest to the star-gazer, is to send to the Sky Publishing Corporation, 49 Bay State Road, Cambridge, Mass. 02138, for a sample copy of their fascinating and beautifully illustrated monthly magazine, *Sky and Telescope*.

will find the various objects of interest.

This book will tell you how to find the constellations.

*The*

# YEAR'S CALENDAR

*for*

# STAR-GAZERS

## VII

# THE STARS—ANY HOUR—ANY NIGHT

IN THE section of this primer which follows, the reader will find the Year's Calendar for Star-Gazers.

This Calendar has been planned on the basis of a regular schedule of star-gazing at a particular time each night—namely, about an hour after it is dark enough to see most of the brighter stars.

This time, however, may not be convenient for some. The Hour-and-Date Diagram on the following page has therefore been constructed to make the Calendar and all charts and text usable at any hour of any night.

The diagram is based on the simple fact already stated in these pages—that all stars steadily "march" or drift westward, progressing each day by the distance they "march" in about four minutes. This brings them back to approximately the same point in one year; the variation from that exact point is so slight that, in your lifetime, you will not be able to detect the difference with the naked eye.

The procedure for using this diagram is very simple.

You will find the months, divided into thirds, running horizontally across the top. Down each side are the hours of the night and early morning—and please note that these hours are given in STANDARD TIME—the only time that can be conveniently used winter and summer in figuring star positions. If your watch is keeping any other kind of time except Standard, you must deduct an hour from your watch time to get Standard Time.

Run across the top of the diagram to get the date. Then run down that column to get the time you want to do your star-gazing.

The diagonal line that cuts across nearest to that point will tell you which section of the Calendar to use at that time,

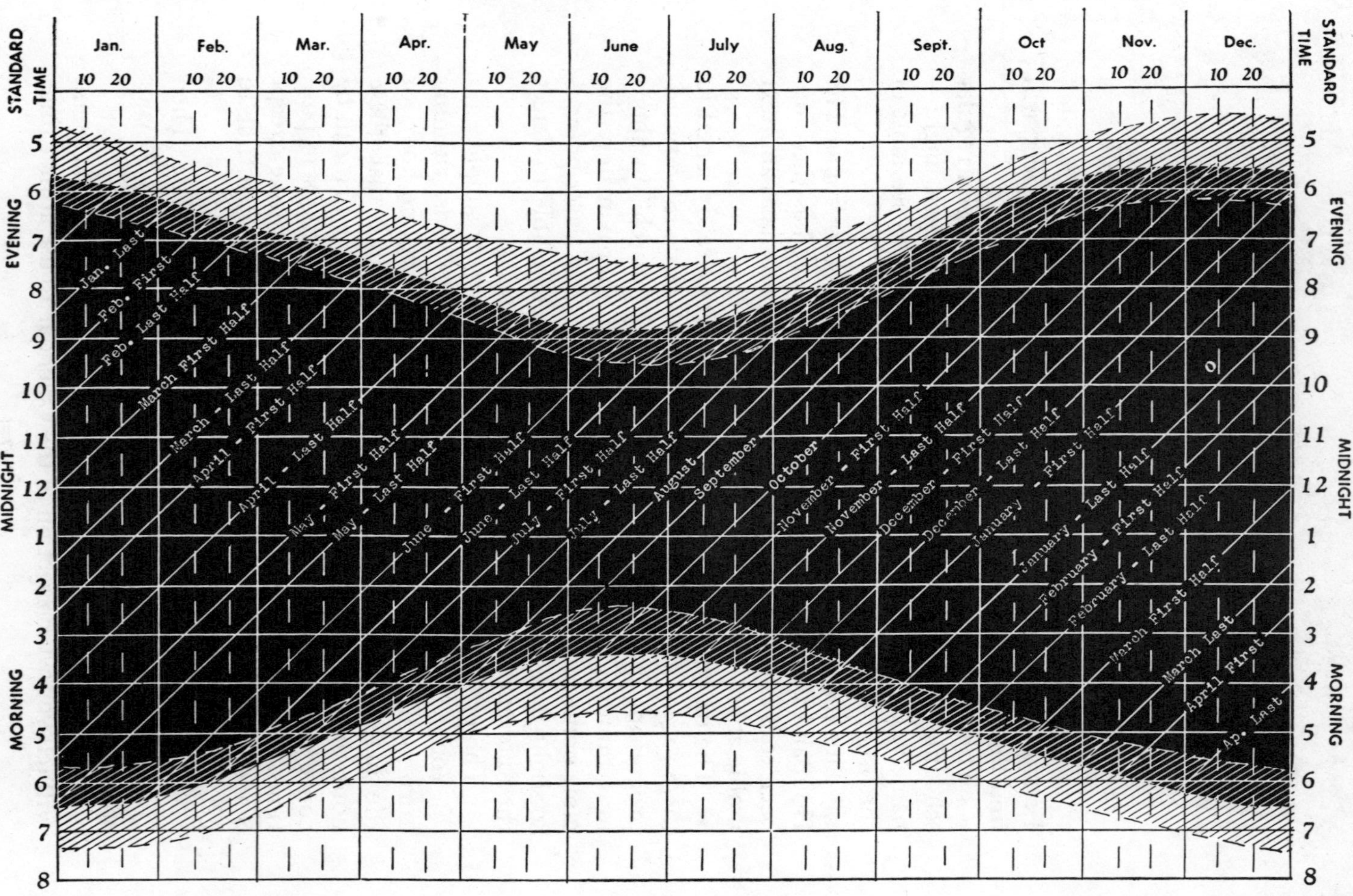
STANDARD TIME
Jan. 10 20
Feb. 10 20
Mar. 10 20
Apr. 10 20
May 10 20
June 10 20
July 10 20
Aug. 10 20
Sept. 10 20
Oct 10 20
Nov. 10 20
Dec. 10 20
EVENING
MIDNIGHT
MORNING
5 6 7 8 9 10 11 12 1 2 3 4 5 6 7 8
Jan. Last
Feb. First
Feb. Last Half
March First Half
March - Last Half
April - First Half
April - Last Half
May - First Half
May - Last Half
June - First Half
June - Last Half
July - First Half
July - Last Half
August
September
October
November - First Half
November - Last Half
December - First Half
December - Last Half
January - First Half
January - Last Half
February - First Half
February - Last Half
March First Half
March Last
April First
Ap. Last

even though that section may be given for a different month.

Let us take an example:

It is a night in the first half of January. We decide to go out at 4 o'clock in the morning (STANDARD TIME, PLEASE! !).

We put a pencil at the top where January 10 is indicated —or approximate the exact date if we wish. The difference will not be important.

Then we run the pencil down that column until we come to the horizontal line indicating 4 o'clock in the morning.

We note that the nearest diagonal line says "April—Last Half."

"But," you may object, "this is January. It won't be the last half of April for three and a half months."

*That does not make any difference. At 4 o'clock in the morning during the first half of January, we will find all of the stars in the same positions they will occupy an hour after dark during the last half of April.*

So we forget that it is January and turn to the Calendar instructions for the last half of April and we will find that all of those instructions, and the charts and maps they refer to, are accurate—all, that is, except the dates of meteor showers, which remain constant regardless of the hour.

In this diagram, which is the basis for similar computations for each constellation or group of constellations in the book, you will notice two curving, shaded bands.

They represent the morning and evening twilight times approximately.

The lighter part of the band indicates that there will be too much daylight for star-hunting. The darker part indicates roughly the times when—though it is not completely dark—the brighter stars can be quite clearly seen.

Do not expect this shaded band to be accurate to a few minutes. The times of sunset, sunrise and end and beginning of twilight vary with your latitude on earth and, as this book attempts to cover from Latitude 30 degrees north (the Gulf Coast) to latitude 50 degrees north (approximately the Canadian border), we have to be satisfied with a reasonable average.

As the object of this book is nothing beyond the simple identification of stars and constellations, the difference is of no importance.

You will find a similar Hour-and Date Diagram for every group of stars given in this book. This is for the convenience of star-gazers who may not want to explore the whole sky but who desire only to locate a particular group at some particular time.

The date and hour are found on the diagram by the method already described and the nearest diagonal line will tell you which chart to use at that time and will specify a certain line if one is necessary. Follow the instructions and the book will cover the stars you are hunting.

# JANUARY

THE YEAR'S CALENDAR

*First Half*

*Easy Groups for Beginners*

North sky circle to be set between 01 and 02. Big Dipper too low for southerners. Cassiopeia at top of its circle.

Chart 1

Brilliant Capella dominates northeast sky, halfway up. Use line BB.

Chart 15

Under Capella is the wedge of Gemini. Use the picture "as is."

Chart 19

Above Capella, stretching across overhead is the Yacht. Use line BB.

Chart 43

To the right of east, brilliant Orion is well up. Use the picture "as is."

Chart 4

Above Orion is Taurus with the twinkling Pleiades quite high. Use line AA.

Chart 10

From southeast to beyond the south point are the more difficult groups given below for advanced star-gazers.

Southwest, Capricornus is setting. Use the picture "as is."

Chart 28

Above Capricornus is the Great Square of Pegasus. Use line AA.

Chart 32

In the northwest, Cygnus is plunging downward. Use the picture "as is."

Chart 39

Great Draco coils between northwest and north. See the north sky circle with top between 01 and 02.

# JANUARY



*Groups for Advanced Star-Gazers*

In the northeast, Lynx is well up. Use line CC.

Chart 92

Monoceros is coming up east but is not yet high enough to be clear. If you want to try it, use line AA.

Chart 93

Turning toward the south, we have several of the less distinct groups. Eridanus, the River, winds high in the southeast. Use line CC.

Chart 90

High over the south is Cetus with Fornax and Sculptor to left and right. Use line FF.

Chart 89

Above Cetus, and to the right, is the indistinct V of Pisces. Use line HH.

Chart 88

Far-southerners can still see the stars of Grus. Use line FF.

Chart 96

The five little groups associated with Cygnus are still high enough in the northwest to identify. Use line NN.

Chart 91

*Zodiac, Milky Way and Meteor Showers*

Look out for deceptive planets in the Zodiac—Cancer, Gemini, Taurus, Aries, Pisces, Aquarius, Capricornus.

The Milky Way is in fine position for binoculars, arching high across the sky from east to west. Perseus, Cassiopeia and Cygnus are particularly rich in star fields.

Meteor-hunters plan an all-night vigil January 2-3 for the Quadrantids, radiating from the area near the word "Draco" in the north sky circle, Chart 1. Consult the Hour-and-Date Diagram if you plan to join the hunt.

THE YEAR'S CALENDAR

*Last Half*

*Easy Groups for Beginners*

In the north, the Big Dipper is coming up but Draco is getting too low for far-southerners. Set the top of the map at 03.

Chart 1

East and southeast, the sky is brilliant. Well up over the east, we find Gemini. Use line AA.

Chart 20

Above Gemini is Auriga, with the brilliant star Capella unmistakable. Use line CC.

Chart 15

The four constellations that compose the Yacht have now passed to the west of overhead. Use line CC.

Chart 43

Down over the horizon in the southeast gleams Sirius, brightest star in the sky.

Chart 47

Above Sirius is the great Orion.

Chart 5

Look above Orion and you will find Taurus and the twinkling Pleiades. Use line BB.

Chart 10

The south and southwest sky is filled with the more difficult groups best left to advanced star-gazers. In the west, we see the last stars of Aquarius. Use line AA.

Chart 28

Higher in the western sky is Pegasus with his Great Square. Use line BB.

Chart 32

In the northwest, Cygnus is virtually standing on his head on the horizon and brilliant Vega is low in the haze. Use AA.

Chart 39

*Groups for Advanced Star-Gazers*

Cancer, Leo Minor and Lynx are now up in the northeast. Use line DD.

Chart 92

To the right of east, we find Monoceros, between the Dog Stars, Procyon and Sirius. Use BB.

Chart 93

Eridanus, the River, winds from Orion down to the south point on the horizon. Use line DD.

Chart 90

In the southwest, we have Sculptor, low over the horizon, with Cetus above him. Use line GG.

Chart 89

Higher and to the right is the V of Pisces, now turned over sidewise. Use line JJ.

Chart 88

Most of the little groups around Cygnus are now too low to be clear but Lacerta is still halfway up the sky. Use line OO.

Chart 91

*Zodiac, Milky Way and Meteor Showers*

Planets may be found in any of the constellations of the Zodiac now visible. They are Cancer, Gemini, Taurus, Aries, Pisces, and Aquarius.

The Milky Way arches high across the sky from southeast to northwest and overhead. It is in fine position for sweeping with binoculars.

On the seventeenth look for meteors radiating from the upper wing-tip of Cygnus as it rises. This is an early-morning job, however, and requires Chart 35, either AA or BB depending on your choice of time. Consult the Hour-and-Date Diagram for Cygnus.

## THE YEAR'S CALENDAR

### *First Half*

### *Easy Groups for Beginners*

The Pointers of the Big Dipper are now high enough in the northeast for all of us to see but far-southerners had better forget Draco. Turn the book to make the top of the circle 04.

Chart 1

The northeast sky is filled with more difficult groups for advanced star-gazers. The easy groups begin in the east where the Sickle has risen. Use line AA.

Chart 53

Halfway up the sky is Gemini. Use line BB.

Chart 20

Higher than Gemini, almost overhead, is brilliant Capella, marking the kite of Auriga. Use line AA.

Chart 16

Comfortably over the horizon southeast shines Sirius, brightest star in the sky.

Chart 48

Halfway up the sky above Sirius is brilliant Orion. Use line AA.

Chart 6

Still higher than Orion is Taurus, now crossing the meridian. Use line AA.

Chart 11

The southwestern sky is filled with difficult groups best left to more experienced star-gazers.

Due west, the winged horse, Pegasus, is standing on his head on the horizon. Use the picture "as is."

Chart 33

The Yacht with its four constellations fills the sky from the Great Square to overhead. Use line AA.

Chart 44

In the northwest, Cygnus, the Swan, has plunged his head below the horizon. This is a good chance for beginners to try using a regular star map to find what is left of the Swan. Use line PP as directed.

Chart 91

*Groups for Advanced Star-Gazers*

Cancer is well up in the east with Lynx above and Leo Minor below, both to the left. Use the line EE.

Chart 92

Monoceros is in good position near the southeast, between Procyon and Sirius. Use the line CC.

Chart 93

Eridanus, the River, winds down the whole southern sky. Use the line EE.

Chart 90

The shapeless Cetus fills the southwest sky. Use the line HH.

Chart 89

To the right of Cetus is the V of Pisces, lying over on its side. Use the line KK.

Chart 88

Lacerta is all that is left of the group around Cygnus. Use the line PP.

Chart 91

The head of the Hydra has now emerged—none too good, but worth looking for nevertheless. Use the line AA.

Chart 94

*Zodiac, Milky Way and Meteor Showers*

If there are planets in the sky, they will be found in one of the Zodiac constellations. The Zodiac groups now visible are Leo, Cancer, Gemini, Taurus, Aries, Pisces.

The Milky Way is at its very best for binoculars and telescopes. It mounts straight up overhead from the southeast to the northwest.

On February 5, look for "shooting stars" radiating from the bright star Capella, in Auriga. The correct chart to use will depend on what hour of night you choose. At midnight, it will be Chart 17, line BB.

THE YEAR'S CALENDAR

*Last Half*

*Easy Groups for Beginners*

For the north sky, turn the book until 05 is at the top of the circle. The Big Dipper is now well up over the northeast and Cassiopeia over the northwest.

Chart 1

The Sickle, in Leo, is conspicuous over the east point. Use the picture "as is."

Chart 53

More than halfway up the eastern sky is the wedge of Gemini with bright Procyon under it. Use line CC.

Chart 20

From southeast to south, Sirius and his neighbor stars are bright over the horizon.

Chart 49

To the south, Orion is crossing the meridian. Use the line BB.

Chart 6

Overhead, the kite of Auriga is at its highest point in the sky. Use line BB.

Chart 16

Just to the right of Orion is Taurus, the Bull, starting down the western sky. Use BB.

Chart 11

To the right of the west point, Pegasus has sunk part way under the horizon. Use AA.

Chart 33

Above Pegasus are the four groups that make up the Yacht. Use the line BB.

Chart 44

Just over the horizon to the right of northwest is the bright star Deneb in Cygnus, the Swan, but the group is now too low to be of interest.

*Groups for Advanced Star-Gazers*

Canes Venatici has risen above the horizon under the Big Dipper but is not yet in good position. If you want to try for it, use the north sky circle with 05 at the top. It is fairly good for Canadians; not worth while for southerners.
Chart 1

Cancer, Lynx and Leo Minor are halfway up the easterly sky. Use line FF.
Chart 92

To the right of east, on the horizon, we have little Sextans and the head and "neck" of Hydra. Use line BB.
Chart 94

Monoceros is halfway up the sky in the southeast. Use line DD.
Chart 93

To the right of south, Eridanus, the River, winds down below the horizon from Orion. Use line FF.
Chart 90

The lower sky in the southwest is filled by the amorphous form of Cetus. Use line JJ.
Chart 89

Pisces, due west, fills the lower half of the sky. Use line LL.
Chart 88

Little Lacerta is still in the northwest but the rest of the Cygnus groups have set. Lacerta can be located by the north sky circle. It is at figure 22. Turn 05 to top.
Chart 1

*Zodiac, Milky Way and Meteor Showers*

Beware of planets in any of the constellations of the Zodiac. At this time, they are Leo, Cancer, Gemini, Taurus, Aries, Pisces.

The Milky Way is still in its best position for binoculars or telescopes. It arches overhead from southeast to northwest.

There are no regular meteor showers during the last half of February.

## THE YEAR'S CALENDAR

### *First Half*

### *Easy Groups for Beginners*

The north sky circle should be turned so the top is between 06 and 07. The Big Dipper is now high in the northeast.

Chart 1

In the east, the great Virgo Triangle is beginning to emerge from the horizon. Use line AA.

Chart 58

Nearly halfway up the eastern sky is the Sickle in Leo. Face east when you use the picture.

Chart 54

Due south, we find Sirius and his bright neighboring stars at their highest points. Use line AA.

Chart 50

Higher than Sirius and to the right is bright Orion. Use line CC.

Chart 6

To the right of Orion is Taurus with the glittering Pleiades. Use the line AA.

Chart 12

Between west and northwest, the four groups that form the Yacht are nearing the horizon. Use line CC.

Chart 44

Above the Yacht, brilliant Capella marks the kite in Auriga. Line CC.

Chart 16

Almost overhead for far-southerners is the wedge of Gemini. Use AA.

Chart 21

### *Groups for Advanced Star-Gazers*

Canes Venatici and Coma Berenices are now up in the northeast. Use line AA.

Chart 95

# MARCH



High in the eastern sky are Cancer, Lynx and Leo Minor. Use line GG.

Chart 92

In the southeast, Hydra and Sextans are well up. Use line CC.

Chart 94

Monoceros is crossing the southern meridian. Use line EE.

Chart 93

In the southwest, Eridanus, the River, winds down below the horizon. Use line GG.

Chart 90

To the right of Eridanus, Cetus has sunk part way below the horizon. This is his annual farewell appearance. Line KK.

Chart 89

Pisces is also making its farewell appearance to the right of Cetus. Use line MM.

Chart 88

*Zodiac, Milky Way and Meteor Showers*

The Zodiac, pathway of the planets, arches high across the sky from east to west. It runs through Virgo, Leo, Cancer, Gemini, Taurus, Aries and Pisces.

The Milky Way is showing signs of descending to the west but is still fine for binoculars and telescopes. It starts in Puppis, to the left of south, mounts up through Monoceros, between Gemini and Orion, past Taurus and Auriga and through Perseus and Cassiopeia to the horizon.

From March 10 to 12, look for meteor showers from the star Zeta in the constellation of Boötes. This is best located by the charts of the Northern Crown, in which Zeta is seen between Arcturus and Serpens. For the correct chart to use after midnight, consult the Hour-and-Date Diagram.

THE YEAR'S CALENDAR

*Last Half*

*Easy Groups for Beginners*

Turn the north sky circle so that 08 is at the top. The Big Dipper will be high in the northeast. Only far-northern Canadians will see Cygnus at the bottom of the circle.

Chart 1

The little Northern Crown is on the horizon northeast but too low to be clear at this time. To the right of northeast, the brilliant star Arcturus is unmistakable and forms one corner of the Virgo Triangle. Use line BB.

Chart 58

High in the sky to the right of east is the Sickle in Leo. Face E-SE (halfway between east and southeast).

Chart 54

To the right of south, brilliant Sirius and its neighbors have passed the meridian. Use line BB.

Chart 50

Almost overhead for far-southerners is the wedge of Gemini. Use line BB.

Chart 21

The great Orion is nearly halfway up the sky in the southwest.

Chart 7

To the right of Orion is Taurus, the Bull, with the twinkling Pleiades. Use line BB.

Chart 12

Above Taurus is the kite of Auriga, with the great star Capella making it unmistakable. Use line AA.

Chart 17

In the northwest, the Yacht is making its last complete appearance. More and more of it will be below the horizon from now on.

Chart 45

*Groups for Advanced Star-Gazers*

Canes Venatici and Coma Berenices are well up in the northeast. Use line BB.

Chart 95

Cancer, Lynx and Leo Minor are overhead. Use line HH.

Chart 92

Hydra is rearing high in the southeast with Corvus, Crater, Antlia and Sextans all above the horizon. Use DD.

Chart 94

Monoceros has now passed the meridian but is still halfway up the sky. Use line FF.

Chart 93

Eridanus, the River, is passing out of our evening skies. It is under Orion in the southwest. Use line HH.

Chart 90

Cetus and Pisces are almost entirely gone in the west and are not worth while.

*Zodiac, Milky Way and Meteor Showers*

Planets may appear in the constellations of the Zodiac. The groups now above the horizon are Virgo, Leo, Cancer, Gemini, Taurus and Aries.

The arc of the Milky Way that has been with us for many months is now obviously descending the western sky. It arches from south to north above Orion and Taurus and still offers good "sweeping" with binoculars and telescopes.

There are no regular meteor showers during the last half of March.

THE YEAR'S CALENDAR

*First Half*

*Easy Groups for Beginners*

The top of the north sky circle should be at 09. Only far-northerners will see Cygnus at the bottom. The Big Dipper is now high enough to give you a crick in the neck.

Chart 1

Hercules, the Northern Crown and Boötes are becoming conspicuous over the northeast horizon. Use line AA.

Chart 63

The great Virgo Triangle is now well up over the east. Use the picture "as is."

Chart 58

The Sickle in Leo is approaching the meridian. Use line AA.

Chart 55

Sirius and its bright neighbors fill the lower sky from south to southwest.

Chart 51

To the right of southwest is brilliant Orion, now getting down toward the horizon. Use the picture "as is."

Chart 8

Above Orion is the wedge of Gemini. Use line AA.

Chart 22

Coming down over the west point is the bright star Aldebaran in Taurus, with the twinkling Pleiades to his right.

Chart 13

Above Taurus we find the kite of Auriga, with the brilliant star Capella more than halfway up. Use line BB.

Chart 17

Only a part of the Yacht is still above the horizon in the northwest. Use the line AA.

Chart 45

*Groups for Advanced Star-Gazers*

Canes Venatici and Coma Berenices are halfway up the sky in the east. Use the line CC.

Chart 95

Cancer, Lynx and Leo Minor are passing overhead. Use the line JJ.

Chart 92

The southeast sky is filled by the Hydra and his four neighboring faint groups. Use line EE.

Chart 94

Monoceros is about halfway up in the southwest. Use line GG.

Chart 93

To the left of west, we find only a vestige of Eridanus, the River. Use line JJ.

Chart 90

*Zodiac, Milky Way and Meteor Showers*

The Zodiac now arches up from east to west through Virgo, Leo, Cancer, Gemini, Taurus and Aries.

The Milky Way is now only about halfway up the western sky and this half of the glowing circle will soon set and the opposite half will rise over the east. At present, there is still good sweeping with binoculars and telescopes through Monoceros, Taurus, Gemini and Perseus.

There are no regular meteor showers during this period.

*Last Half*

*Easy Groups for Beginners*

The top of the north sky circle should be between 10 and 11. The Big Dipper is now at its highest point, almost overhead for far-northerners. The Pointers point straight down at Polaris.
Chart 1

That brilliant star just above the horizon haze in the northeast is Vega. It is included with Cygnus in our position pictures but that group is not yet high enough for identification. You will find Vega between 18 and 19 on the north sky circle.

To the right of Vega and much higher is the Northern Crown, now well up. Use the picture "as is." Chart 63

Hercules can be seen in the Northern Crown pictures but it is shown in more detail in its own. Use line AA. Chart 68

The great Virgo Triangle fills the mid-sky over the southeast.
Chart 59

Leo, with the conspicuous Sickle, is passing across the southern meridian, not far from overhead. Use line BB.
Chart 55

Low over the southwest, we find Sirius and the stars of Puppis setting.
Chart 52

Orion is almost resting on the western horizon. Use line AA.
Chart 8

To the right of Orion, Taurus is bidding us his annual farewell. Use line AA.
Chart 13

Above Taurus is the kite of Auriga with brilliant Capella the most conspicuous object in the northwest sky. Chart 18

Directly above Orion, the wedge of Gemini is pointing straight down. Use BB.
Chart 22

Only the top of the sail of the Yacht is left in the northwest. Perseus is still high enough to be good. Chart 46

### *Groups for Advanced Star-Gazers*

Coma Berenices and Canes Venatici are high over the east. Use line DD.

Chart 95

Hydra and his associated groups stretch all the way across the southern sky. Use line FF.

Chart 94

Monoceros is getting low between southwest and west. Use line HH.

Chart 93

Above Monoceros we have Cancer and Leo Minor with Lynx to the right. Use line KK.

Chart 92

### *Zodiac, Milky Way and Meteor Showers*

If planets are in the sky, they will be in Virgo, Leo, Cancer, Gemini or Taurus.

The Milky Way has now sunk quite low over the western sky. It is good for binoculars and telescopes only in the early evenings and the best areas are from above Sirius in the southwest, between Gemini and Orion, over Taurus and through Auriga and Perseus. Cassiopeia—a rich region—is too low to be good.

On the twentieth, look for the meteor shower known as the Lyrids, radiating from around the brilliant star Vega. Lyrids begin shortly after the fifteenth, reach maximum the night of the twentieth and early morning of the twenty-first, when very bright, swift "shooting stars" may be expected to average one every five or six minutes. They continue intermittently through May and June. For midnight use Cygnus picture, Chart 35. For other times use the Cygnus Hour-and-Date Diagram.

*First Half*

*Easy Groups for Beginners*

Turn the book upside down to bring the figure 12 to the top of the north sky circle. The Big Dipper is now overhead for far-northerners in Canada. They will see Cassiopeia low on the northern horizon but it will be no good for southerners.

Chart 1

In the northeast, Cygnus, with gleaming Vega, is now far enough up for identification. Use line AA.

Chart 35

Over the east point, Ophiuchus and his Serpent have emerged far enough to enable us to trace them. Use AA.

Chart 73

Above Ophiuchus is Hercules with the Great Cluster high enough to test eyesight and binoculars. Use the picture "as is."

Chart 68

Above Hercules is the neat little Northern Crown with bright Arcturus higher and to the right.

Chart 64

In the southeast, far-southerners will see red Antares just over the horizon but he is still too low for the rest of us. The stars of Libra, however, are well up above him. Use AA.

Chart 78

The Virgo Triangle is starting its crossing of the meridian in the south. Use the line AA.

Chart 60

High over the southwest, we find the Sickle of Leo. It is best to face south and use the line CC.

Chart 55

Low over the western horizon, we can still see the bright star Betelgeuse in Orion but the mighty hunter has sunk too far below the horizon to be traced. Above Betelgeuse is the wedge of Gemini.

Chart 23

# MAY

A PRIMER FOR STAR-GAZERS

To the right, brilliant Capella marks the kite of Auriga now approaching the horizon. Use the line AA.

Chart 18

Only the tips of the horns of Taurus, the Bull, remain above the horizon under Auriga. Use the line BB.

Chart 13

The stars of Perseus are all that remain of the four groups that formed the Yacht. They are very low, between northwest and north. Use AA.

Chart 46

*Groups for Advanced Star-Gazers*

Coma Berenices and Canes Venatici are starting across the meridian overhead. Use line EE.

Chart 95

Hydra and the dim groups associated with him fill the southwest sky. Use the line GG.

Chart 94

Cancer, Lynx and Leo Minor are halfway up the sky in the west and northwest. Use the line LL.

Chart 92

Monoceros is very low over the horizon in the west. Use the line JJ.

Chart 93

*Zodiac, Milky Way and Meteor Showers*

If there are planets in the sky, they will be in the Zodiacal constellations—Scorpius, Libra, Virgo, Leo, Cancer, Gemini, Taurus.

The Milky Way now extends virtually all the way around the horizon, everywhere too low to be good for binoculars or telescopes, although the western arc is not too bad immediately after dark.

From the first to the sixth of this month, we look for

"shooting stars" radiating from the Water Jar in Aquarius. These meteors are usually swift moving and make long streaks across the sky. The Water Jar rises just before dawn. Use Chart 24.

Beginning about May 11, meteors may be seen radiating from the star Zeta in Hercules—the star in the kite nearest the Great Cluster in our pictures. These meteors reach maximum later in the month but are worth watching for earlier. Around midnight use the Hercules Chart 70 but check it for your time with the Hour-and-Date Diagram.

*Last Half*

*Easy Groups for Beginners*

Turn the book almost upside down to bring the figure 13 to the top of the north sky circle. Southerners will not see Cassiopeia at the bottom. The end of the Big Dipper's handle is about overhead for far-northerners.

Chart 1

Cygnus is almost clear of the horizon in the northeast with brilliant Vega well up. Use line BB.

Chart 35

To the right of Vega is Hercules with the Great Cluster halfway up the sky. Face east.

Chart 69

Above Hercules is the neat little Northern Crown.

Chart 64

Below Hercules and to the right we find Ophiuchus and his Serpent. Use picture "as is."

Chart 73

Southeast, the red star Antares is clear of the horizon with Libra above him and the stars of Centaurus sprinkled over the horizon to the south point. Use the picture "as is."

Chart 78

The Virgo Triangle is now crossing the southern meridian, in the upper half of the sky. Use the line BB.

Chart 60

Halfway up the sky in the west, we find the Sickle in Leo. In using the picture, face halfway between west and southwest (W-SW).

Chart 56

Just clear of the horizon, to the right of west, we have the wedge of Gemini with bright Procyon due west. Use AA.

Chart 23

In the northwest, the kite of Auriga is on the horizon but the great star Capella is still conspicuous. Use BB.

Chart 18

## THE YEAR'S CALENDAR

### *Groups for Advanced Star-Gazers*

Vulpecula is beginning to show under Cygnus in the northeast but is still rather low to be good. If you want to try for it, use line AA.

Chart 91

The whole lower sky in the southwest is filled by Hydra and his little companions. Use line HH.

Chart 94

Cancer, Lynx and Leo Minor are west and northwest. Use line MM.

Chart 92

Canes Venatici and Coma Berenices are overhead. Use FF.

Chart 95

### *Zodiac, Milky Way and Meteor Showers*

Look out for planets in the constellations of the Zodiac—which, as now visible, are Scorpius, Libra, Virgo, Leo, Cancer and Gemini.

The half of the Milky Way circle that has been in the west has now sunk below the horizon. The opposite branch is rising in the east but is not yet high enough to be very good. Northerners who own good binoculars can find many beautiful fields in Cepheus and Cygnus and far-southerners will be rewarded for sweeping through Scorpius and Centaurus.

On May 24, we get the maximum of the meteor shower that radiates from the star Zeta, where the tail joins the kite in our pictures of Hercules. After midnight use Chart 70 but check for instructions with the Hercules Hour-and-Date Diagram.

About the end of the month, we look for a shower of very fast meteors in Pegasus, radiating from the star shown in our pictures just above Scheat in the horse's leg. Hunting these meteors is an early-morning job, as the star is not satisfactorily above the horizon until around midnight. Use Chart 29 and consult the Hour-and-Date Diagram for instructions.

# JUNE



*First Half*

*Easy Groups for Beginners*

The book should be turned to bring the figures 14 and 15 to the top of the north sky circle. Far-southerners will not see any of the stars below Cassiopeia. Boötes will be overhead. The Big Dipper is now very high in the northwest.

Chart 1

From east to northeast, Cygnus and its bright companions, Vega and Altair, dominate the lower sky. Use the picture "as is."

Chart 35

High over the east, above Vega, is the kite of Hercules with the Great Cluster in fine position. To use the picture, face E-SE (halfway between east and southeast).

Chart 69

Below Hercules, in the southeast, is Ophiuchus with his great Serpent.

Chart 74

Halfway between southeast and south, Scorpius is clear of the horizon, except for far-northerners.

Chart 79

Boötes is leading the Northern Crown across the overhead point. Use line AA.

Chart 65

The Virgo Triangle is high over the southwest.

Chart 61

The Sickle in Leo is coming down over the west point. Face west to use the picture.

Chart 56

To the left of northwest, the two bright stars near the horizon are Castor and Pollux. This is a good chance for the beginner to try using regular star maps. Use the line NN.

Chart 92

To the right of northwest, the bright star in the horizon haze is Capella but the rest of Auriga is below the horizon.

*Groups for Advanced Star-Gazers*

**Star-gazers north of the United States-Canadian border are not likely to have much success with these fainter groups at this time. At latitude 50° north, there is some twilight all night during June.**

The little groups around Cygnus are now high enough in the northeast for identification. Use line BB.

Chart 91

The sky over the horizon from south to southwest is filled by the Hydra and his associated faint groups. Use line JJ.

Chart 94

Coma Berenices and Canes Venatici are now past the overhead point and coming down in the west. Use line GG.

Chart 95

From west to northwest, we find Cancer, Lynx and Leo Minor. Use line NN.

Chart 92

*Zodiac, Milky Way and Meteor Showers*

If there are planets in the sky, they will be confined to the constellations of the Zodiac. At this time the constellations are Sagittarius (half below the horizon southeast), Scorpius, Libra, Virgo, Leo, Cancer, Gemini.

The Milky Way has now come up to a fairly good arc over the eastern horizon. Owners of binoculars and telescopes should sweep all around Cygnus, Aquila, part of Ophiuchus, Scorpius and Centaurus.

Star-gazers who like to stay up until the wee sma' hours will be out until dawn from June 2 to June 17 to count the "shooting stars" radiating from near the great red star Antares in Scorpius. After midnight, use Chart 81 but consult the Hour and-Date Diagram for morning hours.

# JUNE



*Last Half*

*Easy Groups for Beginners*

Turn the book to bring the figures 15 and 16 to the top of the north sky circle. Even far-southerners should now be getting a glimpse of Cassiopeia on clear nights. Draco is in its best position for tracing the convolutions of the long body.

Chart 1

Cygnus and his bright neighboring stars, Vega and Altair, are now well up from east to northeast. Use line AA.

Chart 36

Below Cygnus, a few stars of Pegasus are showing but the group is not yet high enough to use the Pegasus charts.

Very high up, getting ready to cross overhead, is Hercules. You'll have to lie flat on your back to examine the Great Cluster now. Use line AA.

Chart 70

Down in the southeast, we can now see the Teapot in Sagittarius, not yet high enough for Canadians. Use AA.

Chart 83

Above the Teapot is Ophiuchus, struggling with his great Serpent. Use the picture "as is."

Chart 74

Due south, the sky over the horizon is sparkling with the bright stars of Scorpius and his neighbors.

Chart 79

While you are facing south, look up overhead for the neat little Northern Crown. Use line BB.

Chart 65

The great Virgo Triangle is halfway up the southwestern sky.

Chart 61

Low over the horizon, just to the right of west, is the Sickle, in Leo.

Chart 57

*Groups for Advanced Star-Gazers*

**Star-gazers much north of the United States-Canadian border are not likely to have much success with these**

**fainter groups at this time. At latitude 50° north, there is some twilight all night through June and into July.**

All five of the little groups associated with Cygnus are now well above the horizon in the northeast. Use CC.

Chart 91

In the southwest, most of Hydra has gone below the horizon, but Sextans, Corvus and Crater are still up. Use KK.

Chart 94

Coma Berenices and Canes Venatici are coming down the western sky but are still more than halfway up. Use HH.

Chart 95

Cancer is halfway below the horizon in the northwest but Lynx and Leo Minor can still be seen. Use line OO.

Chart 92

*Zodiac, Milky Way and Meteor Showers*

Planets are likely to be low in the sky at this time. The visible part of the Zodiac includes Sagittarius, Scorpius, Libra, Virgo, Leo, Cancer.

The Milky Way is now well up over the eastern horizon. Good sweeping for binoculars and telescopes all through Cygnus, and northward around Cepheus and Cassiopeia and southward around Sagittarius and Scorpius.

Enthusiasts who haunt the hours between midnight and dawn looking for showers of "shooting stars," or meteors, have nothing spectacular scheduled this month, though there are three fairly reliable events on our books.

From the middle to the end of the month, Cepheus gives us a fairly continuous performance. On the twenty-fifth, we look for showers from the star Etamin in the head of Draco, the Dragon. From the twenty-seventh to the thirtieth, showers come from the part of Draco toward which the Little Dipper points. All of these can be located by the north sky circle, Chart 1 and its Hour-and-Date Diagram.

# JULY



*First Half*
*Easy Groups for Beginners*

Turn the north sky circle until the top is between 16 and 17. The bright star Capella, at the bottom, will be seen only by far-northerners. Both the Big Dipper, northwest, and Cassiopeia, northeast, are in good position for all of us and Draco is at his best.

Chart 1

The stars of Andromeda are in the horizon haze in the northeast but not yet high enough to be good. Between northeast and east, however, Pegasus is fairly well up and half of the Great Square can be seen. Use line AA.

Chart 29

Above Pegasus, the middle eastern sky is filled by Cygnus and his two bright companions, the stars Vega and Altair. This is a good time for novices to try their hand at regular star maps, using the line DD in Chart 91. If you are afraid of maps, use line BB.

Chart 36

Capricornus and Aquarius are emerging from the horizon from east to southeast. Use line AA.

Chart 24

To the right of southeast, low, the Teapot in Sagittarius is now in good position and all but Canadians will see the little Southern Crown under the Teapot.

Chart 83

Scorpius is at his highest point in the sky, due south.

Chart 80

Above Scorpius is Ophiuchus, struggling with his Serpent. Use line AA.

Chart 75

While facing south, lie well back and locate Hercules overhead. Use line BB.

Chart 70

Just to the right of Hercules is the neat little Northern Crown, now past the meridian. Use line CC.
Chart 65

Halfway down the sky, southwest to west, is the great Virgo Triangle. Use the picture "as is."
Chart 62

To the right of the west point, the Sickle in Leo is ready to sink into the horizon haze.
Chart 57

*Groups for Advanced Star-Gazers*

**Star-gazers much north of the United States-Canadian border are not likely to have much success with these fainter groups at this time. At latitude 50° north, there is some twilight all night during the first part of July.**

The five little companions of Cygnus are now in fine position in the eastern sky. Use line DD.
Chart 91

Coma Berenices and Canes Venatici are halfway up the sky over the west. Use line JJ.
Chart 95

*Zodiac, Milky Way and Meteor Showers*

The constellations now visible in the Zodiac, in which planets may appear, are Capricornus, Sagittarius, Scorpius, Libra, Virgo, Leo.

The Milky Way now arches from north to south halfway up over the eastern horizon. There are many beautiful star fields for binoculars and telescopes all through this branch of the luminous stream.

About the middle of this month, enthusiastic followers of "shooting stars," or meteors, begin to watch for one of the most famous showers, the Perseids, radiating from the area between Cassiopeia and Perseus. It is best to use the north sky circle, Chart 1, to locate this area. Consult the Hour-and-Date Diagram.

## JULY



*Last Half*

*Easy Groups for Beginners*

The top of the north sky circle should be between 17 and 18. The brilliant star Capella, now at his lowest point, will be seen only by far-northerners. Cassiopeia, Cepheus, Draco and the Big Dipper are now in fine position for all of us.

Chart 1

In the northeast, the stars of Andromeda and Perseus are emerging from the horizon haze and we can begin to see the figure of the imaginary Yacht in which they are included. Only part of it is yet visible.

Chart 40

The flying horse, Pegasus, is now becoming quite clear over the eastern horizon. The entire Great Square can be seen. Use line BB.

Chart 29

Above Pegasus, more than halfway up the sky, is Cygnus, with his two bright companions, the stars Vega and Altair. Use line CC.

Chart 36

From east to southeast, Aquarius and Capricornus are now clear of the horizon. Use line BB.

Chart 24

Just to the left of the south point is the Teapot in Sagittarius, with the dim little Southern Crown below it. Canadians should not be too hopeful of seeing the Crown.

Chart 84

To the right of the south point, Scorpius has passed his highest position.

Chart 81

Above Scorpius is the great Ophiuchus with his Serpent. Use line BB.

Chart 75

Overhead we find Hercules, just clearing the meridian. Use line CC.

Chart 70

THE YEAR'S CALENDAR

The Virgo Triangle is getting low in the west. Use the picture "as is."

Chart 62

Above the Virgo Triangle is the neat little Northern Crown, starting its descent of the western sky. Use DD.

Chart 65

*Groups for Advanced Star-Gazers*

There are five little groups around Cygnus in the eastern sky—Vulpecula, Sagitta, Delphinus, Equuleus and Lacerta. They are now in comfortable position for examination. Use line EE.

Chart 91

In the northwest, we find Coma Berenices and Canes Venatici nearly halfway up the sky. Use line KK.

Chart 95

Leo Minor, northwest, and Lynx, just to the left of north, are above the horizon but too low for satisfactory observation except by far-northerners. If you want to try for them, use Chart 92 but remember that both groups now rest on the horizon.

*Zodiac, Milky Way and Meteor Showers*

The Zodiac now runs along almost its lowest path in the southern sky. Planets may appear in Aquarius, Capricornus, Sagittarius, Scorpius, Libra and Virgo.

The Milky Way now arches high up across the eastern sky from the north horizon to the south and offers many fine star fields to owners of binoculars and telescopes. From Cassiopeia, up through Cygnus and down through Scorpius, it repays many hours of sweeping.

The last half of July and the first half of August bring good hunting for enthusiasts who watch for showers of "shooting stars," or meteors. The famous Perseid shower, which usually begins mildly early in July, will be increasing in richness now, to reach its maximum about August 11. The meteors will radiate from the area between Perseus and Cassiopeia, and the north sky circle, Chart 1, will be the best to use for them in conjunction with its Hour-and-Date Diagram.

From July 18 to August 4, bright, slow-moving meteors leaving long trails may be looked for radiating from the star Algiedi in the head of Capricornus, the Sea-Goat. Around midnight, use Chart 26 but consult Hour-and-Date Diagram for the line to be used at the time you select.

Two meteor showers are usually seen on the night of July 25. One radiates from Perseus, between the stars Marfak and Algol. Use instructions above for Perseids. The other shower radiates from the star Skat in Aquarius, shown in the Capricornus pictures. Use instructions for Algiedi above.

THE YEAR'S CALENDAR

**In August, September and October, it is not necessary to divide the months into halves. The stars still maintain their steady drift westward but darkness comes rapidly earlier every night during these three months so that our hour-after-dark schedule finds the stars only slightly displaced during any thirty-day period.**

*Easy Groups for Beginners*

Turn the north sky circle so that the top is between 18 and 19. Only northerners will see the stars at the bottom of the map as held this way. The best part of the northern sky, however, is now in ideal position.

Chart 1

Our imaginary figure of the Yacht is beginning to emerge from the horizon in the northeast. Use line AA.

Chart 41

Pegasus, the flying horse, is well up over the east. Use the picture "as is."

Chart 29

Cygnus is high above Pegasus with the bright star Vega overhead. Use AA.

Chart 37

In the southeast, Aquarius and Capricornus are clear of the horizon and southerners will see the bright star Fomalhaut.

Chart 24

The Teapot in Sagittarius is at its highest point over the south.

Chart 85

Between south and southwest, Scorpius is beginning to descend toward the horizon.

Chart 81

Above Scorpius is the great figure of Ophiuchus with his Serpent. Use line CC.

Chart 75

# AUGUST

## A PRIMER FOR STAR-GAZERS

Hercules is above Ophiuchus and is now well past the meridian. Use DD.

Chart 70

Low in the west, the Virgo Triangle is making its farewell appearance. Use AA.

Chart 62

Above the Virgo Triangle is the little Northern Crown. Use line AA.

Chart 66

### *Groups for Advanced Star-Gazers*

The indistinct stars of Pisces are emerging under the Great Square of Pegasus and Andromeda, not yet in favorable position but possible with patience. Use line AA.

Chart 88

The five little neighbors of Cygnus are high in the sky at this time. Use FF.

Chart 91

From west to northwest, Coma Berenices and Canes Venatici are in the lower half of the sky. Use line LL.

Chart 95

### *Zodiac, Milky Way and Meteor Showers*

The Zodiac is now at its lowest arc above the southern horizon. If there are planets in the sky, they will be in Pisces, Aquarius, Capricornus, Sagittarius, Scorpius, Libra, Virgo.

The Milky Way arches high across the eastern sky from Perseus in the northeast, up through Cygnus, and down through Scorpius in the southwest. The Perseus-Cassiopeia area, just coming well up, is particularly rich in gems for owners of binoculars and telescopes.

Star-gazers who are enthusiasts about "shooting stars," or meteors, look forward to a continuing treat during August.

The shower that radiates from the star Skat in Aquarius

THE YEAR'S CALENDAR

continues through this month until about the twenty-fifth. Skat is shown in our pictures of Capricornus. At midnight, use line BB in Chart 26; for other times, consult the Hour-and-Date Diagram.

This diagram can also be used for early-morning observation of a shower radiating from near the head of Capricornus during the first four nights of August.

One of the best of the regular showers—the Perseids—can be seen all through the first part of the month with a brilliant maximum usually on the eleventh and a decreasing number nightly until the twenty-second. The radiant point wanders along the strip of sky between Cassiopeia and Perseus and is best followed by means of the north sky circle, Chart 1, and the Hour-and-Date Diagram.

All through August and well into September, we usually see many moderately bright meteors radiating from the little constellation of Lacerta, which can be found on the north sky circle at the figure 22. Use the Hour-and-Date Diagram for your chosen time.

The sky between Cygnus and Draco usually gives us several showers from the tenth to the end of the month. The star Deneb in Cygnus marks the center of another shower all month. Both of these areas can be located on the north sky circle, Chart 1.

The same chart and Hour-and-Date Diagram can be used for a shower beginning the twelfth and continuing through the rest of the month and September from around the brilliant star Capella, shown inside the figure 05 on the north sky circle.

**Again, as explained in the note at the beginning of the August schedule, it is not necessary to divide the month into two parts.**

*Easy Groups for Beginners*

The top of the north sky circle should be turned to about one-quarter of the way past 19 toward 20. The Big Dipper is now getting low in the northwest. Cassiopeia is about halfway up the sky in the northeast.

Chart 1

The Yacht is now fairly well up in the northeast, with the stars Hamal and Sheratan clear of the haze. Use line BB.

Chart 41

Pegasus is nearly halfway up the sky over the east point. Use line AA.

Chart 30

High above Pegasus is Cygnus, now preparing to cross the overhead point. Use line BB.

Chart 37

Low in the southeast, the "lonely star," Fomalhaut, can be seen by all of us except Canadians. Aquarius and Capricornus are high above it.

Chart 25

The Teapot in Sagittarius is just past the meridian in the south.

Chart 85

To the right of the Teapot, Scorpius and Libra are preparing to go below the horizon but they are still good. Use the picture "as is."

Chart 82

Above Scorpius in the southwest we find Ophiuchus with his Serpent. Use the picture "as is."

Chart 76

Higher than Ophiuchus and to his right is the kite of Hercules with the Great Cluster still in fine position. Use line AA.

Chart 71

THE YEAR'S CALENDAR

Halfway up the sky, due west, is the neat little Northern Crown with bright Arcturus below it. Use line BB.

Chart 66

*Groups for Advanced Star-Gazers*

The indistinct V of Pisces is almost entirely above the horizon, though the star Al Rischa is not yet in sight. Use line BB.

Chart 88

The five little groups around Cygnus are high in the eastern sky and will soon pass over to the west. Use GG.

Chart 91

Coma Berenices is ready to set between west and northwest with Canes Venatici above it and to the right. Use MM.

Chart 95

*Zodiac, Milky Way and Meteor Showers*

The Zodiac is now in its lowest arc in the southern sky. If planets are visible, they will be in Pisces, Aquarius, Capricornus, Sagittarius, Scorpius or Libra.

Some of the richest star fields in the Milky Way are now in fine position for sweeping with binoculars or telescopes. The luminous stream starts northeast in Perseus, mounts almost straight up through Cassiopeia and Cygnus and descends through Ophiuchus and Scorpius.

From September 7 to 15, look for meteors from the region in the Yacht pictures just "ahead" of the stars Marfak and Algol if the Yacht were sailing normally. About midnight, use line CC in Chart 42; for other times, consult the Hour-and-Date Diagram.

The shower from Capella in Auriga that began last month continues through this month even though it is not spectacular. Auriga is shown on the north sky circle, Chart 1, at the figure 05. Consult the Hour-and-Date Diagram.

# OCTOBER



**Again, as explained in the August schedule, it is not necessary to divide the month into two parts.**

*Easy Groups for Beginners*

Turn the north sky circle so that the top is between 20 and 21. Cygnus, at the top, will be overhead. The Big Dipper is now quite low in the northwest and will soon be too low for far-southerners.

Chart 1

In the northeast, the Yacht is clear of the horizon and offers a good test for your imagination. Use the picture "as is."

Chart 41

Very low, to the left, of the Yacht, is the brilliant star Capella and to the right, even lower, are the Pleiades. Neither is high enough yet to be good.

Halfway up the sky in the east is the Great Square of Pegasus. Use line BB.

Chart 30

Between southeast and south gleams the "lonely star," red Fomalhaut, and above it are Aquarius and Capricornus. Use line AA.

Chart 26

To the right of the south point we find the Teapot in Sagittarius.

Chart 86

While facing south, lie back and find Cygnus overhead. Use line CC.

Chart 37

Only the red star Antares and a few of the stars of Scorpius and Libra remain above the horizon in the southwest and these are no good for Canadians. Use line AA.

Chart 82

Above Scorpius and Libra is Ophiuchus with his Serpent. Use line AA.

Chart 76

# OCTOBER

THE YEAR'S CALENDAR

Halfway up the sky in the west is Hercules with the Great Cluster still good for observation. Use line BB.

Chart 71

Below Hercules is the little Northern Crown, with gleaming Arcturus low over the horizon to the right. Use line CC.

Chart 66

*Groups for Advanced Star-Gazers*

The indistinct V of Pisces is now clear of the horizon over the east point. Use line CC.

Chart 88

The first few stars of Cetus, the Sea Monster, are emerging above the horizon between east and southeast. Use line AA.

Chart 89

Sculptor and Grus may be seen (but not by Canadians) very low between southeast and south. Use line AA.

Chart 96

Overhead are the five little groups in the neighborhood of Cygnus. Use line HH.

Chart 91

Coma Berenices has set in the northwest but Canes Venatici is still above the horizon. Better use the north sky circle in conjunction with the chart.

Chart 95

*Zodiac, Milky Way and Meteor Showers*

The Zodiac still arches low over the southern sky from east to west. Planets may be found in Aries, Pisces, Aquarius, Capricornus, Sagittarius, Scorpius or Libra.

The Milky Way starts at the northeast horizon, arches straight up overhead through Cygnus and descends to the southwest horizon in Scorpius. It is in fine position for sweeping with binoculars and telescopes.

Meteor showers are fairly continuous through October and several reach maximum.

The most notable and dependable is known as the Orionids because it radiates from the constellation of Orion. The point of radiation is in the giant's upraised right hand—the one holding the club in our pictures. This shower begins about the ninth and reaches maximum from the eighteenth to the twentieth. Orion is not visible in the early evenings. Use Chart 4 at midnight and consult the Hour-and-Date Diagram for other times.

On October 2, look for a shower from the fourth star from the end of the tail of Draco, the Dragon. On the ninth, a shower from the Dragon's head may be expected. Use the north sky circle, Chart 1, and the Hour-and-Date Diagram.

A shower radiating from Aries reaches its maximum usually on October 15. It begins the twelfth and continues until the twenty-third. Aries is a part of our figure of the Yacht. Use Chart 43, line BB, at midnight.

# NOVEMBER

## THE YEAR'S CALENDAR

*First Half*

*Easy Groups for Beginners*

The top of the north sky circle should be between 21 and 22. The Pointers of the Big Dipper are now too low to be useful to far-southerners. Cassiopeia, however, is easily identifiable high over the northeast and Polaris is not difficult to locate from Cassiopeia.

Chart 1

The brilliant star Capella is so conspicuous over the northeast horizon that he must be identified at this time, even though the rest of Auriga may be none too clear. Use line AA.

Chart 14

To the right of Capella, the twinkling little cluster of the Pleiades is in evidence but the rest of Taurus is not yet high enough for a picture. High above the Pleiades is the Yacht with its four interesting constellations and the Great "Nebula" of Andromeda in fine position. Use line AA.

Chart 42

High up in the southeast sky, we find the flying horse, Pegasus, with his Great Square. Use line CC.

Chart 30

Capricornus and Aquarius are now crossing the southern meridian with the star Fomalhaut the brightest object in the southern sky unless there happens to be a planet there. Use line BB.

Chart 26

While facing south, lie back and find Cygnus and his neighbors, now just past the overhead point. Use DD.

Chart 37

The Teapot in Sagittarius is coming down close to the horizon in the southwest. Use the picture "as is."

Chart 87

Low over the west point and southward of it we find the giant Ophiuchus with his Serpent.

Chart 77

To the right of Ophiuchus and a little higher is the kite of Hercules. The Great Cluster is still in good position but will not be so much longer. Use the picture "as is."

Chart 72

# NOVEMBER



Below Hercules is the little Northern Crown, also getting ready to leave our evening skies.

Chart 67

*Groups for Advanced Star-Gazers*

The indistinct V of Pisces is halfway up the eastern sky. Use the line DD.

Chart 88

Below Pisces is the shapeless Cetus stretching from east to southeast. Use line BB.

Chart 89

Sculptor and Grus cover the horizon from southeast to south (no good for Canadians) and far-southerners may also see a bit of Phoenix. Use line BB.

Chart 96

High up in the sky in the southwest are the five little groups that surround Cygnus. Use the line JJ.

Chart 91

*Zodiac, Milky Way and Meteor Showers*

Planets may be found in any of the constellations of the Zodiac now visible—Taurus, Aries, Pisces, Aquarius, Capricornus, Sagittarius.

The Milky Way is a happy hunting ground for owners of binoculars or telescopes. It starts in the northeast and mounts straight up to cross overhead in Cygnus and descend to the southwest in Sagittarius.

From November 1 to 17, slow-moving meteors may be looked for radiating from the star marking the left eye of Taurus, the Bull. Use Chart 10, line BB, at midnight and for other hours consult the Taurus Hour-and-Date Diagram.

From the tenth to the seventeenth, we have the famous swift Leonid meteors radiating from the Sickle, in Leo. This group does not rise until after midnight at this time of year. At 2 A.M. use Chart 53.

THE YEAR'S CALENDAR

*Last Half*

*Easy Groups for Beginners*

The north sky circle is almost in correct position as it stands. The top should be between 22 and 23. Far-southerners will now get no satisfaction from the Big Dipper. They will have to locate the North Star (Polaris) from Cassiopeia now very high in the northeast.

Chart 1

Brilliant Capella is well up over the northeast horizon. Use line BB.

Chart 14

To the right of Capella, the twinkling Pleiades and bright Aldebaran mark Taurus, the Bull. Use line BB.

Chart 9

Above Taurus, the Yacht fills the upper sky. Use BB.

Chart 42

Aquarius is now astride the southern meridian with the great star Fomalhaut below it and Capricornus to its right. Use line CC.

Chart 26

High above Aquarius, Pegasus is beginning to cross the meridian. Use line AA.

Chart 31

The Teapot in Sagittarius has now begun to set in the southwest. Use line AA.

Chart 87

Due west, most of Ophiuchus is below the horizon and the stars that remain can best be identified from the picture of Hercules, now to the right of west. Use line AA.

Chart 72

High in the western sky, Cygnus, with the bright stars Vega and Altair, is headed downward toward the horizon. Use line AA.

Chart 38

# NOVEMBER



The neat little Northern Crown is low over the horizon near the northwest point. Use line AA.

Chart 67

*Groups for Advanced Star-Gazers*

Lynx is above the horizon to the right of north, between the distorted C of Ursa Major and Auriga, but it is good only for Canadians and is best located at this time by the north sky circle.

Chart 1

Cetus is well up over the horizon in the southeast. Use the line CC.

Chart 89

Sculptor and Grus with some of the stars of Phoenix cover the low horizon to the south, in good position for southerners but useless to Canadians. Use CC.

Chart 96

Above Cetus is the dim V of Pisces, now in the upper half of the sky. Use line EE.

Chart 88

Lacerta is overhead and the four little groups near bright Altair are high in the southwest sky. Use KK.

Chart 91

*Zodiac, Milky Way and Meteor Showers*

Any planets which may be in the sky will be in one of the constellations of the Zodiac now visible—Taurus, Aries, Pisces, Aquarius, Capricornus, Sagittarius.

A rich area of the Milky Way is rising above the northeast horizon in Auriga and Perseus with the sparkling star fields spread through Cassiopeia and Cygnus and running down to the southwest horizon.

Enthusiastic hunters of "shooting star" (meteor) showers have none scheduled for the last half of November. In almost all of the older star books, you will find a shower known as the Andromedids listed as among the best and to be looked for this month. That used to be true. In recent years, however, something seems to have happened to the stream of minute particles that caused these shooting stars as the earth rushed through them and burned them to a blazing vapor with the friction of its atmosphere. Possibly the gravitational pull of one of the planets has displaced their orbit so that they no longer lie in the path of the earth as it rushes around the sun at its breakneck speed of some 18½ miles a second. At any rate, it looks as if the once-famous Andromedids will have to be crossed off from our meteor-hunting date book.

# DECEMBER



*First Half*
*Easy Groups for Beginners*

The north sky circle requires no turning. To be strictly accurate, its top should be between 23 and 00. Most of the Big Dipper is below the northern horizon for far-southerners, and those who live in the middle latitudes will require a very clear night to use it. Polaris is best located by practically dropping a plumb line (in imagination) from the star Caph in Cassiopeia and finding the star just to the left of its mid-point.

Chart 1

From east to northeast, the sky is bright with fine stars but the brightest is Capella, now well up above the horizon.

Chart 14

To the right of Capella, the twinkling Pleiades and gleaming Aldebaran mark Taurus, the Bull. Use line AA.

Chart 9

Below Taurus, due east, a part of Orion is emerging from the horizon. Use line AA.

Chart 4

From the Pleiades up almost to overhead, the imaginary Yacht is sailing. Use line CC.

Chart 42

Pegasus, the flying horse, with his Great Square is crossing the meridian. Use line BB.

Chart 31

In the southwest, Capricornus is headed for the horizon, followed by Aquarius and the great star Fomalhaut.

Chart 27

Very-far-southerners may see some of the Teapot in Sagittarius to the right of southwest but it is no good for the rest of us. Our next conspicuous group is Cygnus, the Swan, diving from midway up the sky straight down at the west point. Use line BB.

Chart 38

From west to northwest, low on the horizon, we find Hercules and the head of Ophiuchus. This is the last annual chance to see the Great Cluster. Use line BB.

Chart 72

*Groups for Advanced Star-Gazers*

Lynx is now well enough up in the northeast for all of us to see. Use line AA.

Chart 92

From east to southeast, the first curving line of Eridanus, the River, is arching above the horizon. Use AA.

Chart 90

To the right of Eridanus we see Fornax, low, and Cetus, fairly high. Use DD.

Chart 89

Above Cetus, the indistinct V of Pisces is high in the sky. Use FF.

Chart 88

Sculptor, Phoenix and Grus are now at their highest point south, best, of course, for far-southerners. Line DD.

Chart 96

In the west, the five little groups that are neighbors of Cygnus are still in good position. Use line LL.

Chart 91

*Zodiac, Milky Way and Meteor Showers*

Confusing planets may appear in one of the constellations of the Zodiac now visible—Taurus, Aries, Pisces, Aquarius, Capricornus, Sagittarius.

The Milky Way arches up from east to west with the sparkling fields of Taurus and Auriga now well above the horizon. Perseus, Cassiopeia, Cepheus and Cygnus well repay search with binoculars or telescopes.

There is a good meteor shower due this month, known as the Geminids because it radiates from the constellation Gem ini, now half above, half below the horizon to the right of northeast in early evening. These "shooting stars" can be seen frequently all through the month but reach maximum December 12-13. A note in that fine magazine for amateurs, *Sky and Telescope*, says, "In recent years, this shower has proved to be the most brilliant of the better known displays. Last year, we counted 20 Geminids in the half hour just before midnight of the 12th."

Use Chart 20, line CC, at midnight and consult the Hour-and-Date Diagram for other times.

Take the advice of a man whose teeth have chattered on many a winter's night—wrap up much more warmly than you think is necessary.

## THE YEAR'S CALENDAR

### *Last Half*
### *Easy Groups for Beginners*

The north sky circle is almost in correct position as it stands in the book. More accurately, the top should be halfway between 00 and 01. The Pointers of the Big Dipper are now headed upward and will soon be seen again by far-southerners. The M of Cassiopeia is at its highest position, with Polaris directly under it.

Chart 1

The long wedge of Gemini is low over the horizon between northeast and east. Use line AA.

Chart 19

Above Gemini is the kite of Auriga with the brilliant star Capella. Use AA.

Chart 15

To the right of Auriga, the twinkling Pleiades make Taurus, the Bull, easy to locate.

Chart 9

Below Taurus, the giant hunter Orion is now clear of the horizon and the parade of brilliant winter stars is under way. Use line BB.

Chart 4

Overhead we have the imaginary Yacht preparing to cross the meridian. Use line AA.

Chart 43

The Great Square of Pegasus has passed the meridian and is on its way down the western sky. Use line CC.

Chart 31

In the southwest, Aquarius and Capricornus are getting ready to set. Use line AA.

Chart 27

Halfway up the sky, from west to northwest, we find Cygnus with Vega and Altair below it. Use line CC.

Chart 38

# DECEMBER

A PRIMER FOR STAR-GAZERS

The last stars of Hercules are low over the northwest horizon but the kite is too low now to be of interest.

*Groups for Advanced Star-Gazers*

Lynx is high enough in the northeast to be identified even by far-southerners. Use line BB.

Chart 92

Eridanus, the River, is above the horizon southeast for far-southerners but much of it is still hidden from Canadians. Use line BB.

Chart 90

Well up in the sky from southeast to south is the amorphous form of Cetus, the Sea Monster. Use line EE.

Chart 89

Above Cetus is the indistinct V of Pisces now straddling the meridian. Use line GG.

Chart 88

In the south, Grus is beginning to set but Sculptor and Phoenix are at their highest points. No good for Canadians. Use line EE.

Chart 96

In the westein sky we have the five little groups that are neighbors of Cygnus. Use line MM.

Chart 91

*Zodiac, Milky Way and Meteor Showers*

The Zodiac is climbing higher in the sky and planets may be in any of its constellations now visible—Gemini, Taurus, Aries, Pisces, Aquarius, Capricornus.

The Milky Way arches from east to west almost overhead with fine sweeping for binoculars and telescopes in Auriga, Perseus, Cassiopeia and Cygnus.

The Geminid meteor shower continues to be worth watching through the month though it is past maximum. Just after midnight, use line AA in Chart 21 and use Hour-and-Date Diagram for other times.

From December 28 to January 4, we look for the "Quadrantids" radiating from between Draco and Boötes between the figures 14 and 15 on the north sky circle, Chart 1. Use Hour-and-Date Diagram to find the position for the time you choose.

# EASY GROUPS

*for*

# BEGINNERS

## VIII

# THE NORTH SKY CIRCLE

In several places in the preceding pages I have emphasized the value to the beginner of first concentrating all his efforts on the identification of the principal groups around Polaris, the North Star, and have advised him not to go wandering about the sky until he feels thoroughly at home in this north sky circle.

Now we are ready to get at the job of locating any of these stars at any time on any night that suits us.

First of all, I will ask you to recall that one-hour photograph of the northern sky. If you were to measure those star arcs accurately, you would find that each one of them is a shade less than one-twenty-fourth of the complete circle of which it is a part.

In other words, it would require about 24 hours for these stars to make a complete revolution and come back to the same place.

We have learned that the actual time is about four minutes less than 24 hours by our earthly clocks so that we can regard the north sky circle as a huge clock that gains about four minutes a day on our earthly clocks.

As a matter of fact, the most valuable and accurate clocks in the world are the "sidereal" (or star) clocks in the great observatories and they keep the time that is kept by this north sky circle and not by regular clocks. The sidereal clocks are checked constantly by the stars and all earthly clocks are checked by time signals sent out by the observatories—time signals which are computed from the star time shown by the sidereal clocks.

Thus it is this north sky circle that governs the hours by which we manage our daily lives, though few people know that it is the stars by which we check our clocks.

Therefore, instead of saying that the star clock runs fast by four minutes a day, we really ought to say that all our clocks are running slow by four minutes a day.

For many reasons, however, that would prove most inconvenient. For one thing, the zero hour, marking midnight on the sidereal clock, can occur at any time, either day or night, and to have midnight at noon would be most confusing to anyone except an astronomer.

So we will regard this north sky circle as a clock that runs fast by four minutes a day and then our next job is to make a table or a graph or diagram from which we can translate one kind of time into the other. When we do that, we can predict exactly where we will find any of these stars whenever we want to go outdoors and look for them.

Fortunately, such a diagram is easy to make and simple to understand and use. There is one on the next page and Chart 1 shows the north sky circle.

With this diagram, all you need do is run your finger along the top row of months to the date you want, run down that column to the chosen hour of STANDARD time and the diagonal line nearest that point will give you the approximate star time.

If you want to sound scientific, you can refer to this as either sidereal time or the Right Ascension of the Meridian—they mean the same thing.

It is equally easy to grasp the idea of the north sky circle as a clock. It is a different kind of clock, to be sure, but not at all complicated. It is a clock with only one hand and that is imaginary. This hand remains fixed and immovable, pointing straight up the sky from Polaris, while the circular card or face, containing the hour-figures (accurately known, even though they are invisible in the sky) revolves *counter-clockwise,* bringing one hour-figure after the other up to the tip of the stationary hand.

You will do well to regard the map of the north sky circle in Chart 1 as such a clock. The marginal figures represent the

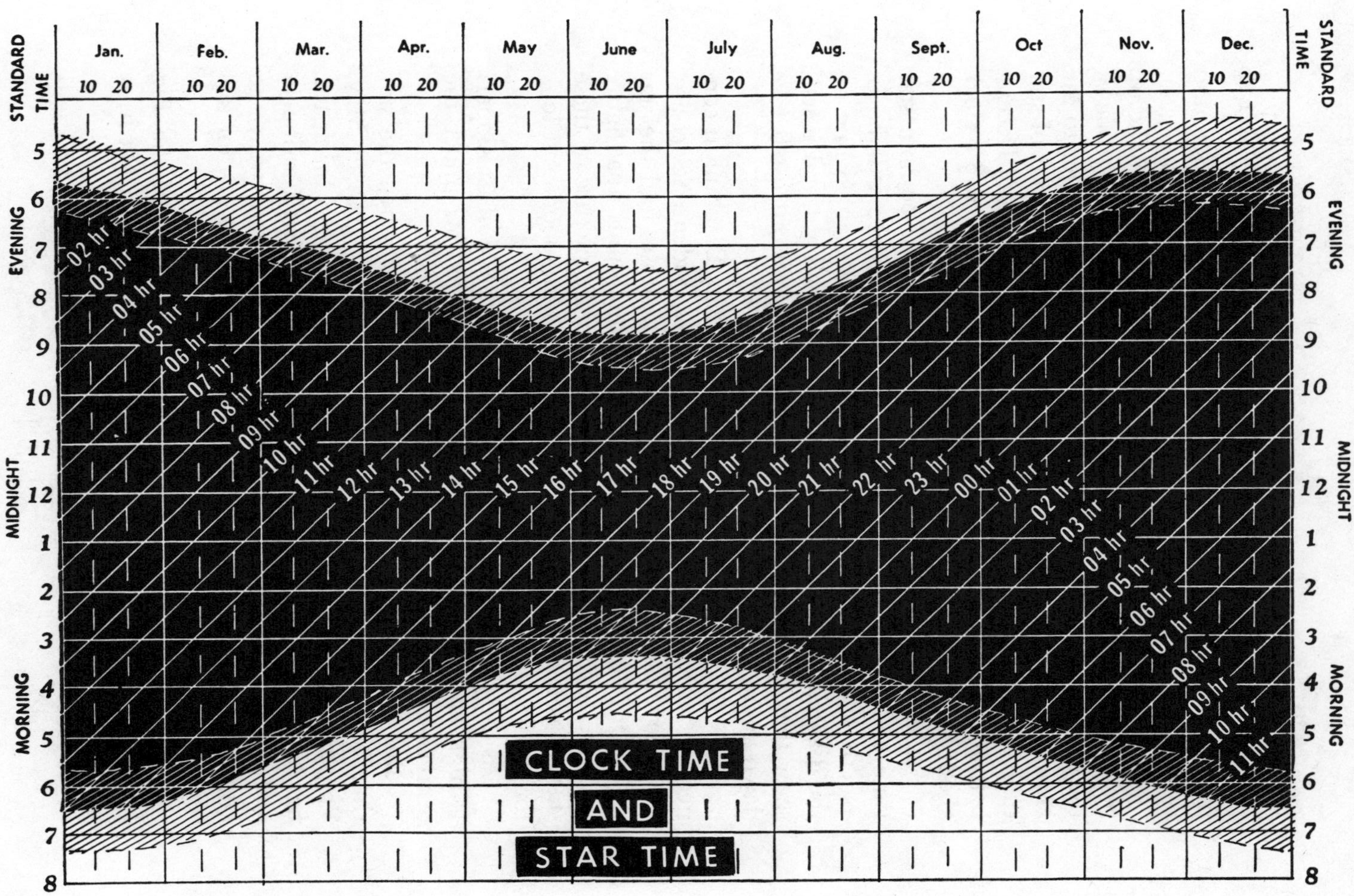
CLOCK TIME
AND
STAR TIME
STANDARD TIME
Jan. Feb. Mar. Apr. May June July Aug. Sept. Oct Nov. Dec.
10 20
EVENING
MIDNIGHT
MORNING
5 6 7 8 9 10 11 12 1 2 3 4 5 6 7 8
02 hr 03 hr 04 hr 05 hr 06 hr 07 hr 08 hr 09 hr 10 hr 11 hr 12 hr 13 hr 14 hr 15 hr 16 hr 17 hr 18 hr 19 hr 20 hr 21 hr 22 hr 23 hr 00 hr 01 hr 02 hr 03 hr 04 hr 05 hr 06 hr 07 hr 08 hr 09 hr 10 hr 11 hr

hours of sidereal (star) time from 00 hour all the way around to the end of 23 hour, when we start at 00 hour again.

If you will imagine this fixed hand pointing straight up from Polaris in the picture, you will see that the star time of the circle as it stands in the book is 00 hour. Now refer to the Hour-and-Date Diagram and you will see that 00 hour of star time can come at 6 o'clock about the twenty-second of December, at 7 o'clock about the seventh of December, at 8 o'clock about the twenty-second of November, etc.

At all of those times on those dates, it will be 00 hour star time and all of the stars in the north sky circle will be in exactly the positions shown. You can follow that 00 line on the diagram all the way along to morning twilight and it will show that these stars will be in the same position just before dawn about the eighth of August.

Now the usefulness of the Hour-and-Date Diagram in connection with the north sky circle becomes evident. Select any hour (STANDARD time) on any night you please, find the star time from the diagram, turn the book around until that figure is at the top, and you will have an accurate picture of these stars as you will then find them if you go outdoors and look for them.

As the picture stands now, at 00 hour, the M of Cassiopeia is high above Polaris and the Big Dipper is low under the center—too low for southerners to see clearly.

But suppose you had chosen a clock time when the star time was 12 hour—say, 9 o'clock about the eighth of May. You would have to turn the book upside down to bring the figure 12 to the top and then you would find that Cassiopeia and the Big Dipper had reversed their positions, with the Dipper now high above Polaris and Cassiopeia too low for far-southerners.

Incidentally, whenever you see the Pointers of the Big Dipper directly above Polaris, pointing straight down at it, it is 11 hour star time.

In every section of the Calendar for Star-Gazers you will

## CHART 1

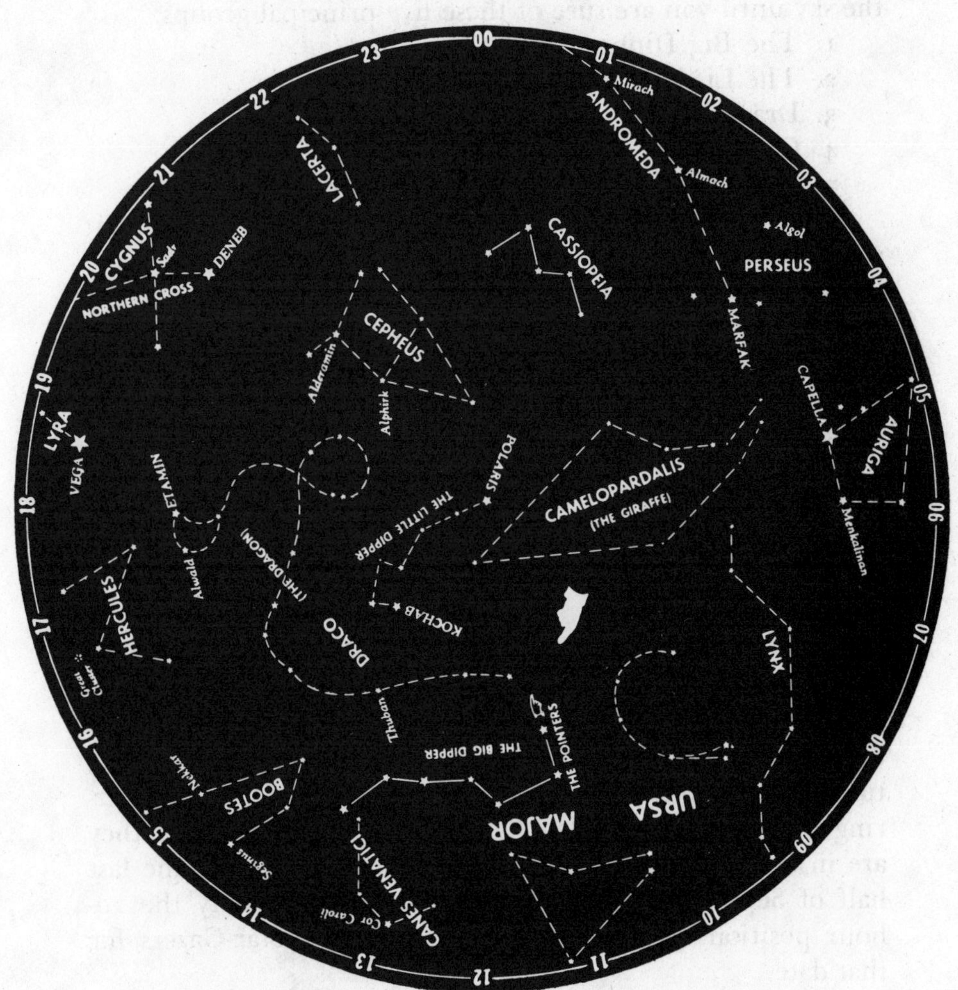


DETAILS and star names of the Big Dipper, the Little Dipper and Draco are on Chart 2; of Cassiopeia and Cepheus, on Chart 3.

notice that I start by giving the star time for setting this north sky circle and so locating your first and most important stars. As a veteran, let me again urge you not to leave this area of the sky until you are sure of these five principal groups:

1. The Big Dipper
2. The Little Dipper and Polaris
3. Draco
4. Cassiopeia
5. Cepheus

Next in order of ease and importance are the two brilliant stars Capella in Auriga (near 05 and 06) and Vega, in Lyra (between 18 and 19). One or the other is always in sight at any time on any clear night and, for Canadians, Capella never goes below the horizon and Vega dips under only briefly for observers along the northern United States border. These are the two brightest stars in the northern hemisphere of the sky.

### *The Dippers, Polaris and Draco*

Chart 2 shows a picture of the Big Dipper, the Little Dipper and Draco, the Dragon, as a modern sky map maker would connect the stars by solid or dashed lines to lead the eye from one to the other and show which ones belong together.

The star time is 20 hour and we see them as we face between north and northwest. Check this by the north sky circle, turning the book to bring 20 hour to the top. Then, by referring to the Hour-and-Date Diagram, you will see that they are in this position about an hour after dark during the last half of September and you will find approximately the 20-hour position specified in the Calendar for Star-Gazers for that date.

The little circle near Polaris in the picture is the actual center of the north sky circle and is known as the North Celestial Pole.

It can be seen that the Big Dipper itself is not a whole

constellation. It is simply a figured group of stars within a constellation.

Our ancient nomad or primitive star-hunter about whom we have talked so much in this book included the Big Dipper, the distorted C of stars to the right in the picture and the bent-in triangle under the Dipper all in one group and somehow or other managed to turn it, in imagination, into a huge bear.

The Big Dipper is supposed to outline his rump and tail, the bowl being the rump and the handle making a tail far longer than that of any bear ever seen by living man. The star Muscida is supposed to be his nose and Talitha the tip of one forepaw while the bent-in triangle locates his hind legs.

This traditional figure of the big bear came from the most remote antiquity and has been handed down to us through the Latin name for the whole constellation—Ursa Major, the Greater Bear.

Ursa Minor, containing the Little Dipper, is the Smaller Bear, also with an impossibly long tail with Polaris, the North Star, at its tip.

There have been many stories about these two bears but the one that has had the widest acceptance comes from Greek mythology.

This legend concerns the infatuation of the great god Zeus for the beautiful nymph Callisto. Such an affair, of course, could not long be kept from Hera, the jealous wife of Zeus, who swore vengeance on the nymph.

Zeus learned of this and, in order to save his sweetheart, turned her into a bear.

In this form, Callisto wandered in the forests of Arcadia, safe from harm, until one day her own son, Arcas, hunting in the forest, spied the bear and raised his spear to kill her.

But Zeus saw the danger just in time and instantly changed Arcas into a bear cub. Then, to avoid further danger, he placed both bears in the sky among the stars.

Hera, however, finally had her revenge. With the aid of

# CHART 2

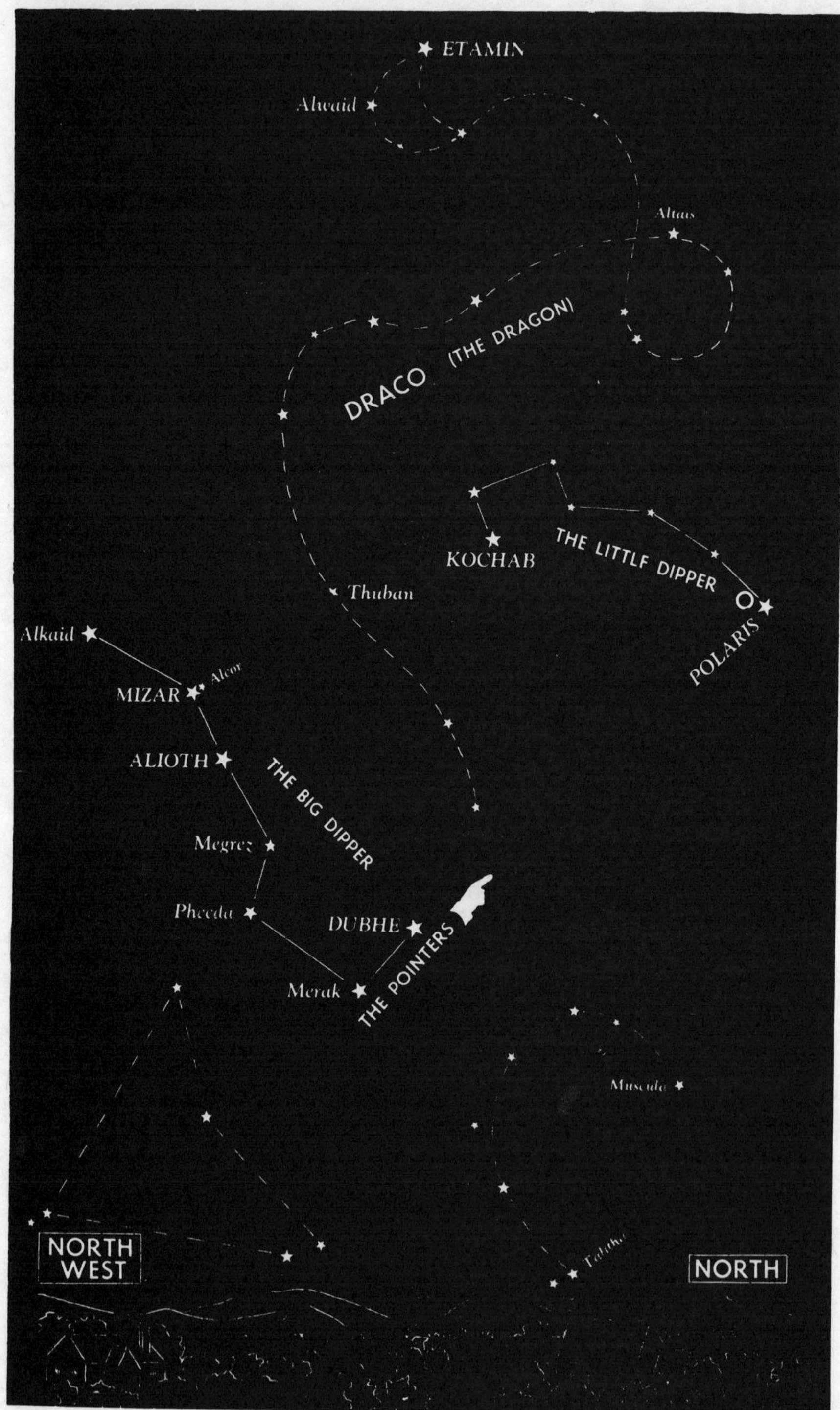

ETAMIN
Alwaid
Altais
DRACO (THE DRAGON)
KOCHAB
THE LITTLE DIPPER
POLARIS
Thuban
Alkaid
Alcor
MIZAR
ALIOTH
THE BIG DIPPER
Megrez
Phecda
DUBHE
Merak
THE POINTERS
Muscida
Talitha
NORTH WEST
NORTH

PRONUNCIATIONS

*URSA MAJOR*—"erse-a may-j'r." the "erse" rhymes with "purse."
DUBHE—"dubb-ee." Accent "dubb."
MERAK—"mee-rack." Accent "mee."
PHECDA—"feck-da." Accent "feck."
MEGREZ—"mee-grez." Accent "mee."
ALIOTH—"alley-oth." "Alley" rhymes with Sally. "Oth" rhymes with "cloth."
MIZAR—"my-zar." Accent "my."
ALKAID—"al-kade." Accent "kade."
TALITHA—"tay-lith-a." Accent "tay."
MUSCIDA—"mew-see-da." Accent "mew."
ALCOR—"al-kore." Accent "al."
*DRACO*—"dray-ko." Accent "dray."
ETAMIN—"et-a-minn." Accent "et"; rhymes with "get," "bet." This star is also known as Eltanin, pronounced "el-tay-nin"; accent "tay."
ALWAID—"al-wade." Accent "wade."
ALTAIS—"al-taze." accent "al."
THUBAN—"thoo-ban." Accent "thoo," the "th" soft as in "think" or "thank."
*URSA MINOR*—"erse-a my-n'r." Accent on "erse" and "my."
POLARIS—"pole-air-iss." Accent "air."
KOCHAB—"ko-kab." Accent "ko" (rhymes with "go").

other gods, she had the two bears sentenced to revolve eternally around the visible sky, never being allowed to seek a daily rest beneath the horizon.

So, today, Callisto, the Big Bear, and Arcas, the Little Bear, are eternal warnings against the sin of being found out.

The novice star-gazer will find little of interest in Ursa Major except the Big Dipper but that is a group of the utmost importance. Our British cousins calls this figure the Plough.

The two most important stars are Dubhe and Merak, the Pointers. No matter in which part of its circle in the sky the Big Dipper is found, Dubhe and Merak will always point to Polaris, the North Star.

But the most interesting stars to the beginner are Mizar and its little neighbor, Alcor. These two are not physically connected but are in the same line of sight from the earth.

Consequently they seem inseparable and visually they are, except to a person with perfect eyesight.

The Arabs called this pair "the horse and rider;" American Indians called it "the squaw with the papoose on her back."

See if you can separate them without the use of binoculars. Then, if you have binoculars, use them all around these stars. It is a beautiful region of the distant sky, with its beauties beyond the reach of the naked eye.

Of the seven stars in the Big Dipper, the five inner ones all apparently belong to a mysterious and loosely joined swarm of stars, possibly including our sun, that are hurtling through space at about the same speed and in the same direction. These five are all at distances from 70 to 100 light-years from the earth.

The two end stars, however—Dubhe and Alkaid—are rushing at even greater speeds in the opposite direction and are more than 300 light-years from the earth.

These opposing motions will slowly alter the form of the Big Dipper and, in the course of several hundred centuries, it will no longer resemble a dipper at all.

Just as the two outer stars of the Big Dipper have a special name—the Pointers—so the two outer stars of the Little Dipper are assigned a celestial function. They are called "the Guardians of the Pole."

Kochab is the brighter one and is a navigational star—that is, the *Nautical Almanac* and the *Air Almanac* give complete data about it for every night in the year and every hour of the night so that navigators may use it to determine their positions at sea or in the air. Whenever, in any of the sky pictures in this book, you see a star name spelled in capital letters, you will know that it is one of these navigational stars.

The other "Guardian" is not so bright as Kochab and is usually known simply by the Greek letter Gamma, though it has an old Arabian name, Pherkad.

Polaris, the North Star, is one of the most interesting objects to owners of good telescopes. To the naked eye, the star seems to be only a single point of light but, with a good glass, it is seen to have a small companion, very close to it.

The experts in the great observatories, however, have scientific instruments which prove it to be more complex than a simple "double." The brighter star of the two is itself a triple system. It consists, first, of two stars that revolve around a common center of gravity in 3.97 days, causing a partial eclipse when one passes in front of the other, which makes Polaris lose about 10 per cent of its light at each eclipse point in each revolution.

At the same time, these two stars have a third one bound to them by gravity and the three revolve about *their* common center of gravity in about twelve years.

### *Cassiopeia and Cepheus*

There is an ancient myth that is still useful to the star-gazer of today because it serves to gather into one area of the sky the principal characters in the story and thus aid his memory.

Fortunately, too, these characters are so placed that they make their entrances on the sky-stage in proper order after the celestial curtain goes up at the same time each year.

The story is an old legend of the ancient kingdom of Ethiopia.

King Cepheus had as his queen the dazzlingly beautiful Cassiopeia. We find them placed today in our northern sky, doomed—like the Bears—to circle eternally around the Celestial Pole and never permitted to retire to rest beneath the horizon.

Cassiopeia's marvelous beauty became famous far and wide and, as its fame grew, so grew her vanity. She began to boast of her beauty, even after the birth of her lovely daughter, Andromeda.

At last the queen's vanity became so uncontrollable that

she committed what was, at that time, considered a deliberate insult to the gods; she boasted that, in her person, there had at last been created a woman more beautiful than the divine sea nymphs.

Now a boast like that could not be permitted to go unpunished. There would be no stopping the impudence of these puny mortals if the gods permitted it.

So they passed sentence on Cassiopeia. She must give up her lovely daughter, Andromeda, to a horrible death.

It was decreed that Andromeda should be chained to the rocks on the shore of the sea. At the appointed time, Cetus, a horrible sea monster and champion of the nymphs, would emerge from the waves and devour her in full view of the horror-stricken parents and their subjects.

So it was arranged. Andromeda was bound to the rocks with chains and King Cepheus and Queen Cassiopeia and all the despairing people waited for the awful Cetus to come for the doomed girl.

But they reckoned without the hero Perseus, who seems to have been an ancient version of the United States Marines, who always arrive just in the nick of time.

Perseus, the son of Zeus, riding his winged horse, Pegasus, was on his way home from one of his most famous exploits—the slaying of Medusa, the lady who had poisonous snakes for hair but whose most charming attribute was the fact that anyone who looked at her was immediately turned into stone.

Perseus had slain Medusa and cut off her head, snaky locks and all, and was returning with the deadly head concealed in a bag so that no one should become petrified by looking at it.

As he flew on Pegasus through the air, he saw the Ethiopians on the shore, very evidently in trouble.

Descending, he was at once smitten with the loveliness of Andromeda. He learned just in time what the trouble was. Even then, the monster Cetus, in a great tidal wave of foam, was hurtling toward the shore to claim his victim.

Perseus shouted a warning to all the people to close their

eyes, closed his own, pulled the head of Medusa from the bag at his side and Cetus—looking to see what this puny human was trying to do—stared straight at the snaky locks.

At once, the monster was turned to stone and Andromeda was saved, to marry Perseus and, of course, to live happily ever after. The mighty Hercules was their grandson.

So impressed were the gods with the cleverness and bravery of Perseus, that they transferred all the actors to the sky, little dreaming that humans would later use the flying horse for an oil company's trademark or the name of the Perseus star, Marfak, for a system of car lubrication.

Chart 3 shows us the groups of stars representing King Cepheus and Queen Cassiopeia at about the lowest point in their eternal circling around the Celestial Pole. This position may be considered the "between performances" period in our mythological drama. Here the actors are resting briefly before rising for another season of nightly appearances for their audience of star-gazers. It is star time 13 hour, in case you want to refer back to the map of the north sky circle.

I have refrained from giving the traditional mythological drawings of these two characters because they are both beyond the imagination of a modern star-gazer and would only be confusing to the novice.

Cassiopeia is popularly known as the "Lady in the Chair" but it is a difficult figure to visualize and the group becomes much more striking and conspicuous when considered as the capital letter W below the Pole or M when above it.

Cepheus is pictured in the old star atlases as having his feet almost on the Pole and his head and shoulders out where we see the star Alderamin and the lesser group of Delta, Epsilon and Zeta. This old figure, too, requires a primitive type of imagination and it is far easier for a modern to regard the stars as forming a child's attempt to draw a church and steeple.

We find these two characters in our mythological drama rising to introduce the other players at about 14 or 15 hour star time. About an hour later than this—16 hour star time—the center of the "church" in Cepheus will be as high above the horizon as Polaris, the North Star. Then we can prepare for the rest of the dramatic cast.

At 17 or 18 hour we will see Andromeda above the horizon in the northeast (Chart 40). Half an hour after this, Pegasus, the winged horse, will be in full view (Chart 29), and, in another half-hour after that, we will see the hero Perseus (Chart 41). Of course, during all this time, all the characters will continue to climb higher in the sky.

If, however, we do not care to stay out so late, but want to confine our observations regularly to the schedule of an hour or so after darkness, we shall have to wait until August for all of the figures to be above the horizon and then consult the Calendar to get the correct pictures for each one.

Before we leave this old story it may be well to mention the fate of Cetus, the Sea Monster, the villain of the piece. He too has been placed in the sky but removed from his intended victims so that he can never threaten them again. He rises in the southeast but not until long after the other characters are well up. His supposed figure covers a large area of the sky but it is dimly marked with no notable stars and is included among the more difficult groups. The group is shown in Chart 89.

The two constellations of Cepheus and Cassiopeia have many objects of interest to the star-gazer.

First of all, these are two of the constellations bordering upon or in the marvelous star fields of our local galaxy, forming that luminous belt around the sky which we call the Milky Way. Such areas of the heavens make a good pair of binoculars worth twice whatever they cost. There is fine "sweeping" all through Cassiopeia, especially the region marked "Field of Stars," and the "foundation" of the Cepheus "church."

Cepheus also contains the remarkable and historic star that bears the Greek letter Delta.

Delta is a variable star—that is, its light varies. At maximum brightness, it sends us about twice as much light as at minimum. And it is as regular as clockwork.

From minimum to minimum, or from maximum to maximum, the time is 5 days, 8 hours, 47 minutes and 39 seconds. At maximum, it is white; at minimum, yellow. It rises quickly from minimum to maximum in about a day and a half and uses the longer part of its cycle fading from maximum to minimum.

Fortunately for the noninstrumental amateur who is interested in watching these changes, there are two steady stars near Delta which furnish comparisons by which its fluctuations can be estimated after a little practice.

At maximum, Delta is just as bright as Zeta; at minimum, it is a shade less bright than Epsilon.

Long study of the recorded observations of Delta has gradually led to the development of a method by which we can arrive at a very close estimate of the distances of many celestial objects which are so far away that any attempt to make direct measurements would be hopeless.

In the first place, it was discovered that Delta fluctuates in brightness, not because it is subject to partial eclipse by a darker companion star, as Algol is (page 212), but because it is actually a pulsating star. It swells up and contracts and again swells up and contracts like the huge chest of some giant breathing regularly in his sleep.

Why any star should do this—in fact *how* it is possible for it to act so—is one of the many unsolved mysteries of the universe in which we live. Pulsation, however, is by no means an uncommon state. Our catalogues contain several thousand stars which do the same thing. When the pulsations are regular in their schedules, we call such stars "Cepheids" because they are like Delta in Cepheus.

Painstaking study of the nearest of the Cepheid type variables—those near enough to have their distance and brightness measured by instruments—revealed the fact that there was a definite relationship between the "period" of the star

# CHART 3

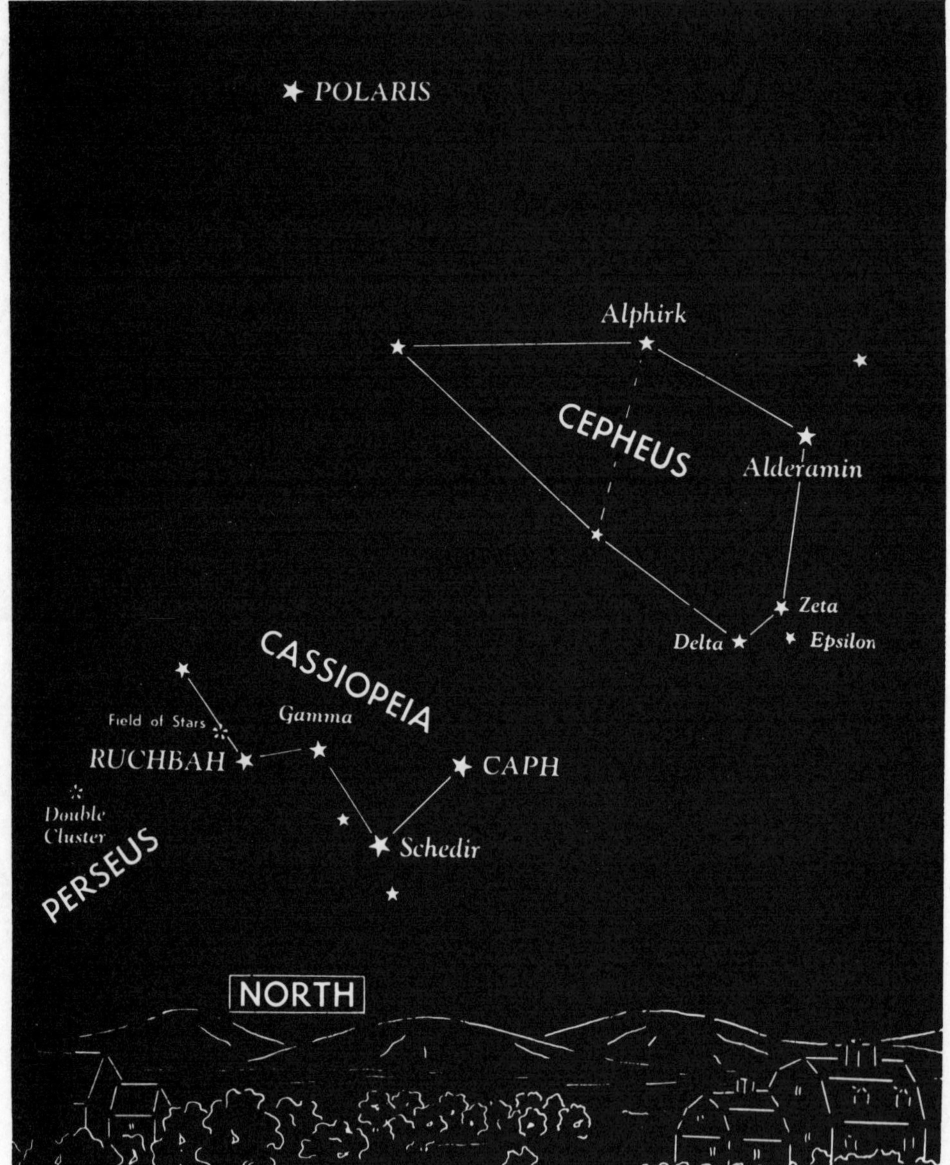

POLARIS
Alphirk
CEPHEUS
Alderamin
Zeta
Delta
Epsilon
CASSIOPEIA
Gamma
Field of Stars
RUCHBAH
CAPH
Double Cluster
Schedir
PERSEUS
NORTH

PRONUNCIATIONS

*CEPHEUS*—"see-foos." Accent "see."

ALDERAMIN—"al-derr-a-minn." Accent "derr."

ALPHIRK—"al-firk." Accent "al."

DELTA, EPSILON and ZETA (pronounced "zay-ta") are not proper names; they are the English spellings of the Greek letters that have been assigned to these stars.

*CASSIOPEIA*—"kass-ee-oh-pee-ya." Main accent on "pee" with secondary accent on "kass."

SCHEDIR—as if spelled "shedder." Accent "shed." Many authorities seem to favor the spelling Schedar.

CAPH—as though spelled "kaff."

RUCHBAH—"ruck-bah." Accent "ruck."

GAMMA—this is the English spelling of the Greek letter that has been assigned to this star. The star is generally known, even among serious scientists, as "Gamma Cass."

(the time for one complete cycle of its variability) and its actual luminosity. The longer the period, the greater the luminosity and vice versa.

Incidentally, in speaking of stars, scientists make a distinction between the words "brightness" and "luminosity." Brightness is used to express the amount of light it seems to send us as we see it from our earth, with no knowledge of its distance. A dim star may actually be emitting a tremendous amount of light but be so far away that it seems dim to us. On the other hand, a very ordinary star may look much brighter to us because it is much nearer.

Therefore brightness means the light we receive without regard to the amount of light actually sent out by the star. There are many tremendously bright stars which are so far away that they are not visible even in the greatest telescopes. They have so little "brightness" that we cannot see them.

"Luminosity," on the other hand, has nothing to do with distance or even with whether the star is visible to us or not. It is a measure of the actual amount of light emitted by a star.

In order to reach a uniform standard of comparison and measurement, we assume a distance of about 33⅓ light-years (one light-year is six million million miles) and then we ask our mathematicians to figure out just how bright each star would look to us if it were placed at this standard distance.

The result is what we call the star's luminosity, or intrinsic brightness or absolute magnitude. Our own sun, if moved away to this standard distance, would no longer appear to us to be a great ball of dazzling fire but would be so dim that we would not see it at all if there were any moonlight or much street lighting around us. Fortunately for us, our sun is only about 8⅓ light-*minutes* away.

Delta in Cepheus is about 275 light-years away—or nearly nine times the standard distance.

The information gained from the near-by Cepheid variables enabled our mathematicians to figure the exact relationship between a Cepheid's period and its luminosity. They already knew how to figure the effects of distance and other factors on a star's apparent brightness. So the method of calculation became a simple one: the period of the variable enabled them to calculate the luminosity; the difference between actual luminosity and apparent brightness enabled them to calculate the distance.

This yardstick has given us a totally new approach to the problems of many remote and independent universes of stars, such as the Great Nebula (which should be called Galaxy) in Andromeda described and pictured on page 197 and the Great Cluster of Hercules, on page 258.

Experts examine observatory photographs and records of these systems covering many years; they locate and analyze the Cepheid variables and thus arrive at an estimate of the distance.

Turning now from Cepheus to the W or M of Cassiopeia, we meet another variable much more mysterious than Delta in Cepheus. This is the star Gamma in Cassiopeia.

There is no satisfactory explanation for the unpredictable

behavior of Gamma Cass. It might almost be compared to a man who, for many years, had lived a steady and respectable life and then had suddenly tired of respectability and decided to become a gay dog and stage a series of wild parties to shock and scandalize his neighbors.

Prior to the year 1927, Gamma Cass was a staid and respectable citizen. Incidentally, when I say that something happened there in 1927, I really should say about the year 1600, because it takes the light of Gamma Cass about 325 years to reach the earth. But accepting earthly reckoning, Gamma was only a little brighter than the near-by star Caph (which is marked in the pictures) up to 1927.

Then, without warning, it suddenly began to show violent changes, not only in brightness, but in diameter, temperature, color and physical and chemical characteristics as recorded in various observatory instruments.

For ten years, it increased in brightness until it was brighter than the star Alioth in the Big Dipper. Then it decreased with even more rapidity and in three years was only as bright as the near-by star Ruchbah.

Since then it has fluctuated constantly but not so violently in brightness. Its color and temperature, however, have shown wide and inexplicable variations. At its brightest, it has been 3½ times as bright as at its minimum.

But its apparent diameter has varied even more widely. During the many years of its respectability, it had a diameter about 8⅓ times that of the sun; in 1934, it was 15½ times; in 1936, 10.6 times; in 1937, 18 times; in 1939, 9.8 times.

Needless to say, Gamma Cass is being constantly watched today by the experts in most of the big observatories, and the records which they are gathering with their instruments are being endlessly studied by physicists and mathematicians, all striving to find some acceptable explanation for this strange behavior.

The one now receiving most attention is that Gamma Cass is spinning on its axis with amazing rapidity. This produces, around its equator, a tremendous centrifugal force that gradually makes its gases bulge out farther and farther until a "breaking strain" is produced, when the outer belt of atoms is hurled out into space and the star, relieved of this excess, settles back to begin the process all over again.

IX

## ORION, THE MIGHTY HUNTER

ORION is the most brilliant constellation to be found in the sky. Its bright stars and the unmistakable pattern of their placement make it the easiest group for the novice to identify and it dominates the early evening heavens from December to mid-April.

To the amateur with good binoculars or a telescope, it offers in its Great Nebula one of the most thrilling of celestial objects, rivaling in interest the famous Andromeda Galaxy, the Great Cluster in Hercules and the Double Cluster in Perseus—all visible to the naked eye as dim and hazy specks, becoming thrilling with enlargement by good lenses, and striking us almost speechless with awe and unbelief when we see them as revealed in long-exposure photographs made with great observatory telescopes.

Orion, too, gives to the scientist other objects which lead to endless debate.

Here we find vast clouds of opaque, interstellar dust that entirely black out the stars behind them. Will this matter—millions of centuries in the future—be gathered into the makings of new stars and galaxies?

The famous Great Nebula shows spots that seem to indicate that its gases, acting under forces of light pressure and gravitation, are beginning to form into apparently denser knots here and there.

Are these knots an evidence of great stars in the actual process of gestation?

Here we find two immense stars, Rigel and Betelgeuse, apparently at two entirely different periods in a star's existence. Rigel, the most intrinsically luminous of all stars and one of the hottest, is apparently just reaching the prime of life and the height of manly vigor in the time span of a star.

Betelgeuse, comparatively dull and red and diffuse, expanding and contracting spasmodically, is like an old man with

*Photo by Yerkes Observatory*

THE GREAT NEBULA OF ORION

his strength almost entirely spent, panting in the asthmatic decrepitude of old age.

Is this the correct interpretation of these phenomena? There is much evidence to justify it as a theory. But—like almost every question that concerns the mysteries of the heavens—there is only one answer: we do not know.

The Great Nebula of Orion is easily seen with the naked eye. Its identification is made simple by its position relative to the bright stars of the group as shown in our pictures and the fact that even naked-eye observation reveals it to be not a clear and distinct point of light like a star, but an obviously diffuse bright spot that is dim but unmistakable.

A nebula is a concentration or cloud of gas and dust in space. That world "concentration" must not be understood as implying that the gas is gathered in a dense mass; as a matter of fact, the Orion nebula is probably so diffuse as to have little more density than what we would consider a good vacuum in a physics laboratory.

But here we are dealing with such vast spaces that even this sparse scattering of matter results in such countless billions of atoms and molecules that they completely hide from our line of sight the stars that may be behind or beyond them.

In the case of the Great Nebula, many bright stars are apparently immersed in this cloud and surrounded by it and their radiation excites and illuminates the atoms of the cloud so that these atoms, in turn, send light to us, some by reflection and refraction, perhaps, but most by their own excitation, which causes them to radiate.

The Great Nebula is believed to be on the order of a thousand light-years from us and the distance between it and us seems to be increasing at the rate of about 600 miles a minute. The total mass of the cloud—tenuous as it is—is about 10,000 times the mass of the sun, and the sun has over 333,000 times the mass of our great earth. All of this mass in the nebula is, however, so scattered as to occupy a space almost inconceivable in extent—so vast that light, traveling at a speed of 11,000,000 miles a minute, would require 3¼ *years* to cross it.

When we come to the famous Horsehead dark nebula in Orion, we find something different in two ways. First of all, it

*Photo by Mt. Wilson Observatory*

THE "HORSEHEAD" NEBULA IN ORION

is not visible, even in a large telescope. It requires a long exposure even in the most efficient of instruments to give us a photograph that shows it clearly.

Secondly, the Horsehead is a great cloud of cosmic dust such as we find scattered in many parts of space. It is this kind of opaque cloud, unilluminated by any near-by stars, that causes the various "coal sacks" and "rifts" in the Milky Way, one of the greatest of these rifts beginning in the constellation Cygnus and another in Ophiuchus.

These clouds are between us and the stars behind them and not close enough to the stars to be excited or illuminated by their light. In many of them—and particularly in this Horsehead—distant starlight is bent or refracted or reflected by the scattered specks of matter on the edges of the cloud, or there are luminous clouds beyond them, and this light

PRONUNCIATIONS

*ORION*—pronounced like the Irish name, "O'Ryan."
BETELGEUSE—"bett-'l-jews." Accent "bett."
RIGEL—"rye-jell." Accent "rye."
BELLATRIX—"bell-lay-tricks." Accent "lay."
MINTAKA—"minn-tack-a." Accent "minn."
ALNILAM—"al-nile-am." Accent "nile."
ALNITAK—"al-nye-tack." Accent "nye" (rhymes with "rye," "eye").
SAIPH—like our word "safe."

serves to give us a clear outline of the main body of obscuring matter.

The photograph of the Horsehead shows this clearly. This amazing object is located between the star Alnitak and the little star under it in the Orion diagram. Unfortunately, as I have said, it is not visible; it can be studied only in pictures.

The diagram is printed for readers who sometimes find such conventionalized arrangements easier to follow than the old picture form in which the stars are enclosed in the mythological figures.

This diagram should be used in connection with the sky pictures shown in Charts 4 to 8, because the names of the individual stars are given on the diagram only.

The ancient mythological stories of Orion are so many and so confused that it is impossible to choose among them. All, however, agree that he was the mightiest hunter in the world and he is shown in the stars with his club upraised in his right hand. Hanging from his upraised left hand is the skin of a great lion he has killed and which he is brandishing in the face of Taurus, the Bull, who is charging down upon him. The lion skin is marked by a neat little string of seven stars, all but the top one known by the Greek letter Pi, numbered from one to six from top to bottom.

Orion's head is marked by a triangle of stars and most beginners are incredulous when a veteran tells them that the full moon would fit into this little triangle. It is a good proof

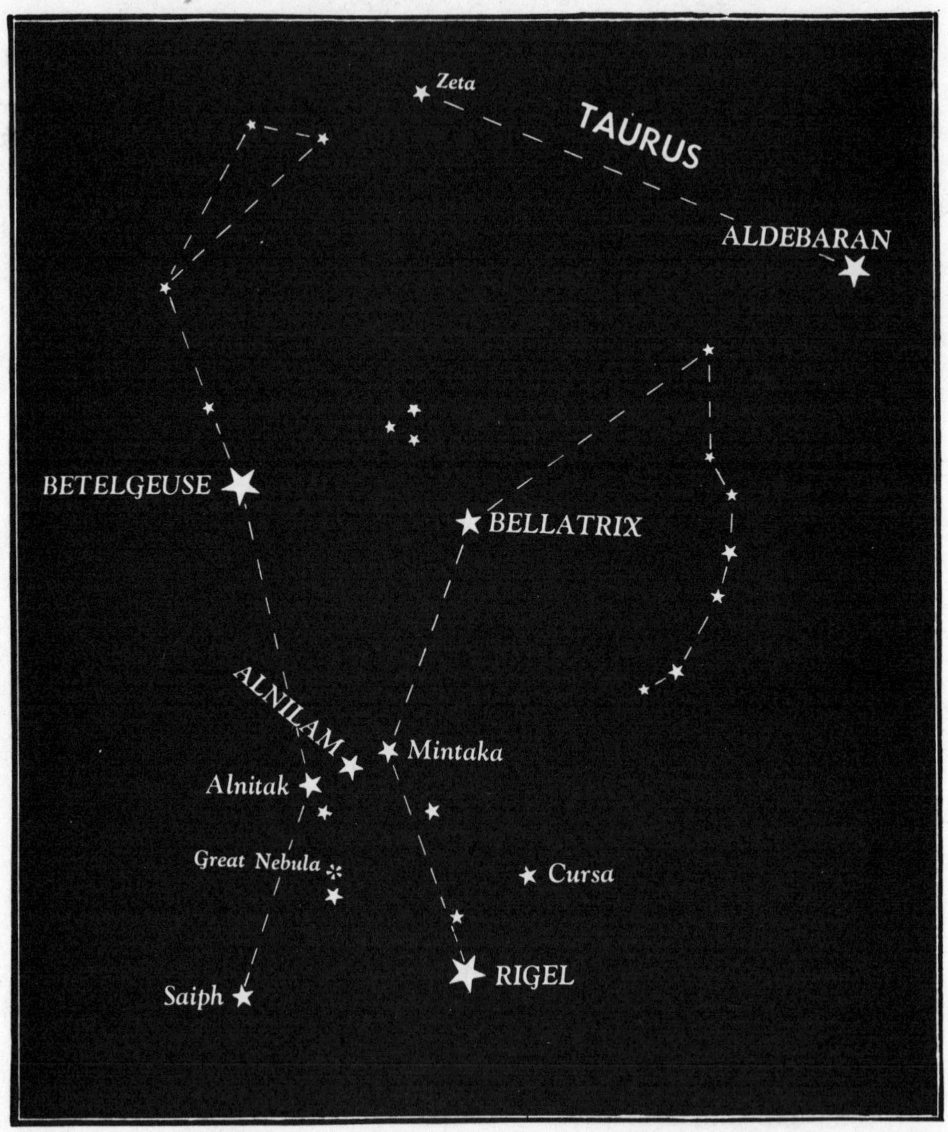


Diagram of Orion showing individual stars and their popular names.

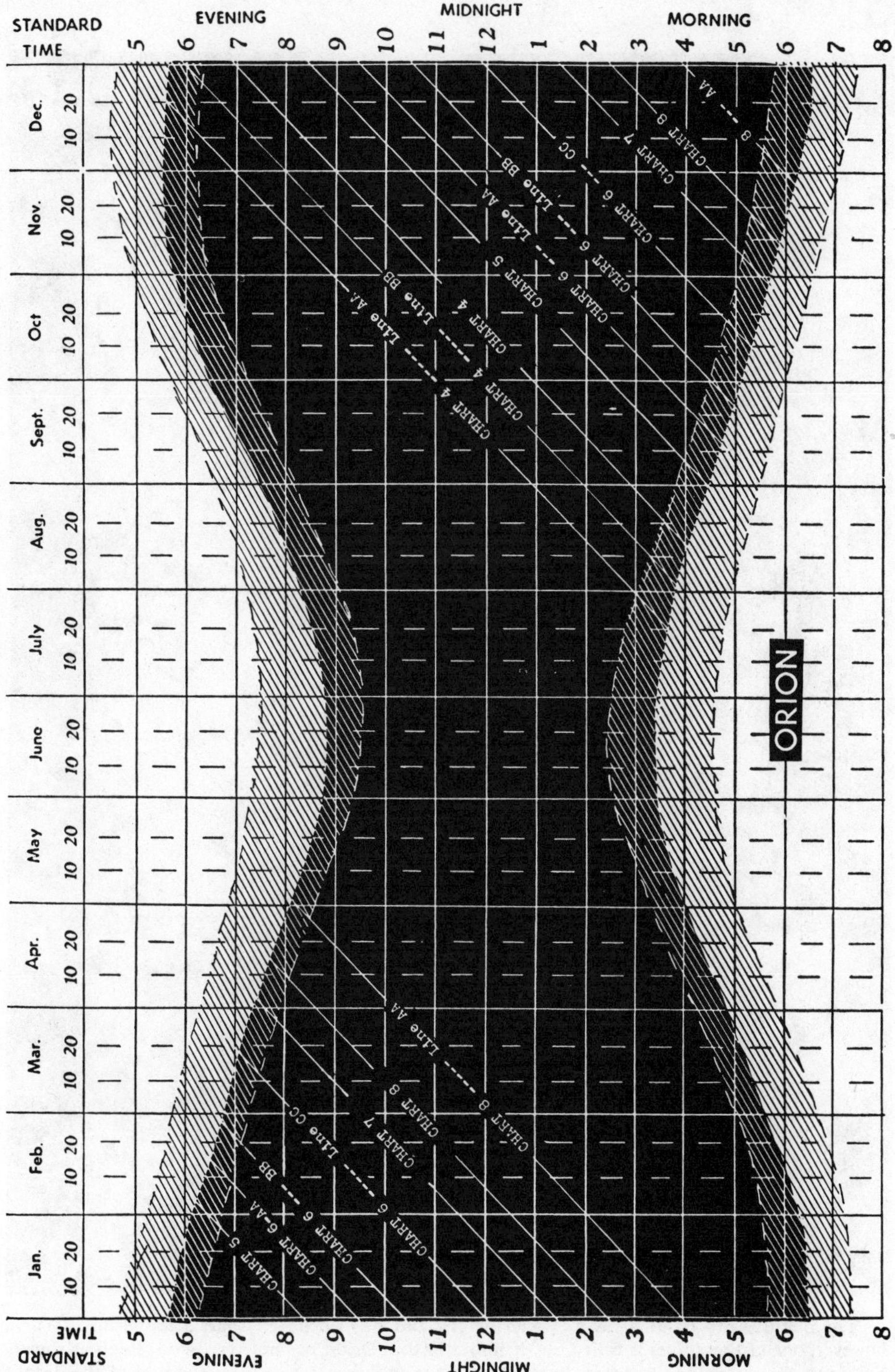


HOUR-AND-DATE DIAGRAM FOR ORION. Diagonal line nearest to hour and date desired shows correct chart and line to use at that time.

# CHART 4

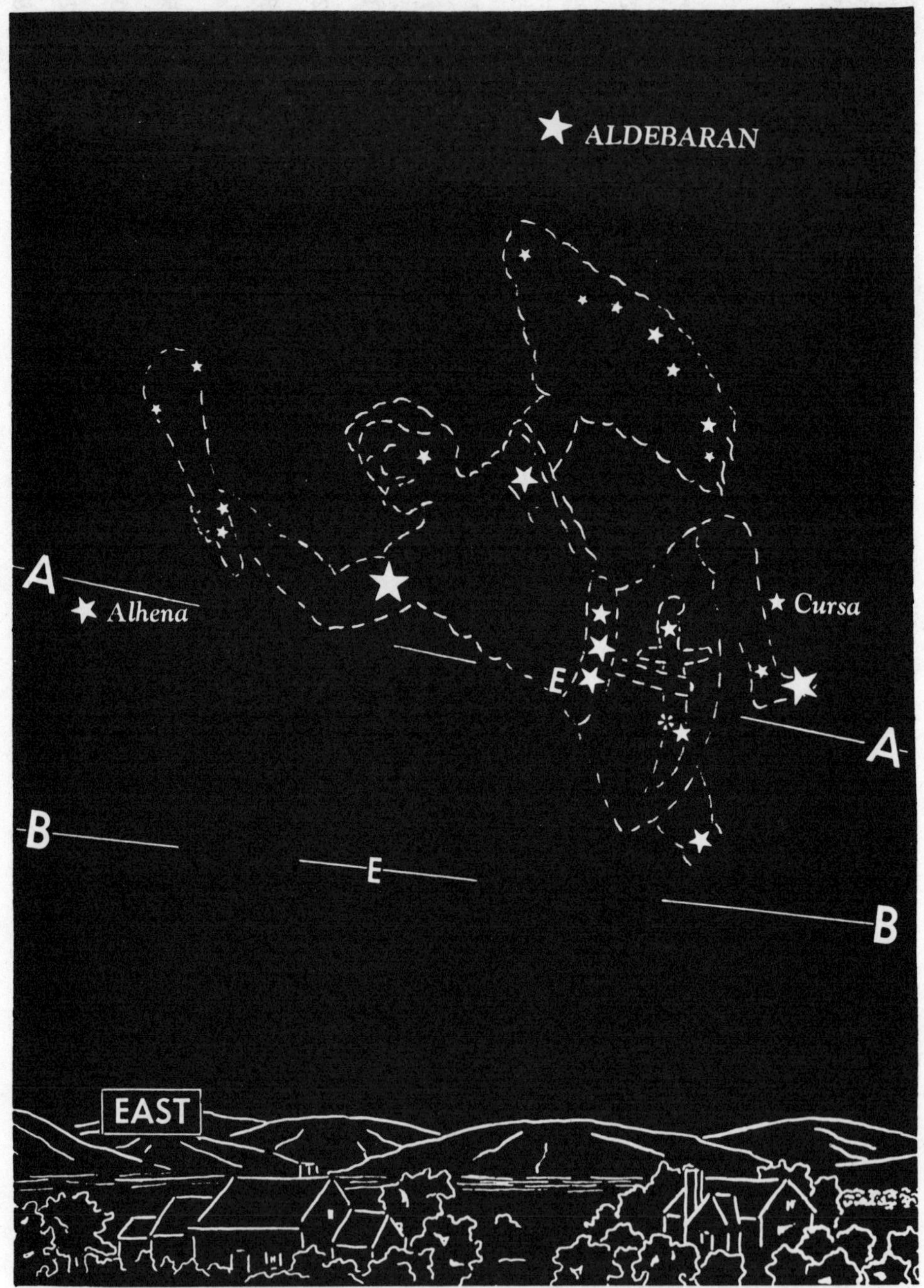


The picture is to be used "as is," ignoring AA and BB, whenever Chart 4 is specified. When, however, one of these lines is called for, it indicates that Orion has not yet risen so high as shown. You must then imagine these stars lowered until the specified line rests on the tops of the distant hills in the landscape. Note how Orion swings southward as he climbs up the sky. The E's mark the east point when either AA or BB is the horizon.

of the illusion of size created by the moon against a background of pin-point stars. A fair-sized pea, held at arm's length, will cover the full moon. If you don't believe that, try it. Hold up a dime at arm's length and see how its diameter compares with that of the moon.

I have already spoken of the two bright stars, Betelgeuse and Rigel, but it is worth while to consider some of their amazing individual details.

Betelgeuse is a "pulsating" star, but so irregular in its habits that no one can predict when it will expand or contract. At maximum size, it is about 460 times the diameter of the sun; at minimum, about 330. The diameter of the sun is about 109 times the diameter of the earth and the diameter of the earth is about 8000 miles. You might like to amuse yourself by figuring the diameters of Betelgeuse from these relations.

Or it might be more impressive to make a comparison by means of familiar things. If you can imagine this earth of ours shrunk to the size of a baseball, then, on the same scale, Betelgeuse would be a globe about two *miles* in diameter. If we could transport our solar system to Betelgeuse with the sun in the center of the star, the planets Mercury, Venus, the Earth and Mars would all revolve around the sun well inside the star with several million miles to spare on the outside of their orbits.

It takes the light from Betelgeuse about 300 years to reach us; our sun, at that distance, would not be visible to us. Yet Betelgeuse has aptly been called a "luminous vacuum." Its average density is so low that it is only about one one-thousandth that of air.

With all its vast surface, however, the actual light emission of Betelgeuse is only about 3600 times that of the much smaller sun.

Rigel, with not much more than a tenth of the diameter of Betelgeuse, is the most luminous star we know—14,000 times more luminous than the sun. Its light requires about 460 years to reach us, and the earth and Rigel are flying away from each other at the rate of some 840 miles a minute. That, however, is infinitesimal when you figure it out in percentage of the distance and it will make no change in the apparent brightness of Rigel for many thousands of years to come.

# CHART 5

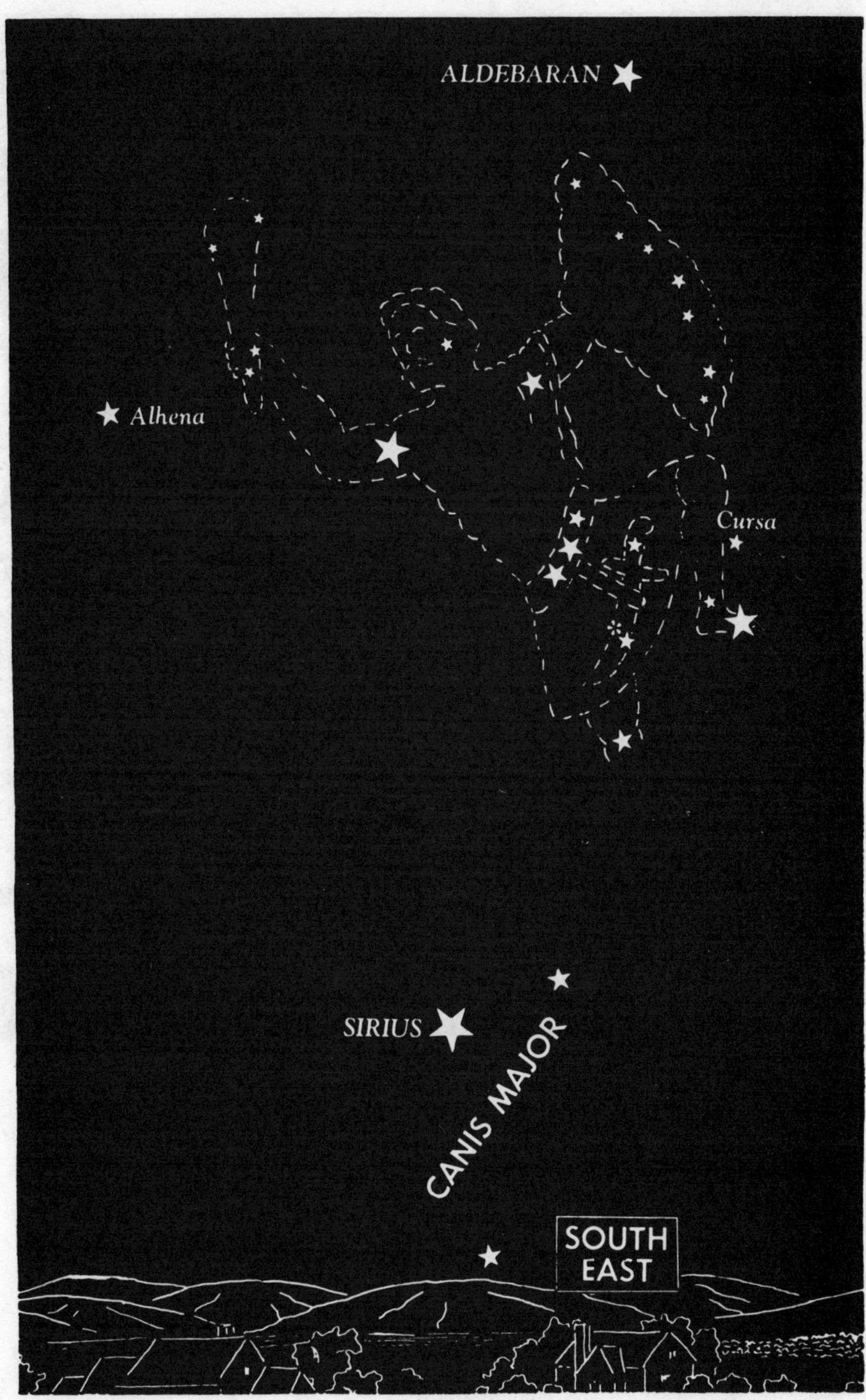


**Orion**: When Orion is in this position, the southeast sky makes a brilliant display, with bright Aldebaran and the twinkling Pleiades above Orion and brilliant Sirius blazing beneath him.

# CHART 6

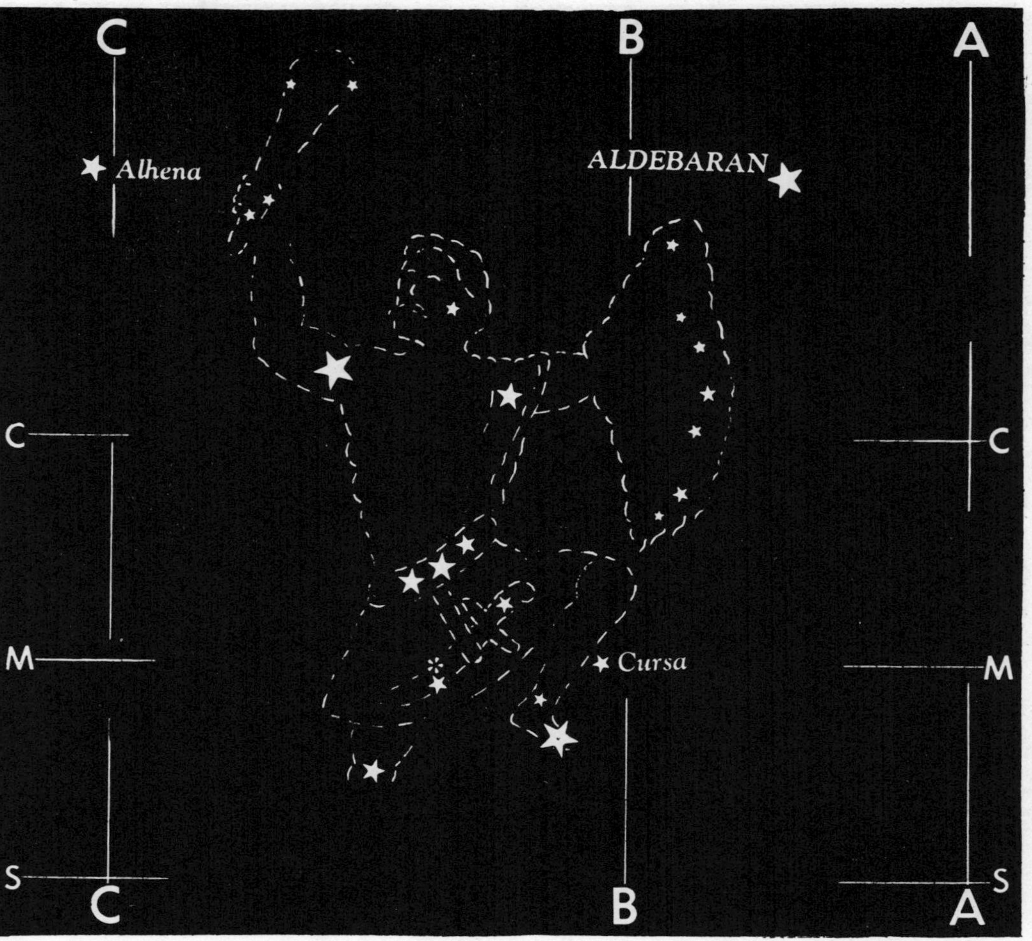


**Orion**: This picture will enable you to locate Orion as he approaches and crosses the southern meridian. Lines AA, BB and CC will be specified at different times. In all cases, face due south, lean back comfortably, shift the book until the specified line is perpendicular to the horizon at the south point, then raise the picture until the cross-line appropriate to your location is halfway up the sky—the C for Canadians, M for mid-United States observers, and S for far-southerners.

# CHART 7

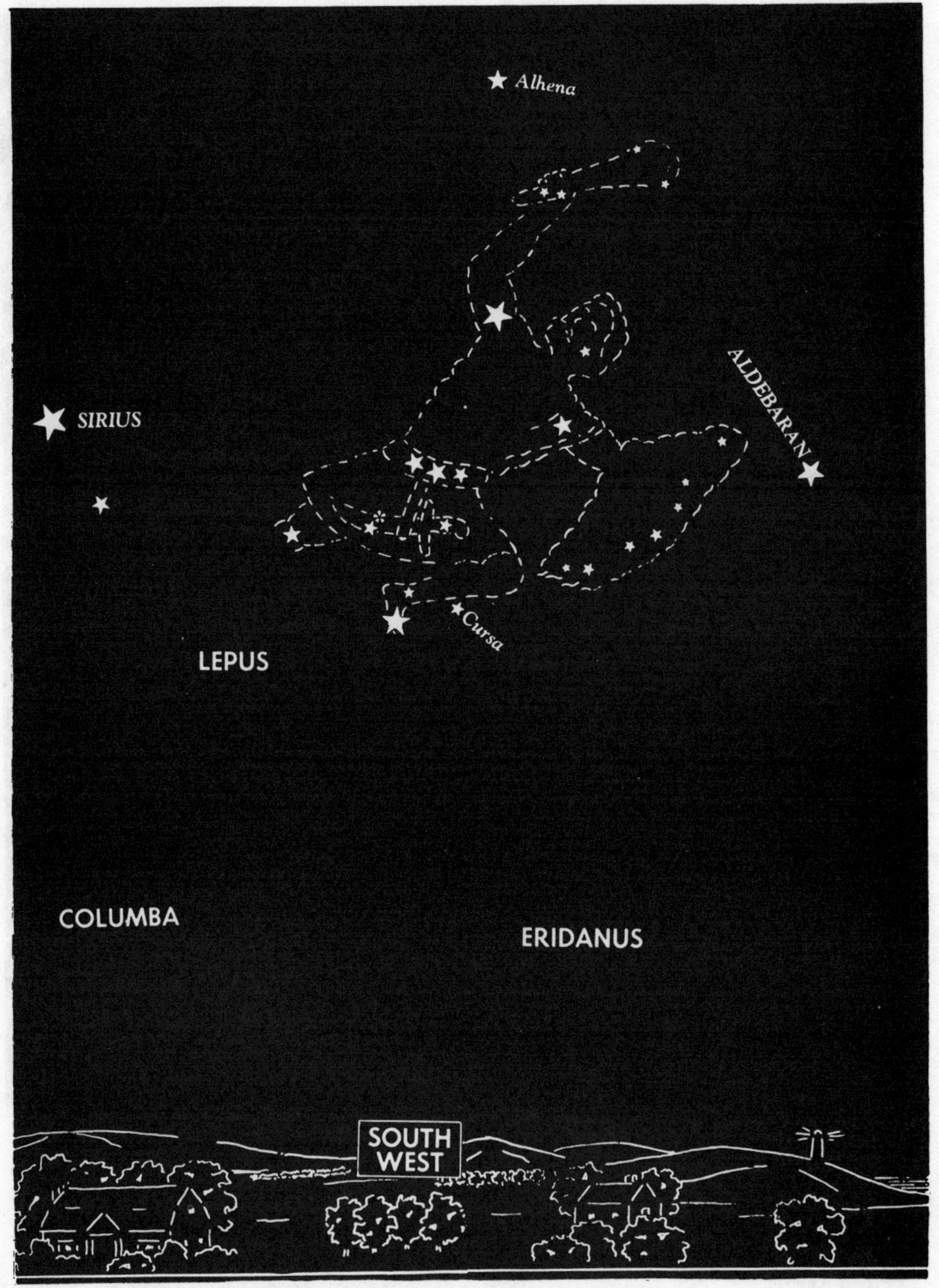


ORION: As he descends the western sky, the great hunter begins to lean over on his left side. Contrast this and Chart 8, with Chart 4, which shows him leaning to the right side.

# CHART 8

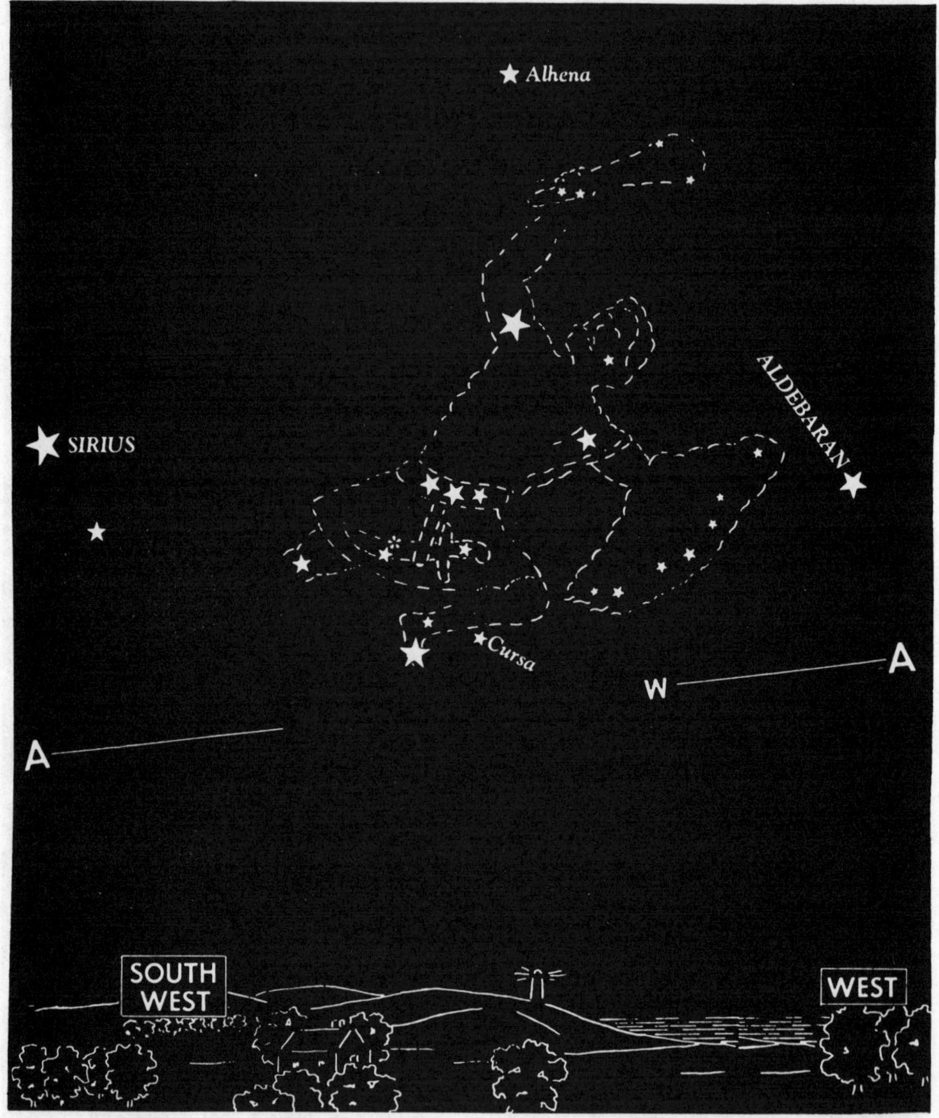


**Orion:** This picture, ignoring the line AA, shows Orion as you will find him whenever Chart 8 is called for. When, however, the line AA is specified, it indicates that these stars are no longer so high and you must imagine them lowered until AA rests on the tops of the distant hills in the landscape.

## X

# TAURUS, THE BULL

WITH the coming of the favorite star group known as Taurus, the Bull, into the early-evening sky in mid-November, star-gazers who own binoculars or telescopes can settle down happily for a whole winter in which to enjoy two of the most fascinating "loose clusters" in the firmament.

These are the famous Pleiades and the even more beautiful but not so famous Hyades.

Without any introduction by an experienced observer, the Pleiades announce themselves unmistakably even to a novice who never heard of them before. Anyone who is having difficulty in locating and recognizing various stars and star figures might very well start with the Pleiades, because there is nothing else like them in the sky and nobody can look very long at the heavens on a winter night without noticing them and wondering what they are.

To the naked eye, this group looks at first like a shimmering little cloud of light. But further examination, aided by good eyesight, will reveal six sparkling stars crowded so close together that most people find it difficult to count them with certainty.

There are some star-gazers who claim to be able to count seven or eight or nine, but such a claim usually arouses skepticism in a veteran.

Good binoculars will reveal a score of stars in the little group while a long-exposure observatory photograph shows about 2000 in the area—all suffused in great clouds and streamers of nebulous light.

Of these 2000 stars, approximately 250 actually belong to the cluster that is called the Pleiades. The others simply happen to be in the same line of sight and are either closer to us, and thus in the foreground, or farther away, and thus in the background.

But the 250 belonging to the group apparently have some real connection. Long observation and study indicate that they are traveling through space in about the same direction and at about the same speed. But most of them are apparently held loosely together like a load of bird shot fired from a shotgun.

Any casual observer of the Pleiades will notice that there is one star in the group unquestionably brighter than any of the others. This is Alcyone (pronounced "al-sigh-oh-nee"; accent "sigh"; rhymes with "high," "my").

The Pleiades are about 350 light-years away from the earth and they occupy such a vast volume of space that the light from a star on the outer edge of the group would require about 35 years to cross through and reach the opposite edge. And, remember, light travels at a speed of six million million miles in one year.

The second loose cluster or group in this constellation of Taurus is known as the Hyades. It covers the region in and around the bent letter V formed by the brightest stars and representing the face of the bull in the old mythological pictures.

There are about forty stars in this cluster and all appear to be hurtling through space together, headed toward a point not far (as seen from the earth) from the objective point of the Pleiades. Possibly the two swarms will some day, in the unpredictable future, join and become one, but at present we can find no connection between them except in the ancient myths, which claimed that the Pleiades were the daughters of the god Atlas by Pleione, while the Hyades were half-sisters of the Pleiades, with Aethra for their mother.

The Hyades are only about 140 light-years from us—less than half the distance of the Pleiades.

When Taurus is in the night sky, it is well worth the while of any star-gazer to beg, borrow or steal a pair of binoculars to view these two clusters, because the most dazzling of the stars are not visible to the naked eye. This is particularly true

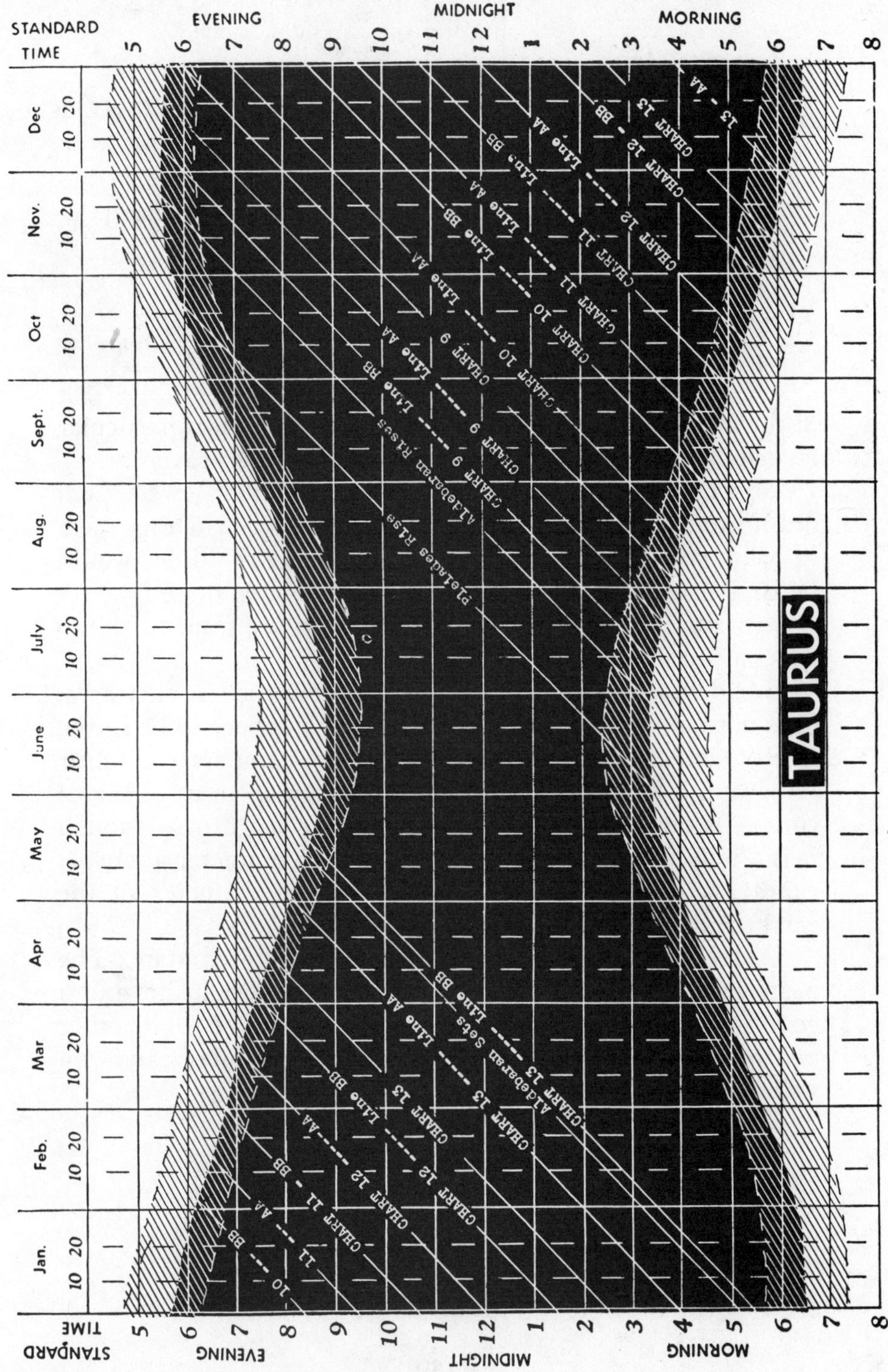


Taurus Hour-and-Date Diagram: Diagonal line nearest to date and hour desired shows correct chart and line to use at that time.

PRONUNCIATIONS

*TAURUS*—like "tore-us." Accent "tore" (rhymes with "bore," "sore").
PLEIADES—"plee-a-deez." Accent "plee."
HYADES—"high-a-deez." Accent "high."
ALDEBARAN—"al-debb-a-ran." Accent "debb."
EL NATH—pronounced as spelled.
ZETA—"zay-ta." Accent "zay." This is not a name; it is the English spelling of the Greek letter that is assigned to this star.

of the area inside the V of the Bull's face—my own particular favorite among all the binocular regions of the heavens.

Some day I hope an imaginative designer of jewelry will duplicate this superb setting of celestial gems, matching them in color, sparkle and design. His only chance of failure would be in trying to improve them. It could not be done.

Invisible as they are, most of these stars are from 50 to 100 times as luminous as our sun.

Incidentally, Aldebaran, the brightest star in this area, does not belong to the Hyades. It simply happens to be in the line of sight from the earth but is in the comparatively near foreground, being only about 55 light-years from us. That, of course, is one reason for its much greater brightness, though it is a notable star in its own right, with a diameter about 35 times that of the sun (or 3500 times the diameter of the earth) and 91 times the sun's luminosity.

Aldebaran is one of the unquestionably red stars. The nearby pure white star, Zeta, at the tip of the right horn, is a good star for comparison. Keep glancing from one to the other and back again, particularly if you have binoculars, and you will see the great difference.

# CHART 9

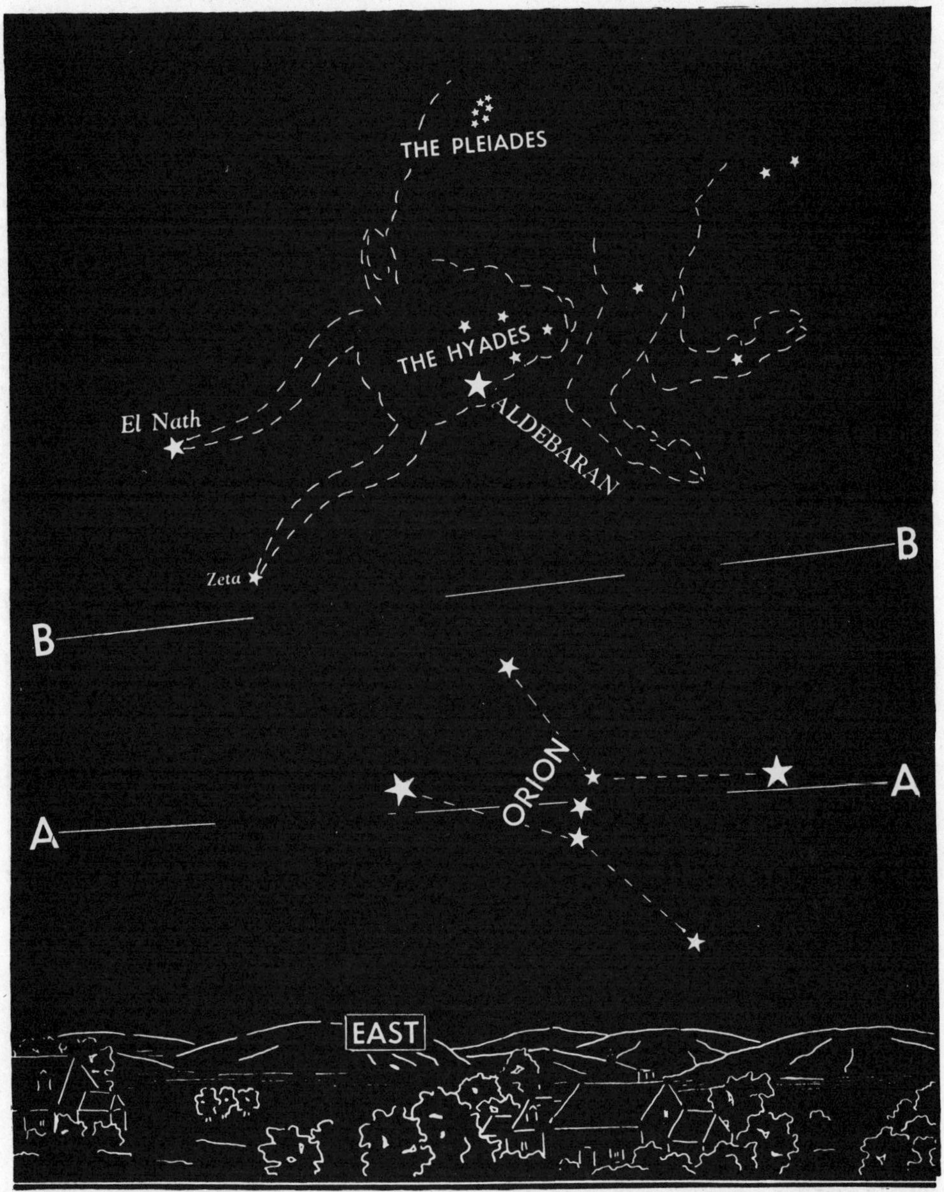


**Taurus:** This picture is to be used "as is," ignoring AA and BB whenever they are not specified. When, however, one of these lines is called for, it means that the stars are not yet so high and you must imagine them lowered until the specified line is resting on the tops of the distant hills in the landscape.

**Planet Warning**

Taurus is in the Zodiac, the path of the wandering planets. If, in using this picture, you see a bright "star" in this area that is not shown here, you may be sure it is a planet.

# CHART 10

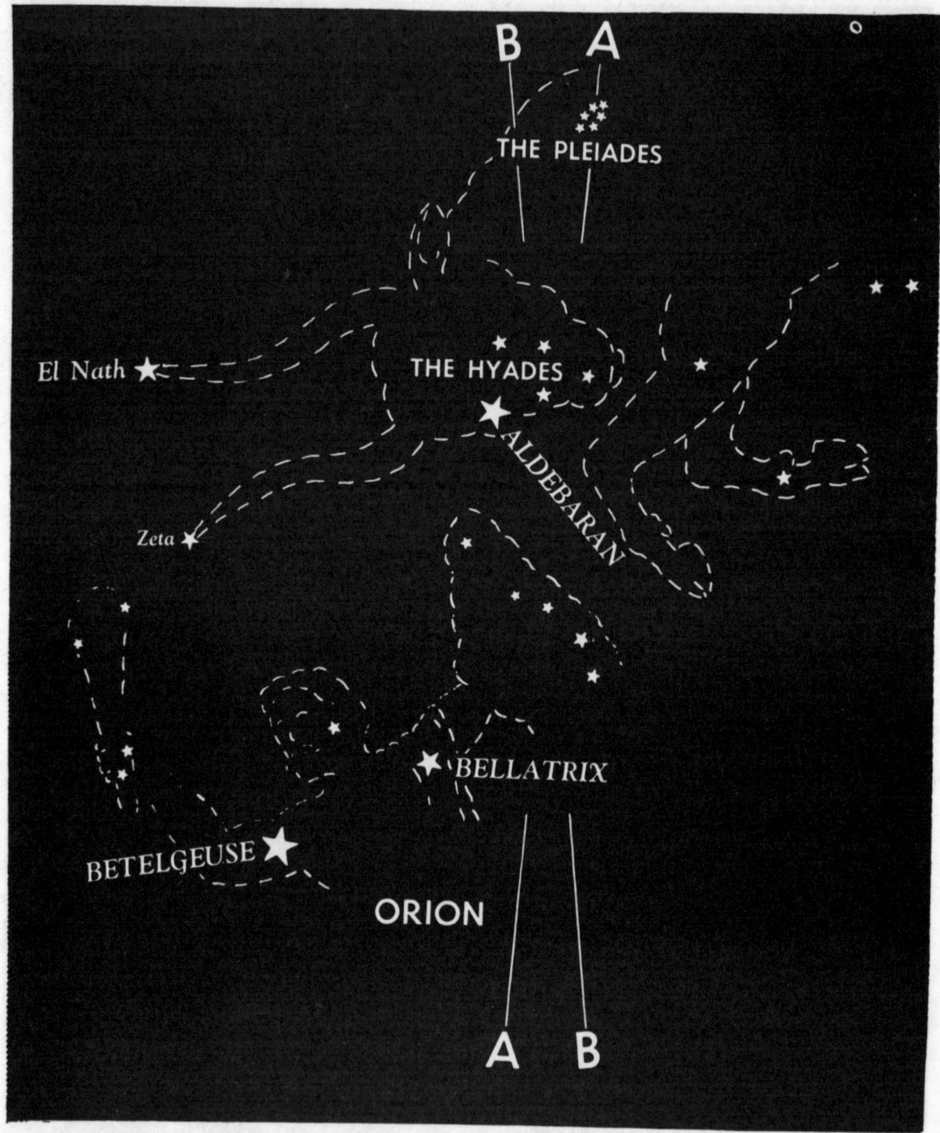


TAURUS: When one of these lines is specified in connection with Chart 10, these instructions must be followed:

Line AA—face halfway between east and southeast; hold AA vertical; raise the picture until the star Aldebaran is halfway up the sky. Look around the edge of the book and you will be looking at Taurus.

Line BB—face southeast; turn line BB to vertical; raise the book until the star Bellatrix is halfway up the sky.

PLANET WARNING

Taurus is in the Zodiac, the path of the wandering planets. If, in using this picture, you see a bright "star" in this area that is not shown here, you may be sure it is a planet.

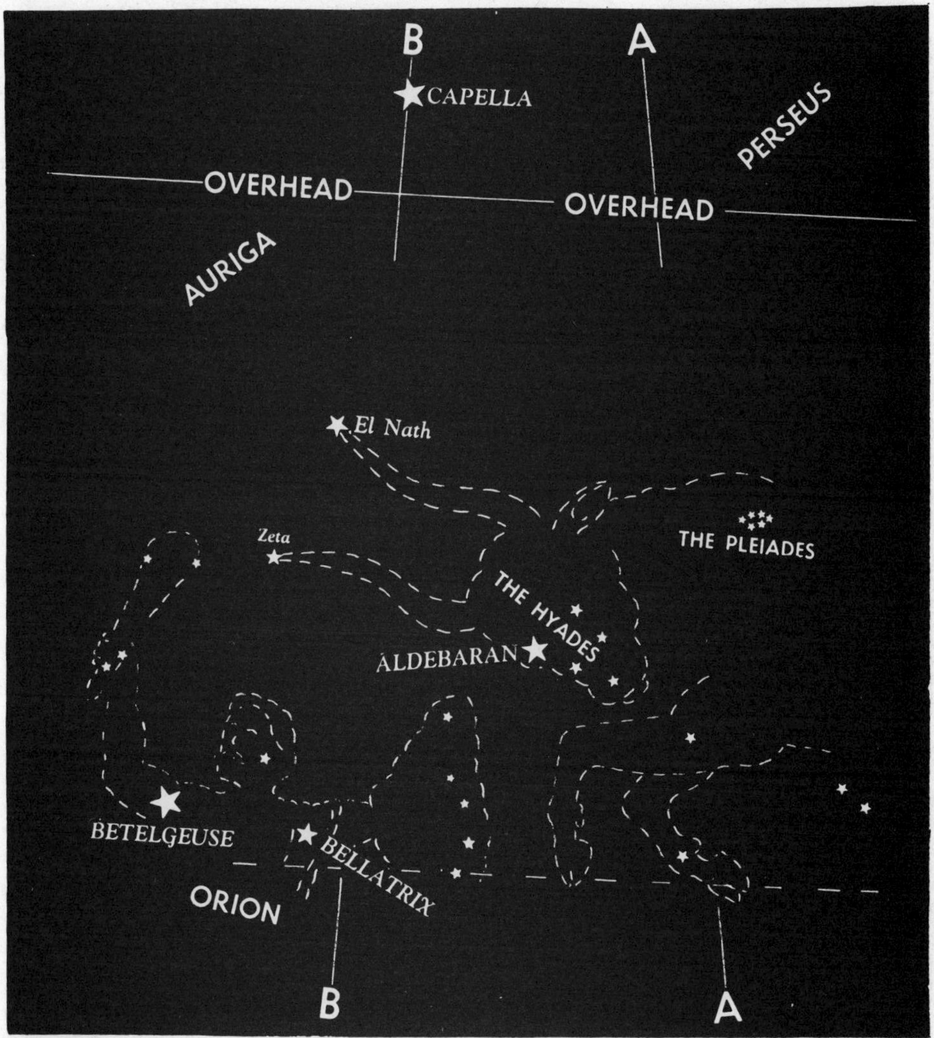


TAURUS: The lines AA and BB in this picture enable you to follow Taurus and his brilliant neighbors as they cross the meridian. To use them, face south, lie back comfortably; raise the picture until the line "Overhead" is overhead; shift the picture to make the specified line bisect your body lengthwise. Look around the edge of the book and you will be looking at Taurus.

PLANET WARNING

Taurus is in the Zodiac, the path of the wandering planets. If, in using this picture, you see a bright "star" in this area that is not shown here, you may be sure it is a planet.

# CHART 12

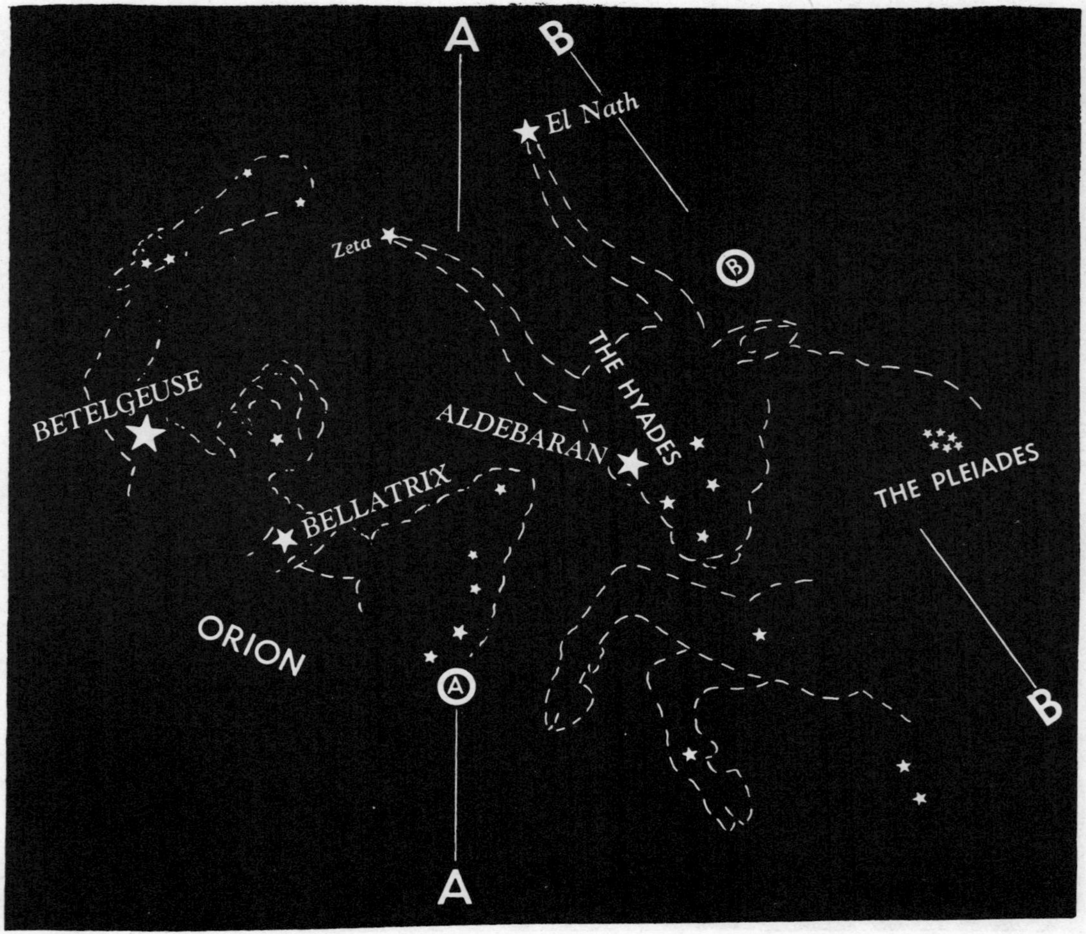

TAURUS: The two lines AA and BB are necessary to follow Taurus down the western sky from his overhead position. In using them, follow this procedure:

Line AA—face southwest; hold AA vertical; raise the picture until the circled A is halfway up the sky. Glance past the edge of the book and you will be looking at Taurus and the Pleiades.

Line BB—face west; turn BB vertical; raise the picture until the circled B is halfway up the sky.

### PLANET WARNING

Taurus is in the Zodiac, the path of the wandering planets. If, in using this picture, you see a bright "star" in this area that is not shown here, you may be sure it is a planet.

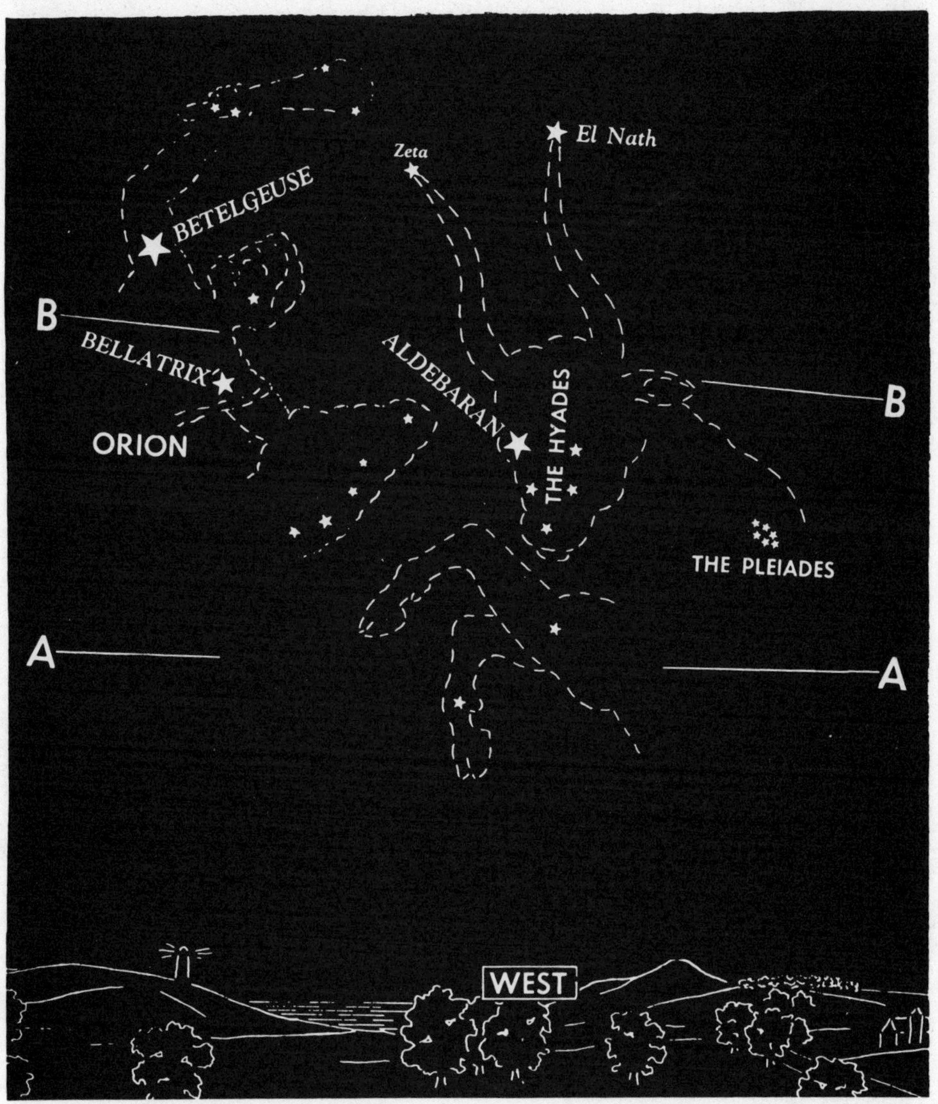


TAURUS: The picture is to be used "as is," ignoring AA and BB when Chart 13 is specified. When, however, one of these lines is called for, it means that these stars are no longer so high and you must imagine them lowered until the specified line is resting on the tops of the distant hills in the landscape.

### PLANET WARNING

Taurus is in the Zodiac, the path of the wandering planets. If, in using this picture, you see a bright "star" in this area that is not shown here, you may be sure it is a planet.

## XI

# THE KITE IN AURIGA

EXPERTS who write books about the stars will frown at you reprovingly if you speak of the "kite" in the constellation of Auriga. They will tell you that there is no authority for such a conception.

That, of course, is true. But go out some night and locate this figure for yourself—and, ever after, it will be a kite to you in spite of the experts.

If you will turn to Chart 14 you will see the principal stars of this constellation with the kite drawn in solid lines. Many star books give maps that show a pentagon, or five-sided figure, made by including the star El Nath in one corner. I have indicated this conventional pentagon by extending dashed lines to that star. If you find it easier to locate this pentagon than my kite, that will be all right. The whole object of star-gazing is to locate stars, and whatever figure your own imagination suggests is the best for you. In fact, you will find it more enjoyable if you get into the habit of hunting among the stars for figures of your own. These are modern times and some of us moderns ought to begin to modernize these musty old conceptions.

If, however, you use the pentagon for Auriga, always bear in mind the fact that the star El Nath does *not* belong to Auriga. Many writers speak of it as being "common" to Auriga and Taurus, but this is not strictly true. By international agreement, the boundaries of the constellations are now rigidly fixed and El Nath belongs to Taurus and nowhere else.

The idea that it is "common" to both arises from the original drawings of the old mythological pictures in which El Nath is the tip of the Bull's left horn and is also in the right foot of the god.

While we are speaking of Taurus, the Bull, it is well to

repeat the warning about wandering planets, given with the Taurus pictures. The stars of Auriga and Taurus are in much the same field; you instinctively see one in combination with the other. Therefore, if one or more bright planets are passing through Taurus, as is frequently the case, they may confuse the pattern. I have seen Saturn and Mars together so close to El Nath that a novice would be unable to tell which was which.

That is another advantage of using the figure of the kite. It keeps Auriga separate and distinct with the long stick of the kite frame always pointing halfway between the conspicuous Pleiades and the bright star Aldebaran.

There is ample justification for being independent in visualizing your own figure for this constellation because the old pictures and the meanings of the star names show a hopeless mixture of antique conceptions.

According to the most ancient legend, Auriga was a goatherd and a patron of shepherds and all who tend flocks.

The Greek legend makes him a famed trainer of horses and the inventor of the four-horse chariot.

The Romans adopted the Greek idea and so he became known as Auriga, the Charioteer.

This confusion of concepts is reflected in the ancient map pictures and the star names. The pictures represent Auriga as holding a whip in his right hand in deference to the Charioteer story, but in his left arm is a kid, and the three stars bearing the Greek letters Epsilon, Eta and Zeta are known as "the Kid" and the star named Capella means "the She-Goat."

This star, Capella, is so bright that no one can fail to identify it after it has risen. When it is over the northeast horizon, the sky will show only one other star to compare with it in brightness. That will be Vega, high up as you face west at that time. Vega is slightly brighter than Capella but you will have to be an experienced observer to estimate the difference with the naked eye.

Capella is the third brightest star to be seen from the

United States or Canada but it can never be mistaken for another of its class because it is alone in its quadrant of the sky.

Arcturus, almost exactly as bright, is sinking in the west as Capella rises above the mists in the northeast. At that time, Vega is high in the western sky. Nearly five hours later, when Capella is approaching its highest point in the sky and Vega is almost hidden in the mists of the northwest, the brightest star in the heavens comes up over the horizon in the southeast. This is Sirius, in the group known as Canis Major.

Two of the stars of Orion—Betelgeuse in his right shoulder and Rigel in his left foot—are nearly as bright as Capella as they are seen by the inexperienced observer, but careful study will show Betelgeuse to be quite a bit less brilliant and Rigel, though brighter than Betelgeuse, will be found to be somewhat dimmer than Capella.

Thus Capella always rules supreme over a very large area of the heavens; it is so bright as to be visible even when a full moon is passing close to it.

Furthermore, Capella is visible at some time of the night every night in the year. You will understand this if you will refer back to that one-hour photograph on page 13.

Capella's distance from the pole would bring its track down into one of the lower corners of that photograph. Consequently, for star-gazers as far north as Canada and New England, it never sets. For mid-United States star-gazers it circles below the northern horizon for only about 5½ hours and for those in the far south it is out of sight only 7 hours.

The light from Capella requires approximately 45 years to reach us here on earth. It is a fairly large star—about 16 times the diameter of the sun (and the sun is 109 times the diameter of the earth)—and it is about 150 times as luminous as the sun.

The star Menkalinan is much more distant than Capella. Any record that we get tonight of an event on Menkalinan is really a record of something that happened there 160 years ago, as we measure years on earth. It takes that long for the light to reach us. And there actually are records of events on Menkalinan which our scientists are watching and studying carefully.

This star is really two stars in one system. It is what we call a "spectroscopic binary." The word "binary" means that there are two stars revolving around their common center of gravity. The term "spectroscopic" indicates that these stars cannot be seen or photographed as separate points but that the double character of the star is proved by the lines in its "rainbow" as revealed in a spectroscope. Incidentally, Capella is also a spectroscopic binary.

Menkalinan's system is composed of two stars of almost equal size, each one about three times the diameter of the sun, and they are of about equal brightness. They revolve about each other in a plane which is so inclined to our line of sight that there is a partial eclipse every time one circles around in front of the other. Thus Menkalinan loses some of its brightness every 3 days, 23 hours, 2½ minutes.

Two of the three little stars forming "the kid" are of particular interest to specialists though their actual mechanism is far beyond the reach of any amateur instrument.

The star called Zeta is a binary system that presents problems that we are only beginning to understand. It seems to be quite well established that the system has a hot star about 4 million miles in diameter revolving with a cooler super-giant which is some 260 million miles in diameter. But this super-giant is evidently very tenuous in composition, its average density being only about one-millionth the density of water.

The orbit, or elliptical path of the smaller hot star about their common center of gravity seems to be some billion miles in diameter. When the small star circles behind the big star and is eclipsed, it does not disappear quickly. Instead, it is gradually dimmed as it passes behind successive layers of the big star's atmosphere, until finally its rays no longer penetrate and it is in total eclipse. Its period is 972 days.

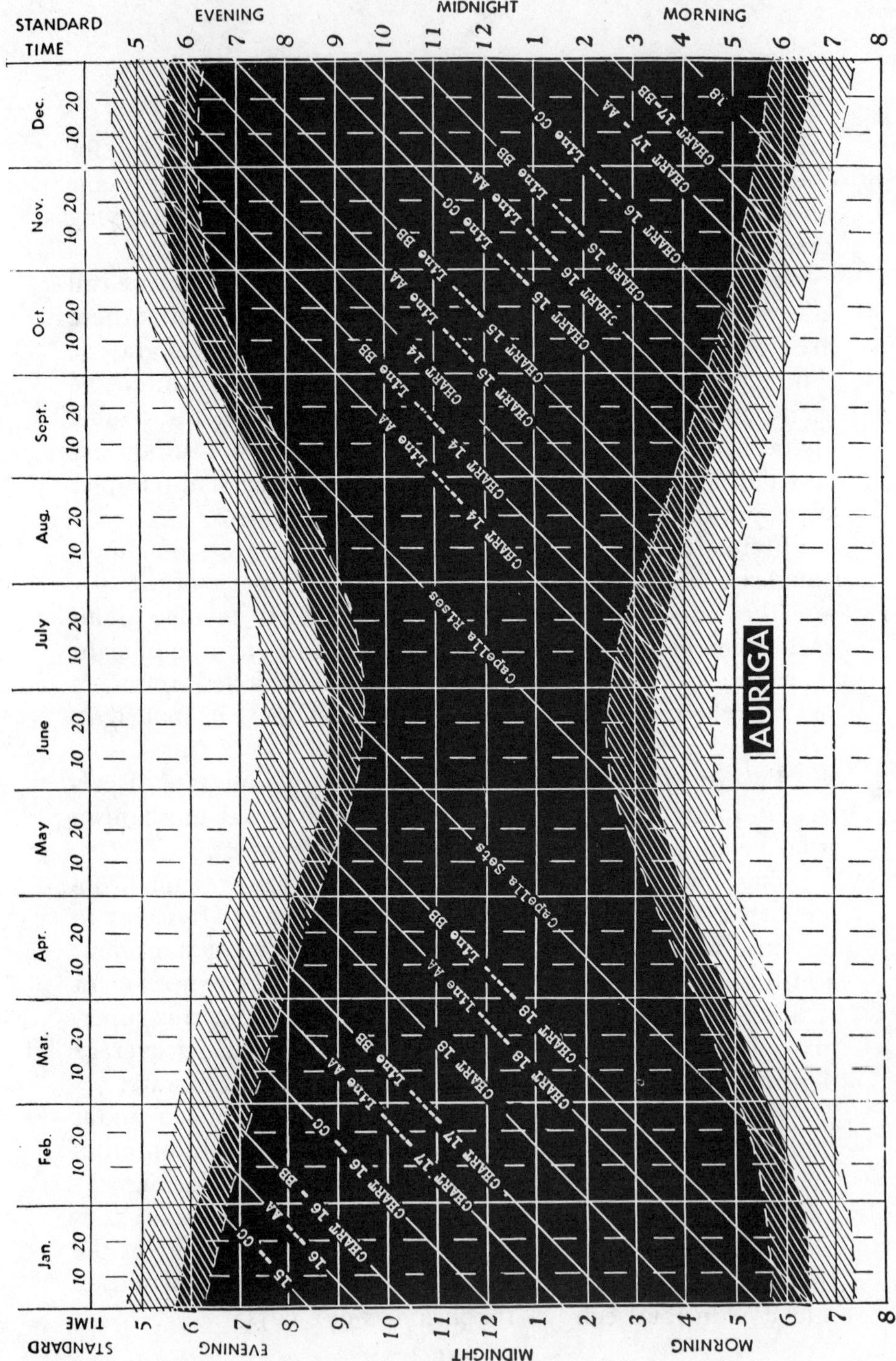


The diagonal line nearest to the date and hour desired shows the correct chart and line to use at that time.

The big star in this system seems to be of almost unbelievable dimensions but it would be the little brother in the amazing binary system of the star Epsilon in the same trio forming "the kid."

Suppose we use my favorite standard of comparison. We imagine this big earth of ours shrunk to the size of a baseball. Then, on that scale, the cool super-giant in the Zeta system would be a globe of gas about a mile and a half in diameter.

But that is the size of the *smaller* star in the Epsilon system. The larger star is a "ghost." It gives us virtually none of the light by which we see Epsilon but, every twenty-seven years, as we see them circling, tilted to our line of sight, the edge of the big dark star grazes across the front of the lower edge of the smaller bright star and the visible Epsilon loses about half its light.

Now for the size of this "ghost" companion.

If the earth is pictured the size of a baseball, the "ghost" star—believe it or not--is a globe *fifteen miles* in diameter.

# CHART 14

PRONUNCIATIONS

*AURIGA*—"or-eye-ga." Accent "eye"; the "g" is hard as in "gct, goat," etc.
CAPELLA—"cap-pell-la." Accent "pell."
MENKALINAN—as spelled. Accent "kal."
Epsilon, Eta (pronounced "ate-a") and Zeta (pronounced "zay-ta") are not proper names. They are the Greek letters assigned to these stars.

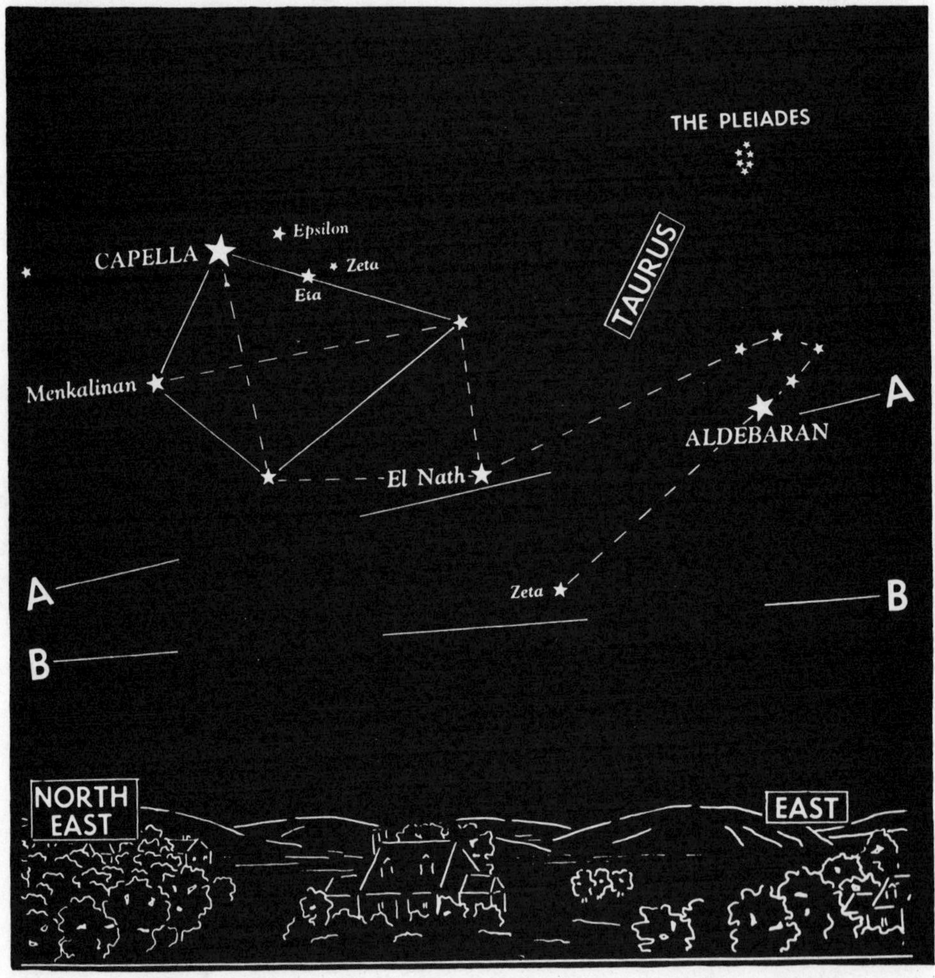


AURIGA: When line AA or BB is not specified in the instructions, this picture is to be used "as is." When one of the lines is called for, however, it means that these stars are not yet so high and you must imagine them lowered until the ·pecified line is resting on the tops of the distant hills in the landscape.

## CHART 15

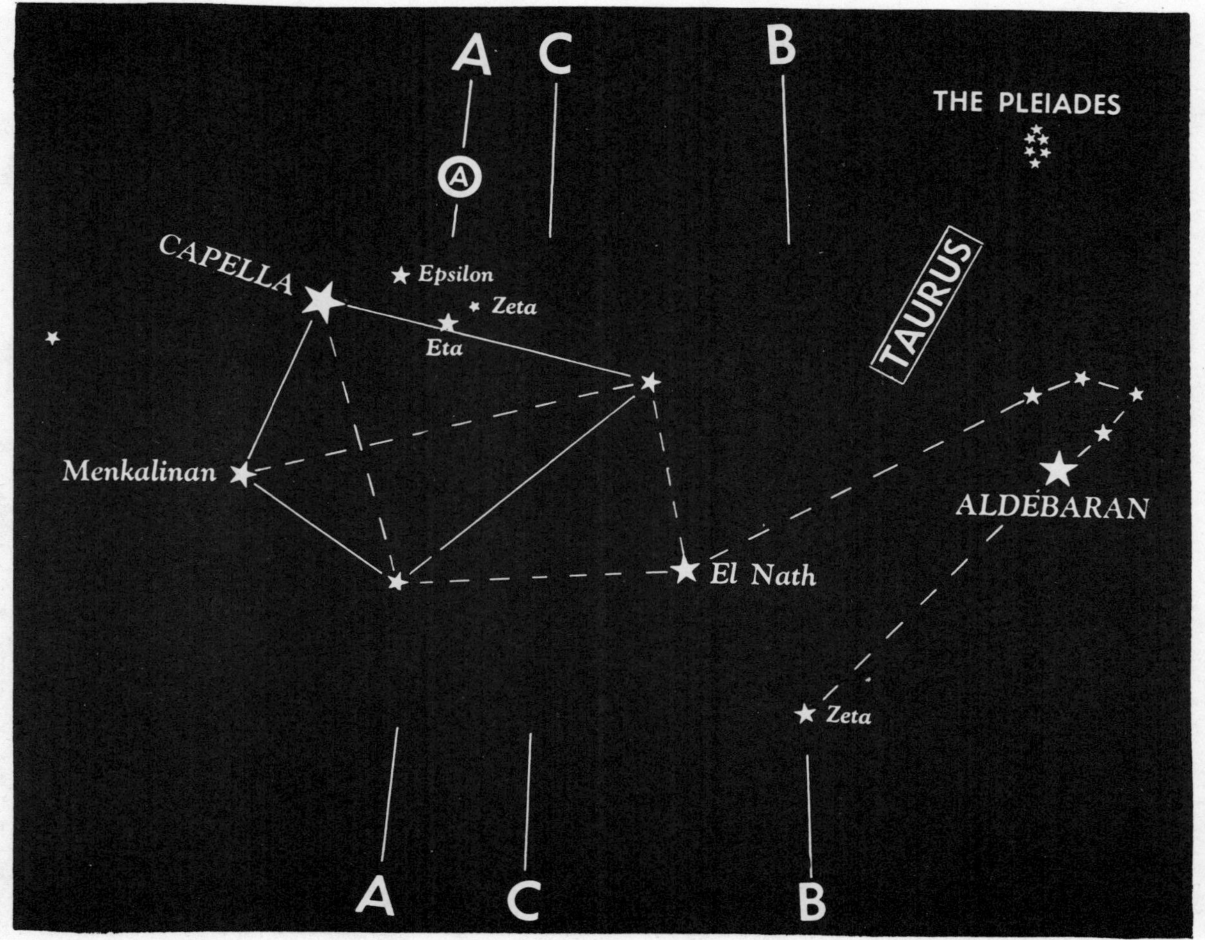


AURIGA: When any one of these lines is specified, proceed as follows:

Line AA — face halfway between east and northeast; make the line AA vertical; raise the book until the circled A is halfway up the sky. The book will then be covering these stars.

Line BB — face east; make BB vertical; raise the book until the name Aldebaran is halfway up the sky.

Line CC — face east; make CC vertical; raise the book until the bottom edge of the picture is halfway up the sky.

## CHART 16

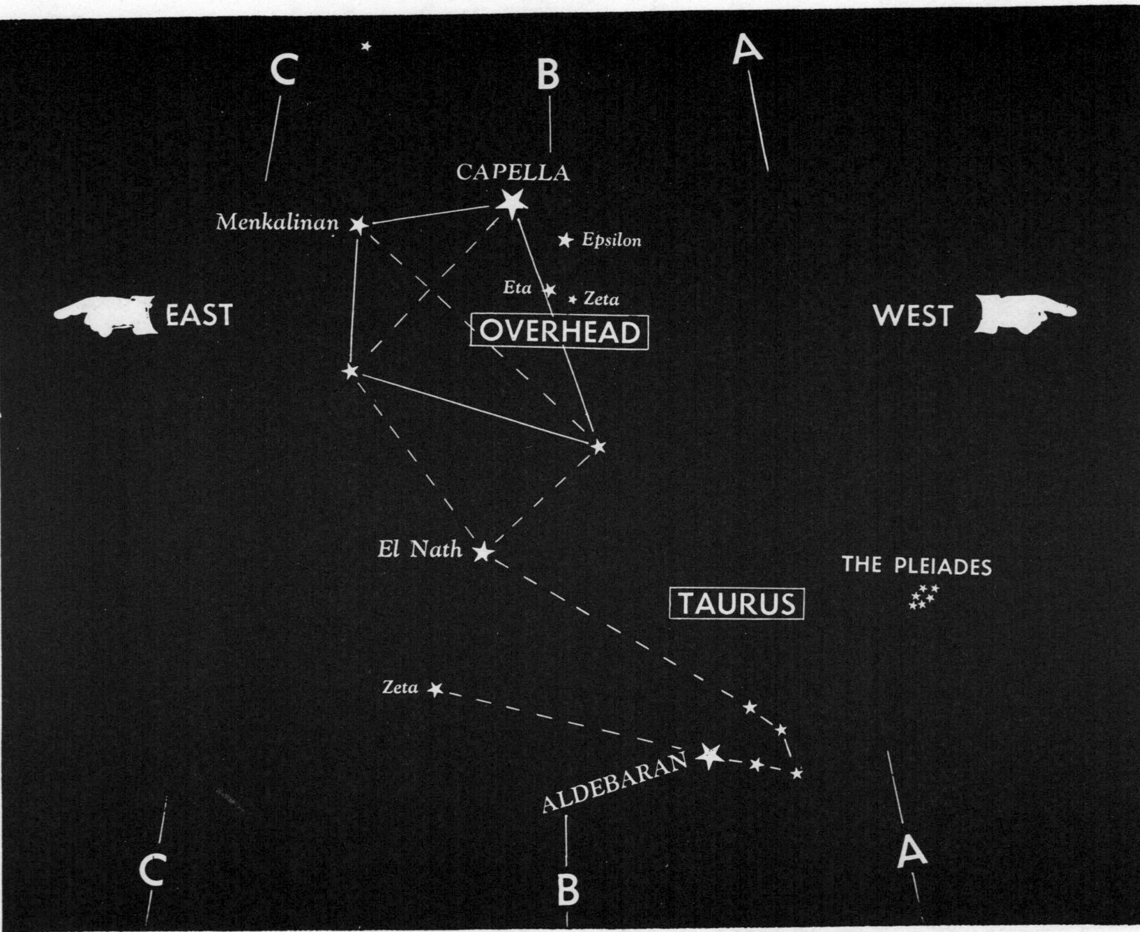


**Auriga:** This chart shows Auriga as it passes overhead. The point marked "Overhead" is for observers in the mid-latitudes. For Canadians, the overhead point will be above the word Capella. For far-southerners, overhead will be between the star El Nath and the kite.

In all cases, face south; lie back comfortably; raise the book to overhead and move it until the specified line cuts through your body lengthwise.

# CHART 17

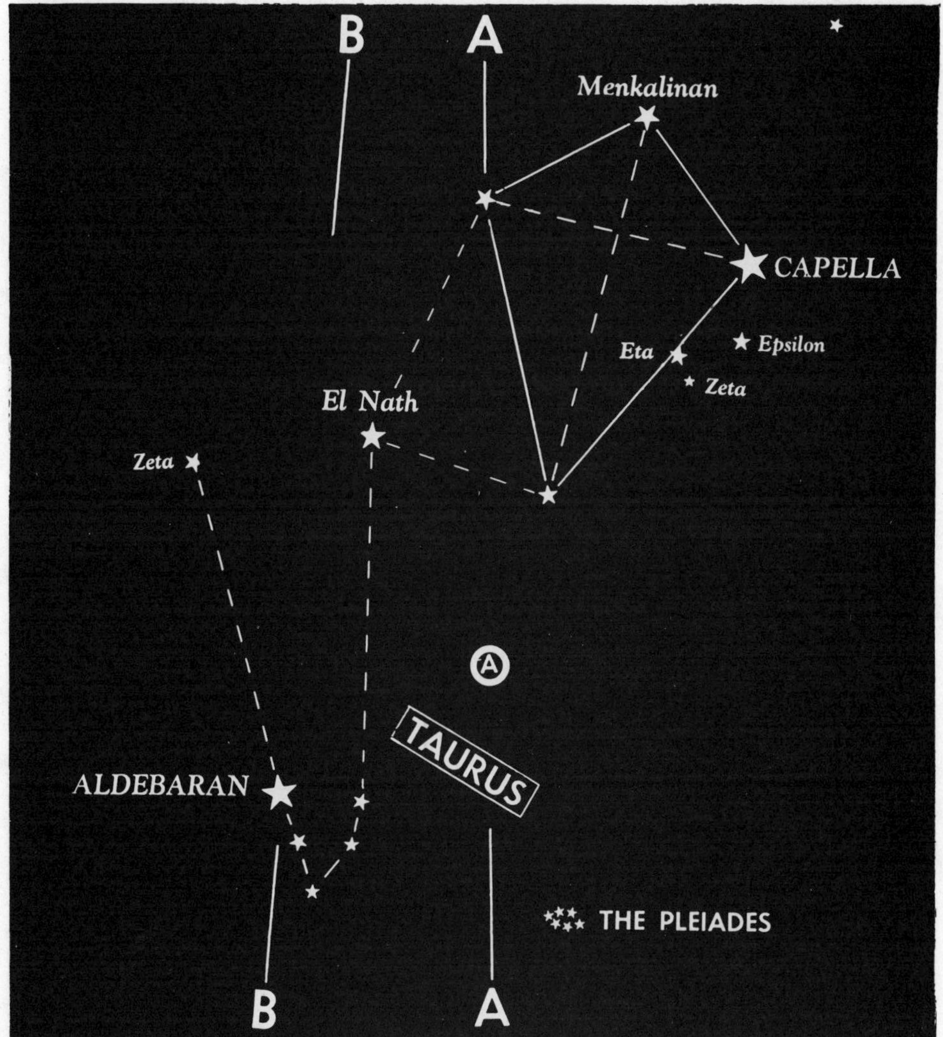


Auriga: The lines AA and BB will be specified in the instructions at different times. In either case, face west and tilt the book to make the specified line vertical. Then:

Line AA—raise the book until the circled A is halfway up the sky; look over the top of the book and you will be looking at the stars shown in the chart.

Line BB—raise the book until the star El Nath is halfway up the sky.

# CHART 18

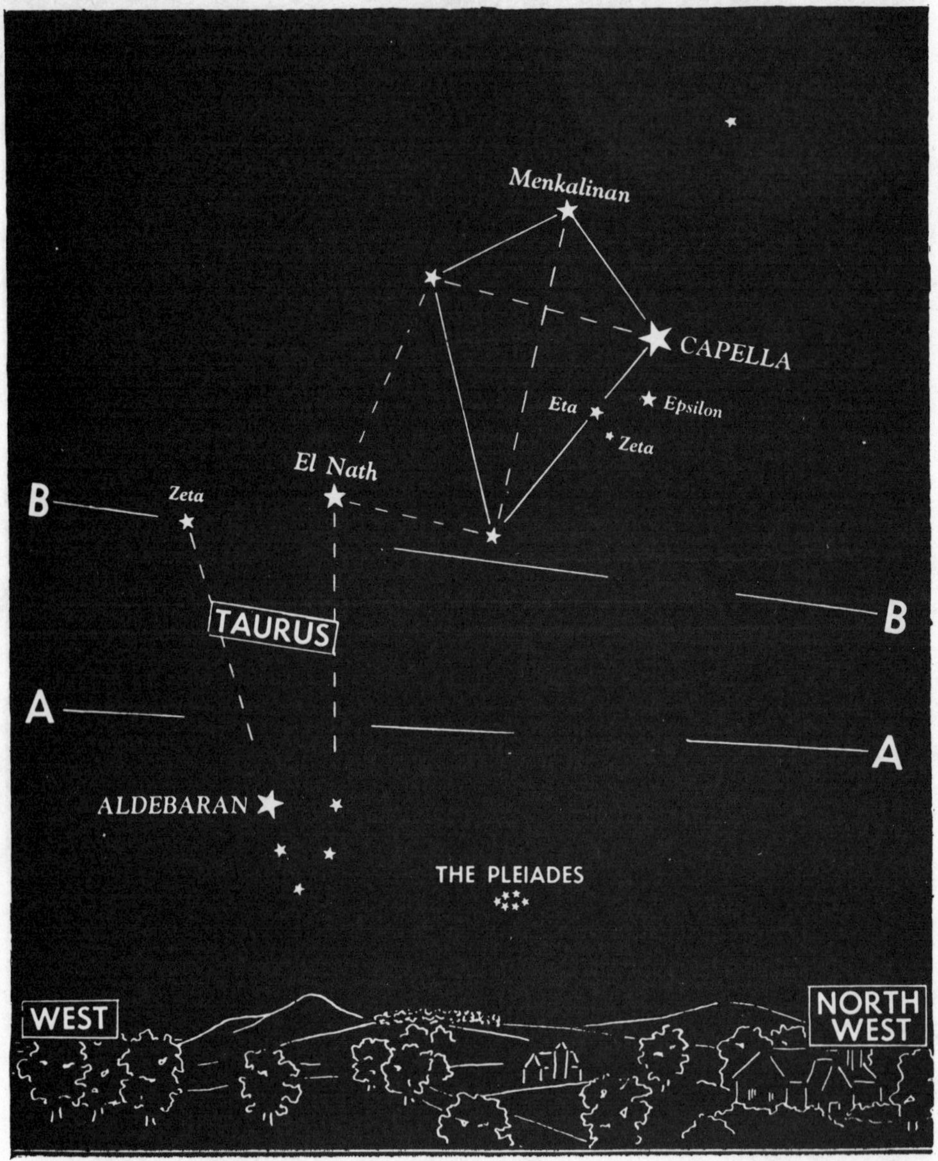


AURIGA: This picture is to be used "as is," ignoring AA and BB when Chart 18 is specified. When, however, one of these lines is stipulated, it means that the stars have sunk below this position and you must imagine them lowered until the line is resting on the tops of the distant hills in the landscape.

## XII

# THE LONG WEDGE OF GEMINI

THE fame of two of the outstanding heroes of antiquity is preserved to us today in two entirely different ways—first, in a constellation of bright stars; second, in a slang ejaculation.

The constellation is Gemini, the Twins. The ejaculation is "By Jimminy!"—a popular corruption of the ancient "By Gemini!"

The Twins of mythology were Castor and Pollux, sons of Zeus and Leda and brothers of that Helen whose face launched a thousand ships and caused the Trojan War.

Castor and Pollux figure in scores of the ancient folk tales. They were warriors, adventurers, and famous navigators.

Their names are handed down to us by St. Paul for we find in the eleventh verse of Acts 28:

"And after three months, we departed in a ship of Alexandria which had wintered in the isle, whose sign was Castor and Pollux."

Macaulay, too, helped immortalize them in his poem, "The Battle of Lake Regillus," and the old lore of the sea declares that St. Elmo's fire first appeared when it descended upon the heads of these two adventurers after they saved the ship of the Argonauts in a tremendous storm. For this they became the patrons of all seafarers, whose oath thereafter became "By Gemini."

The name Gemini has been given to the entire group of stars surrounding the long wedge shown in our sky pictures. Somehow or other, the ancient star-gazers managed to find in these stars the outlines of the two heroes standing close together, their arms over each other's shoulders, but it is hopeless for a modern to try to duplicate this feat of imagery.

The star Castor is supposed to be in the head of one twin and Pollux in the other. Alhena marks one foot.

As in many of these constellations, I have preferred to

indicate a figure which is much easier for star-gazers of today to find, so the three brightest and most unmistakable stars are shown in our pictures as forming a long wedge.

This wedge is quite obvious, once you have located it, and you will always find it with its point aimed straight at Orion, the Great Hunter. Furthermore, the wedge can be seen when the moonlight is so bright as to make the other stars of the constellation invisible.

So I hope the conservative scientists will forgive us if we regard Gemini as a long wedge and not as a pair of very indistinct heroes.

For the owner of a good pair of binoculars, there is fine "sweeping" all about the stars Propus and Meboula and up to include the loose cluster known as M35, dimly visible to the naked eye on a good night. This cluster has more than 500 stars in it. Its distance is about 1500 light-years and its diameter 25 light-years.

There seems to be some evidence that when the two stars, Castor and Pollux, were first chosen to represent the Twins, they actually appeared to be twin stars of equal brightness. If this is so, we must conclude that Castor has faded or Pollux has grown more brilliant, for there is considerable difference between them now. Pollux is much the brighter and is one of the fifty-five standard navigational stars.

Long study of Castor has revealed it to be one of the most interesting stars in the heavens. With the development of the telescope, observers saw that this point of light was two stars. They were found to be revolving around a common center of gravity in a period of about 340 years.

Then it was found that the fainter of these two was itself a binary system, with the stars eclipsing each other every three days, and then came the discovery that the brighter star of Castor was also a binary system with a period of rotation of about nine days.

Still later, a near-by, very faint star, proved to belong to this complex system. This star also proved to be a binary with a period of a little less than twenty hours and the three systems of two stars each were found to be revolving around their common center of gravity apparently in a period of approximately ten thousand years.

Thus Castor, which looks to us like an ordinary bright star, is, in reality, an extremely complicated system of six stars, performing an intricate pattern of intertwined loops in space but so far away (43 light-years) that our eyes see them as only one point of light.

Pollux has also proved to be a group of six stars but is apparently much more simply organized than Castor.

The star Mekbuda is a Cepheid variable (see page 107) with a period of 10 days, 3 hours, 43 minutes. It is an extremely tenuous star, with an average density only one-tenth the density of the air at the earth's surface.

### *Procyon, the Little Dog Star*

We find so many of the stars at such staggering distances from us that it is restful, once in a while, to come to one which is a "near" neighbor.

Such a star is the brilliant Procyon, in the little constellation known as Canis Minor, the Smaller Dog. The Big Dog star is Sirius, in Canis Major.

Procyon is one of the brightest stars in the sky as seen from the earth but this distinction is due entirely to its nearness. It is only seven times as luminous as the sun so, if it were out at the distance of Castor or Pollux, it would command little or no attention from us. Its distance is about 10½ light-years. Castor is thus about four times as far away and Pollux nearly five times.

Procyon is a binary system with its own peculiarities. The smaller star of the two has only one-third the mass of the larger one and the larger one gives about 100,000 times as much light as the smaller one. They revolve about their common center of gravity in about 39 years.

## PRONUNCIATIONS

*GEMINI*—"jem-in-eye." Accent "jem."

CASTOR—"kass-ter." Accent "kass."

POLLUX—pronounced as spelled. Accent "poll" (rhymes with "doll").

ALHENA—"al-hen-a." Accent "hen."

WASAT—"way-sat." Accent "way."

MEBOULA—"meb-bool-a." Accent "bool." This star is also called MEBSUTA—pronounced "meb-sue-ta"; accent "sue."

MEKBUDA—"mek-bew-da." Accent "bew" (rhymes with "due").

*CANIS MINOR*—"kay-niss my-n'r." Accent "kay" and "my."

PROCYON—"pro-see-on." Accent "pro" (rhymes with "go").

GOMEIZA—"go-my-za." Accent "my." The "g" is hard as in "get."

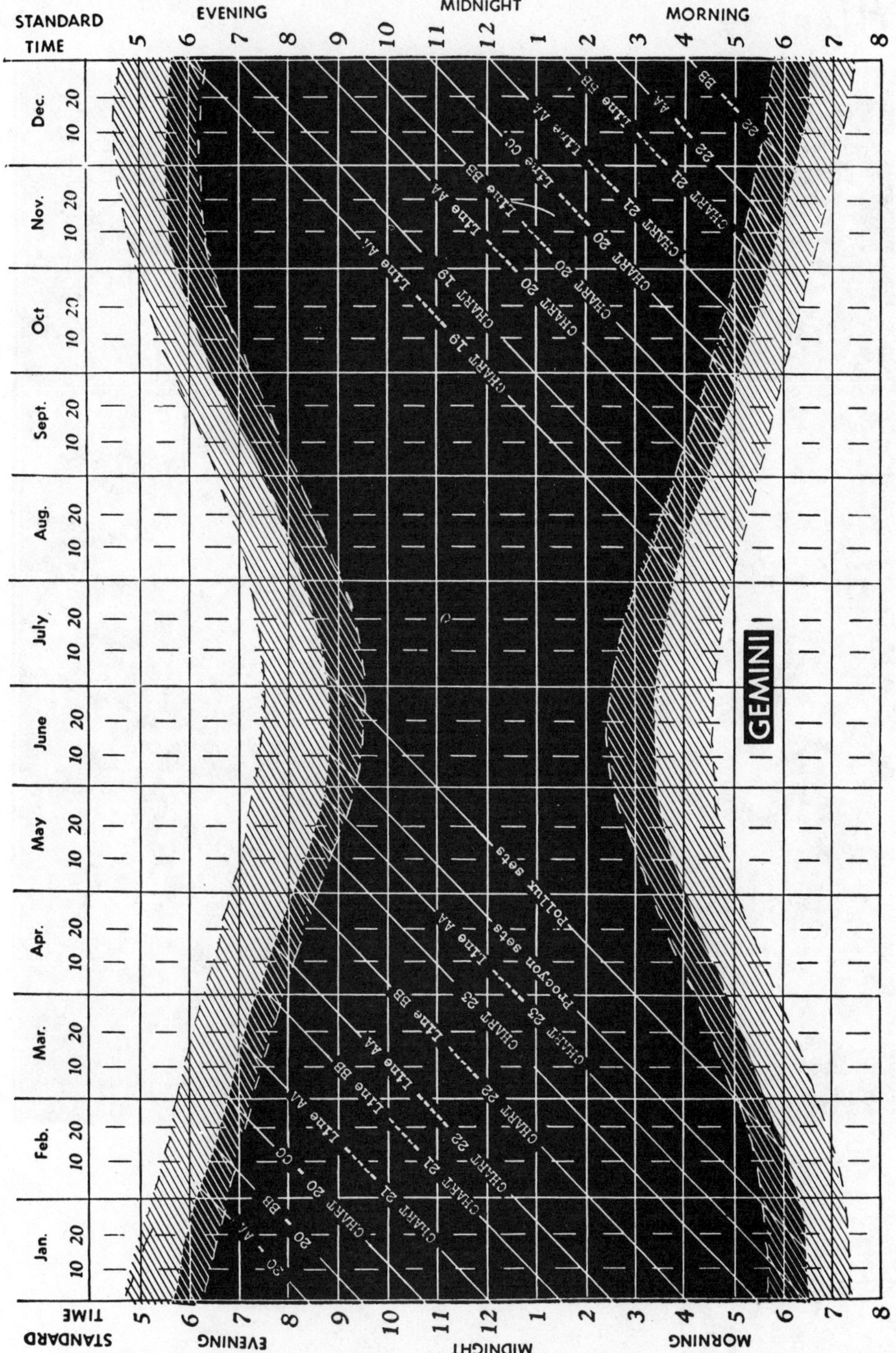


The diagonal line nearest to the hour and date desired shows the correct chart and line to use at that time.

# CHART 19

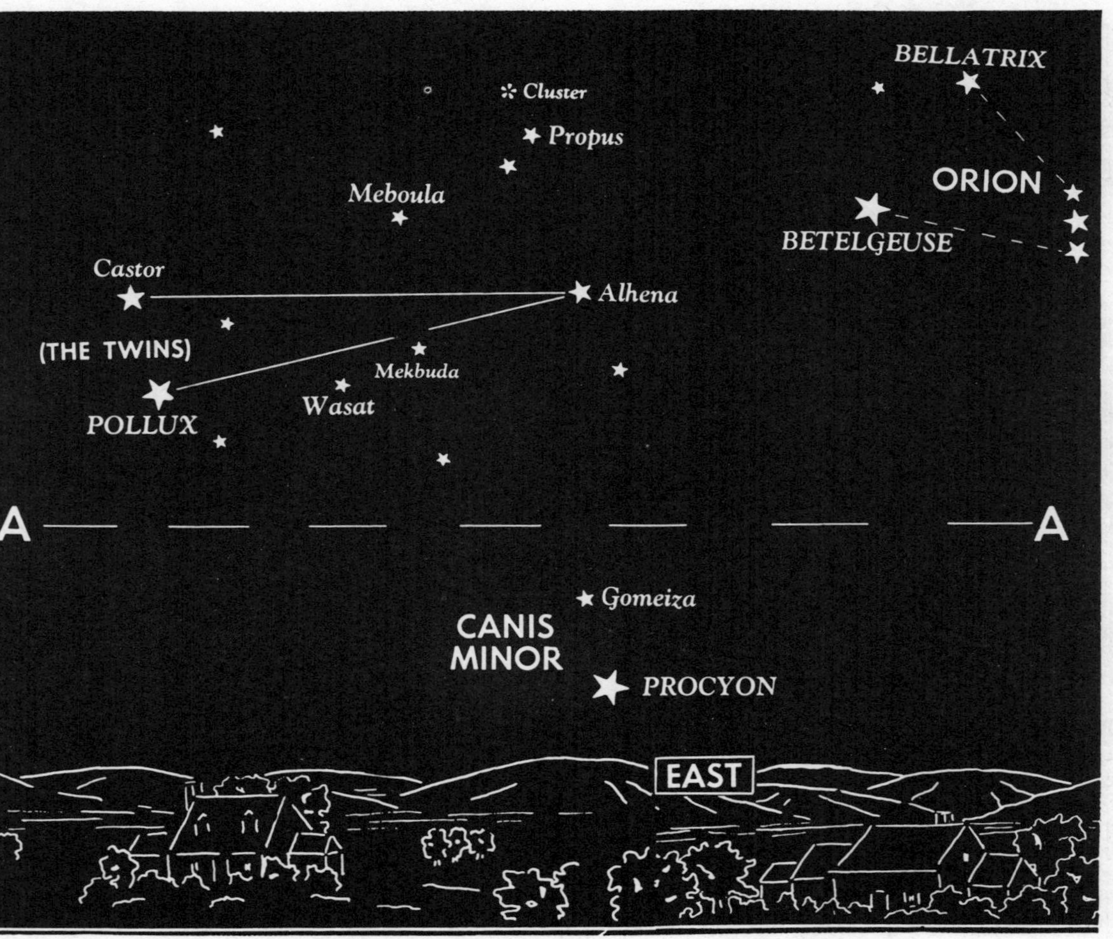


GEMINI: When the instructions specify simply Chart 19, this picture should be used "as is," ignoring line AA. When, however, line AA is specified, it indicates that the stars are not yet so high and you must imagine them lowered until the line AA rests on the tops of the distant hills in the landscape.

The constellation of Gemini is in the Zodiac. Watch out for wandering planets.

# CHART 20

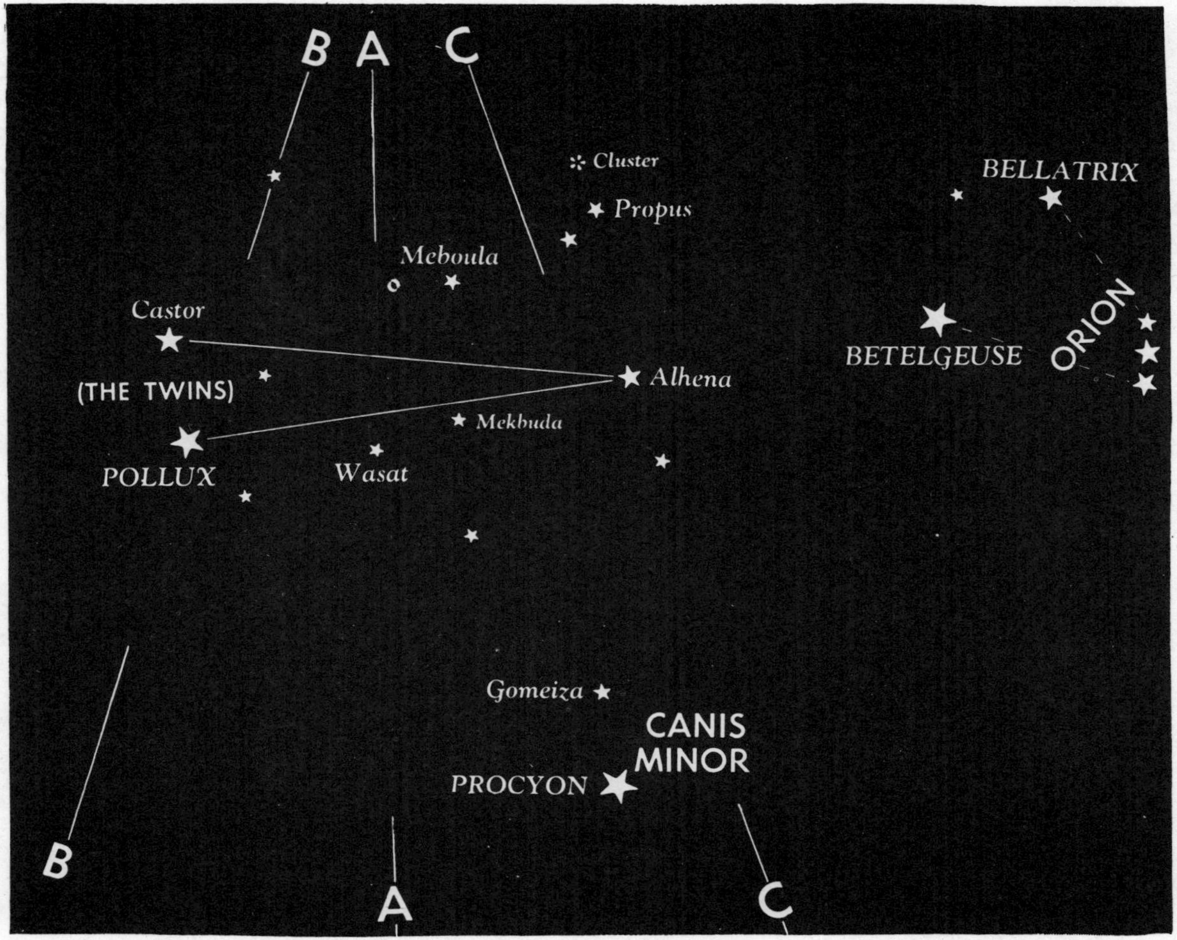

**Gemini:** As the wedge of Gemini mounts the eastern sky, it begins to turn so that these three lines, AA, BB, CC, become useful and the correct one to use at any time will be specified in the instructions.

To use line AA—face east; hold AA vertical; raise the picture until the star Propus is halfway up the sky; glance past the left edge of the book and you will be looking at the Twins, Castor and Pollux.

To use line BB—face east; tilt the book until BB is vertical; raise the picture until the star Pollux is halfway up the sky.

To use line CC—face southeast; tilt the book until CC is vertical; raise the picture until the star Gomeiza is halfway up the sky.

The constellation of Gemini is in the Zodiac. Watch out for wandering planets.

# CHART 21

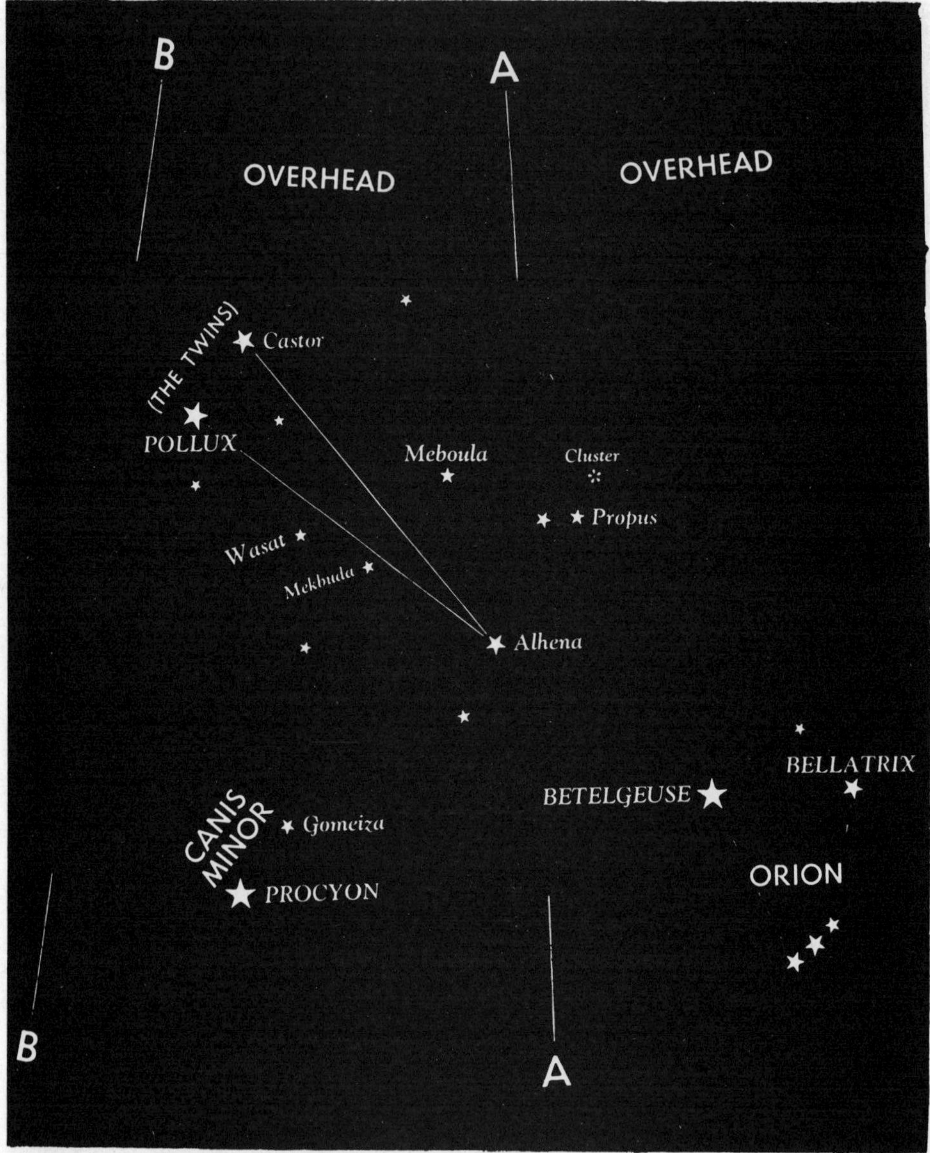


**Gemini:** When it is time for Gemini to cross the meridian, the instructions will indicate whether to use line AA or BB. In both cases, the procedure is the same. Face south; lie back comfortably; raise the picture until "Overhead" is overhead; shift sideways until the specified line bisects your body lengthwise. Glance around the edge of the book and you will be looking at Gemini.

The constellation of Gemini is in the Zodiac. Watch out for wandering planets.

# CHART 22

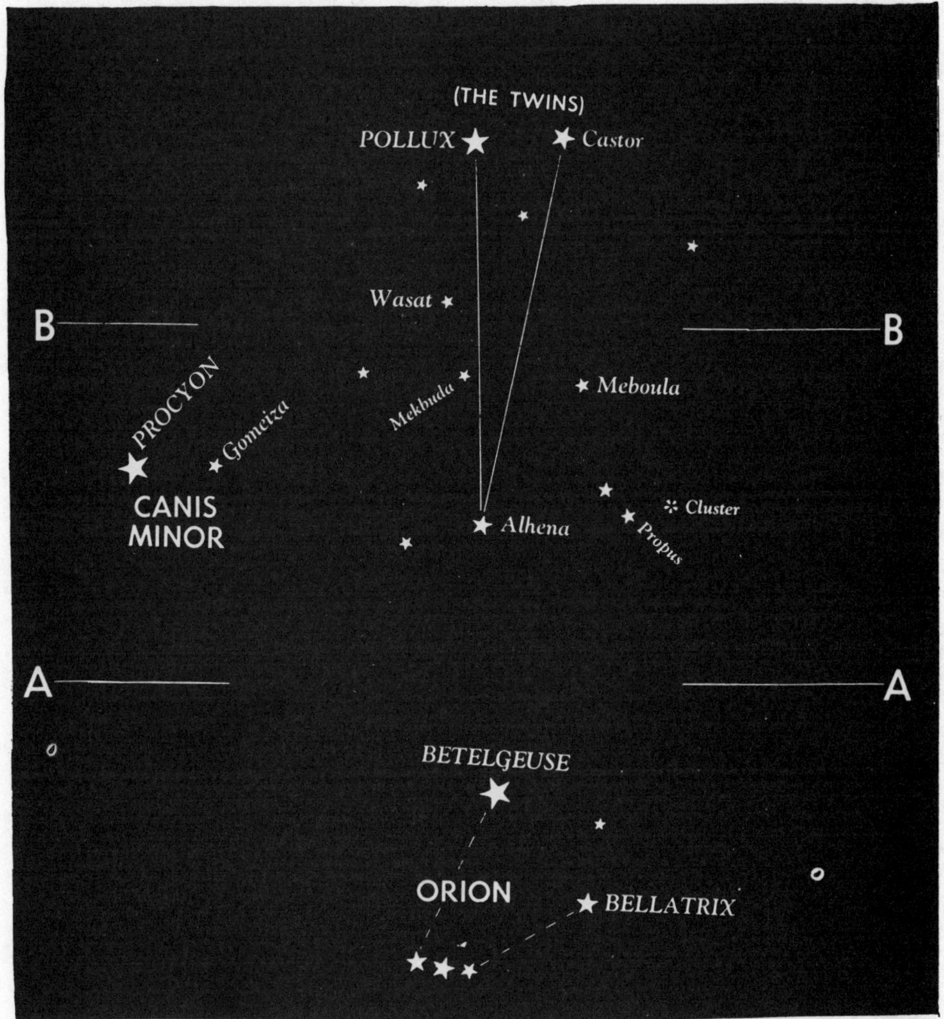


GEMINI: The wedge of Gemini descends the western sky pointing straight down but aimed at different compass points at different times. If the line AA is specified, face halfway between west and southwest and raise the picture until AA is halfway up the sky. For line BB, face due west and raise the book until BB is halfway up the sky.

The constellation of Gemini is in the Zodiac. Watch out for wandering planets.

# CHART 23

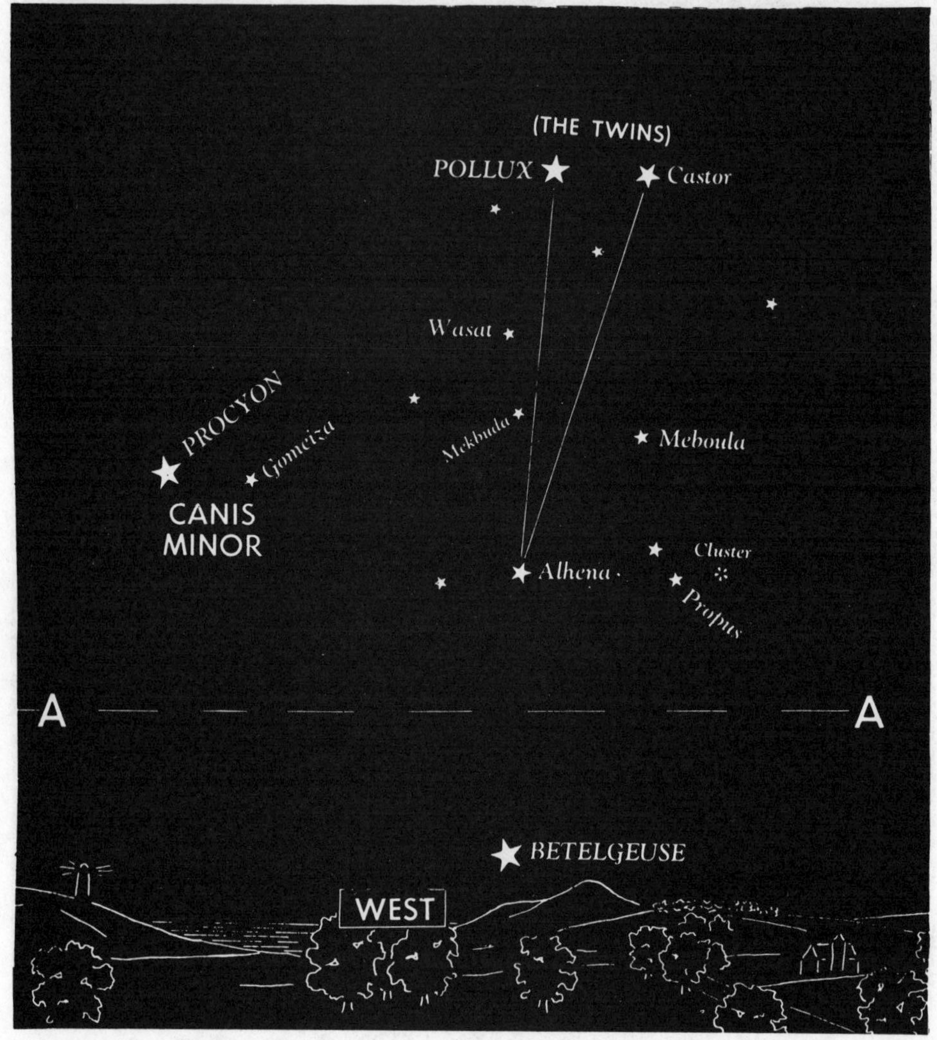


GEMINI: When Chart 23 is specified this picture is to be used "as is," ignoring the line AA. When, however, the line AA is called for, it indicates that these stars are not so high and you must imagine them lowered until the line AA rests on the tops of the distant hills in the landscape.

The constellation of Gemini is in the Zodiac. Watch out for wandering planets.

## XIII

# CAPRICORNUS, AQUARIUS, FOMALHAUT

THE constellation of Capricornus or, as it is usually called, Capricorn, is not conspicuous but is important to the stargazer because of its position in the Zodiac.

Thus if you learn that there is a planet or any other object of interest "in" Capricornus, you will want to be able to locate the constellation. When we speak of a planet being "in" any constellation, we mean that, as it happens to be seen from the earth at that particular time, it is so placed in space that we see it against the stars of the constellation. The stars are in the infinitely distant background; they have no connection whatever with the planet, in spite of the hocuspocus of the astrologers.

In the ancient picture maps of the heavens, Capricorn is represented by the figure of a sea-goat, combining the forequarters and head of a goat and the tail of a fish. This kind of monster might seem unintelligible to us today if we did not know the ancient myth that explains its origin.

According to this bit of folklore, there were some nymphs and goddesses playing in a field one day when the mischievous god, Pan, saw them and joined in the fun.

In order to amuse them, he transformed himself into a goat and leaped into the river. Instantly, the part of his body that was submerged in the water was turned into a fish while the part out of the water remained a goat.

The great god Zeus, passing by, saw the feat and was so highly amused by its cleverness that he decreed the perpetuation of the grotesque figure in the sky.

Hence our constellation—Capricornus, the Sea-Goat.

There are only three stars in Capricorn that are bright enough to be considered even moderately conspicuous, but

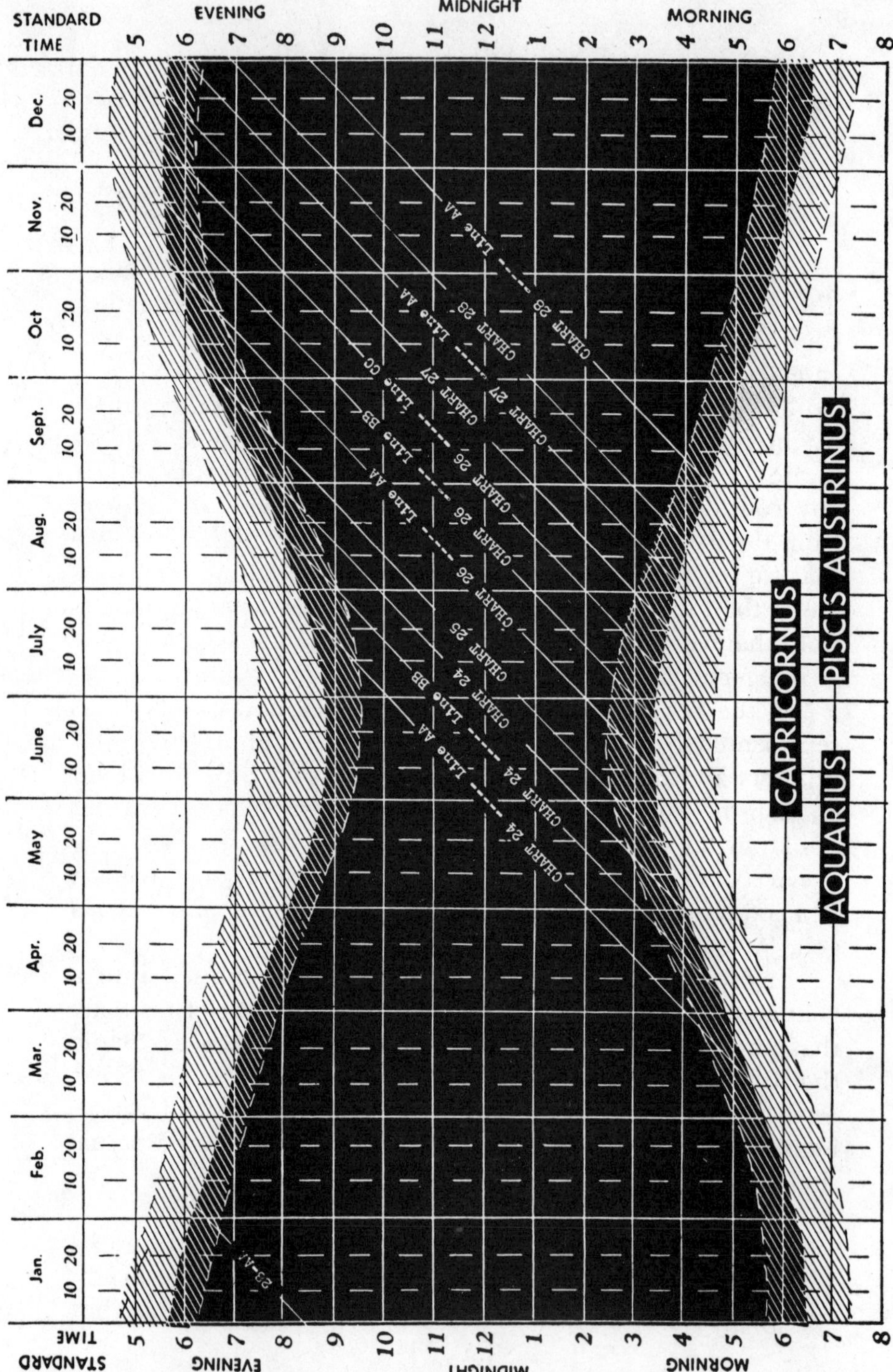


The diagonal line nearest to the date and hour desired shows the correct chart and line to be used at that time.

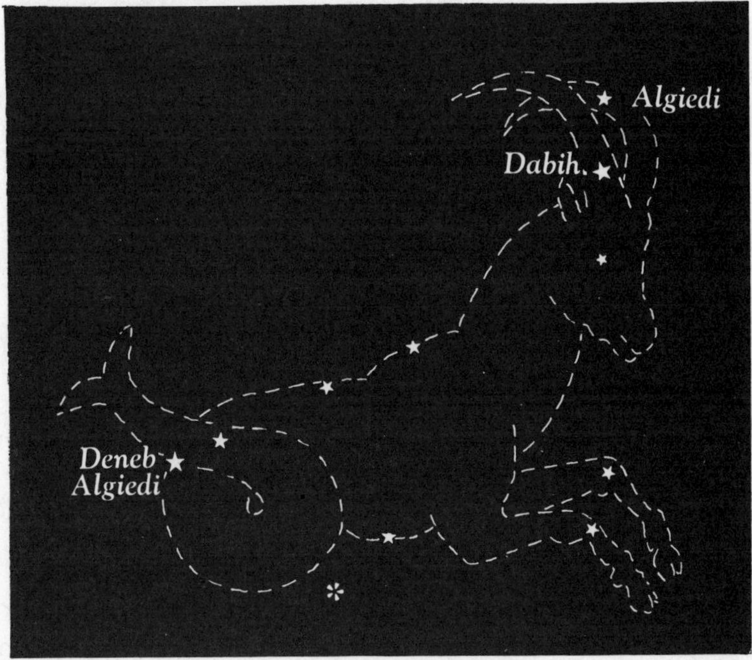


Ancient star-gazers imagined they saw in this constellation the figure of the fish-goat to match their folk tale about the playful god Pan. The imaginary creature is shown in outline in this picture for the benefit of those who want to try to find it. For modern star-gazers, however, connecting the stars with dashed lines in the conventional way is a much easier method of locating this inconspicuous constellation and that is how it is shown in the five charts that follow.

the figure is circled by the brighter stars of Aquarius and followed across the sky, from east to west, by the great star Fomalhaut so that together they present an interesting area and one that the star-gazer should know.

The star Algiedi is a good test for unusually keen eyesight. Many observers, without optical aid, can see that it is really two stars. Experts have discovered that each of these two is a triple system, so that there are really six stars contributing to the pencilpoint of light that we call Algiedi.

Dabih is also a double and some people claim to be able

PRONUNCIATIONS

*CAPRICORNUS*—"kap-ree-korn-us." Accent "korn."
ALGIEDI—"al-jee-dee." Accent "jee."
DABIH—"day-bee." Accent "day."
DENEB ALGIEDI—means "the tail of the goat." "Deneb" always means tail; thus, Deneb in the tail of the Swan and Denebola, in the tail of Leo, the Lion.
*AQUARIUS*—"ack-ware-ee-us." Accent "ware."
SADALMELIK—"sad-al-mell-ick." Principal accent on "mell."
SADALSUUD—"sad-al-sue-ud." Accent "sue."
SKAT—pronounced like our word "skate."
ALBALI—"al-bale-lee." Accent "bale."
*FOMALHAUT*—"foe-mal-ought." Accent "foe" (rhymes with "go," "so," etc.).

to see it so with the naked eye. Opera glasses or binoculars reveal both stars clearly.

The little cluster marked in the pictures is known as M30. It is merely a very faint glow to the naked eye on a clear, dark night and a nebulous spot through binoculars. It requires a six-inch telescope to resolve it into separate stars.

Zeta, looking like a very ordinary star, is, in reality, one of the super-giants of the sky. It is so far away that its true brilliance is lost to us. Yet it has 6000 times the luminosity of our sun and 80 times its diameter—or 8800 times the diameter of the earth.

The appearance of Capricornus above the southeastern horizon where it rises is the signal for the coming of the red star Fomalhaut, one of the four "royal stars," famous among both astrologers and ancient navigators. The other three are Aldebaran, in Taurus; Regulus, in the Sickle of Leo; and Antares in the Scorpion.

Fomalhaut is about 24 light-years away from us and is moving across our line of sight at an unusually rapid rate—though you need not fear that it will alter its position on your star maps and sky pictures during your lifetime. It is too far away for its speed to be evident to the naked-eye observer.

Fomalhaut is the most southerly of all the very bright (so-

# CHART 24

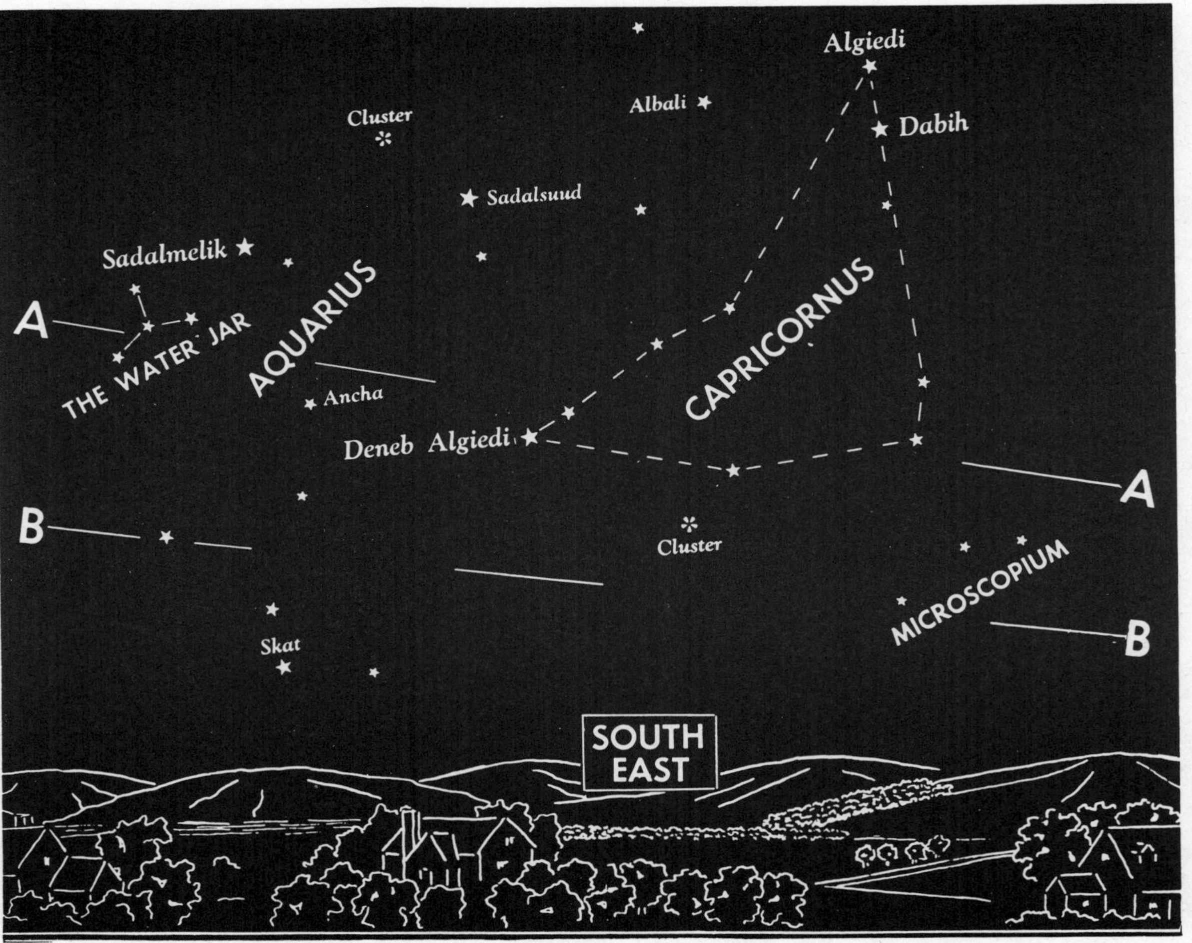


**Capricornus:** Lines AA and BB should be ignored when Chart 24 is specified. If, however, one of these lines is called for, it indicates that the stars are not yet so high and you must imagine them lowered until the line is resting on the tops of the distant hills in the landscape.

The constellations of Capricornus and Aquarius are in the Zodiac—the pathway followed by the wandering planets. Beware of any strange "stars" in either constellation. If they are bright and are not in these pictures, they are planets.

called "first magnitude") stars that can be seen from the United States. It is the only star of this brightness in a considerable area of the sky around it and thus is easily seen and identified and so is of great interest and value to navigators.

Because of this isolation from other stars of its class, Fomalhaut has become known as "the solitary one," or "the lonely star."

This bright star, with the line of little stars near it, is supposed to represent a fish, and the group bears the Latin name of Piscis Austrinus, or Southern Fish.

If you can find any resemblance to a fish in the group, you are a better star-gazer than the author of this book.

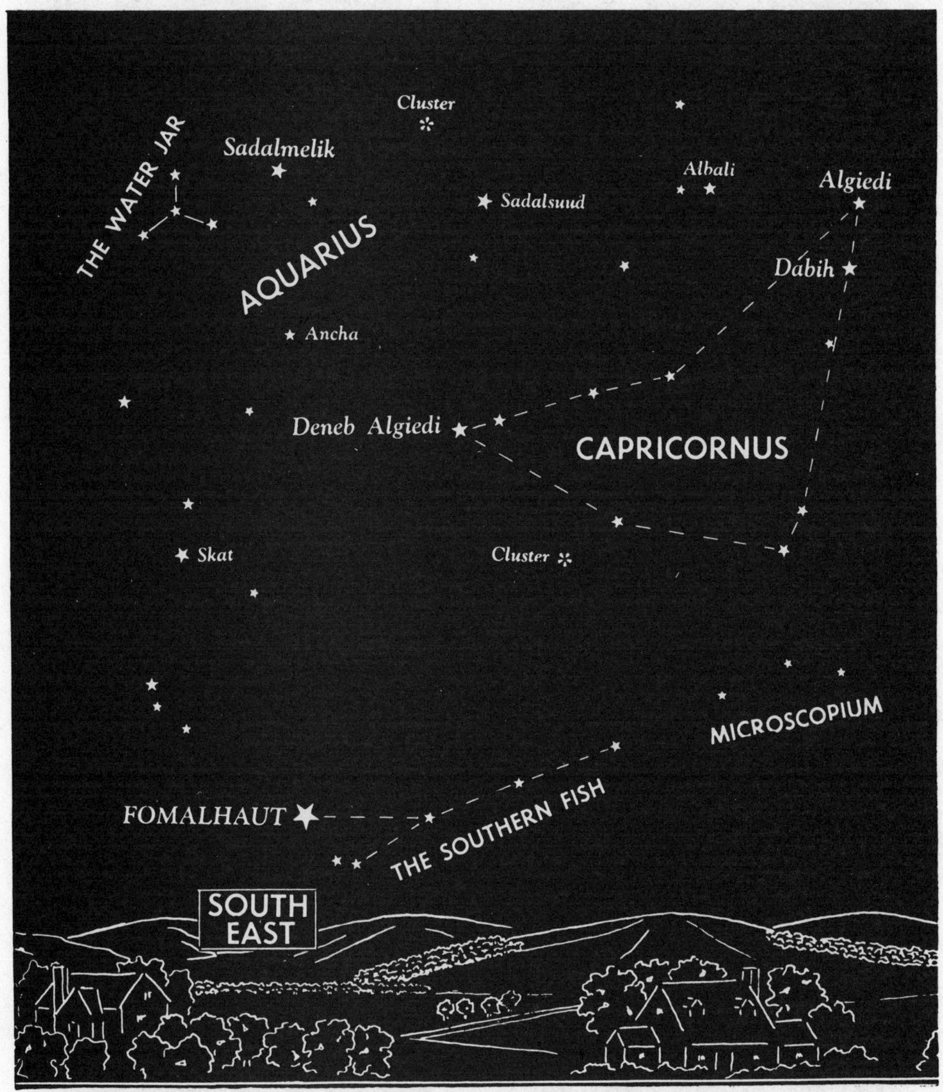


**Capricornus:** The constellations of Capricornus and Aquarius are in the Zodiac—the pathway followed by the wandering planets. Beware of any strange "stars" in either constellation. If they are bright and are not in these pictures, they are planets.

# CHART 26

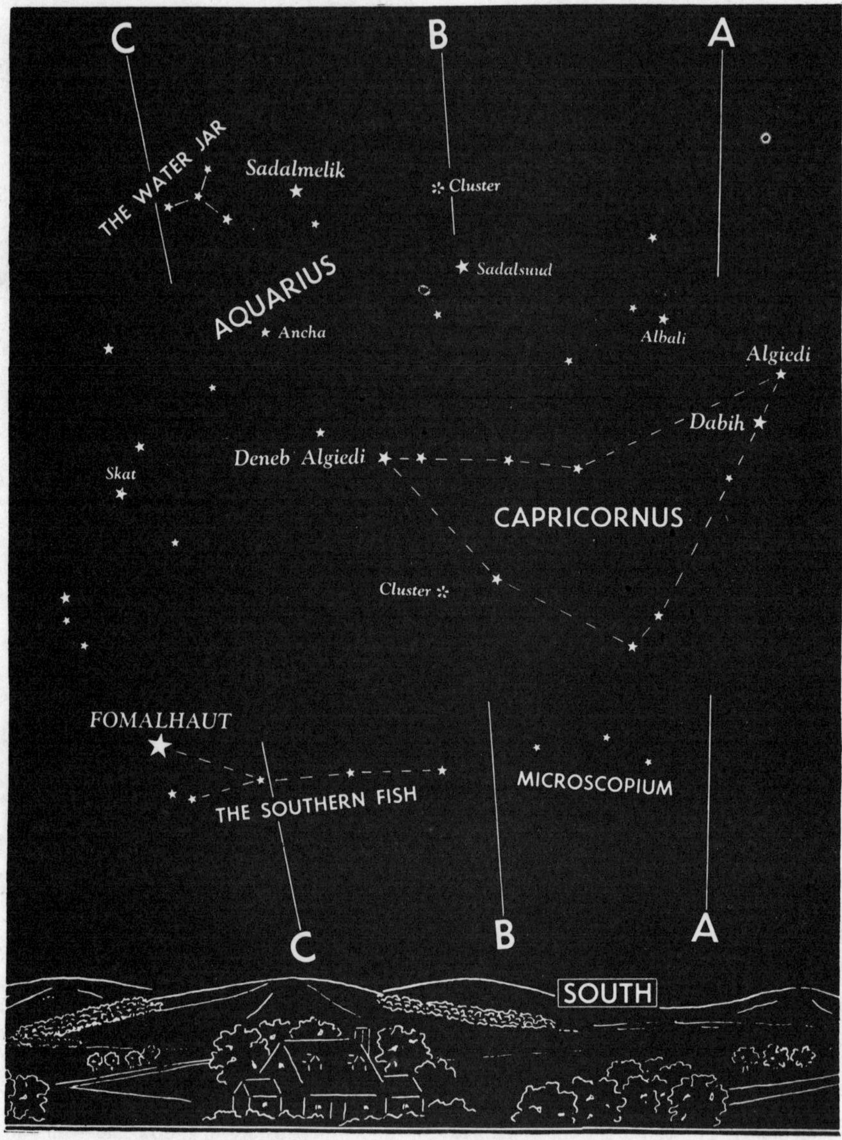


**Capricornus:** With this picture, you can follow Capricornus and his neighbors as they cross the southern meridian. One of these lines, AA, BB or CC, will be specified in the instructions. In all cases, face due south and tilt the book until the specified line is vertical at the south point of the horizon.

The constellations of Capricornus and Aquarius are in the Zodiac—the pathway followed by the wandering planets. Beware of any strange "stars" in either constellation. If they are bright and are not in these pictures, they are planets.

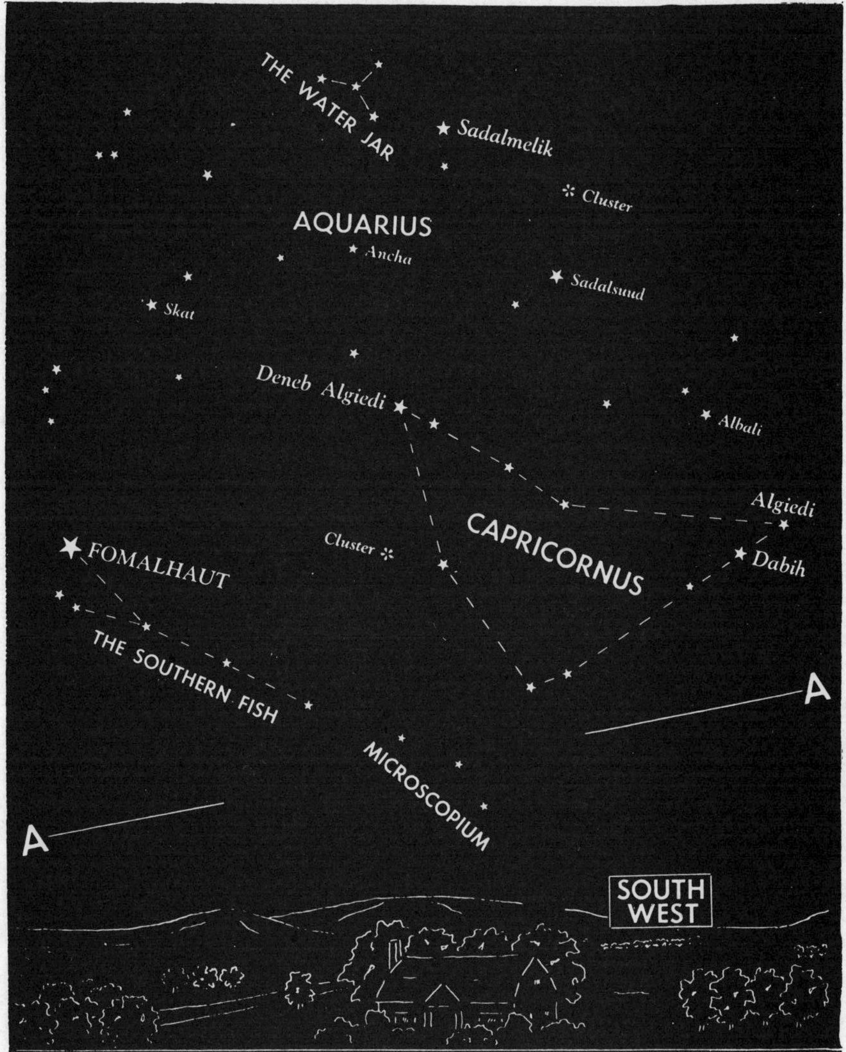


CAPRICORNUS: This picture shows Capricornus and his neighbors as they are descending toward their final position in the southwest. Ignore the line AA if Chart 27 is called for in the instructions. If, however, the line AA is specified, it means that these stars are no longer so high and you must imagine them lowered until AA is resting on the tops of the distant hills in the landscape.

The constellations of Capricornus and Aquarius are in the Zodiac—the pathway followed by the wandering planets. Beware of any strange "stars" in either constellation. If they are bright and are not in these pictures, they are planets.

# CHART 28

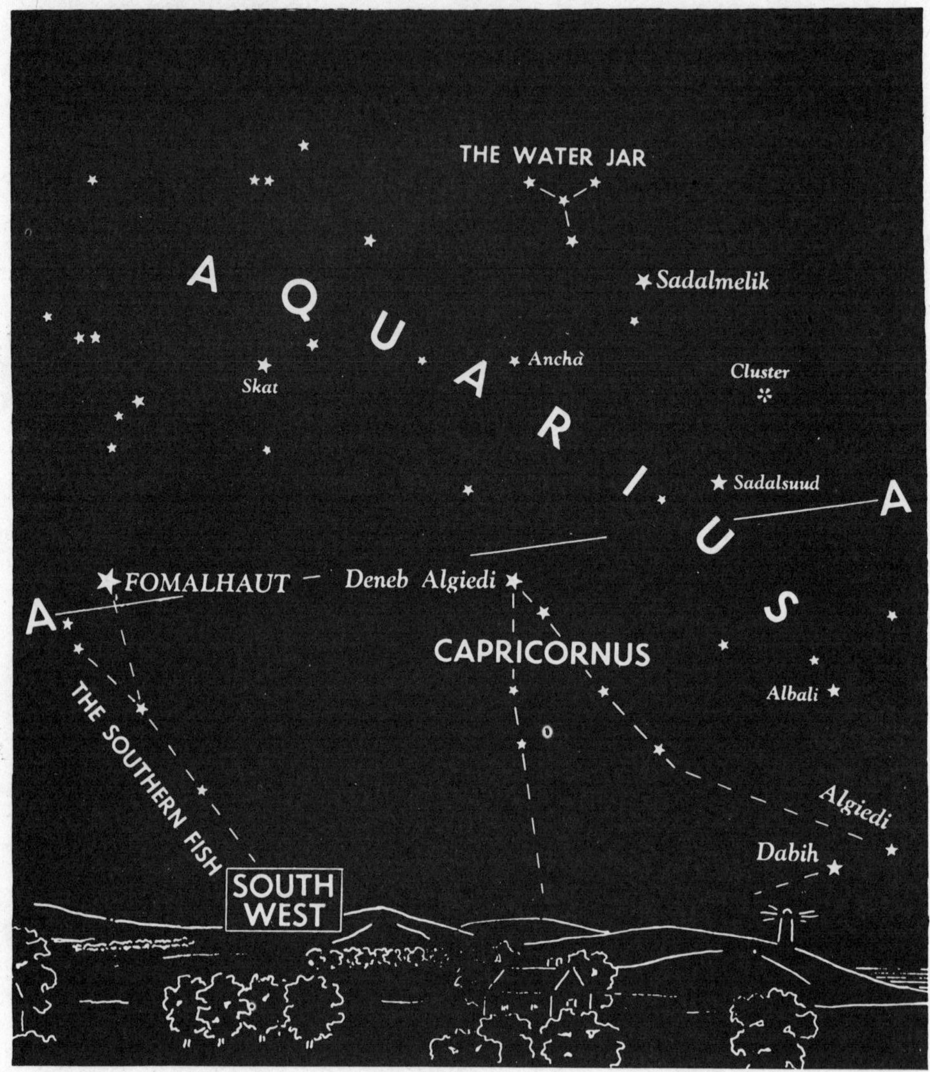


**Capricornus**: Capricornus and his neighbors are bidding us farewell when they are in the positions shown in this picture. Ignore the line AA unless it is called for in the instructions. If, however, the line is specified, it indicates that the stars are no longer so high and you must imagine them lowered until AA is resting on the tops of the distant hills in the landscape.

The constellations of Capricornus and Aquarius are in the Zodiac—the pathway followed by the wandering planets. Beware of any strange "stars" in either constellation. If they are bright and are not in these pictures, they are planets.

## XIV

## PEGASUS

THERE is little of naked-eye interest in the constellation of Pegasus except the famous Great Square. This one figure, however, is such an unmistakable "landmark" in the sky that it is of paramount importance both to the casual star-gazer and to the navigator.

The Square itself has two valuable navigational stars—Alpheratz and Markab—and the nose of the mythical horse contains another—Enif. Furthermore, the Square is surrounded by constellations containing other navigational stars and it acts as a conspicuous and easily found checking point to guide you in your search for groups that are not quite so clearly marked.

Pegasus is an excellent illustration of the extremes to which the ancient star-gazers went to find star formations into which to squeeze the gods and monsters of their old folk tales, whether the formations really fitted the gods and monsters or not.

For a modern star-gazer to claim that he can actually visualize this upside-down half of a flying horse is a masterpiece of imagination—or fiction.

But the Great Square is unmistakable, even though it is slightly battered out of true square shape.

The star Alpheratz does not belong to the constellation of Pegasus. It is supposed to mark the head of the chained maiden, Andromeda, who has a constellation of her own, shown in Charts 40 to 46. Pegasus is the flying horse which carried the hero Perseus to his rescue of Andromeda in the old myth told in connection with the figures of her parents, Cepheus and Cassiopeia, in the text accompanying Chart 3.

To the naked eye, the inside of the Great Square seems

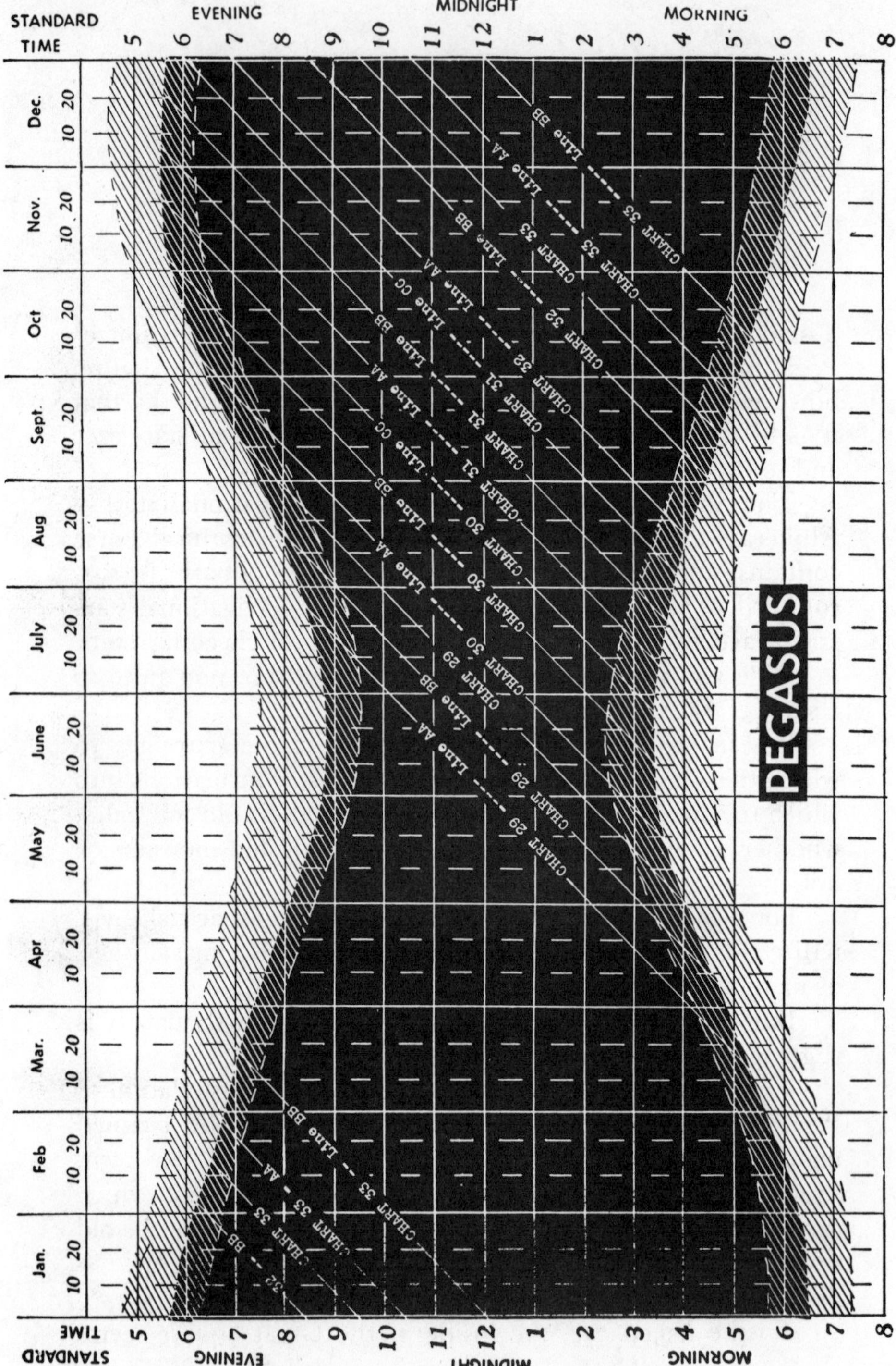


The diagonal line nearest to the hour and date desired shows the correct chart and line to use at that time.

PRONUNCIATIONS

*PEGASUS*—"peg-gas-us." Accent "peg."
MARKAB—as spelled. Accent "mar."
SCHEAT—"shee-at." Accent "shee."
ALGENIB—"al-jee-nib." Accent "jee."
ENIF—"enn-if." Accent "enn" (rhymes with "pen," "hen," etc.).

almost devoid of stars. A few can be seen on a clear night. But aim a pair of binoculars or a telescope at this seemingly blank region and you will find many surprises.

It remains for the long-exposure photographs from the great observatories, however, to reveal the wonders that lie beyond the visible stars of Pegasus in the same line of sight.

The great Mount Wilson telescope has captured a photograph of one small area of Pegasus showing 162 objects, each probably a whole galaxy of millions of great stars, at distances so great that the light requires 100,000,000 years to reach us, traveling at 11,000,000 miles a minute!

# CHART 29

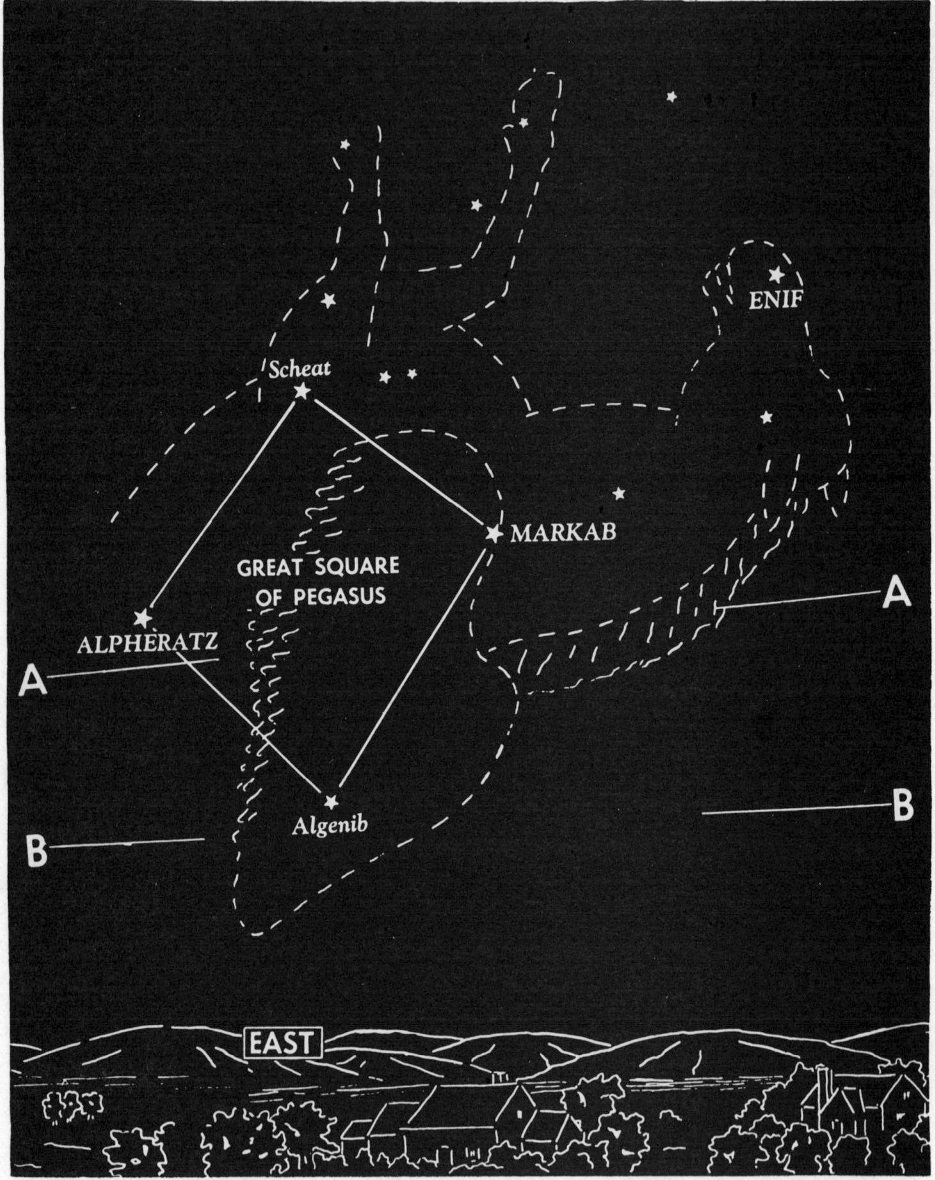


PEGASUS: Ignore the lines AA and BB unless one of them is called for in the instructions. When, however, one of these lines is specified, it indicates that these stars are not yet so high and you must imagine them lowered until the line is resting on the tops of the distant hills in the landscape.

# CHART 30

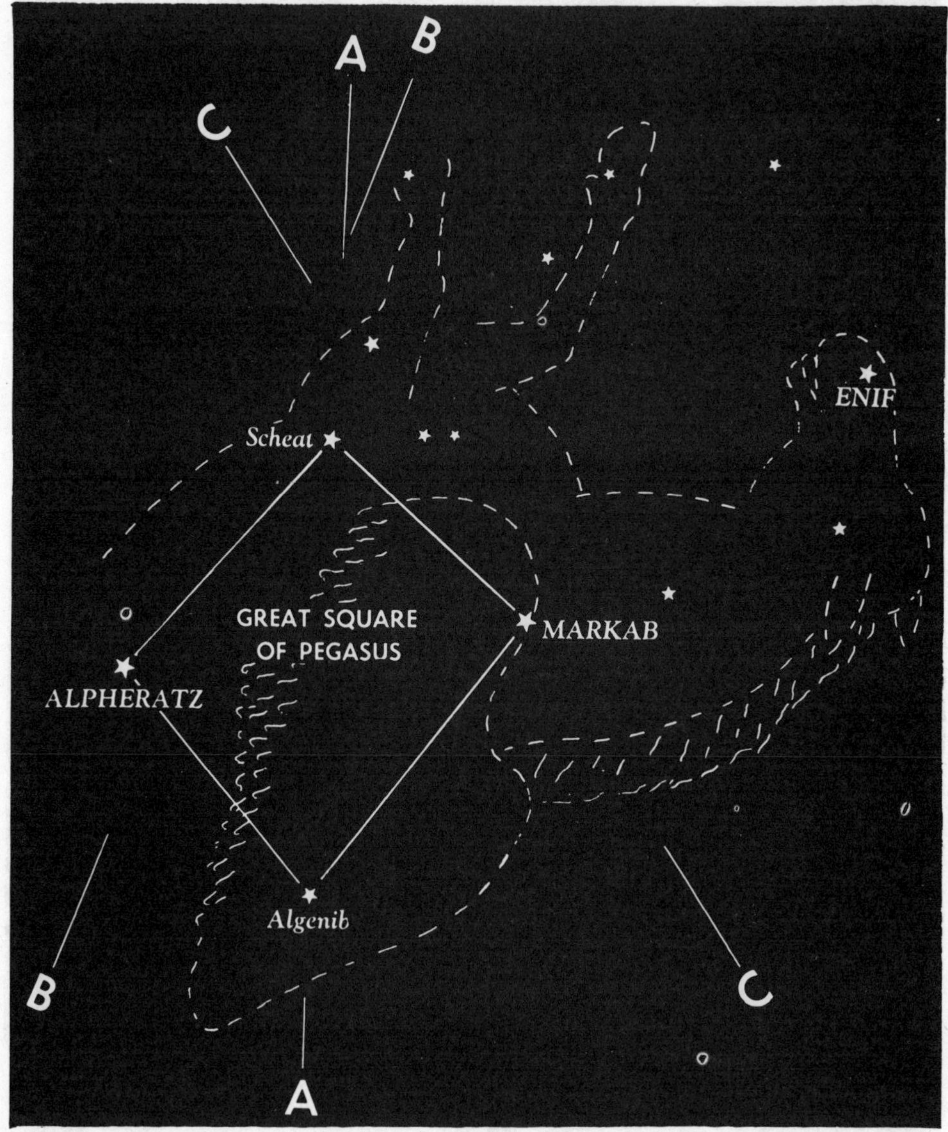


PEGASUS: Pegasus twists around as he mounts the eastern sky, so that these three lines—AA, BB, CC—are needed to locate him in his various aspects.

For line AA—face east; hold AA vertical; raise the book until the star Scheat is halfway up the sky; glance around the book and you will be looking at Pegasus.

For line BB—face east; turn line BB to vertical; raise the book until the star Alpheratz is halfway up the sky.

For line CC—face southeast; turn line CC vertical; raise the book until the star Algenib is halfway up the sky.

# CHART 31

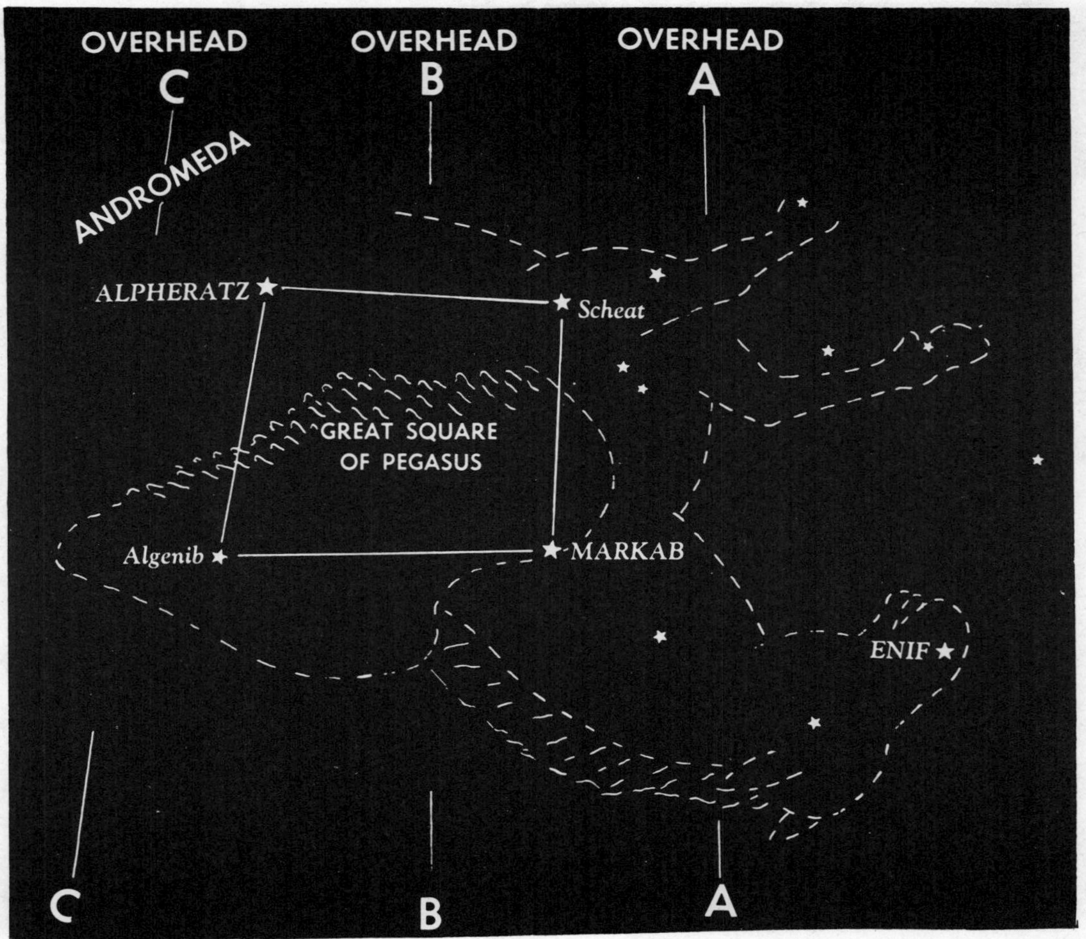


PEGASUS: With the three lines AA, BB and CC you can follow Pegasus in his journey across the overhead sky. In all cases, the procedure is: Face south; lie back comfortably; raise the book until "Overhead" is really overhead; move it to right or left to bring the correct line directly over your body; glance around the edge of the book and you will be looking at Pegasus.

# CHART 32

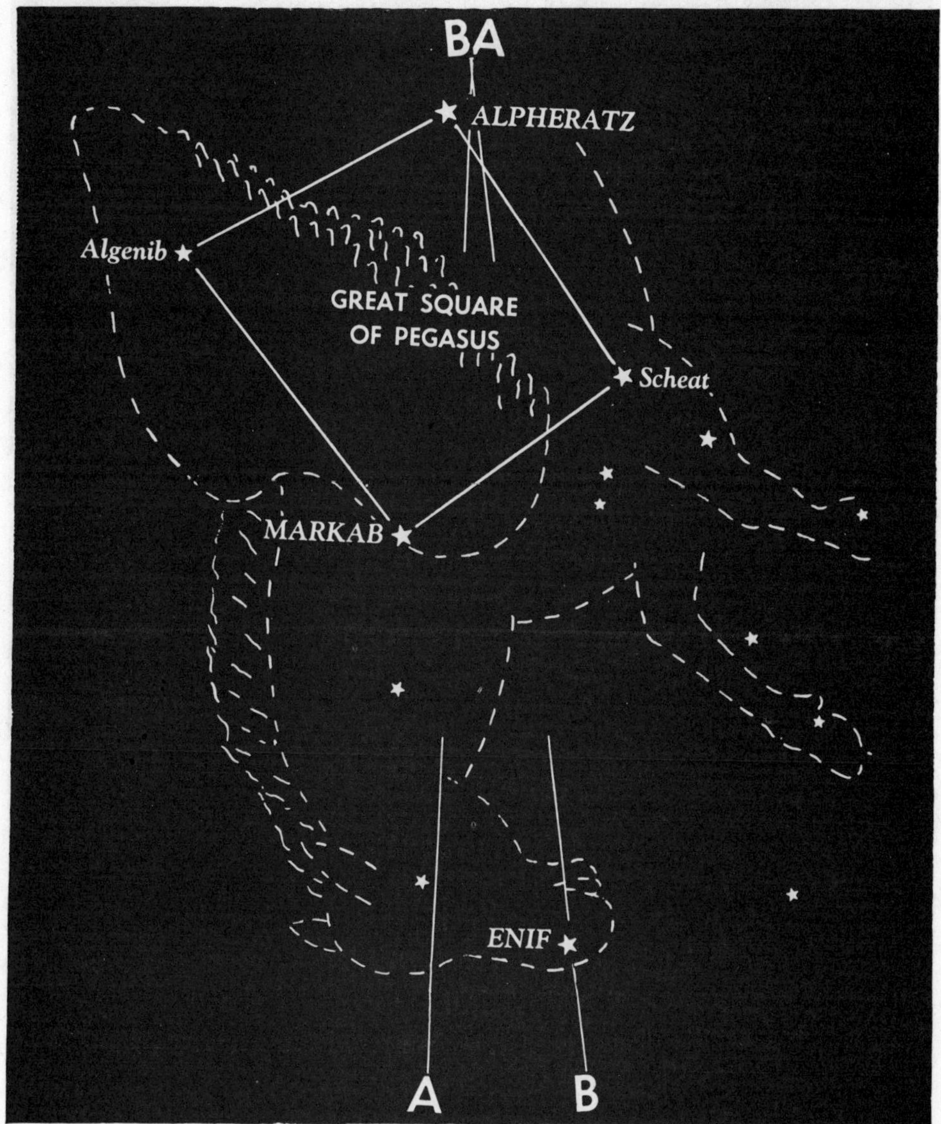


PEGASUS: As Pegasus descends the western sky, we need two vertical lines and two compass directions to locate him at different times.

For line AA—face halfway between west and southwest; hold the line AA vertical; raise the picture until the neck of the horse is halfway up the sky; glance over the top of the book and you will be looking at the Great Square.

For line BB—face due west; make BB vertical; raise the book until the Great Square is halfway up the sky.

## CHART 33

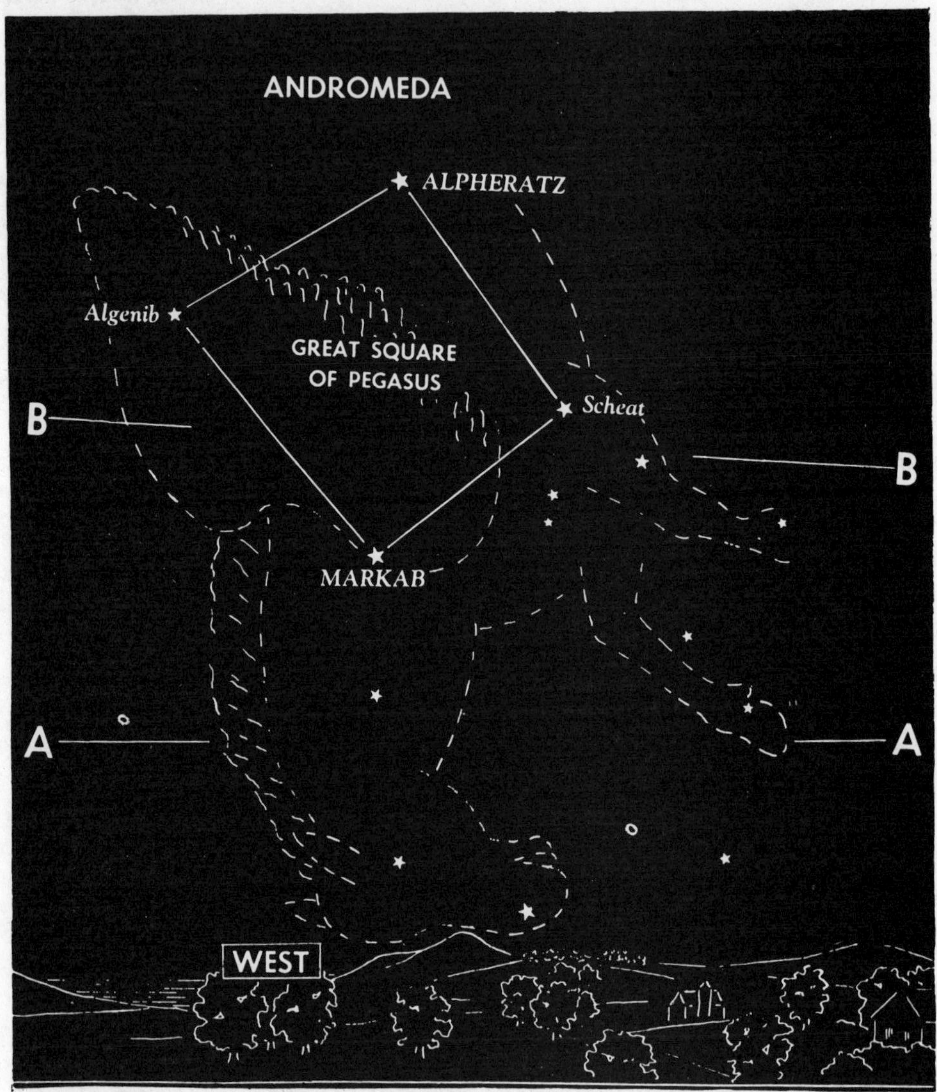


PEGASUS: Ignore the lines AA and BB unless one of them is called for in the instructions. When, however, one of these lines is specified, it means that these stars are no longer so high and you must imagine them lowered until the stipulated line is resting on the tops of the distant hills in the landscape.

## XV

# CYGNUS, LYRA AND AQUILA

TOWARD the middle of June, an hour or so after dark, the fine constellation of Cygnus, with two bright neighbor stars, comes into good position above the horizon, stretching from northeast to east.

This marks the beginning of the happy hunting season for the star-gazer with a good pair of binoculars or a telescope. From now until well into the winter, the millions of sparkling little stars that make up this part of the Milky Way will swing into the early evening sky.

But the naked-eye observer will see the Milky Way only as a glowing, irregular belt of luminosity, with a great black rift dividing it into two streams, beginning with Cygnus and extending down through several of the constellations that follow Cygnus across the sky.

In the space between the stars Deneb, Sadr and Epsilon, he will notice the black void known as the Northern Coal Sack. This Coal Sack and the Rift are vast clouds of matter "floating" in interstellar space and obscuring everything behind them.

Some idea of the unbelievable dimensions with which we are dealing may be gained from the estimate that, on the average, there are less than half a dozen specks of this microscopic matter in each cubic mile of space, yet the total is sufficient to present a solid and impenetrable curtain between us and the more distant stars.

The bright neighbor star that rises just before Cygnus and that precedes the constellation across the sky is Vega. The star that follows, more to the southward, is Altair.

That is the combination that is shown in the charts on the following pages.

Vega and Altair are not in the constellation known as Cygnus, the Swan. They belong to two separate constellations and the details of those two groups will be taken up later.

Here we have three good navigational stars in a comparatively small area of the sky—Vega, Altair and Deneb ("deneb," in the name of a star, always means "tail").

The whole constellation of Cygnus contains a great many stars fainter than those shown in the charts and some just as bright, but as, throughout this book, we emphasize only the stars needed to form the recognizable designs that we want to discover and remember, the superfluous ones are not shown.

If you are curious to make the acquaintance of all of these fainter stars, you will find them in Chart 91, and full instructions for using this map are given in the Calendar for Star-Gazers in the sections devoted to the more difficult groups.

Long before the dawn of recorded history, ancient man had pictured a bird of some kind formed around the nine or ten brightest stars in this group. This conception—with final agreement that the bird was a long-necked swan—was handed down from generation to generation and today we know it by the Latin word for swan—Cygnus.

Now the whole swan can be quite easily pictured on a clear, moonless night, but when the moon passes its first quarter, its light begins to dim out the fainter stars of this figure and leaves only five of the brightest visible to the naked eye.

These five, however, serve our purposes of identification just as well because they are so placed as to form an unmistakable cross—and we know this part of the group as the Northern Cross.

The Swan, of course, is the very ancient picture; the Cross is comparatively modern, but anyone who wants to give his stars a more up-to-date picturization is perfectly justified in seeing this group as a great airplane flying northward, whereas the Swan heads toward the south.

## CYGNUS, LYRA AND AQUILA

Any picture is allowable if it helps fix the three navigational stars in your memory. You may be amused by the perfect baseball game that I find in these stars. It is shown on page 187.

It is my impression that the conception of the Swan is most useful to beginners because, in his long flight across the sky he seems to be trying desperately to fly between Vega and Altair but he never quite makes it. They always manage to keep just a few wingbeats ahead of him.

Here are some amazing facts about some of the stars in these groups.

In the pictures you will find, in the long neck of the Swan, a circle marked "Chi." This denotes a star which you may or may not see. It is one of those mysteries of the heavens—a long-period, irregular variable.

At its brightest, Chi is as bright as the star Eta. At its dimmest, it can be found only with the great observatory telescopes. It is 9500 times brighter at maximum than at minimum and it goes through its cycle in a period of about 410 days, remaining invisible for about six months.

Deneb, the "tail," is one of the most distant of what we call the "nearer" stars. The light by which you see it tonight started from Deneb at least 700 years ago and, according to many recent estimates, this figure may be nearer to 1900 years. It is so far away that exact statements cannot be made, yet we consider it to be in a near-by suburb of the vast star-city which we call our galaxy, whose city lights all around us we call the Milky Way.

If Deneb were as near to us as our sun, we would be blinded by its light and entirely atomized by its heat. It is 4800 times as bright as the sun and 135 times the sun's diameter (or 14,715 times the diameter of the earth) but our little human eyes see it only as a fairly conspicuous but by no means particularly notable star.

A good pair of binoculars will show that Albireo is really

two stars, so close together in our line of sight that our naked eyes see them as a single point of light. There is no evidence, however, that they are physically connected. The nearer one of the pair is distant about 160 light-years from us. In good binoculars, the color contrast between these two stars is most striking. One is definitely orange; the other is blue-white which will appear to some eyes to have a tinge of green.

### *Vega and Its "Family"*

The brilliant star Vega is one of our very close neighbors. Vega's light, at the speed of 11,000,000 miles a minute, requires about 25 years to reach us. And, of the 22 brightest stars, only 4 are closer than 16 light-years, the very closest being 4¼ light-years away.

Vega is an important star to know because it is visible at some time of night or morning for every clear night in the year for star-gazers in the United States and northward.

Vega rules a neat and interesting little group of stars known as the constellation of Lyra, the Lyre. It is shown in detail on Chart 34. In this group are two fascinating stellar systems.

First, there is the star Sheliak, a "binary," or two stars revolving around their common center of equilibrium or around each other, if you prefer to think of it in that way.

This is one of the most massive binary systems yet discovered and one of the most unusual in its actual organization. The larger star has a mass (mass is equivalent to the amount of "stuff" it contains) 50 times that of the sun or nearly 17,000,000 times the mass of the earth. The smaller star is 43 times as massive as the sun. In actual size, too, these stars are impressive. Shrink the earth to the size of a baseball and, on that scale, Sheliak would be two globes, one nearly two *miles* in diameter, the other about a mile and a half. On that same scale, the sun would be only 27½ *feet* in diameter.

These two immense stars of Sheliak are less than one-third as far from each other as the earth is from the sun. This nearness means that the atmospheres of the two great stars overlap and mingle in the space between them. As they revolve around each other, there is a constant flow of atoms and minute particles from one, around the other and back again. Some of these particles are constantly being ejected into space and, over a period of millions of years, have formed a tenuous but luminous shell of gases surrounding the whole system.

Once every 12 days, 21 hours, 45 minutes, one of these great globes circles around in "front" of the other (as seen from the earth) and we have a partial eclipse that cuts off much of the total of light by which we ordinarily see Sheliak.

At maximum brightness, Sheliak appears to us to be as bright as the near-by star Gamma (sometimes called Sulafat).

During eclipse, Sheliak is only as bright as the near-by stars Zeta and Kappa.

This whole change can be seen by the naked eye and thus Sheliak is a favorite object with experienced star-gazers who specialize in keeping track of variable stars.

If you have binoculars, you will enjoy "sweeping" all around these stars.

Between Sheliak and Gamma, but a little nearer to Gamma, is the famous Ring Nebula in Lyra. You will find a picture of it on the next page. Unfortunately your binoculars will not show it but this photograph, made with the great Mount Wilson 100-inch telescope with a one-hour exposure, reveals it clearly.

The generally accepted theory is that, millions of years ago, the star shown in the center exploded—an actual atomic bomb in nature—and hurled out great masses of gas, and it is known that this surrounding gas is still expanding. We see the star now through the thin part of this envelope of gas. The "ring" effect is caused by the fact that we are looking through

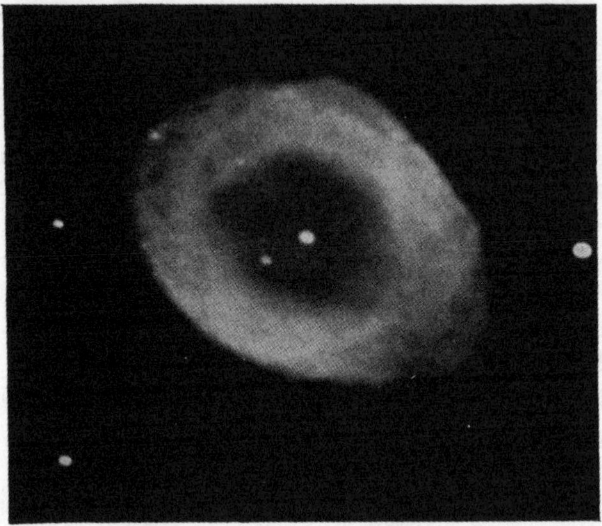

*Mount Wilson Photograph*
THE RING NEBULA IN LYRA

the rim lengthwise, as it were, and therefore there is much more gas in our line of sight and the refraction of the light from the star makes it more luminous, because each particle acts as a prism or mirror, and reflects the rays to us.

Another great favorite in Lyra is the star Epsilon, quite near to Vega. Here is a test of good eyesight even more severe than that furnished by Mizar and Alcor in the Big Dipper (Chart 2).

Unusually good vision on a clear dark night will reveal Epsilon as undoubtedly two little stars together. This feat is just about the limit of perfect vision, but binoculars make the two stars clearly visible. A telescope will show that each of these two stars is, in turn, a double, and observatory instruments prove that the brightest of the four is double. So we have a system of five stars, revolving intricately about each other and about a common center of gravity in periods that probably range from hundreds to thousands of years.

## CYGNUS, LYRA AND AQUILA

### PRONUNCIATIONS

*LYRA*—"lie-ra." Accent "lie."
- VEGA—"vee-ga." Accent "vee." The "g" is hard, as in "go," "get."
- SHELIAK—"shell-yak." Accent "shell."
- GAMMA—English spelling of Greek letter assigned to this star. It is sometimes known as SULAFAT (pronounced "sue-la-fat"; accent "sue").

*AQUILA*—"ack-will-a." Accent "ack."
- ALTAIR—"al-tare." Accent "tare."
- ALSHAIN—"al-shane." Accent "shane."
- TARAZED—"tar-a-zed." Accent "tar" (rhymes with "bar," "far," "car").
- ETA—"ate-a." Accent "ate." English spelling of Greek letter.
- IOTA—"eye-oh-ta." Accent "oh." English spelling of Greek letter.

### *Altair and Its "Family"*

Sheliak, in Lyra, gives us a good example of a variable star whose fluctuation in light is due to an eclipsing system.

The little constellation of Aquila, with Altair as its brightest beacon, gives us a good example of a variable whose light changes because the star actually pulsates, or expands and contracts. This kind of variable, when it has an exactly timed period, we call a "Cepheid" variable, as explained in the text relating to Chart 3.

Eta, in Aquila, is a Cepheid variable. At brightest, it equals Alshain; at dimmest, it is only as bright as near-by Iota. Its period is 7 days, 4 hours, 14 minutes. For 40 hours, it is at maximum. Then, for 66 hours, it "deflates" until it reaches minimum size and brightness. For 30 hours, it is equal to Iota only and then, slowly, it expands and brightens until it rivals Alshain again.

Like most Cepheids, Eta is an extremely tenuous star, its average density being only a little more than one-third the density of our atmosphere at sea level. It is about 650 light-years from us—one of our "neighbors," as we measure the vastness of the universe.

The star Altair is a very average body, with a diameter only about half again as great as the diameter of our sun and

## CHART 34

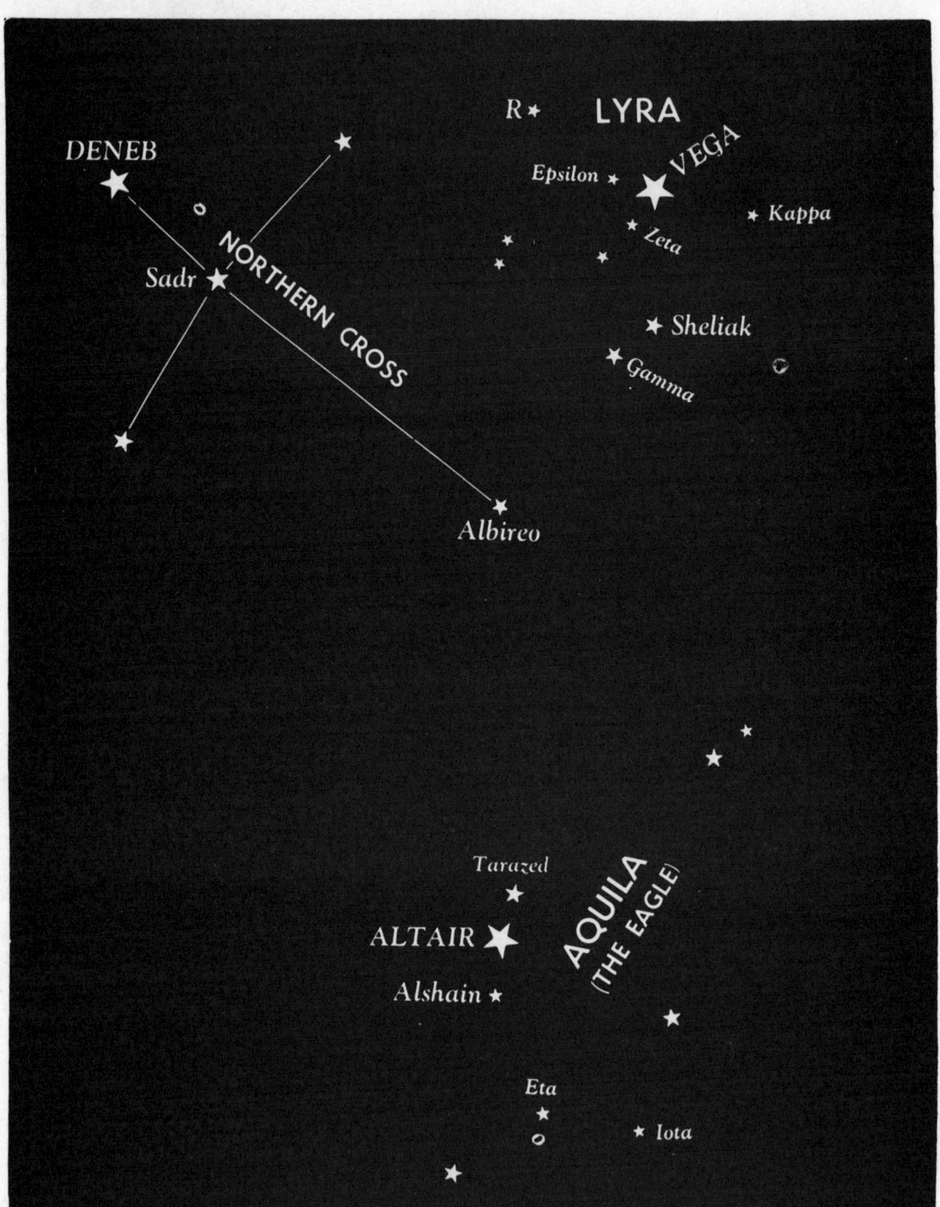

R
LYRA
DENEB
VEGA
Epsilon
Kappa
Zeta
NORTHERN CROSS
Sadr
Sheliak
Gamma
Albireo
Tarazed
AQUILA
(THE EAGLE)
ALTAIR
Alshain
Eta
Iota

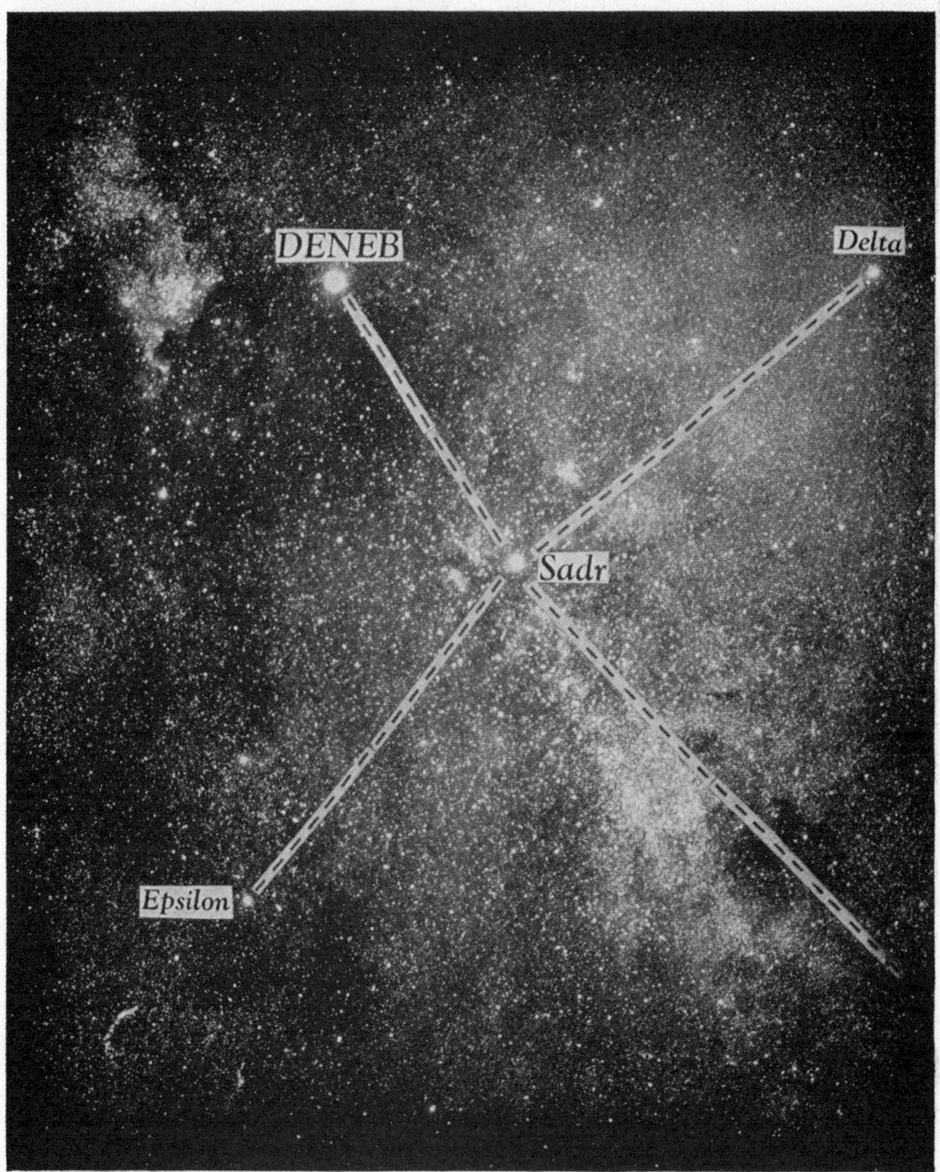


THE MILKY WAY IN CYGNUS

This photograph from the Ross-Calvert *Atlas of the Northern Milky Way* shows the famous North American Nebula in the upper left-hand corner and the wisps of the Veil Nebula in the lower left.

a luminosity only about nine times as great, this being due to a somewhat higher surface temperature as well as to greater radiating surface. Its conspicuous brightness among the much greater stars in the heavens is due to the fact that it is a mere 15½ light years from us.

### *Some Wonders in Cygnus*

On the preceding page you will find a photograph which strikingly demonstrates some of the wonders that the great observatory telescopes find in our Milky Way. This picture is a part of one of the plates in the great Ross-Calvert *Atlas of the Northern Milky Way,* published by the University of Chicago Press. The picture was taken by Frank E. Ross with a three-hour exposure.

In order that you may be able to locate this marvelous region exactly, I have inserted lines and names which you can check with the chart of Cygnus on the page facing it. You will not be able to see any of these wonders with your naked eyes or binoculars, though binoculars will reveal amazing clusters of sparkling little stars all around this region. Cygnus alone is worth the cost of the best binoculars you can buy.

In the upper left-hand corner of the photograph, you can find a luminous cloud shaped much like a map of North America and this shape gives it its name—the North American Nebula. Of course, the nebula in its entirety does not have this shape. The form is due to the fact that much of the luminosity is totally obscured by a dense and opaque cloud of interstellar matter, and this cloud can be plainly seen against the brightness of the Nebula in the background. The individual stars that can be seen against this black cloud are on this side of it—in other words, nearer to us than the cloud is.

Down in the lower left-hand corner of the photograph are two wisps of luminous material that are also among the famous objects in the sky. Together they are known as the Veil Nebula and it is believed that, if it were not for obscuring

## CYGNUS, LYRA AND AQUILA

### PRONUNCIATIONS

*CYGNUS*—"sig-nuss." Accent "sig" (rhymes with "big").
DENEB—"den-ebb." Accent "den."
SADR—pronounced like our word "sadder."
ALBIREO—"al-beer-ee-oh." Accent "beer."

The other stars in the Swan are not generally known by popular names but are marked with the English spelling of the Greek letters that have been assigned to them. The pronunciation of these Greek letters follows:

PHI—"fie" (rhymes with "pie," "rye").
CHI—"kye" (same rhymes as above).
ETA—"ate-a." Accent "ate."
ZETA—"zay-ta." Accent "zay."
EPSILON—"epp-sill-on." Accent "epp."
DELTA—as spelled. We use this letter in speaking of the "delta" of a river.
THETA—"thay-ta." Accent "thay," the "th" soft as in "think."
IOTA—"eye-oh-ta." Accent "oh."
KAPPA—pronounced as spelled. Accent "kapp."

matter, we would see that they are simply two edges of one great cloud.

On the following page, we get an amazing "close-up" of the wisp on the inner side. This is the so-called Filimentary Nebula. The photograph was made at the Mount Wilson Observatory after seven hours' exposure with the huge 100-inch-diameter reflecting telescope.

Compare this picture with the smaller image and you will be able to check all the details. The little star in the center of the wisp, whose light is probably responsible for the luminosity of the long filament of cloud, can be seen in both pictures. The dark streak of obscuring matter that runs down to the right of the wisp can also be noted and the individual stars that show against it are nearer to us than the obscuration and so can be seen against it.

There are five indistinct little groups near Cygnus, always included in the Calendar among the groups for advanced stargazers. They are Vulpecula, Delphinus, Sagitta, Equuleus and

*Mount Wilson Photograph*

FILIMENTARY NEBULA IN CYGNUS

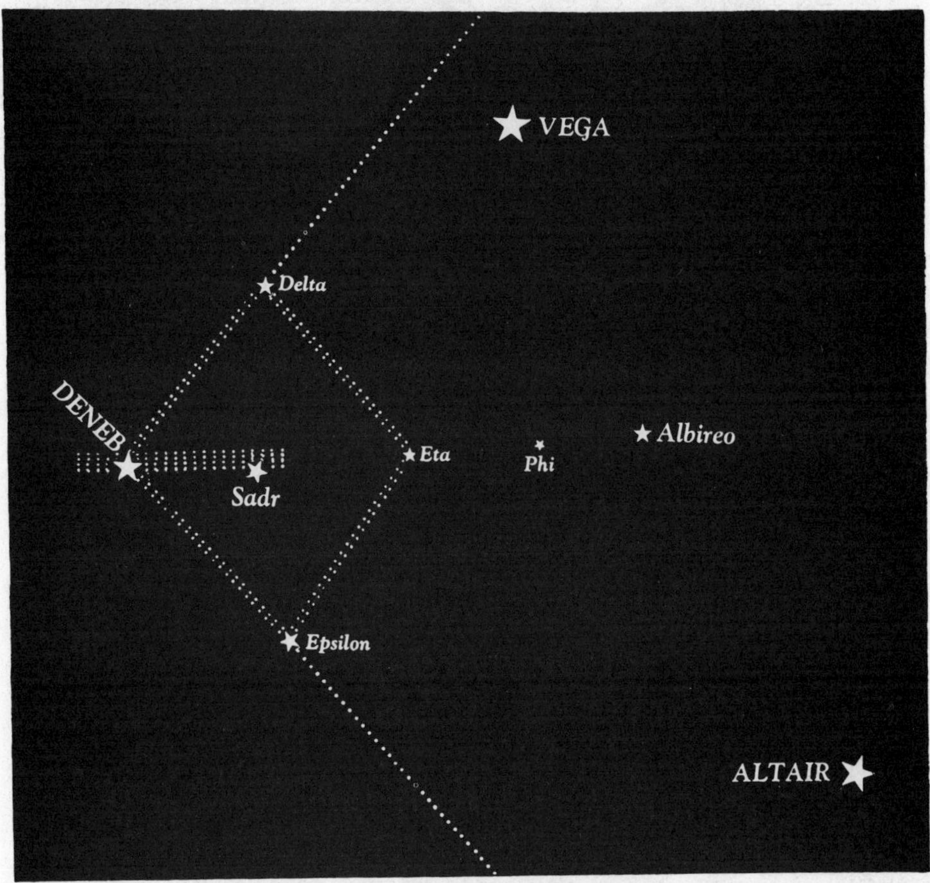


A BASEBALL GAME IN THE SKY: Study the stars in the picture of Cygnus in Chart 35 and then see if you can find this baseball game. The batter has hit a high fly to center. Albireo is running in to get it and second-baseman Phi is also out after it. Shortstop Eta has run over to cover second for Phi and left-fielder Vega is running in to back up third in case of trouble.

Lacerta. The novice star-gazer should use them as his introduction to regular star maps because the presence of conspicuous Cygnus, with Vega and Altair, among them helps locate them. They are shown in detail on Chart 91.

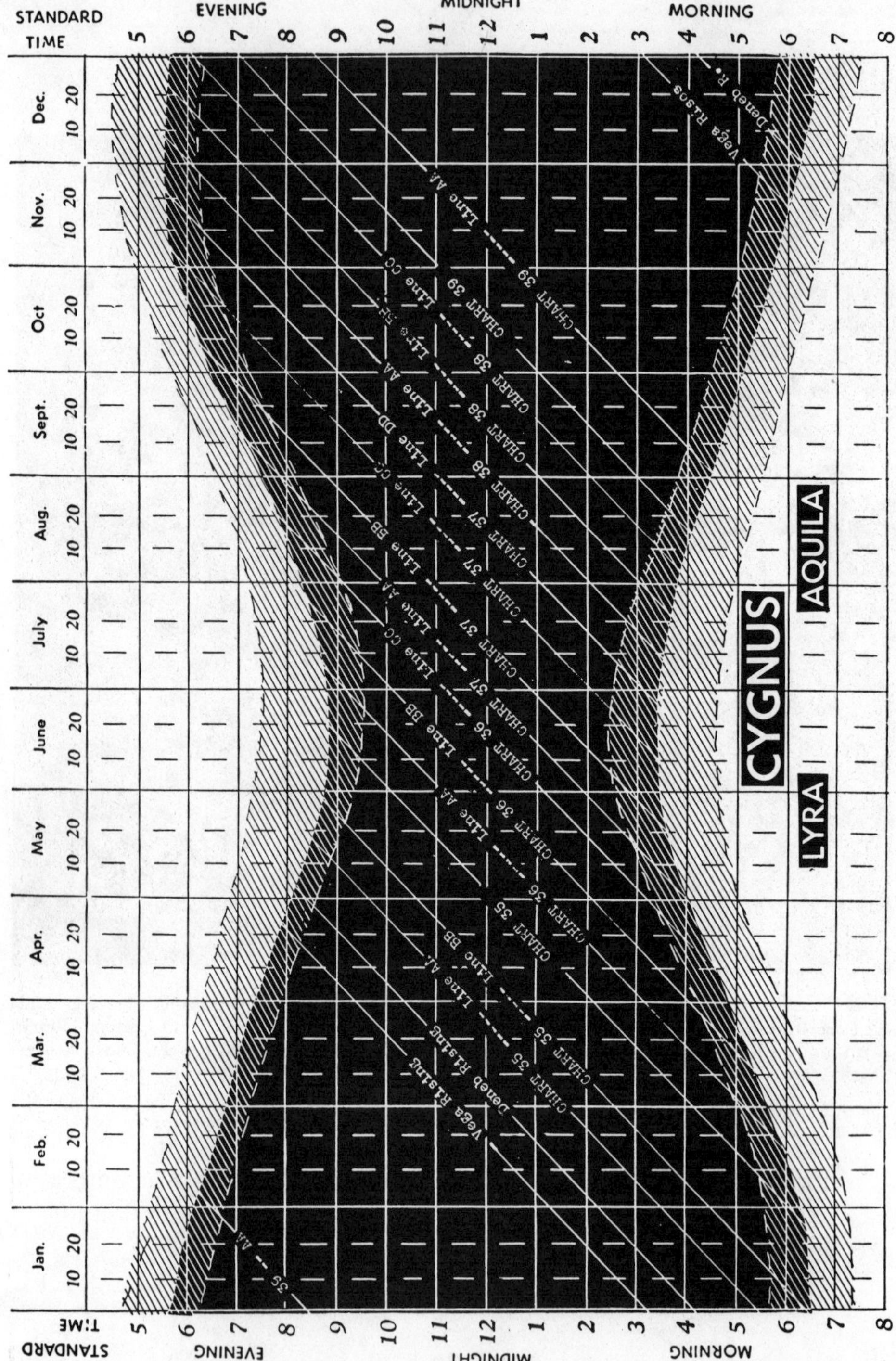


The diagonal line nearest to the hour and date desired shows the correct chart and line to use at that time.

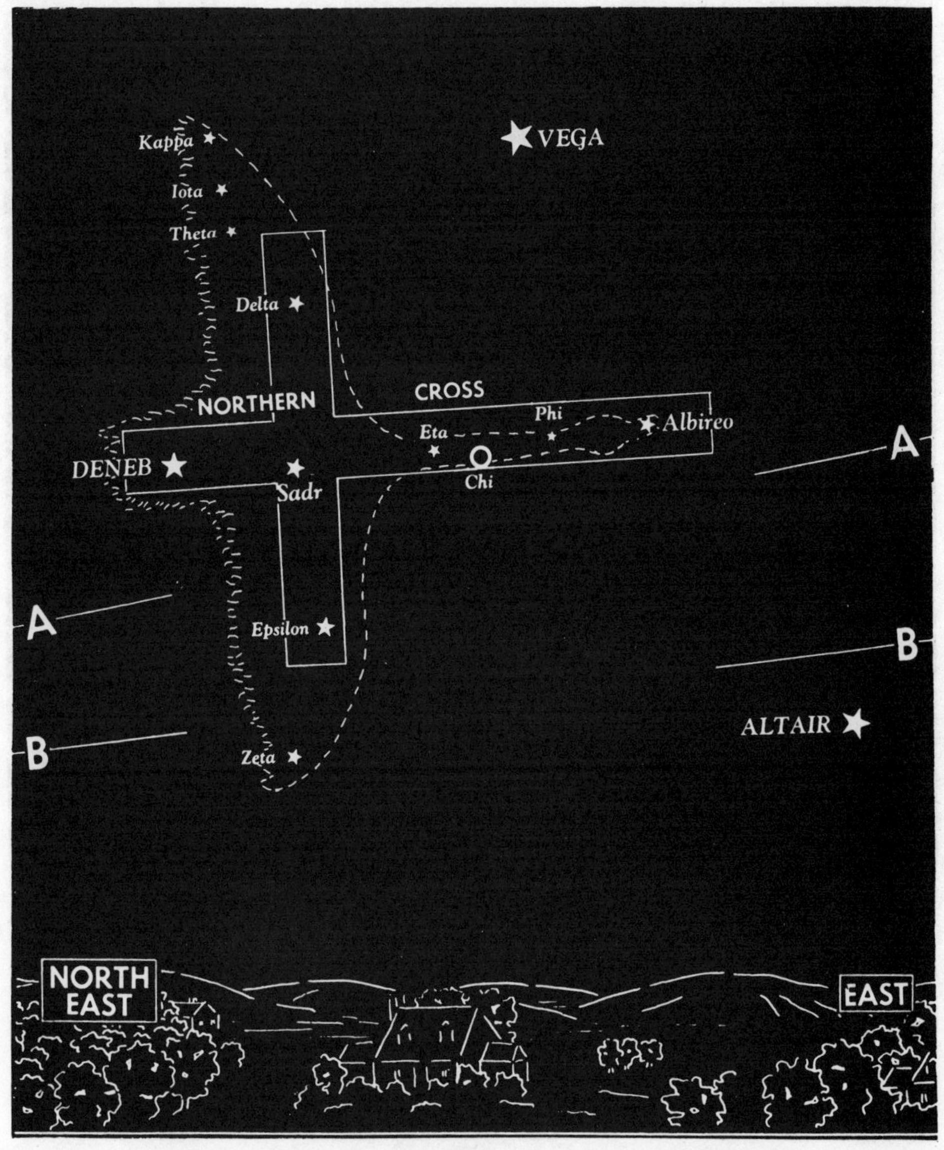


CYGNUS: This picture shows the stars of Cygnus as they are used to form two different familiar images—the Swan and the Northern Cross. Ignore the lines AA and BB, unless they are specified. When, however, either line is called for, it means that the stars are not yet so high and you must imagine them lowered until the specified line is resting on the tops of the distant hills in the landscape.

## CHART 36

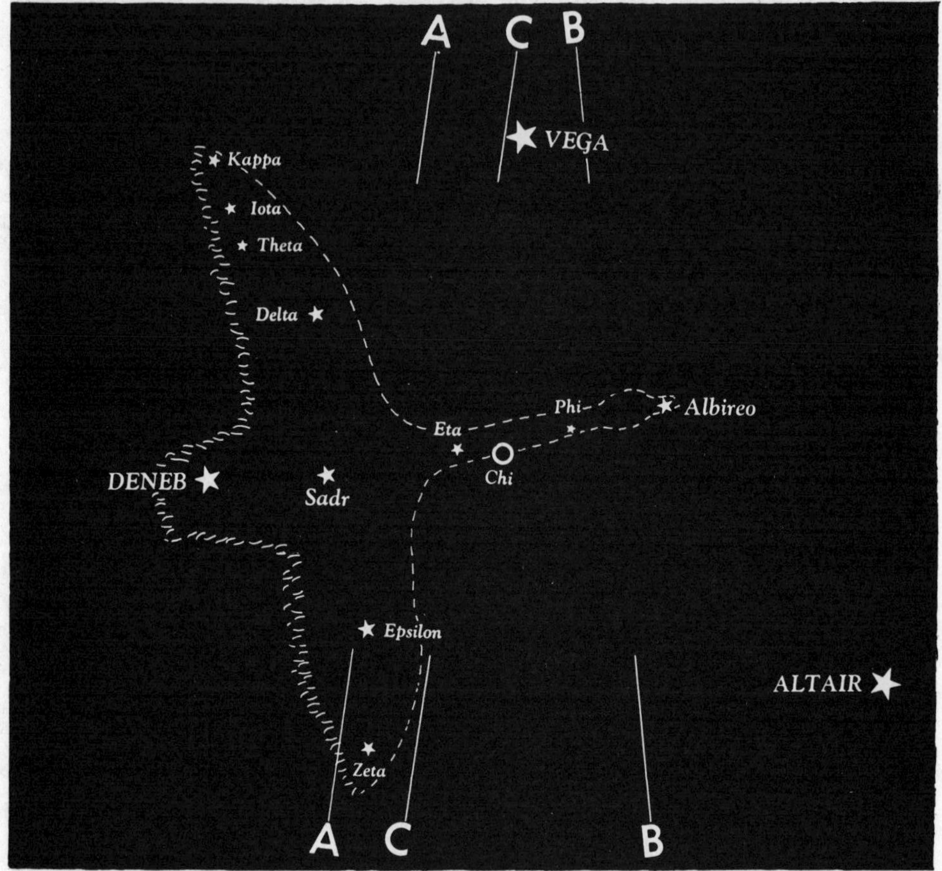


CYGNUS: The three lines, AA, BB, CC, are useful in locating Cygnus and his companions as they climb the eastern sky. The method of using them follows:

Line AA—face E-NE (halfway between east and northeast); tilt the picture to make the line AA vertical; raise it so that the star Delta is halfway up the sky, glance past the edge of the book and you will be looking at these stars.

Line BB—face east; make BB vertical; raise the picture to bring Deneb halfway up the sky.

Line CC—face east; make CC vertical; raise to bring Zeta halfway up the sky.

# CHART 37

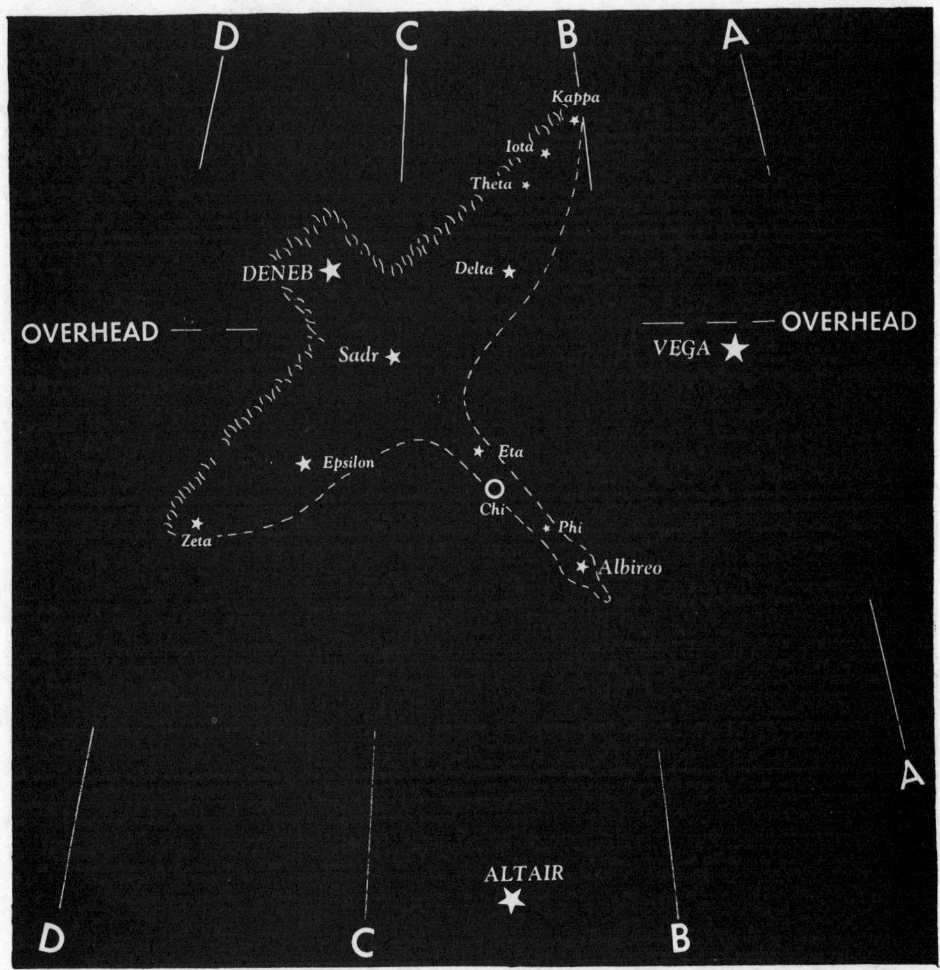


CYGNUS: Cygnus and his companions occupy a large area of the sky so they take a long time crossing the overhead meridian. These lines will be used at different times but in all cases the procedure is the same. Face south; lie flat with head north, feet south, hold the book above you so that "Overhead" is really overhead; then move it right or left until the specified line cuts lengthwise directly through your body.

# CHART 38

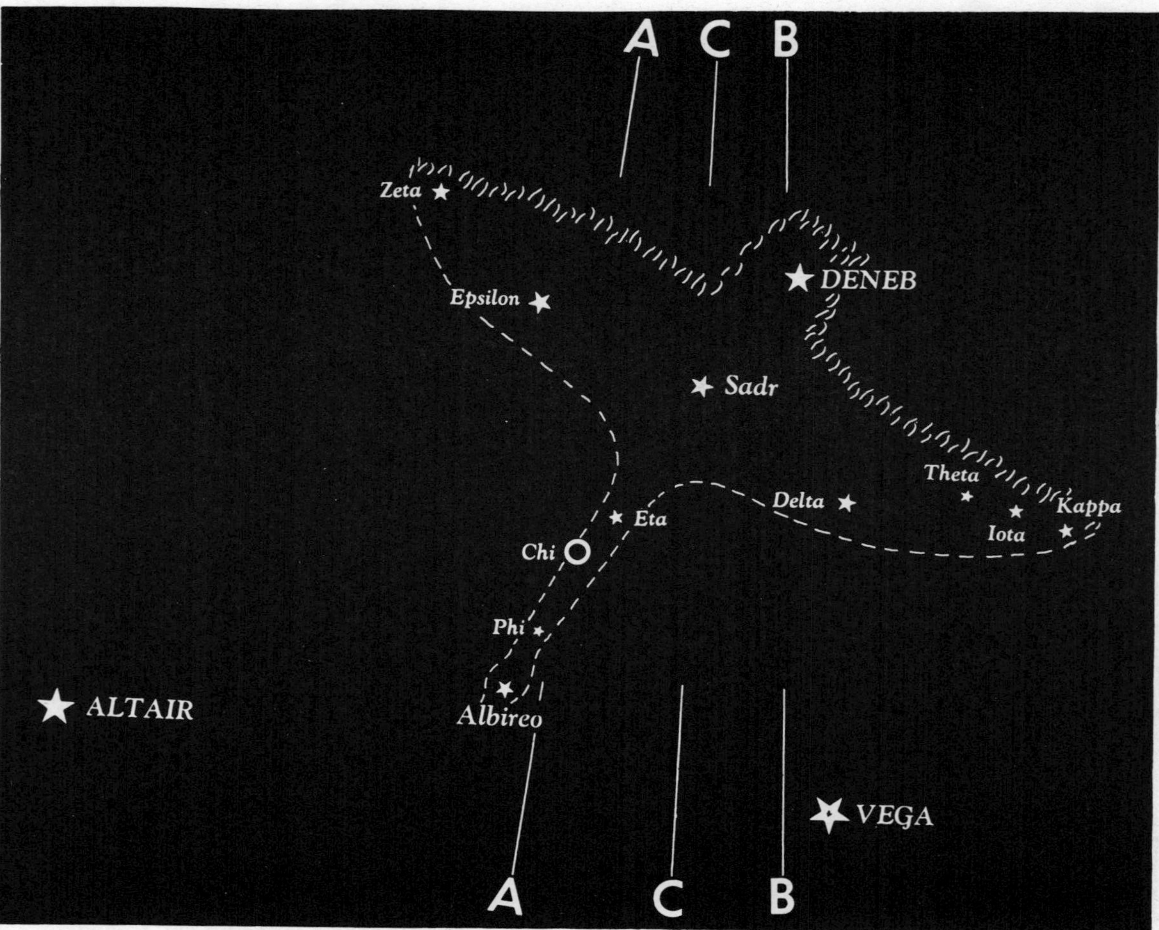


CYGNUS: In all instructions for Chart 38 the three lines AA, BB, CC are used to locate Cygnus as he descends the western sky.

Line AA—face west; make AA vertical; raise the picture until Vega is halfway up the sky. Glance around the edge of the book and you will be looking at these stars.

Line BB—face halfway between west and northwest; make BB vertical; raise the book to make the circle Chi in the Swan's neck halfway up the sky.

Line CC—face halfway between west and northwest; make CC vertical; raise the book until Sadr is halfway up the sky.

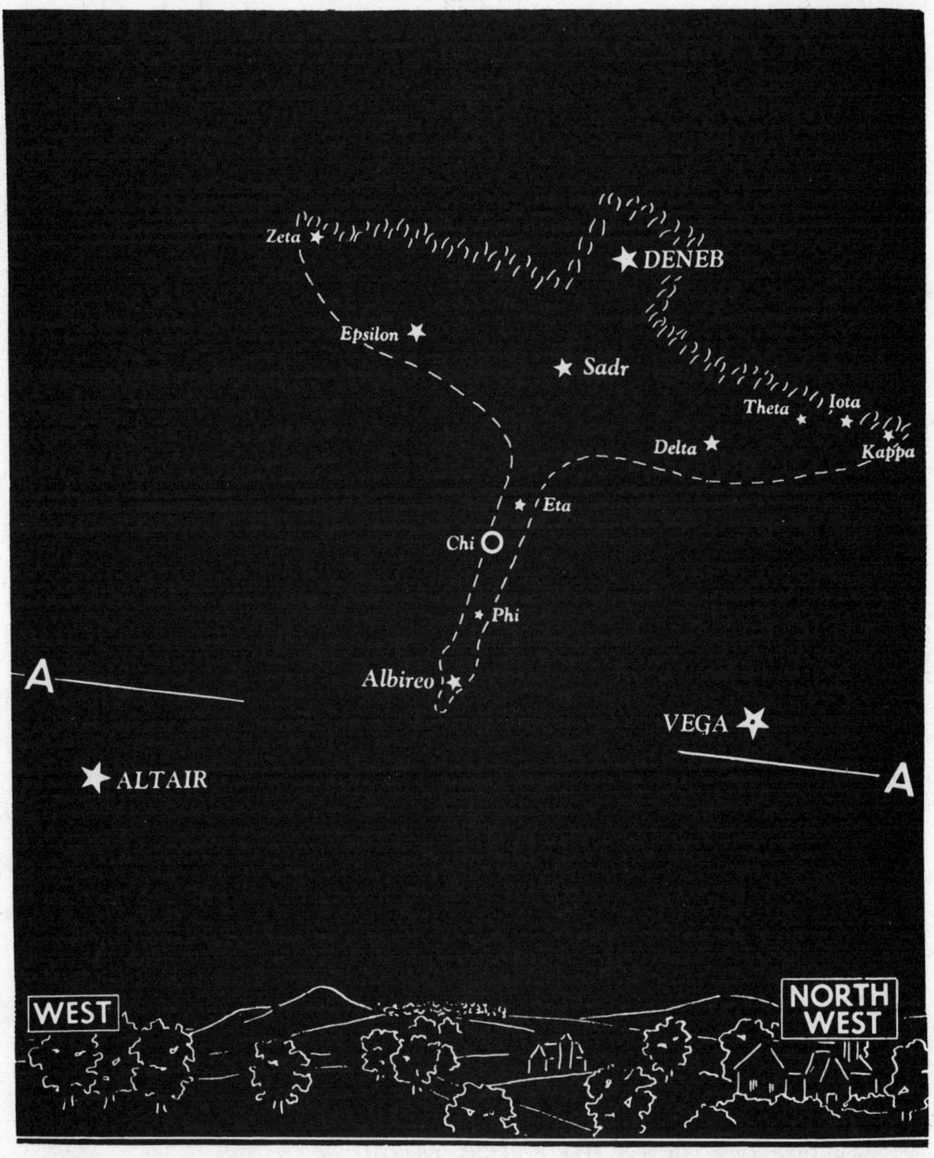


CYGNUS: If you will look at Chart 35, you will see that the Swan rose flying horizontally; now we find it plunging head down into the horizon as it prepares to set. This chart shows it just before it has gone low enough for the horizon haze to dim the star Albireo. At times, the instructions will specify the use of horizon AA. Then you must imagine the landscape raised to meet that line and Albireo will be too low—practically on the horizon—to be seen well.

## XVI

# THE YACHT

**The Yacht is an imaginary figure formed in the sky by the constellations of Andromeda, Perseus, Aries and Triangulum. It is *not* a figure that is recognized by authorities.**

—

Yet there really is a Yacht in the sky.

If you will take the trouble, you can find it and it does not require nearly as great a stretch of the imagination as many of the traditional figures allegedly seen by ancient star-gazers.

It is a graceful sloop with mainsail, topsail and jib set and the Great Square of Pegasus can easily be visualized as the yacht club dock past which it has just sailed, close-hauled into the east wind.

But, to complete the whole picture of the Yacht, we need four constellations—Andromeda, Perseus, Aries and little Triangulum. So it is best to consider them one at a time as they rise above the horizon in the northeast or follow each other as the Yacht sails (unfortunately backward) across the sky from rising to setting.

That means that the constellation of Andromeda comes first, and Perseus follows. This will have special significance if you have read the text describing Chart 3 in which was told the ancient myth of the hero Perseus, his flying horse Pegasus and the rescue of the maiden Andromeda, daughter of the vain queen Cassiopeia, whose constellation accompanies the Yacht across the sky like a great sea gull.

You must not expect to find any recognized authority for this Yacht. It is a figment of my own imagination just as is the baseball game I find in Cygnus but I have always liked the Yacht because it is most useful in helping to locate the various objects of interest included in its outlines, particularly one of the most amazing and fascinating objects in the whole sky—the so-called Great Nebula of Andromeda.

To the naked eye, this is only a dim and indistinct speck, like a little star veiled behind a curtain of clouds. If there is moonlight or street lighting near you, you will have a hard time seeing it.

You must forgive this speck for being so dim and tired-looking. And you will when you realize that, as you see it tonight, this light has been traveling well over 750,000 years—possibly 1,000,000—to reach you—traveling all that time at the tremendous velocity of 11,000,000 miles a minute.

As you look at the Andromeda Nebula tonight (and we are not going to call it a "nebula" much longer) you cannot say, "It *is* of such-and-such a shape." You must say, "It *was*."

Because you will be doing something that no one else in the world except a star-gazer can do; you will actually be seeing the past.

In this case, it is (or was) in the very remote past as we count our chronology here on earth, for tonight's light left Andromeda in the days when apelike creatures here had only recently begun to evolve into the form that we now call man.

The light that you are now getting is more than 100 times older than the Pyramids; the distance that it has traveled is so inconceivable that even to write the number of miles in figures is meaningless.

Yet, in that dim little speck, we have an entire system of worlds with a total mass that it would take some 100 *billion* of our suns to equal.

This far-distant system probably gives us one of the best pictures we have of the structure of our own system, which contains the earth and the planets and the sun and all of the countless stars which we can see or photograph, plus the billion or more forever invisible to us, whose combined light we see only as the irregular band of glowing sky which we call the Milky Way.

Most of our bright stars would be pygmies if they were in

the Andromeda Galaxy and, if our sun were there, it would be so insignificant that we could not see it from the earth even with our most powerful telescopes nor photograph it on our most sensitive plates.

You will note, in the paragraph above, that I have stopped calling this object by its historic name of Nebula. Instead we are going to call it the Andromeda Galaxy.

The word "nebula," in its strict sense, refers to a cloud—Latin, *nebula*; a cloud, mist, vapor. The word as used by star-gazers should therefore be confined to its exact meaning—a cloud, either luminous or dark, of gas or scattered microscopic cosmic dust. If the cloud is luminous, it shines because its atoms are excited by radiation from near-by stars or by refracting or reflecting their light. But a nebula is primarily a cloud, even though it may have stars enmeshed in it as is the case with the Great Nebula in Orion.

A galaxy, however, is primarily an aggregation of stars with more or less organization into a system, even though there is certain to be a great deal of nebulous matter involved throughout its structure.

In deference to its historic fame, I am using the name "Nebula" in the charts because the change to the term "galaxy" has not yet been widely accepted.

The Andromeda Galaxy was named Nebula because its tremendous distance made it appear as a nebulous cloud until development of the great telescopic cameras and photographic technic and other scientific advancements captured the imprint of thousands of its stars. Then modern methods, particularly the law of the Cepheid variables, gave us the yardstick for measuring its distance and its dimensions. If you forget that law, read the text describing the star Delta in Chart 3.

In many books about the stars, you will find this Galaxy referred to as M31 and that designation in itself gives an interesting sidelight showing the rapid progress that has been made in the scientific study of such objects.

"M31" merely indicates that the Andromeda Galaxy was

*Yerkes Observatory Photograph*

THE ANDROMEDA GALAXY M31

number 31 on a list of indistinct celestial objects which were *nuisances* to an old comet-hunter named Messier. Messier made his list because, in his search for comets, he had (as he thought) wasted much valuable time watching these dim specks and measuring their positions night after night to detect the motions among the fixed stars which would prove them to be comets. That was what he was interested in—comets.

In the telescope which he used, these objects were not revealed in their true form; they looked like nebulous and amorphous specks of luminosity, as distant comets look. Therefore when, after many nights watching and checking up on them, he found that they did not move among the stars and so proved they were not his beloved comets, he decided to catalogue them in order not to waste any more of his valuable time on such unimportant intruders.

Messier's list contains the positions of 103 such "nuisances." Today, that list is a catalogue of many of the most amazing and most important objects in the sky, their true structure and significance having had to await the development of present-day celestial photography, spectroscopy, astrophysics and the methods of measurement which we classify as astrometry.

As these branches of science progressed, it was natural that their devotees should turn to Messier's list as a good start for their investigations. If these 103 mysterious objects were not comets, what were they?

It was these investigations that revealed the universe as we picture it today—a countless myriad of isolated systems, each in itself an organized universe of unnumbered stars and perhaps planets and the nebulous material from which stars and planets are possibly evolved or which, perhaps, they eject in their mad whirl through space—and all going through birth and life and death in the far reaches of a space that is totally beyond the little boundaries of the human imagination to picture.

Messier's immortality rests today entirely upon his list of "nuisances" which he considered not worth an hour of a scientist's time; his lifework on comets could be thrown into the wastebasket and science would be none the poorer for its loss.

It is a queer freak of fortune that a man's most serious mistake should prove to be his most valuable contribution to human knowledge. Christopher Columbus gained fame the same way.

Observatory photographs of this Andromeda Galaxy and other comparable systems give us a fairly clear idea of approximately the kind of system which science now believes surrounds the earth and the sun and the planets.

If you can project yourself in imagination into the swarm of stars revealed by the telescopic camera, you can begin to find explanations of some of the phenomena which we on earth see in our own sky on any clear night.

Examine the photograph of the entire Andromeda Galaxy made at the Yerkes Observatory.

At first glance, this appears to be an elliptical body of luminous matter, streaked through with dark patches. The picture on the following page, however, shows, on a greatly enlarged scale, just the "upper" tip of this spiral as recorded on a plate attached to the great 100-inch reflecting telescope of the Mount Wilson Observatory.

In this latter photograph, and by means of other new scientific methods, we get proof that this apparent cloud is really the glow of the combined light of billions of great stars, and every one of the minute white dots in the picture represents a super-giant. An ordinary star like our sun would make no impression at that distance.

It can be clearly seen that there is much true nebulosity involved with these stars just as there is among the stars of our own system. The dark patches about in the center of the picture may not be in the Andromeda Galaxy; they may be

This Mount Wilson photograph of the tip of the Andromeda Galaxy shows a portion of the system on a greatly enlarged scale and reveals the images of individual stars.

opaque clouds in our own system which intervene and shut out our view of the luminosity behind them. The few individual stars seen against this dark curtain are in our own system, between the earth and the dark clouds.

Yet the Yerkes picture of the whole system shows distinctly that there are great circular streaks of dark material involved with the Galaxy stars all the way around the swarm and this kind of dark band is seen in the photographs of virtually all such systems, and becomes particularly striking in those galaxies which we see "edge on," as we see the one in the constellation of Coma Berenices. It seems that these whirling universes tend to throw outward around their equators or belts, much of the "stuff" of which dark nebulae are composed.

On the following pages, you will find photographs that show variations in form and also show that these systems are oriented in different ways as we see them from the earth.

The Andromeda Galaxy is obviously tilted part way over from a strictly edge-on view so that we look at it obliquely. On the other hand, we have the two extremes—strictly edge-on and strictly at right angles—plentifully represented among the thousands of such objects that have sat for their portraits by our skilled observatory photographers.

If you have a very vivid imagination, these photographs will give you the clearest possible idea of the way our scientists now picture our own galaxy, our own position in that galaxy and why we see that impressive luminous band that we call the Milky Way surrounding the earth in a great belt.

Suppose now you were an astronomer living in one of these galaxies and that you used a great telescope to photograph the system in which our earth is embedded.

When you had your picture developed and printed, you would look in vain for the earth or even the sun. Both would be too insignificant to make even a microscopic speck on your negative.

What you would see on your plate would be almost a duplicate of one of these photographs. Just which one would

An "Edge-on" Spiral Galaxy: This object is in the constellation of Coma Berenices. The photograph was made with a five-hour exposure through the Mount Wilson sixty-inch reflecting telescope.

present the closest resemblance, we do not know. Some theorists favor the well-organized and smoothly formed Andromeda Galaxy; others think they have evidence that your picture would show the lack of complete organization and the loosely attached spiral streamers shown in the photograph of the galaxy listed as M33 in the constellation of Triangulum.

Then examine the striking universe of stars and "stuff" that our telescopes reveal in the little constellation of Canes Venatici. This is the famous "Whirlpool Nebula" (but we will hereafter, I hope, call it the Whirlpool *Galaxy*). It was number 51 on the list of nuisances that irritated old man Messier.

Those who favor the Canes Venatici form use, as added evidence, that odd and mysterious cloud of luminous matter at the end of one of the octopus tentacles. They claim that our own system shows a similar characteristic in what we call the Magellanic Clouds—two great, shining areas in the southern skies, not visible from the United States, but conspicuous objects in the night skies of star-gazers in the southern hemisphere.

Whichever form your photograph showed, we will assume that it aroused your interest and you decided to come here and inspect our galaxy in more detail. So you entered your atomic space-ship and started this way.

As you neared, you would see that our galaxy definitely was more or less disc shaped with a huge, inflated central core probably like the one in the picture of the edge-on spiral. This core would be surrounded by a roughly flat and not very thick belt of what looked from a distance like luminous material, possibly with spiral arms or tentacles of some sort. You will find it discussed in our chapter on Sagittarius.

Closer approach would reveal two important facts:

1. The whole system is in rapid rotation about the "inflated" central core.

2. The system is not, as it seemed in your photograph, a great cloud of luminous gas—a mere nebula—but an aggregation of several billion stars of various sizes, from super-

A Loose Spiral Galaxy: This object is listed as M33 and is in the little constellation of Triangulum, shown in our pictures of the Yacht. The photograph was made at Mount Wilson.

giants to pygmies, and of various colors and temperatures from blazing blue-white, with temperatures so high that virtually all atoms are stripped of their outer electrons, to dim and barely visible dull red, cool enough for atoms to combine into molecules—all interspersed with vast clouds of interstellar particles or microscopic specks of dust. The entire disc would quite possibly be surrounded by a belt of this "stuff" that had been hurled out into space by the centrifugal force of the rapidly rotating wheel of stars.

In fact, it would all bear a strong family resemblance to the galaxy you had just left.

Plunging through this outer obscuring belt, you would come into the main body of the galaxy and here, all around you, you would begin to see the individual stars. As you looked straight ahead through the almost endless vista of the disc, the most distant stars would be so far away that they would not appear as distinct individuals to your unassisted eyesight but their combined light would form a luminous band all around you, like a nighttime photograph of New York or any other great city, with the near-by windows (stars) clearly defined but the distant horizon made visible only as a glowing streak against the black sky.

"Ah!" you would say. "They have a Milky Way here too."

And that would be true. That is what our Milky Way is.

Somewhere in your trip through our galaxy—probably a little to the north of the exact slice that would cut the disc into two flat halves and possibly a third of the way in from the outer boundaries toward the swollen center, you would see a star that is unique, so far as we know.

This star would not be notable in itself—not one of the big ones nor yet one of the little ones; not one of the very hot ones nor one of the very cool ones; just an average run-of-the-mill star.

But this star, which we know as the sun, would be the center of a system which presents a most amazing piece of celestial mechanism.

THE "WHIRLPOOL NEBULA": A remarkable galaxy in the constellation of Canes Venatici near the handle of the Big Dipper. This photograph was made at the Mount Wilson Observatory.

Circling around it, almost but not quite in the same plane, would be many small globes, one of which is our earth, and many of these globes, in turn, would have still smaller globes, or moons, circling around them as they circled around the sun, as the sun circled around the galaxy, and as (many scientists believe) the galaxy itself and all the other galaxies circled around some unknown distended center or core or hub of a super-system which we call the Metagalaxy.

To achieve a masterpiece of understatement, it is all rather puzzling.

The Andromeda Galaxy is the most distant object that can be seen with the naked eye.

This requires good eyesight, accurate location and a dark and crystal-clear night with no street or house lighting near. It appears at first to be a very dim star but you will soon notice that it is not a sharp and distinct point, as a star is, but quite obviously hazy and diffuse. Binoculars will make this more obvious but even the best binoculars or small telescopes will not reveal its form.

It may help you to locate this object if a veteran star-gazer gives you his own method of finding it.

Wait until these stars are at least as high as shown in Chart 40. If there is any haze along the horizon, they will have to be as high as in Chart 41, line AA. In early evenings, you will have a good view of Andromeda from the end of July to mid-March.

Your first job, of course, is to locate the Great Square of Pegasus, which you can easily do at any time by referring to the Pegasus Hour-and-Date Diagram and Charts 29 to 33.

Then focus binoculars or eyes on the bright star Alpheratz. Run straight across and get the star Mirach in your field of view. Then run slowly "up" (if it is in the east) to the fairly bright star "above" Mirach, pause a moment to check your bearings and then run up in the same direction and about the

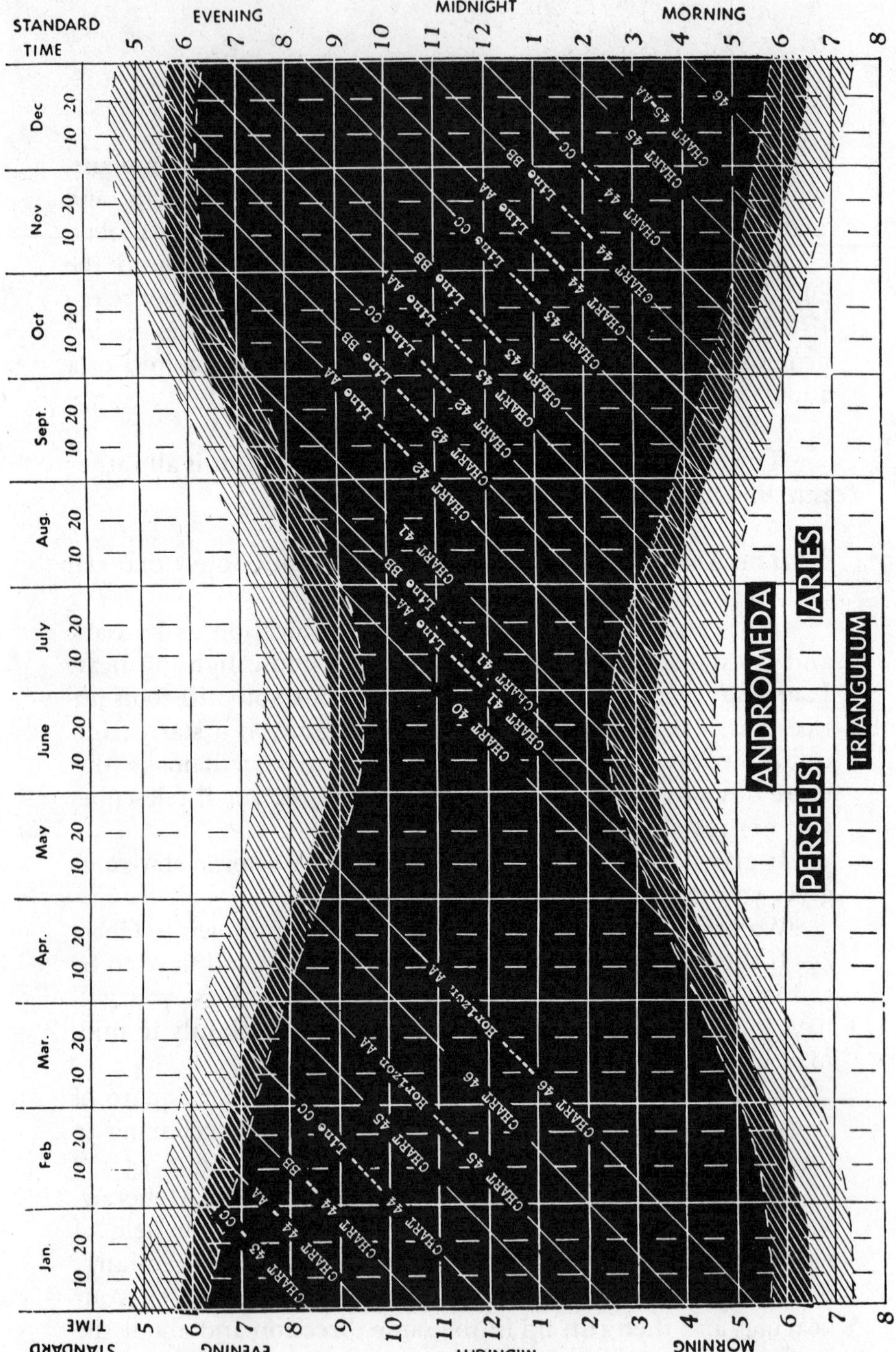


The diagonal line nearest to the hour and date desired shows the correct chart and line to use at that time.

# CHART 40

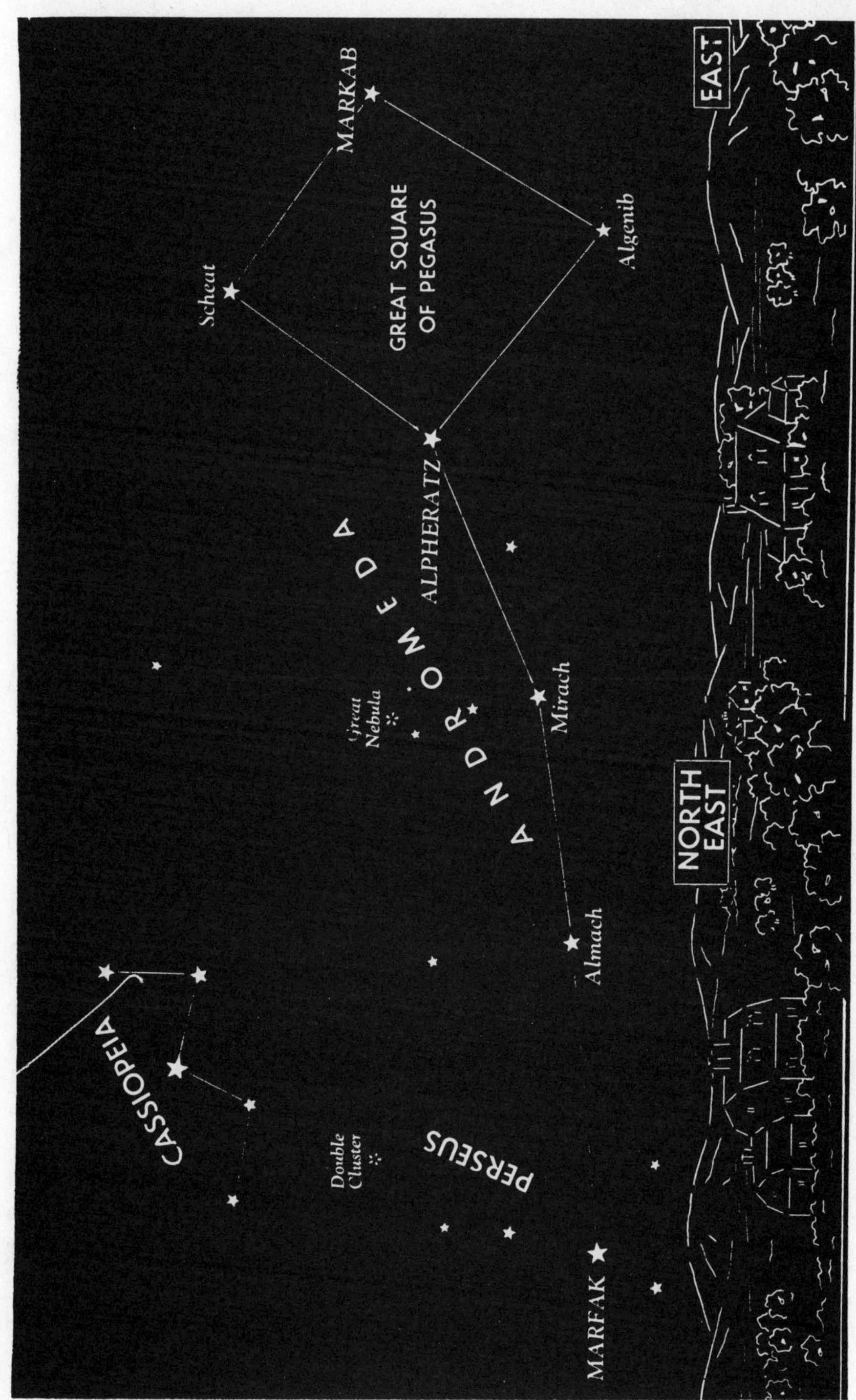


**The Yacht:** This picture does not yet show the form of the Yacht but only the first appearance of two of its constellations—Andromeda and part of Perseus.

PRONUNCIATIONS

*ANDROMEDA*—"an-drom-ee-da." Accent "drom" (rhymes with "Tom").
ALPHERATZ—"al-fee-ratz." Accent "fee."
MIRACH—"my-rack." Accent "my."
ALMACH—"al-mack." Accent "al."
*PERSEUS*—"purz-use." Accent "purz" (rhymes with "furs"). The "use" rhymes with "juice."
MARFAK—as spelled. Accent "mar." This name is also spelled MIRFAK—pronounced "meer-fack." Accent "meer."
ALGOL—as spelled. Accent "al." The "g" is hard as in "go," "get."
*ARIES*—"air-ri-eez"—three syllables. Accent "air." The "i" of the "ri" is short as in "bit."
HAMAL—both "a's" are short. Accent "ham."
SHERATAN—"sher-at-tan." Accent "sher" (rhymes with "her").

same distance. You will find a little triangle of "stars" in your field of view.

This little triangle is your stopping place and I quote the word "stars" because, as you will quickly see, one of them is too hazy to be the distinct and clear image made by even a small star.

That hazy object is the Andromeda Galaxy.

### *Perseus and the "Demon Star"*

THE constellation of Perseus furnishes the stars that form the peak of the mast and sail of our imaginary celestial Yacht and also the surrounding stars that fly ahead and astern.

Perseus is of the greatest interest to the amateur star-gazer for three reasons:

1. From this group radiates one of our finest and most dependable meteor showers, the Perseids, which usually reach maximum about August 11.

2. The group contains the famous "double cluster"—an unusual organization of stars constantly being investigated in the great observatories, quite easily seen with the naked eye and a striking sight in small telescopes or good binoculars.

3. The star Algol, that marks the throat of the gaff of the

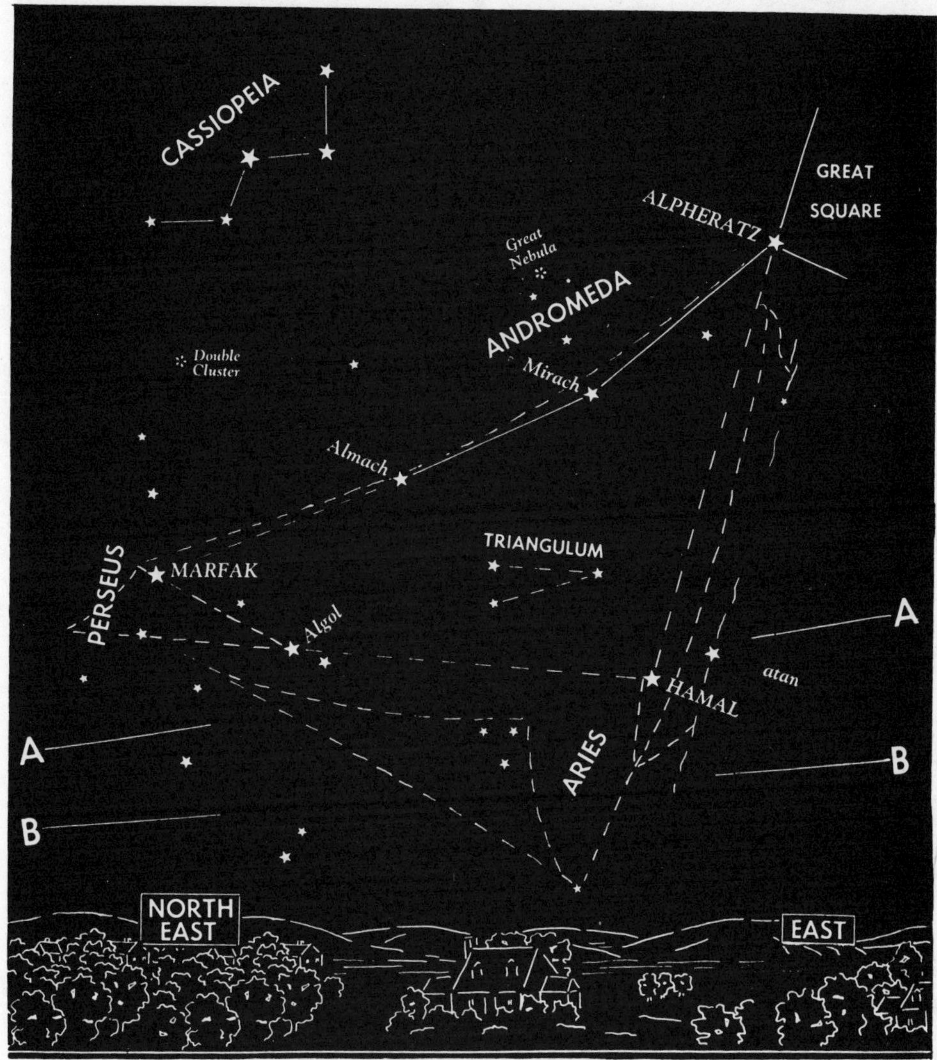


THE YACHT: Ignore the lines AA and BB unless they are called for. When, however, one is specified, it indicates that these stars are not yet so high and you must imagine them lowered until the line rests on the tops of the distant hills in the landscape.

The constellation of Aries is in the Zodiac—the pathway followed by the wandering planets. Beware of strange "stars" in this group. If they are bright and are not in these pictures, they are planets.

Yacht, is an almost perfect example of the "eclipsing binary" star, one which is as regular as clockwork and, best of all, one whose entire eclipse takes less than ten hours from maximum through minimum and back to maximum, so that the whole performance can be watched in one night during October, November and December, when the schedule fits right.

The magazine *Sky and Telescope*, so frequently mentioned in these pages, always carries Algol's complete timetable when the eclipse is visible.

Algol is a system of two stars revolving around their common center of gravity, their motions being almost, but not quite, in our line of sight to them. If it were exactly, or more nearly, in the line of sight, we would have a total eclipse of the brighter, but smaller, star by the larger, dark star and the effect would be even more striking but, as it is, it is an extremely interesting and fascinating phenomenon to watch.

At brightest, Algol is 3⅓ times brighter than at dimmest. The whole eclipse requires 9 hours 40 minutes and it occurs every 2 days, 20 hours, 49 minutes, 08 seconds. At brightest, Algol is exactly as bright as the near-by star Hamal in Aries. At dimmest, it is about equal to the brightest of the three little stars that our charts show in the little group called Triangulum. Thus we have two close standards with which to estimate the progress of the eclipse and any novice can do it with little trouble.

Furthermore it requires only 5 hours for fading down from maximum to minimum; it is at minimum for about 20 minutes during the time it takes the larger dark star to pass across in front of the smaller bright one, and then, in another 5 hours, Algol is itself again.

Algol was known to ancient star-gazers as "the demon star."

If you have good binoculars, sweep all around the star Marfak and on through the Double Cluster to Cassiopeia. There is no part of our Milky Way more thrilling than this region.

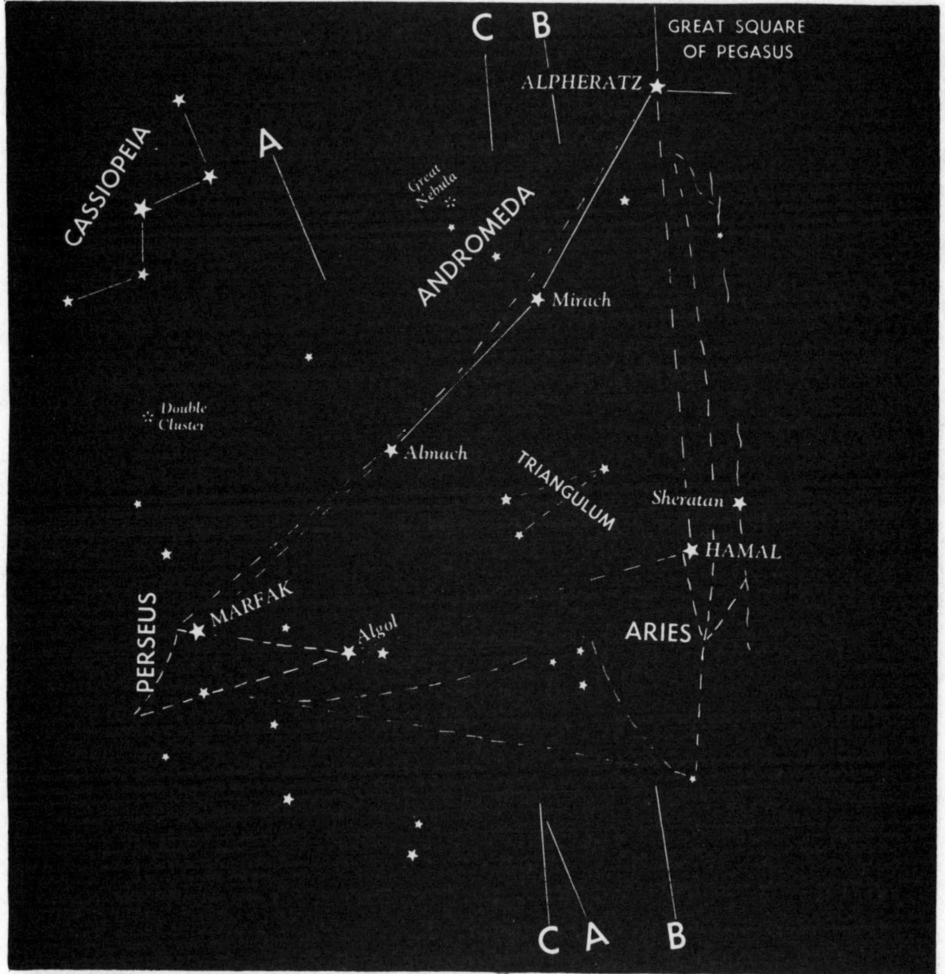


THE YACHT: When this chart is called for, the instructions will specify which line of this picture to use for any particular time. Follow these directions:

Line AA—face halfway between east and northeast; turn the book until AA is vertical; raise the picture until the star Mirach is halfway up the sky. Glance around the edge of the book and you will be looking at the Yacht.

Line BB—face east; make BB vertical; little Triangulum is halfway up the sky.

Line CC—face east; make CC vertical; the Yacht's bowsprit is halfway up the sky.

Aries is in the Zodiac. Beware of strange "stars" in this group. If they are bright and are not in these pictures, they are planets.

# CHART 43

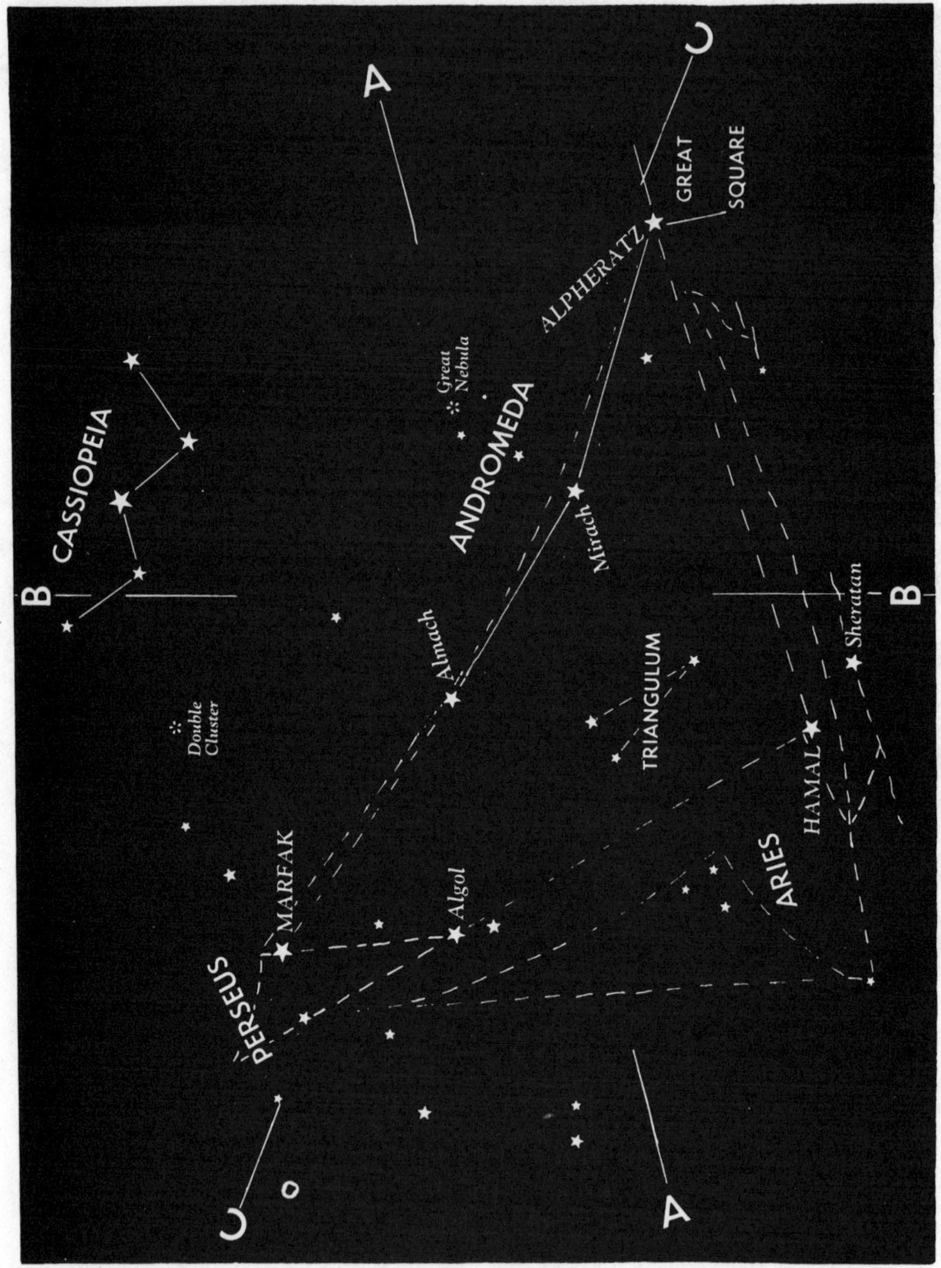


To use line AA—face east; turn the book until AA is perpendicular to the horizon at that point; lie far back and raise the book to bring the Great Nebula symbol overhead.

To use line BB—face south; lie back with the line BB cutting lengthwise through your body; raise the book until Almach and Mirach are overhead.

To use line CC—face west; CC vertical; raise book until star Algol is overhead.

Aries is in the Zodiac. Beware of strange "stars" in this group. If they are bright and are not in these pictures, they are planets.

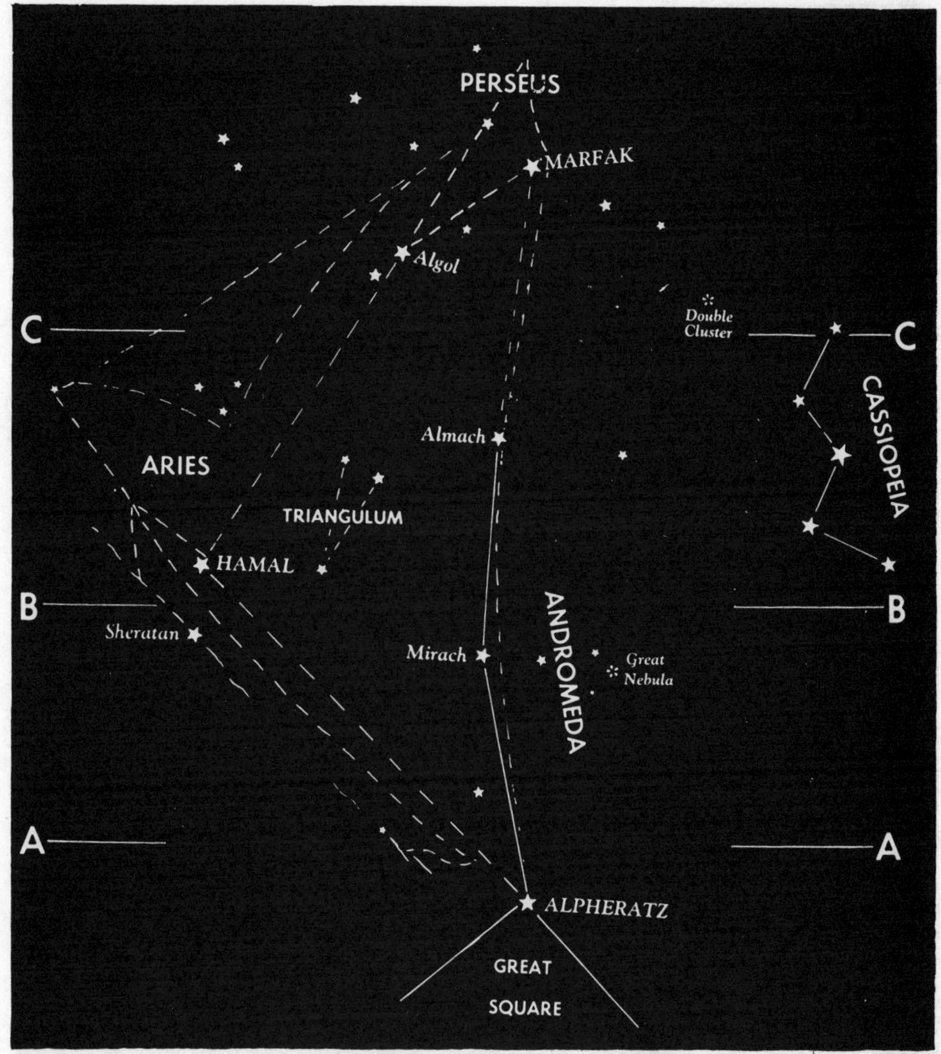


THE YACHT: With this chart, we follow the Yacht as it sails (backward) down the western sky. The three horizontal lines show the parts of the picture that will be just halfway up the sky between horizon and overhead at different times.

For AA—face west; raise the book until the line AA is halfway up the sky. The word "Perseus" will then be overhead.

For BB—face halfway between west and northwest; raise until the line BB is halfway up the sky.

For CC—again face halfway between west and northwest; raise until CC is halfway up the sky. The bottom of the picture will then be on the horizon.

In all cases, check with the unmistakable stars of Cassiopeia.

**Aries is in the Zodiac. Beware of strange "stars" in this group. If they are bright and are not in these pictures, they are planets.**

# CHART 45

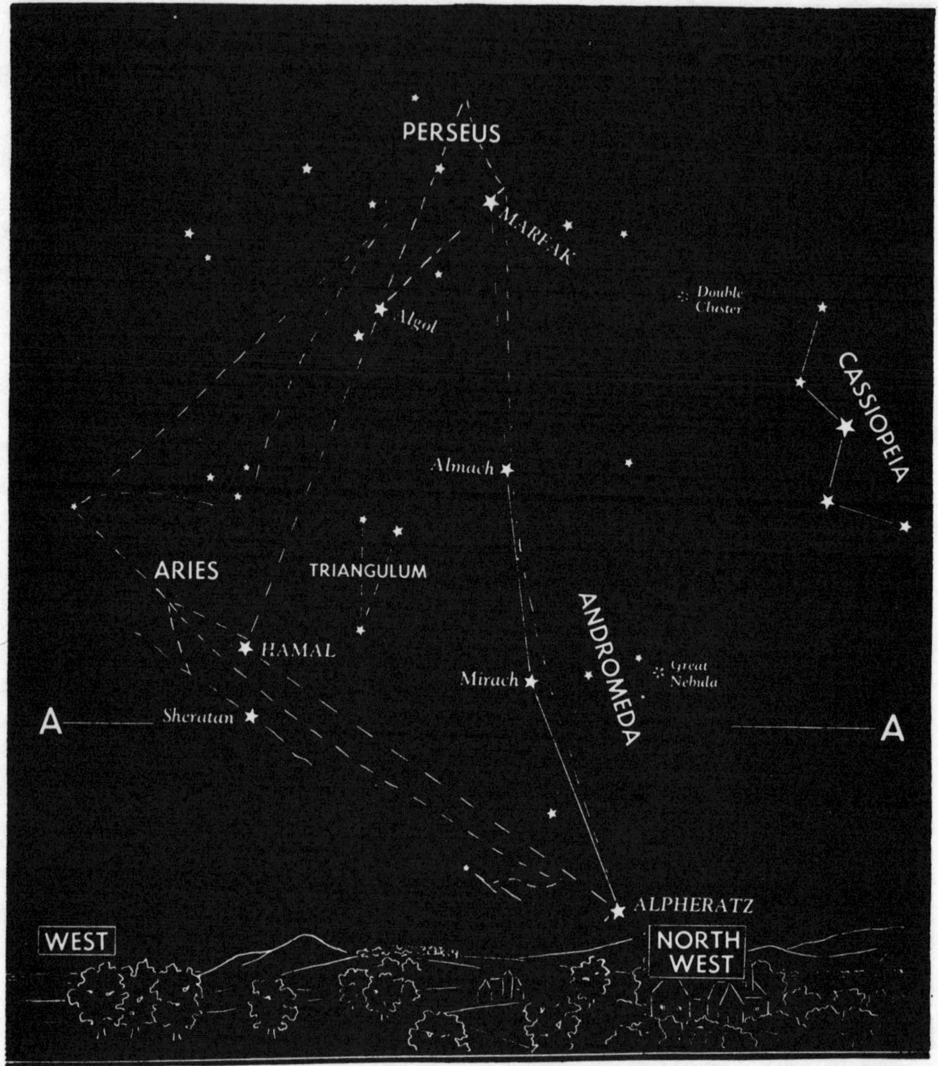


THE YACHT: Ignore the line AA unless it is called for in the instructions. When, however, the instructions are to use horizon AA, it means that these stars have all descended lower and that you must imagine the landscape raised to make the horizon meet the line AA.

Aries is in the Zodiac. Beware of strange "stars" in this group. If they are bright and are not in these pictures, they are planets.

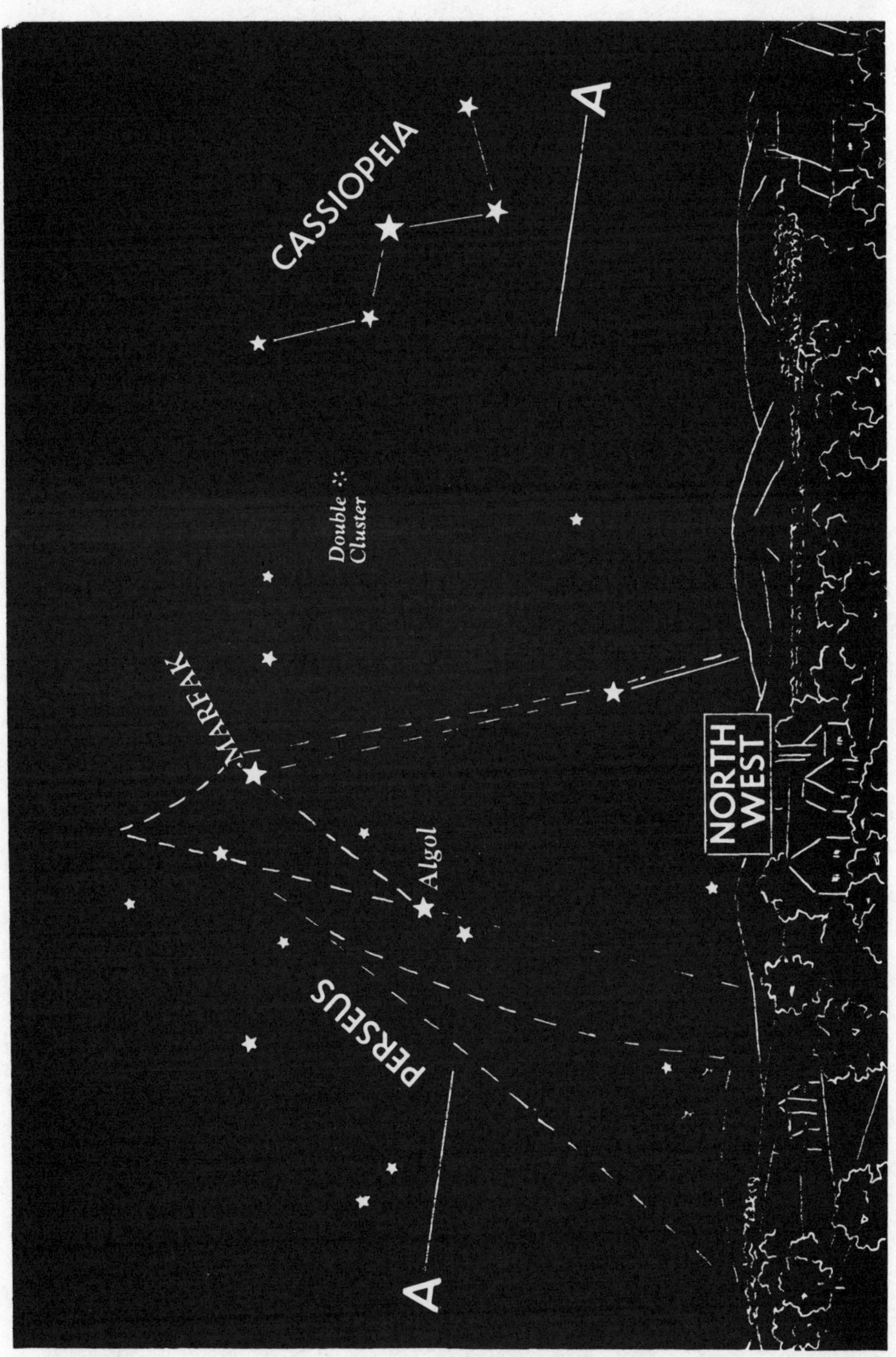


THE YACHT: Ignore line AA unless it is called for in the instructions. When AA is specified, it indicates that these stars are no longer so high and you must imagine them lowered until the line AA rests on the tops of the distant hills in the landscape.

## XVII

# CANIS MAJOR AND SIRIUS

JUST before the sun rises in the first part of August, a dazzling bright star appears over the horizon in the southeast and the "dog days" are with us again.

The star is Sirius, the "Dog Star," brightest star in the whole sky and ruler of the constellation which bears the Latin name Canis Major—the Greater Dog. The bright star Procyon marks Canis Minor—the Smaller Dog (see Charts 19-23).

Like all stars, Sirius rises four minutes earlier every 24 hours and this brings it into our just-after-dark sky during the first half of January and early-to-bedders have it with them from then until the first of May.

Sirius is, of all the naked-eye stars that can be seen from the United States, the nearest to the earth. Its distance is only slightly more than 8½ light-years.

Unless the planets Venus or Jupiter—or Mars at particularly favorable times—happen to be in the sky, the most careless glance about the dome of the heavens will locate Sirius beyond any doubt and, even if those planets are also present, Sirius will be unquestionable ruler in its own section of the sky. It furnishes the final and dramatic climax to that matchless procession of stellar headliners beginning with Capella and the Pleiades through Taurus and Orion and Gemini and Procyon that make our winter skies the never failing delight of the confirmed star-gazer.

Sirius and the group of bright stars near him are supposed to form a dog and they have been imagined as a dog by the primitive star-gazers of many lands and many epochs. But the old-time artists who first drew these concepts on the maps of the skies gave us a tortured and twisted dog such as no modern could possibly imagine. Consequently, in the charts in this chapter I have unblushingly substituted my own better-trained dog whom I have taught to assume a more recognizable position, making it easier for the novice to tie all the stars together into canine plausibility.

So far, we have considered Sirius only from the visually spectacular viewpoint.

But, during the past century or more, scientists have probed and photographed and measured and calculated and deduced facts about this brilliant star that have revealed another of those celestial objects that prove to be almost beyond the bounds of human belief.

As long ago as 1834, it was discovered that Sirius showed slight but unmistakable variations in its motion across the sky. A well-behaved star, traveling through space by itself, goes steadily in what, for thousands of years, will appear to us to be a straight line, covering equal distances in equal times. When an investigator finds a star that violates this invariable rule, he knows that there is something in the star's neighborhood that is causing a disturbance.

Ten years after the first discovery of this trouble with Sirius, Bessel studied all the records, performed a masterpiece of mathematical analysis and announced that Sirius was one star of a binary system—two stars revolving around their common center of gravity or, in other words, revolving about each other.

From that time on, observatories all over the world tried to find the predicted companion but without success. Finally, in 1862, the great telescopic lens-maker Alvan Clark, testing a new eighteen-inch-diameter lens, saw it for the first time and thus silenced those who had begun to scoff at Bessel's mathematics.

This elusive companion of Sirius now proves to be, as I have said, one of the most unbelievable objects that our modern scientific methods have discovered in the skies.

The bright star that we know as Sirius is an average star,

less than twice the diameter of our sun and only about 30 times as luminous and with about 2⅓ times the sun's mass. Only its nearness makes it seem so bright for it would be insignificant if set side by side with some of the super-giants.

The companion, however, is a genuine white *dwarf*. It has a diameter only about three times the diameter of the earth, yet if the two bodies could be weighed on the same scales, this little star would weigh about 250,000 times as much as the earth. That necessarily means that the material of which the star is made is packed together so tightly that we can find nothing with which to compare it.

You may get some idea of this from the fact that the star is some *5000 times as dense as lead.*

If we could transport only a little more than a thimbleful of the star to the earth, it would weigh about a ton.

So great is the gravitational effect that if a man weighing 160 pounds on earth could be transported to the surface of the star, his bones would be crushed, for his body would weigh over 4200 *tons.*

How can a star get into this condition? What process—operating through billions of years—could have pressed that material so densely into so small a body?

And, to add to the questions for which we have no answer, there is a mystery about this system that opens up another area of speculation.

According to theories that have widespread acceptance among scientists, the big star Sirius is a young star, while the little star is in the final stages of an inconceivably long life.

If this is so, how and when did they become imprisoned together in a binary system? Such a system could be reasonably well understood on the basis of contemporary birth—of a simultaneous launching together upon their careers or possibly contemporary condensation from the same vast cloud of floating interstellar nebulous "stuff," if that is how stars are born.

But for "crabbed age and youth" to be found inseparably bound together seems to admit of only one plausible explanation—that the two stars, quite recently as we measure cosmic time, pursuing their individual paths through space, passed so close to each other that their mutual gravitational effect made each swerve toward the other with accelerated velocity until they found equilibrium only in the eternal ellipses which they must henceforth follow around their common center of gravity while, at the same time, that center of gravity is carrying them both around the great wheel of billions of stars that we call our galaxy.

No one must accept that explanation as a statement of fact. When we are dealing with the universe of stars, there is no such word as "fact." It seems to be the only theory that offers a plausible explanation of this Sirius system, but you will find many famous scientists who will not even admit that it is plausible.

If you are a novice at star-gazing (and I am assuming in this book that you are) you will have considerable difficulty in building a mental image of any kind of dog around the stars of this group but that need not discourage you. The five brightest stars make an unusual but very distinct and easily recognized geometrical pattern in the sky and, once you learn to recognize that pattern, you can just forget the dog entirely.

Sirius will present no problem. You will recognize it at once. To the right of Sirius, you will then quite readily find the bright star Mirzam and then, below, you will see the conspicuous triangle formed by the three bright stars Adhara, Aludra and Wesen.

As Sirius, with the rest of the Greater Dog, climbs into the southeastern sky and starts its journey westward, it is followed by an area plentifully sprinkled with fairly bright stars which, however, do not form any easily recognizable pattern.

These stars—much better seen by far-southerners than by the rest of us—mark the constellation of Puppis. This Latin word means the stern of a ship. It is a survival from the records of the first explorers who sailed into the waters of the southern hemisphere and to whom the starry skies around the South Celestial Pole were all new.

To them it seemed that a vast area of that sky was filled with stars that formed the kind of ship in which they sailed—the kind with the oddly shaped bows and the towering high stern made familiar to us in the pictures of the three vessels that Columbus used.

These explorers, however, went to their ancient mythology to name this great ship in the skies. They called it Argo Navis—the ship Argo which Jason and his Argonauts used to recover the Golden Fleece.

This constellation Argo Navis was too big and unwieldy to satisfy later star-gazers so, by general consent, it was divided into four parts—Puppis, the Stern; Vela, the Sail; Carina, the Keel; and Pyxis, the Compass.

Of these, only parts of Puppis and Pyxis can be seen from the mid-United States. Puppis is shown in our charts of Sirius and Canis Major on the following pages and Pyxis can be seen in the lower left-hand corner of the map of Monoceros, Chart 93.

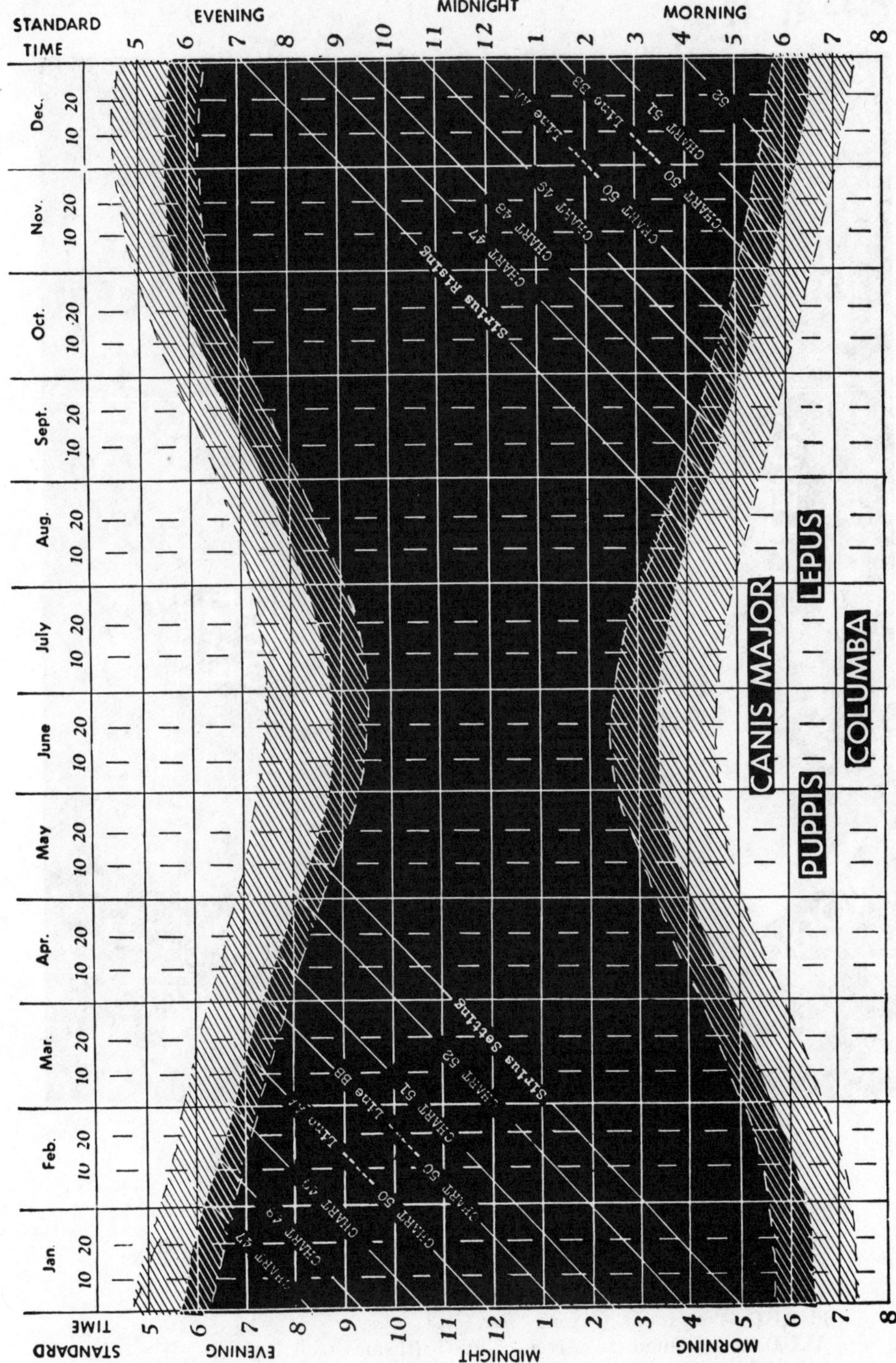


The diagonal line nearest to the hour and date desired shows the correct chart and line to use at that time.

# CHART 47

Canis Major Rising

## PRONUNCIATIONS

*CANIS MAJOR*—"kane-iss may-j'r." Accent "kane" and "may."

SIRIUS—both "i's" are short, as in "bit," "pit." Accent first syllable.

MIRZAM—again the "i" is short as in Sirus. Accent "mir."

ADHARA—"add-day-ra." Accent "day."

FURUD—"few-rood." Accent "few."

ALUDRA—"al-ludd-ra." Accent "ludd" (rhymes with "mud").

WESEN—authorities differ. Some say "way-senn"; some say "wess-en." Take your choice.

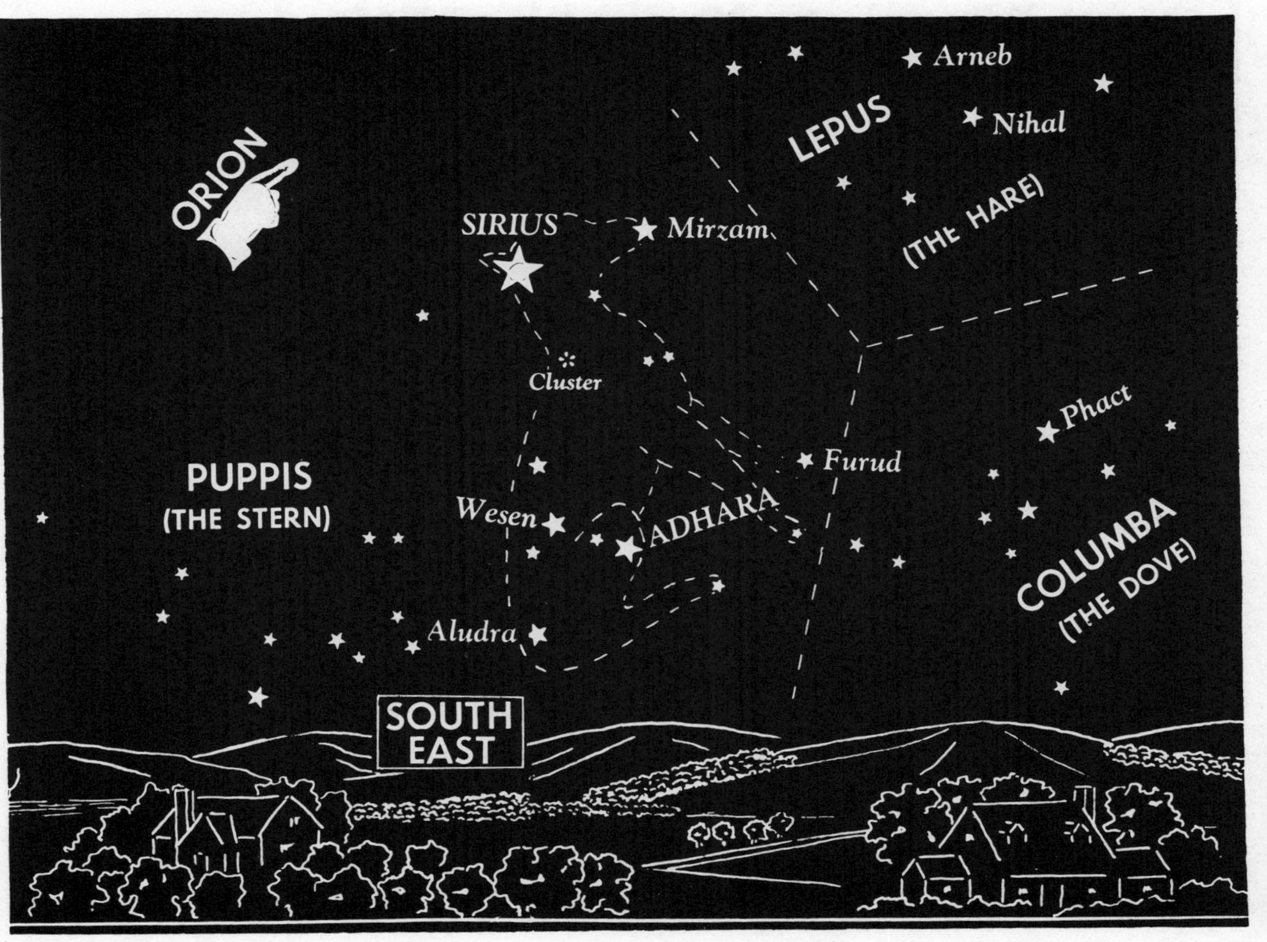


Canis Major, Well Up

# CHART 49

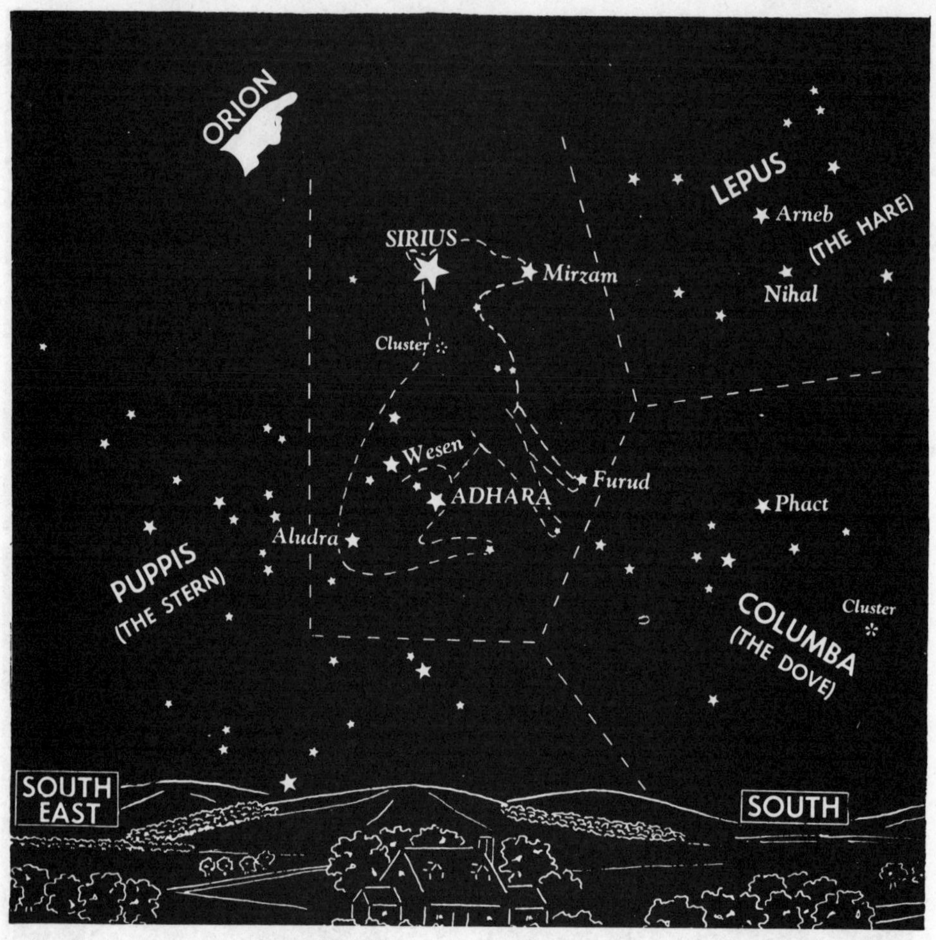


CANIS MAJOR AND PUPPIS

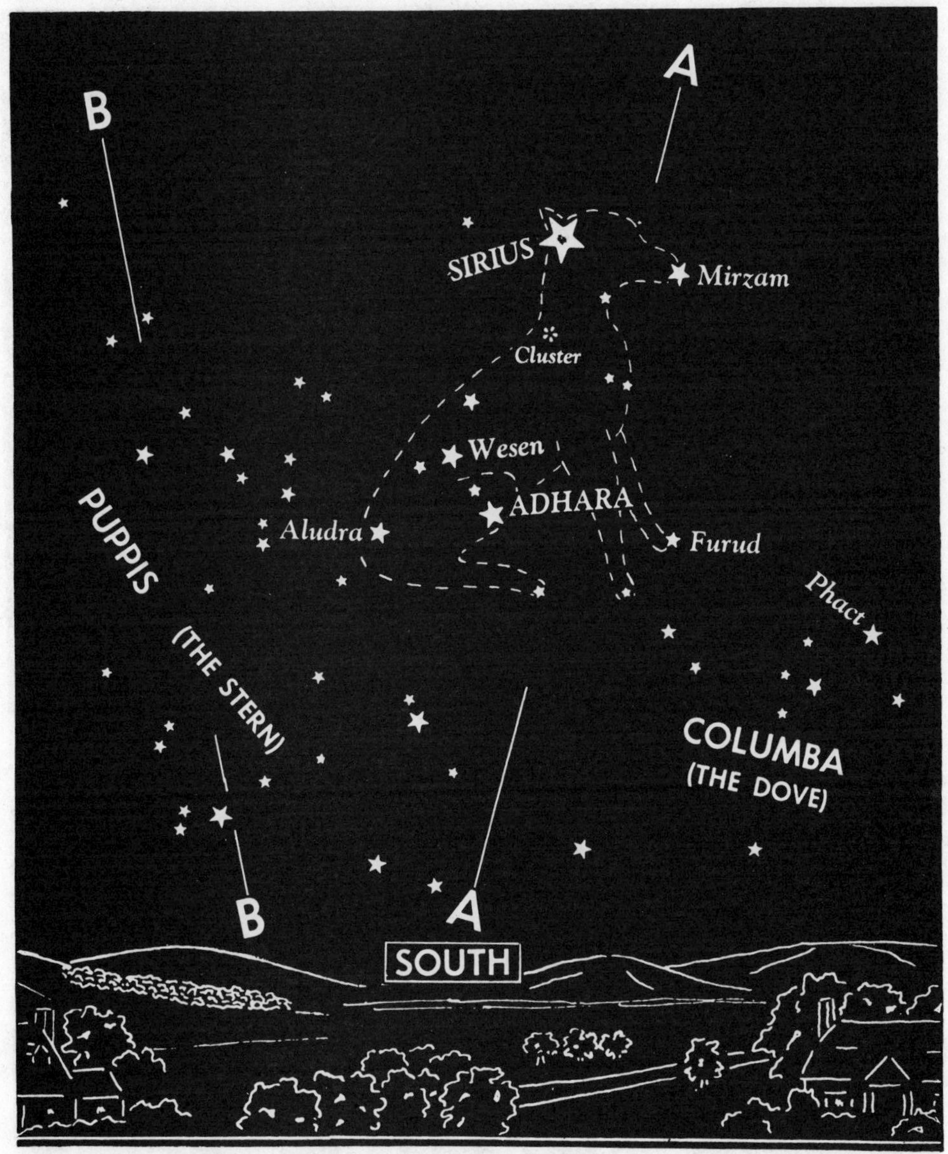


Canis Major at Its Highest: In this chart, brilliant Sirius and its neighbors are crossing the southern meridian—their highest positions. The instructions will stipulate which of the lines is to be turned to vertical at any particular time. In all cases, face due south and turn the book slightly to make the line perpendicular at that point.

## CHART 51

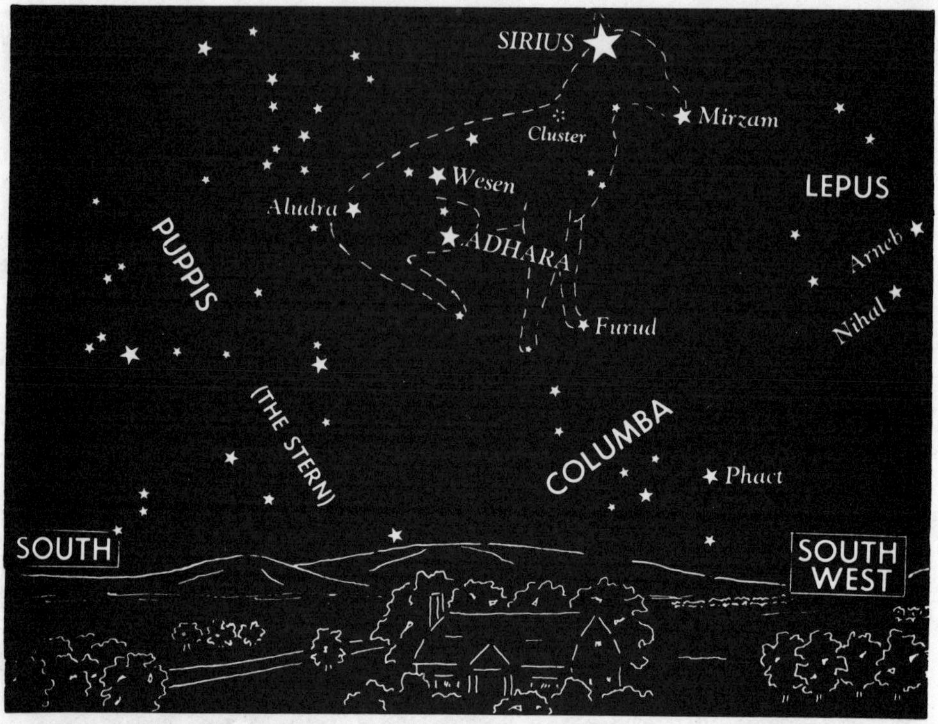

## CHART 52

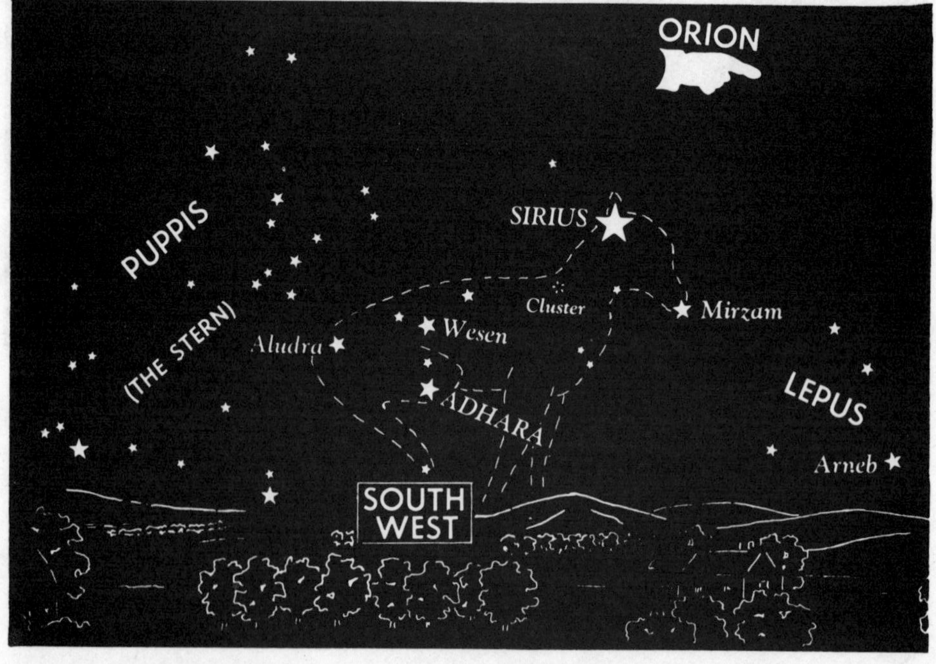

XVIII

# THE SICKLE IN LEO

ANCIENT star-gazers chose four bright stars as "royal stars." They were Fomalhaut, Aldebaran, Antares and Regulus, the Heart of the Lion (Leo).

All four are today among the most important stars for the navigator to know and they are, fortunately, among those most easily identified.

Fomalhaut stands conspicuously alone in his own section of the sky. You will find him with Capricorn in Charts 24 to 28. Aldebaran has an unmistakable position in the unmistakable V of stars in the face of Taurus, the Bull (Charts 9-13). Antares is definitely red and is in another unmistakable formation—the Scorpion (Charts 78-82). And, in this chapter, we deal with Regulus, in the handle of a stellar Sickle that is so plainly marked in the sky that any novice will immediately recognize it, once it is pointed out to him.

This Sickle may be of particular value to the navigator in cloudy weather. Almost any break in the clouds large enough to uncover Regulus clearly will quite certainly show enough of the other stars to reveal the formation, even though there may be enough film of mist over them to dim their brightness.

The Sickle is in the head and forequarters of the ancient figure of Leo, the Lion—a conception that was familiar to the peoples of many lands long before any motion-picture company adopted it as a trademark.

I doubt whether many of us can really visualize that lion in the sky. You can always remember that the star Denebola is in the tail because, as we have learned before, the word "deneb" in any star name means "tail." Denebola will be more important to us when we begin our search for the great Virgo Triangle (Charts 58-62), so in this chapter we will confine our attention to the Sickle.

PRONUNCIATIONS

*LEO*—"lee-oh." Accent "lee."

REGULUS—"reg-you-luss." Accent "reg" (rhymes with "keg," "leg").

DENEBOLA—"den-ebb-oh-la." Accent "ebb."

ALGEIBA—"al-jee-ba." Accent "jee." This name is also spelled ALGIEBA, but the pronunciation is the same.

ZOSMA—"zoze-ma." Accent "zoze" (rhymes with "pose," "rose").

ADHAFERA—"add-day-fer-ah." Accent "day."

CHERTAN—rhymes with "certain," "curtain." Some authorities call this star CHORT.

RASALAS—"rass-al-lass." Accent "rass."

The Sickle, when rising and climbing the eastern sky, is seen cutting upward; when it is crossing the meridian, it is cutting to the right (west) and when it is descending the western sky, it is cutting downward.

Regulus makes its first appearance between east and northeast at dawn during the early part of September and can be seen from that time onward in some part of the sky until mid-July.

Good binoculars may reveal Regulus as a double star, if you have good eyesight and considerable observing experience. If your binoculars fail you on Regulus, turn them on Algeiba. This is one of the most beautiful doubles in the sky and it should be observed in twilight or moonlight to reveal the contrasting colors—one star green; the other delicate yellow.

Another interesting star for the binocular owner is the one at the tip of the curved blade of the Sickle. This star has no popular name but bears the Greek letter Epsilon.

A good glass shows two beautiful twin stars making a fine triangle with the main star.

Adhafera has three companions but they are beyond the power of binoculars, although easy for a small telescope with a lens larger than the usual binocular lenses.

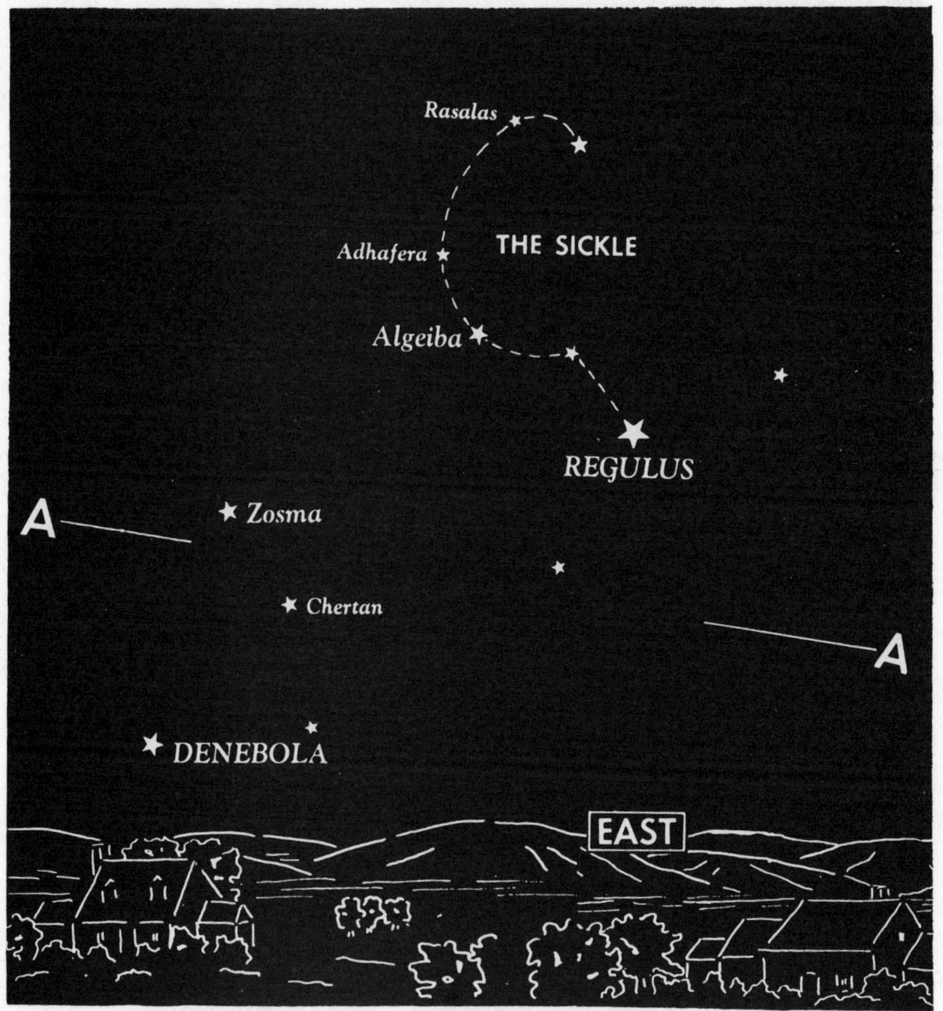


THE SICKLE: The chart shows the whole constellation of Leo, the Lion, as it climbs clear of the horizon haze in the east. Some time before that, however, the famous Sickle is far enough up to be identified. At that time, the line AA represents the horizon and will be specified in the instructions.

Leo is in the Zodiac. Beware of strange "stars" in this constellation. If they are bright and are not shown in this picture, they are planets.

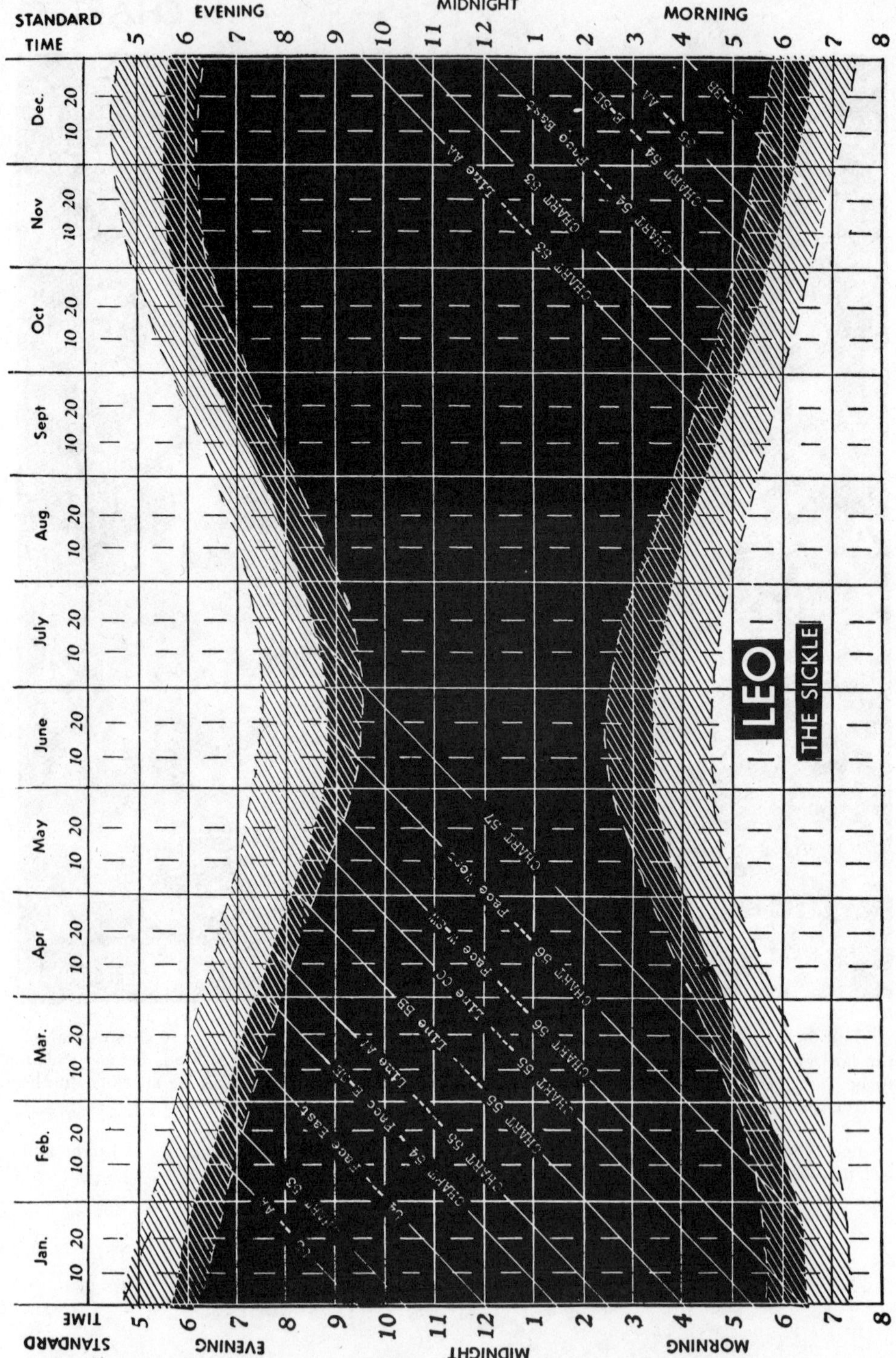


The diagonal line nearest to the hour and date desired will show the correct chart and line to use at that time.

# CHART 54

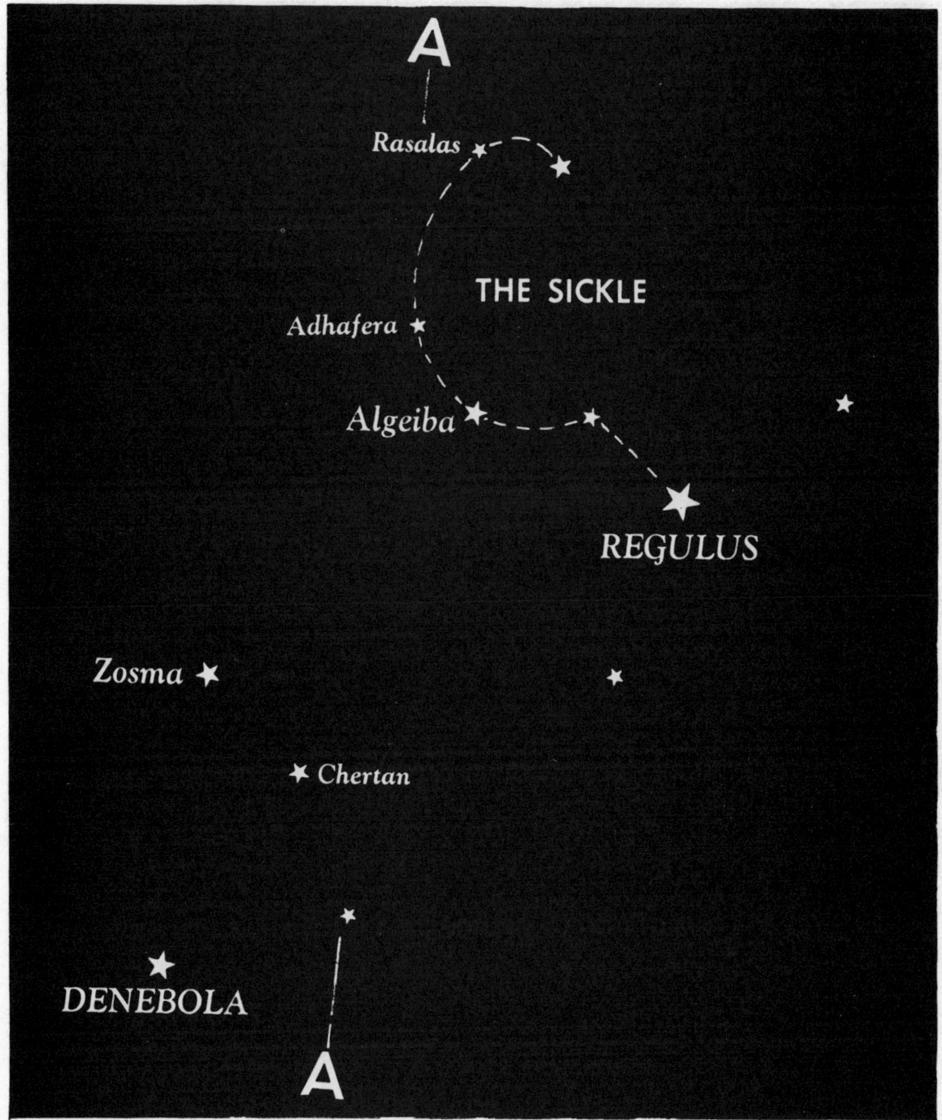


The Sickle: When this chart is to be used, the instructions will specify one of two different compass facings for different times. If you are instructed to face east, do so; make the line AA vertical at the east point; raise the book until the curved blade of the Sickle is halfway up the sky. Glance around the edge of the book and you will be looking at the Sickle. If the facing E-SE is called for, face halfway between east and southeast; make AA vertical; raise the book until the name Chertan is halfway up the sky.

Leo is in the Zodiac. Beware of strange "stars" in this constellation. If they are bright and are not shown in this picture, they are planets.

# CHART 55

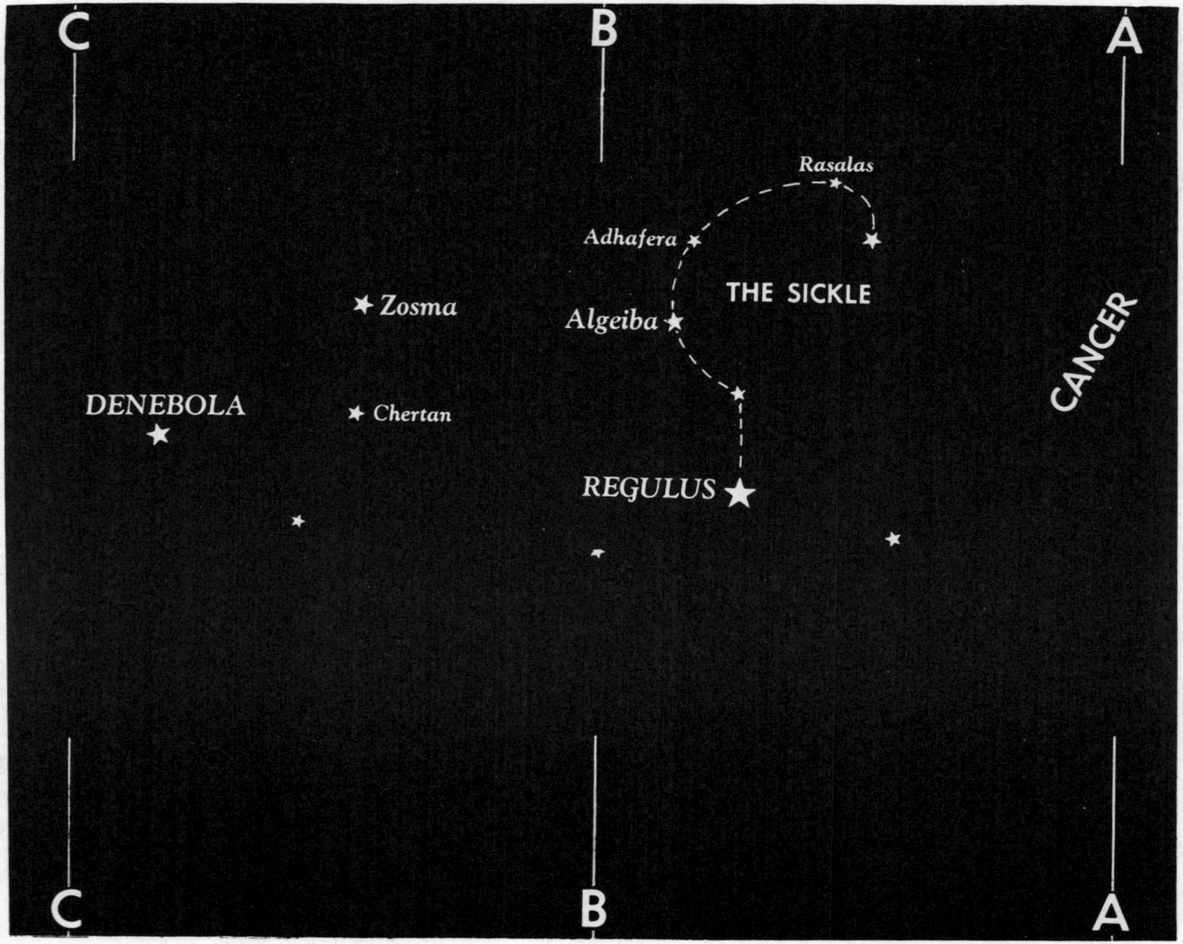

**The Sickle:** This position picture shows the Sickle in its passage across the meridian—its highest point in the sky. The three lines AA etc. are to be used at different times according to the instructions in the Calendar and the Hour-and-Date Diagram. In all cases, first face due south, then lie back comfortably and raise the book until the bottom of the picture is halfway up the sky. The top will then be overhead for southerners and not so far from it for the rest of us. At different periods, each line in turn—AA, BB and CC—should be held to bisect your body lengthwise as the Calendar and Diagram stipulate.

Leo is in the Zodiac. Beware of any strange "stars" in this constellation. If they are bright and are not shown in this picture, they are planets.

CHART 56

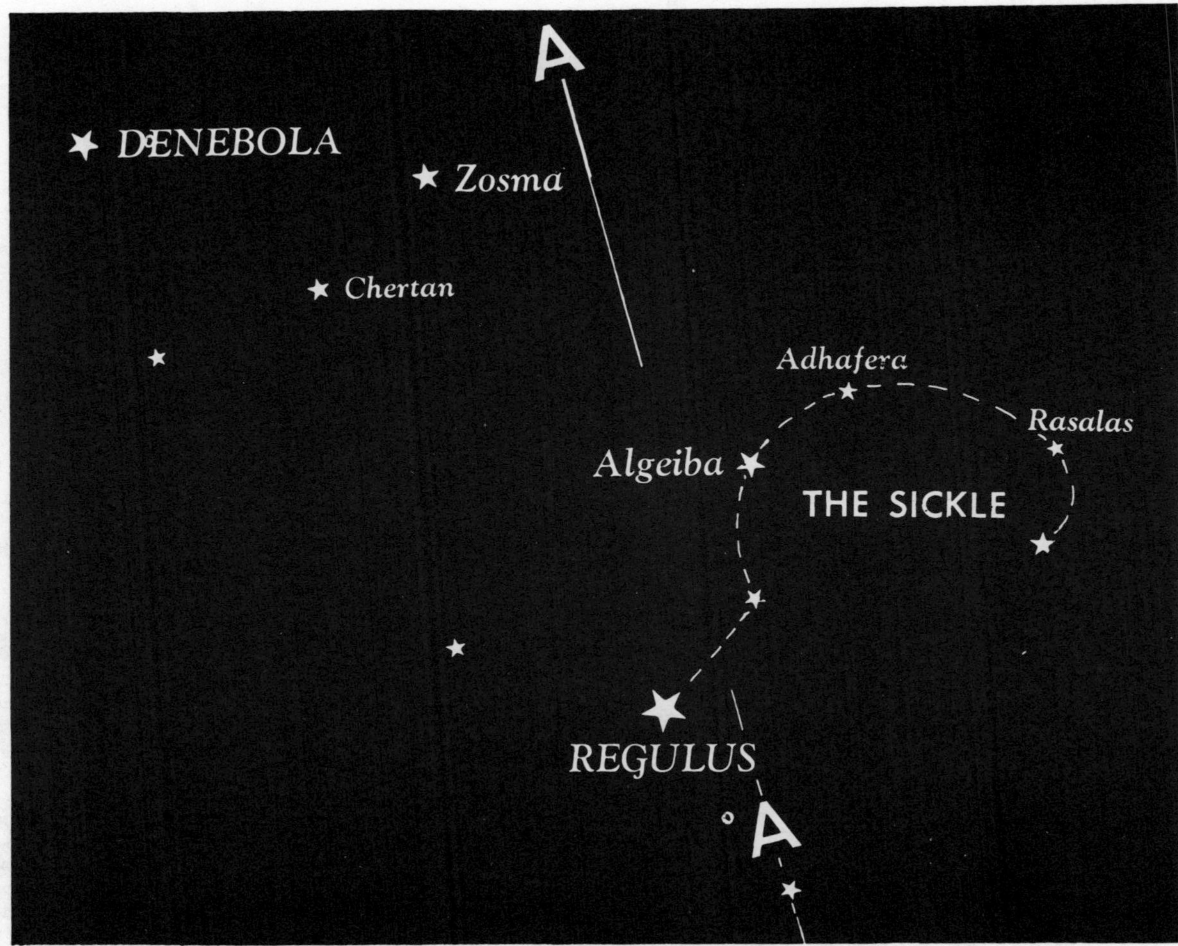


THE SICKLE: The line AA enables you to use this picture at two different periods. The line is to be held vertical in both cases. The Calendar and the Hour-and-Date Diagram will tell you which way to face for the two positions.

Facing W-SW (halfway between west and southwest), hold the line vertical and raise the book until the star Regulus is halfway up the sky. Glance around the edge of the book and you will be looking at the Sickle.

Facing west, hold AA vertical at that point and raise the book until the star Zosma is halfway up the sky.

Leo is in the Zodiac. Beware of strange "stars" in this constellation. If they are bright and are not shown in this picture, they are planets.

# CHART 57

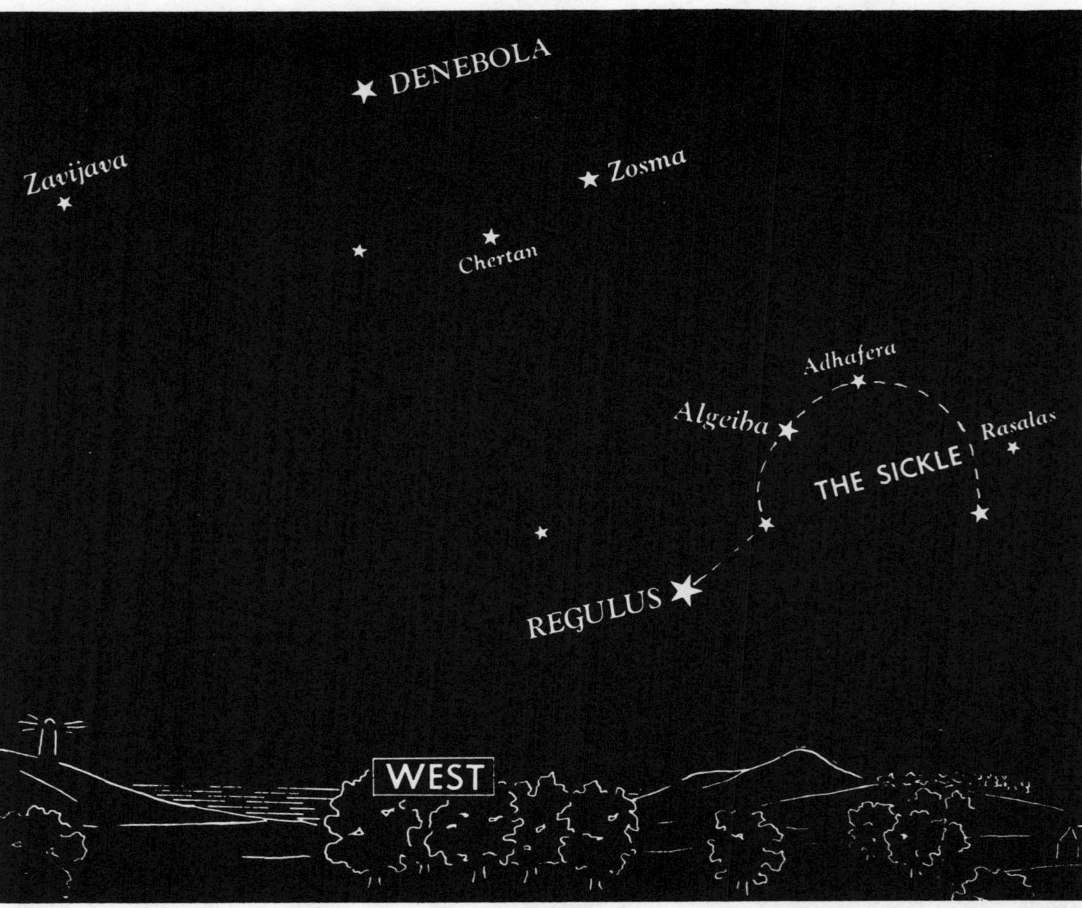


**Soon** after the Sickle reaches this position, it will disappear from our early evening skies. The star Denebola can then be followed by means of its position in the Virgo Triangle, shown on Charts 58 to 62.

Leo is in the Zodiac. Beware of strange "stars" in this constellation. If they are bright and are not shown on this chart, they are planets.

## XIX

# THE GREAT VIRGO TRIANGLE

ANY star-gazer who lives near an observatory should by all means take advantage of a night in April or May when the public is admitted and look through the telescope at the "Field of the Nebulae" in the constellation of Virgo. Incidentally, we will have to begin to ignore the old designation for this Field, even though it is seemingly firmly established, because we now know that the objects in the Field are not nebulae but are galaxies. So let's start right now calling it the Field of the Galaxies in Virgo.

This amazing area covers a third or more of the great Virgo Triangle that is shown in the charts on the following pages. It extends from about the center, marked by the star Vindemiatrix, to the corner marked by the star Spica.

Even a good amateur telescope will reveal many of these distant universes as fascinating objects but it requires the analytical studies of the most expert specialists to give us some idea of the astonishing probabilities represented by these visually indistinct and mysterious-looking specks shown on observatory photographs of the region.

This "Virgo Cloud" as it is called, is quite extensively analyzed by Dr. Harlow Shapley, director of the great Harvard College Observatory, in his fascinating book, *Galaxies*.

In this region of the sky, observatory photographs show a swarm of over three hundred galaxies, so distant from us that their light requires something like *eight million years* to reach us. Compared to the Andromeda and other galaxies, this might seem to represent the extreme outer limits of space but, as a matter of fact, this swarm is considered a "neighbor" group.

In a discussion of stellar distances and the possible outer reaches of space, Shapley says,

"We have photographed galaxies in light that has been *sixteen million centuries* crossing about 9,500,000,000,000,000,000,000 miles of space."

Sixteen million centuries is sixteen hundred million years, compared to which the mere eight million light-years to this Virgo Cluster does indeed seem to be neighborly.

Each one of these three hundred or more galaxies is an entire stellar system in itself, comparable to the system of over two billion stars to which we ourselves belong, yet there seems to be much evidence to support the theory that all of these Virgo objects are actually bound together in some sort of super-system.

The probable total figures become staggering in the light of the assertion by reputable scientists that the average mass of each one of these three hundred galaxies is some two hundred billion times the mass of our sun.

Although we do not see it, these dim Virgo objects emit so much light that it would require one hundred million of our suns to equal each one of them at the same distance. Incidentally, Shapley regards this light factor as indicating that the estimates for the total mass are far too high unless we assume that the space between the galaxies is filled by tremendous clouds of nonluminous and therefore undiscoverable specks of cosmic dust such as we find in great clouds among the stars of our own system and which we have discussed as "dark nebulae" in connection with the famous "Horsehead" object in Orion.

This is the richest field of galaxies that can be seen by a good telescope of amateur size. No member of the swarm is visible to the naked eye.

The brightest star in the constellation of Virgo is Spica, notable for its pure whiteness. The name means "ear of wheat," derived from the ancient pictures of the goddess whose figure was somehow or other traced around the scattered stars

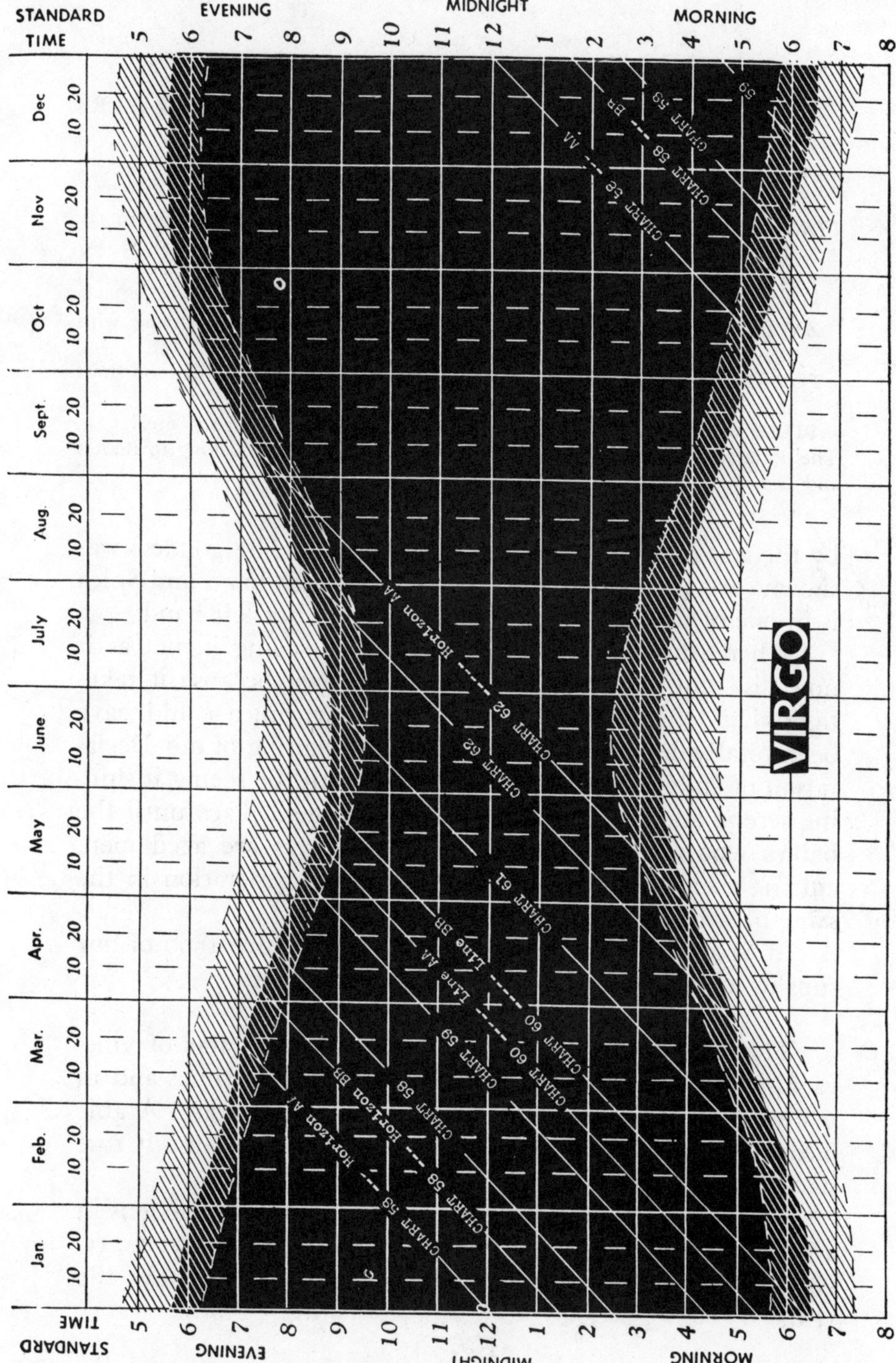


The diagonal line nearest to the hour and date desired shows the correct chart and line to use at that time

## PRONUNCIATIONS

*VIRGO*—classicists stick to the old pronunciation "veer-go." I regret to say that this is no longer authorized and we are now instructed to say "ver-go," with accent on "ver" (rhymes with "her").

SPICA—"spy-ka." Accent "spy."

ZAVIJAVA—as spelled; accents on "zav" and "jav" (both rhyme with "have").

PORRIMA—accent "porr," the "o" short as in "hot." The "i" is also short as in "rim."

VINDEMIATRIX—"vin-dee-mee-ate-tricks." Accent "dee" and "ate."

The other stars shown in the pictures of the Virgo Triangle belong to Boötes and Leo.

by the imagination of primitive star-gazers. The goddess was shown carrying several stalks of wheat in each hand and Spica is in one of the ears of grain hanging from her left hand.

When you look at Spica, you will be seeing it, not as it now "is" but as it was some 235 years ago, because it takes light that long to reach us from the star. Spica could have been totally destroyed at the time of the signing of our Declaration of Independence, yet men would still be seeing it shining serene and undisturbed in its accustomed place until the babies who are now in their mothers' arms are aged men, cursing their rheumatism and the younger generation in the same breath.

At Spica's distance from us, it would require 1500 of our suns to look as bright to the star-gazer on earth.

The star Vindemiatrix has been the patron star of vineyardists and wine makers from the most ancient times and in many lands. The name in Greek, Latin, Persian and Arabic means "grape gatherer," bestowed on the star because it rose just before dawn at vintage time in those countries.

Porrima is a famous double star, a good test for the lens in a small telescope. It is a "binary," or system of two stars, revolving about each other in a period of approximately 180 years.

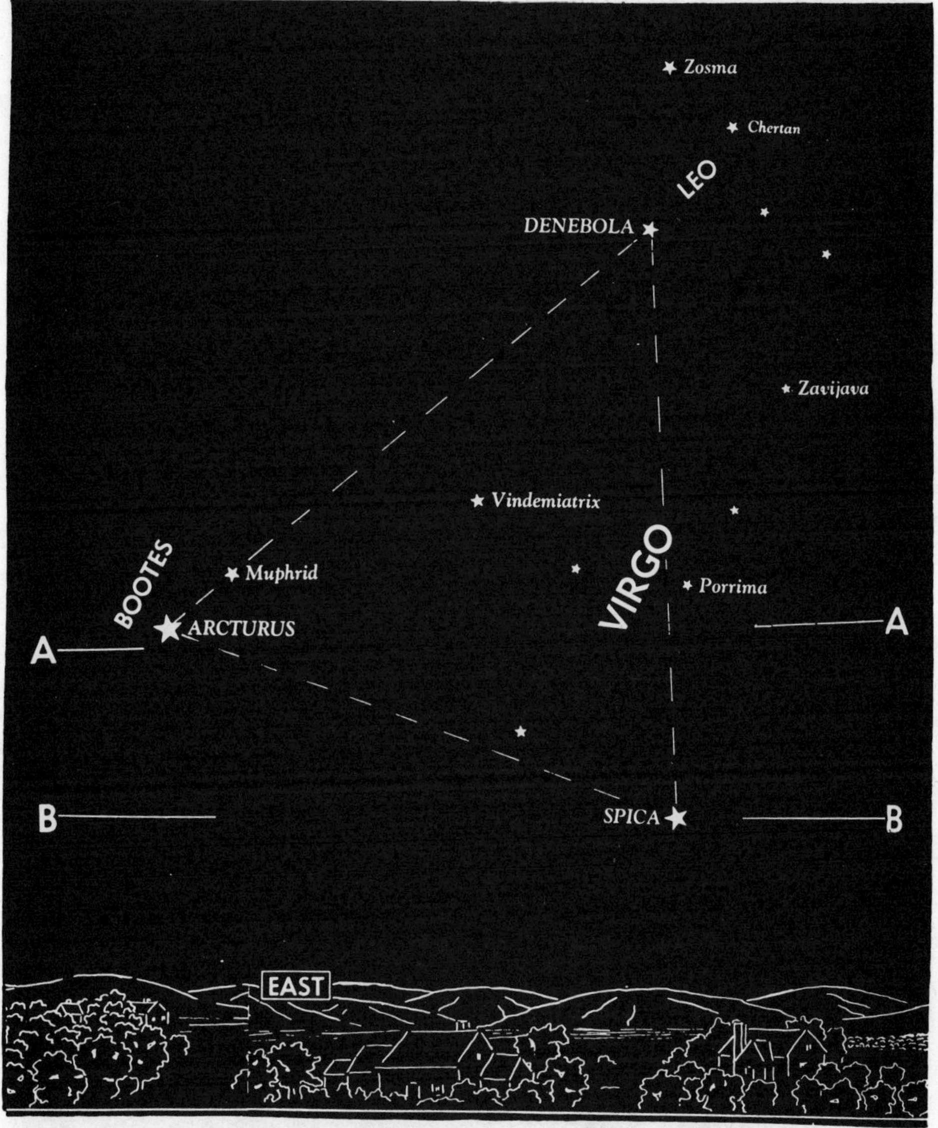


THE VIRGO TRIANGLE: The stars of Virgo begin to be seen in the east before the Triangle is entirely above the horizon. When brilliant Arcturus is first seen dimly in the haze, the line AA is the horizon. Later, when Spica emerges, the line BB is the horizon and we can determine the outlines of the Triangle. Still later, when Spica is clear of the mists, we have the Triangle as shown in the picture, forgetting the lines AA and BB.

Virgo is in the Zodiac. Look our for bright "stars" in this area not given in the picture. They will be planets.

# CHART 59

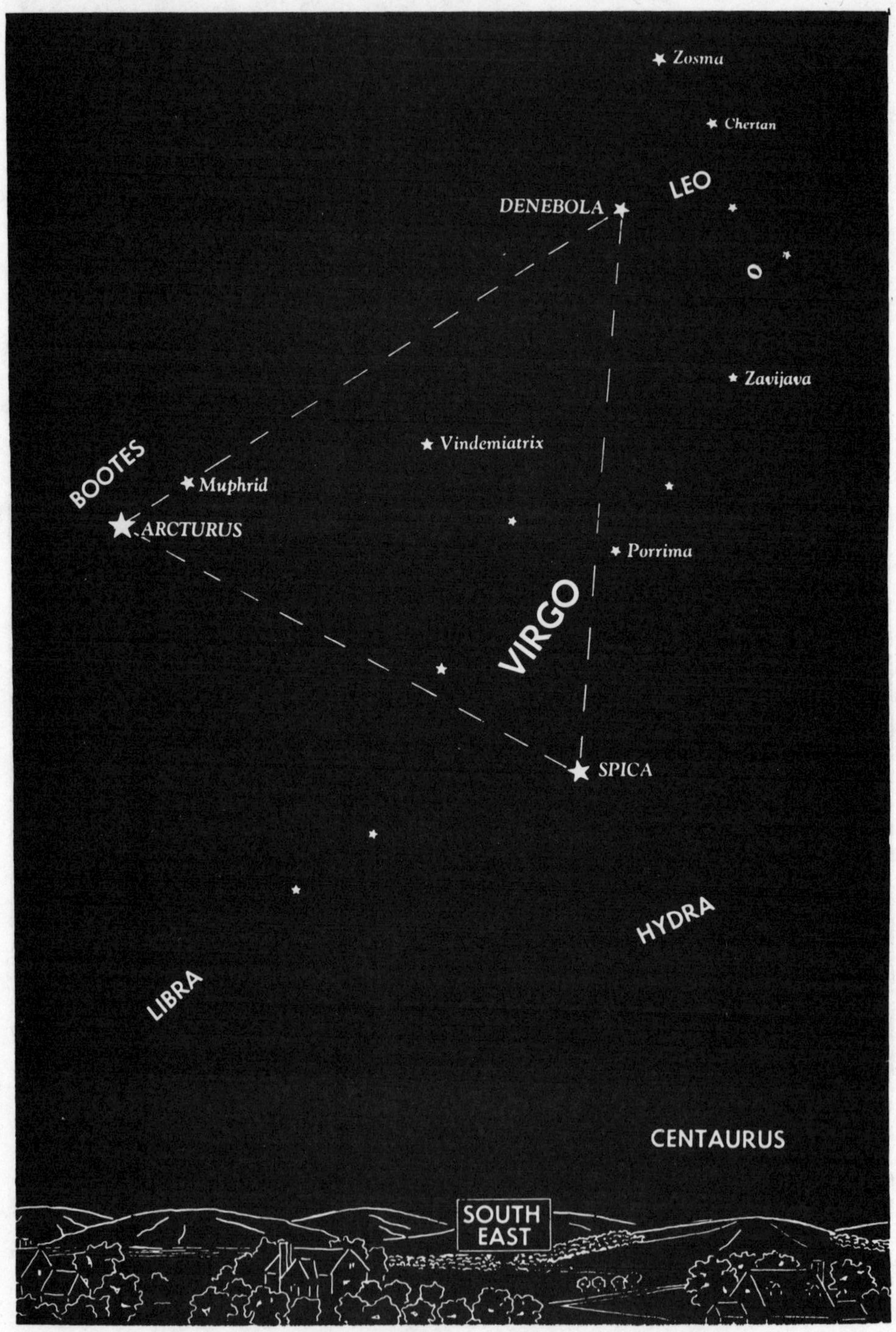


THE VIRGO TRIANGLE: Virgo is in the Zodiac. Look out for bright "stars" in this area not given in the picture. They will be planets.

# CHART 60

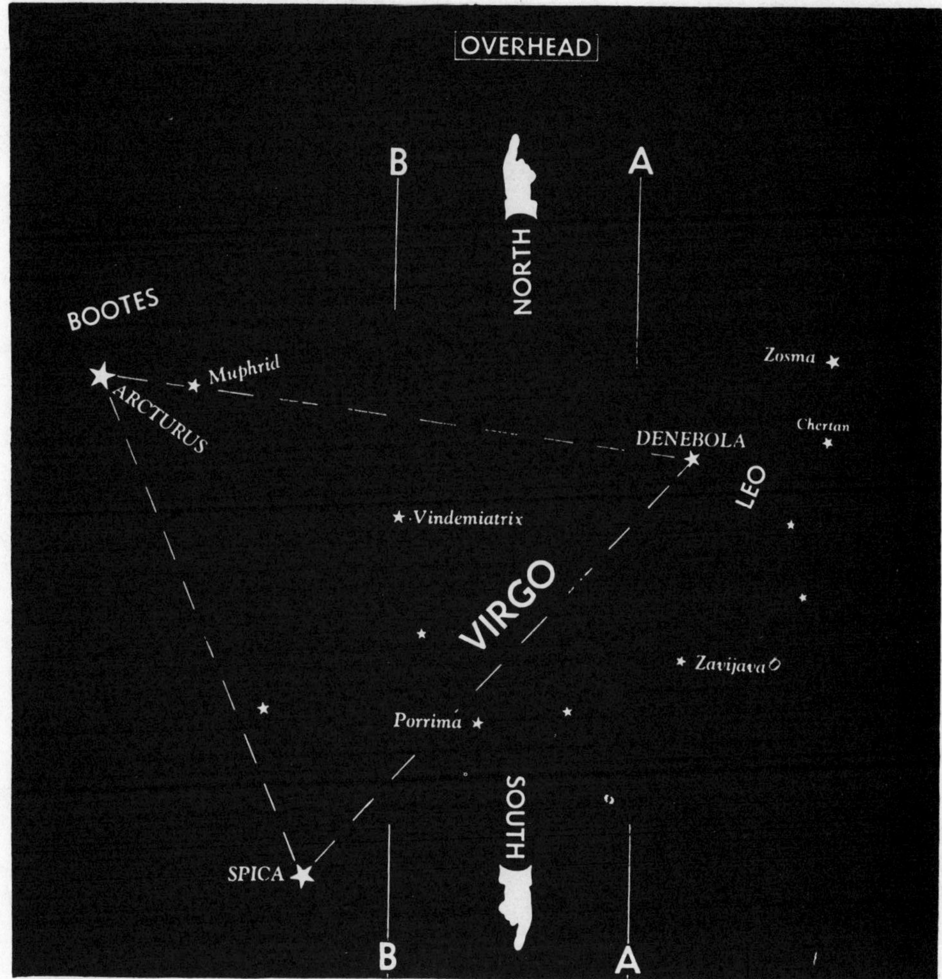


THE VIRGO TRIANGLE: This picture shows the Triangle in its passage across the meridian—its highest point in the sky. In all cases, face due south, lie back comfortably and hold the book above you with "Overhead" really overhead and with one of the lines AA or BB running lengthwise over your body. The line to be used for any particular time is given in the Calendar and the Hour-and-Date Diagram.

Virgo is in the Zodiac. Look out for bright "stars" in this area not given in the picture. They will be planets.

# CHART 61

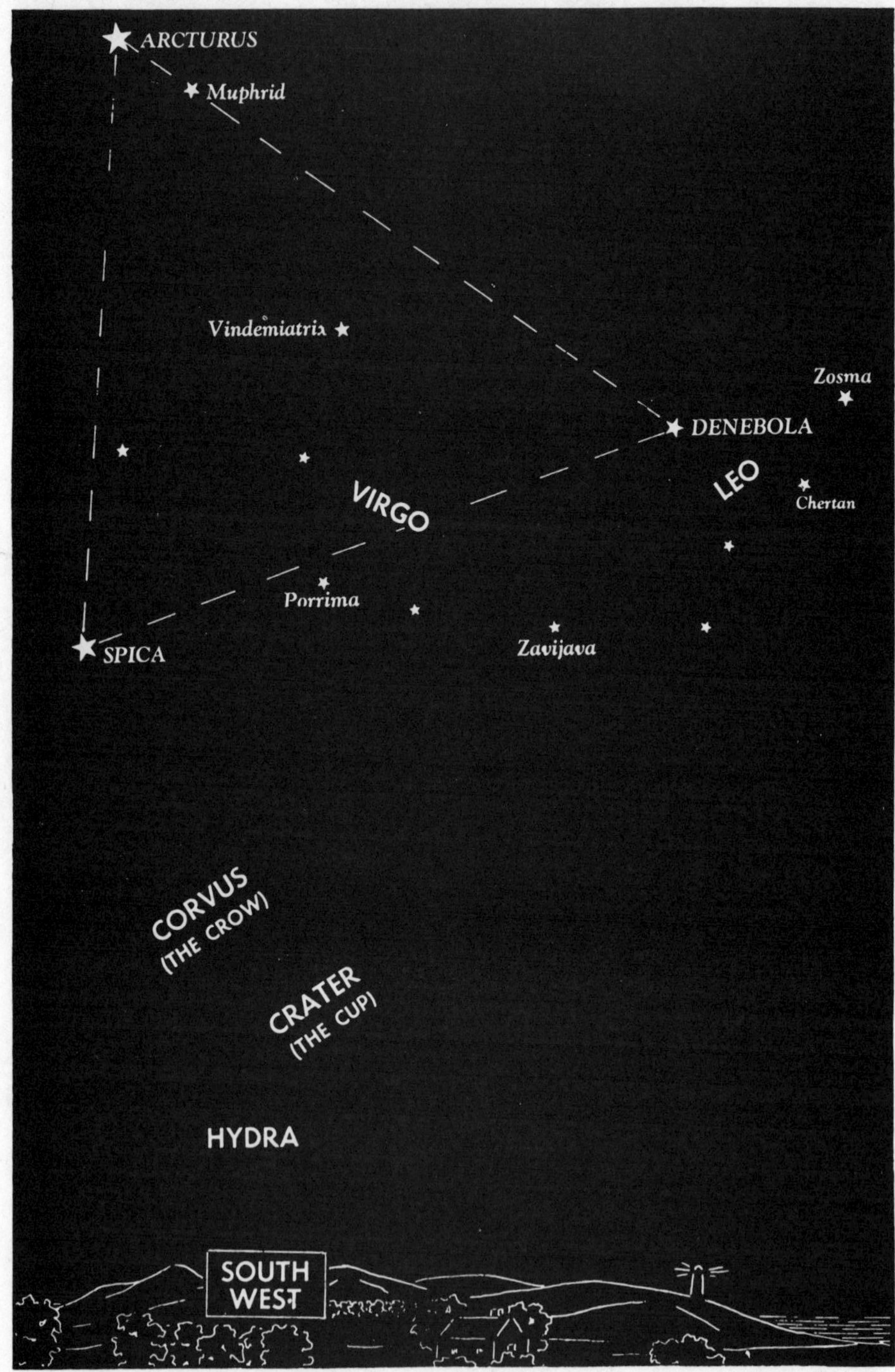


THE VIRGO TRIANGLE: Virgo is in the Zodiac. Look out for bright "stars" in this area not given in the picture. They will be planets. The stars of CORVUS, CRATER and HYDRA are shown in detail on Chart 94.

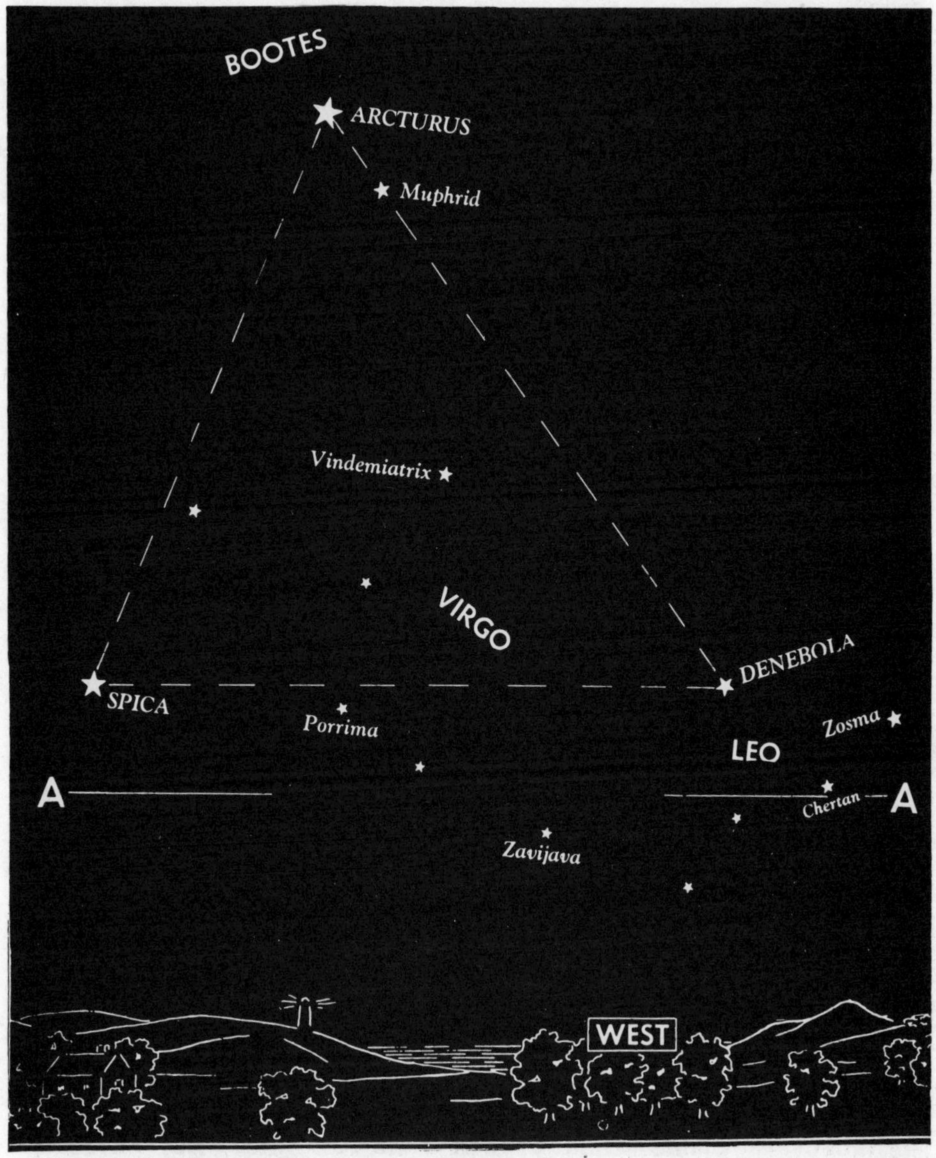


THE VIRGO TRIANGLE: With the Triangle in this position, we have our last chance to identify the stars of Virgo before they sink into the horizon haze. As Virgo descends, the Calendar and the Hour-and-Date Diagram will tell you to use the line AA as the horizon. Spica and Denebola will then be dimmed by the haze. Still later, you can follow Arcturus by the picture of the Northern Crown, Chart 66.

Virgo is in the Zodiac. Look out for bright "stars" in this area not given in the picture. They will be planets.

## XX

## CORONA BOREALIS, THE NORTHERN CROWN

IN SEVERAL places in this book, I have emphasized the value to the navigator of learning the important stars that are part of compact and unmistakable formations that can be instantly recognized through a small break in the clouds during overcast weather.

The little circlet of stars bearing the Latin name Corona Borealis and known in English as the Northern Crown is ideal for this purpose.

The seven brightest stars of the group make the most nearly perfect circle—or major arc of a circle—of any in the sky. The brightest of the seven—Alphecca, sometimes called Gemma or the "Pearl of the Crown"—is included in the navigational lists for which complete data are given in the *Nautical Almanac* and the *Air Almanac*.

For the beginner, the Crown can be located most easily by means of the brilliant near-by star Arcturus, and Arcturus, in turn, can be unfailingly located by means of the simple mnemonic phrase—"Make an arc to Arcturus." That means just this: the stars in the handle of the Big Dipper make a curve that is easily translated into a smooth arc. Continue that imaginary arc about the length of the Big Dipper and you will come to Arcturus or else the curve will show that Arcturus is below the horizon. So remember—"Make an arc to Arcturus." In my days as a Scoutmaster, my Scouts added to that phrase, "And speak to Spica" and thus the phrase located two important stars. The same arc, continued past Arcturus for about the same distance, will come to Spica (see Virgo Triangle, Charts 58-62).

Arcturus precedes the Northern Crown across the sky. There is only one star between Arcturus and Alphecca that can cause a momentary confusion. That is Izar, but a few moments' study will show that Alphecca is brighter than Izar and also brighter than the near-by stars of Hercules, on the opposite side from Arcturus. Consequently, Alphecca will stand out by comparison and the circlet of lesser stars in the Crown will quickly be recognized.

The beautiful crown formation of this group is only momentary, as we count time among the vast reaches of infinity. The stars are all moving in different directions. Seventy-five thousand years from now, they will not even suggest a crown or a circle. Alphecca and the star next to it toward Nekkar have opposing motions and, in the past 75,000 years, have just about changed places.

This "star next to it," bearing the Greek letter Beta and the common name Nusakan, has become extremely interesting to scientists in the last few years. There are evidences that there may be a planet in the system and wherever we see possibilities of a planet, we cannot resist the temptation to speculate on the chance of some form of what we know as "life," whatever that is.

Nusakan has long been known to be a "binary" system—two stars revolving about a center of equilibrium—and its period of revolution is about eleven years. Now it has been found to contain a third and invisible body that seems to emit no light and that apparently has a diameter only about one one-hundredth that of the parent star.

Our earth has only about one one-hundredth the diameter of its parent, the sun, so the possibility of planetary relationship at once suggests itself.

There is another amazing feature about the Northern Crown that makes the little group important to the men who study the remote reaches of space. Far beyond the light-gathering capacity of the human eye, even aided by the most powerful telescope, there is a "field of galaxies" here comparable to the one discussed in our chapter on the Virgo field but much more distant.

Only the photographic plate, with long exposure, can

accumulate enough light to record the images of these faint objects. The great 100-inch telescope in the Mount Wilson observatory has made such a photograph.

The plate covers an area of the sky only about the size of the full moon, yet in that small area, the negative shows some 400 or more faint images, each one an entire universe of stars in itself, like the famous Andromeda Galaxy and the others dealt with in the discussion of our own galaxy.

But looking through the stars of the Northern Crown we have an exceptionally clear view into the remotest space, unclouded by the cosmic dust that veils the distance in so many other parts of the sky. Thus our telescopic cameras are able to penetrate almost without limit and to bring us images of this group of star systems whose light, at a constant speed of 11,000,000 miles a minute, has required 125,000,000 *years* to reach the earth.

The Northern Crown is so closely associated in the observer's sky with the constellation of Boötes that it is convenient to include the latter group in this discussion and the charts that follow.

These charts show all of the principal stars of Boötes but only a portion of Hercules, which has a chapter to itself (Charts 68-72), and part of Serpens, which is combined with Ophiuchus in the text and Charts 73-77.

Back in 1933, the star Arcturus was the object of a great publicity "build-up" that put its name on the pages of virtually every newspaper in the United States.

For Arcturus closed the switch that turned on a huge searchlight that signaled the official opening of the great Century of Progress Exposition in Chicago at 9:15 P.M. on May 27, 1933.

Arcturus was chosen as the star peculiarly appropriate to perform this function. Chicago had had a great World's Fair in 1893—just 40 years before. According to the best estimates of scientists at that time, the light from Arcturus required 40

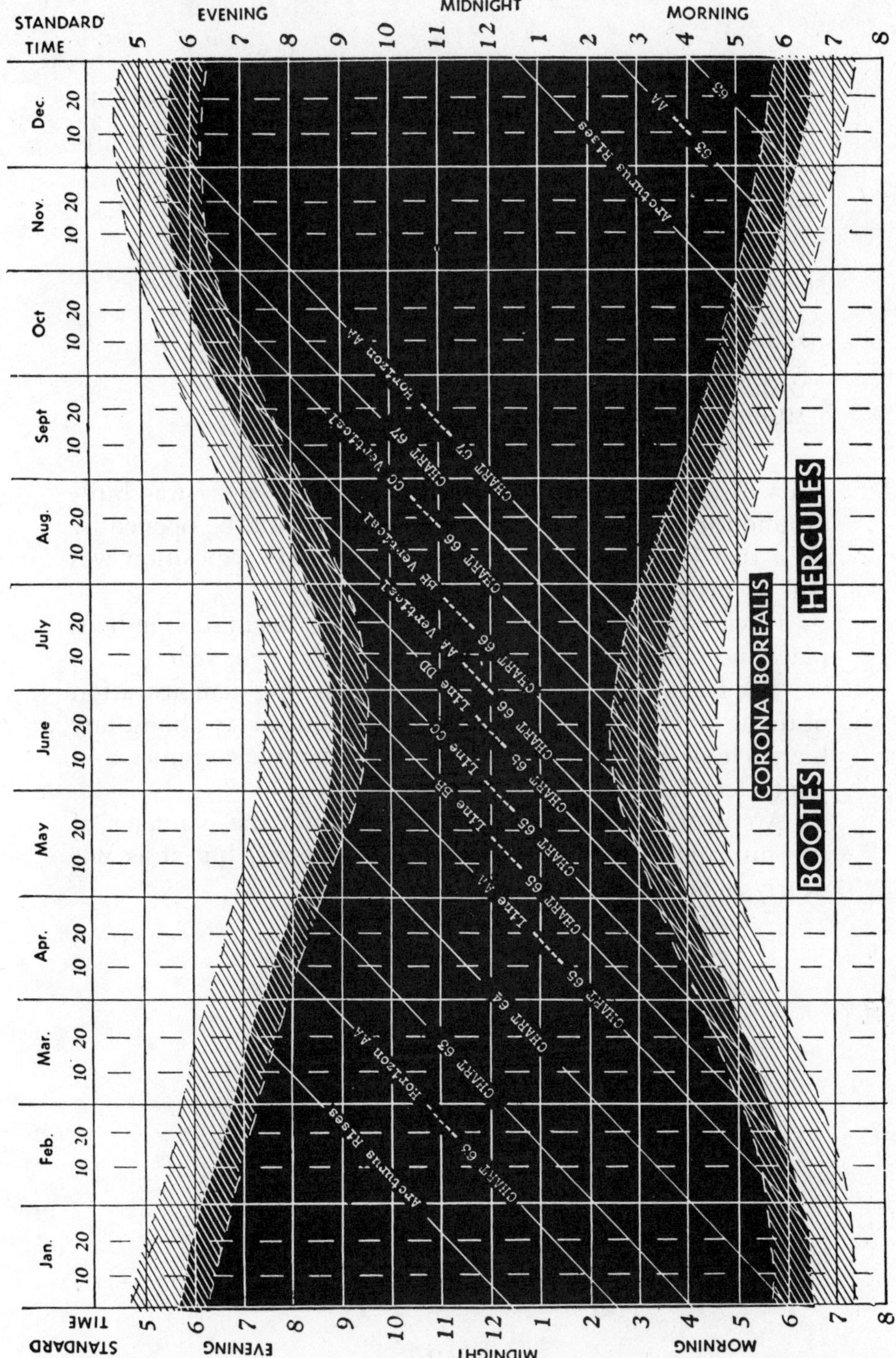


The diagonal line nearest to the hour and date desired shows the correct chart and line to use at that time.

PRONUNCIATIONS

*CORONA BOREALIS*—"kore-oh-na bore-ee-ale-iss." Accent "oh" and "ale."
ALPHECCA—"al-feck-a." Accent "feck."
NUSAKAN—"new-sack-kan." Accent "new."
*BOÖTES*—three syllables, "bo-oh-teez." Accent second syllable, "oh."
ARCTURUS—"ark-tew-russ." Accent "tew" (rhymes with "new," "few").
NEKKAR—"neck-ar." Accent "neck."
SEGINUS—"sedge-eye-nuss." Accent "eye."
IZAR—"eye-zar." Accent "eye."
MUPHRID—"muff-rid." Accent "muff."

years to reach the earth so a great publicity story was built around the fact that the 1933 Exposition would be opened by light that had started its trip while the 1893 exposition was still in progress.

(Incidentally, more recent and more accurate methods place the light-time distance of Arcturus at 37.5 years.)

The feat at that time seemed a most amazing demonstration of the wonders of scientific achievement but today almost any high school boy understands enough about electronics and photoelectric cells to explain it to you.

Arcturus is a huge star, about 25 times the diameter of the sun and possibly 100 times as luminous, but it is not nearly as hot or as dense.

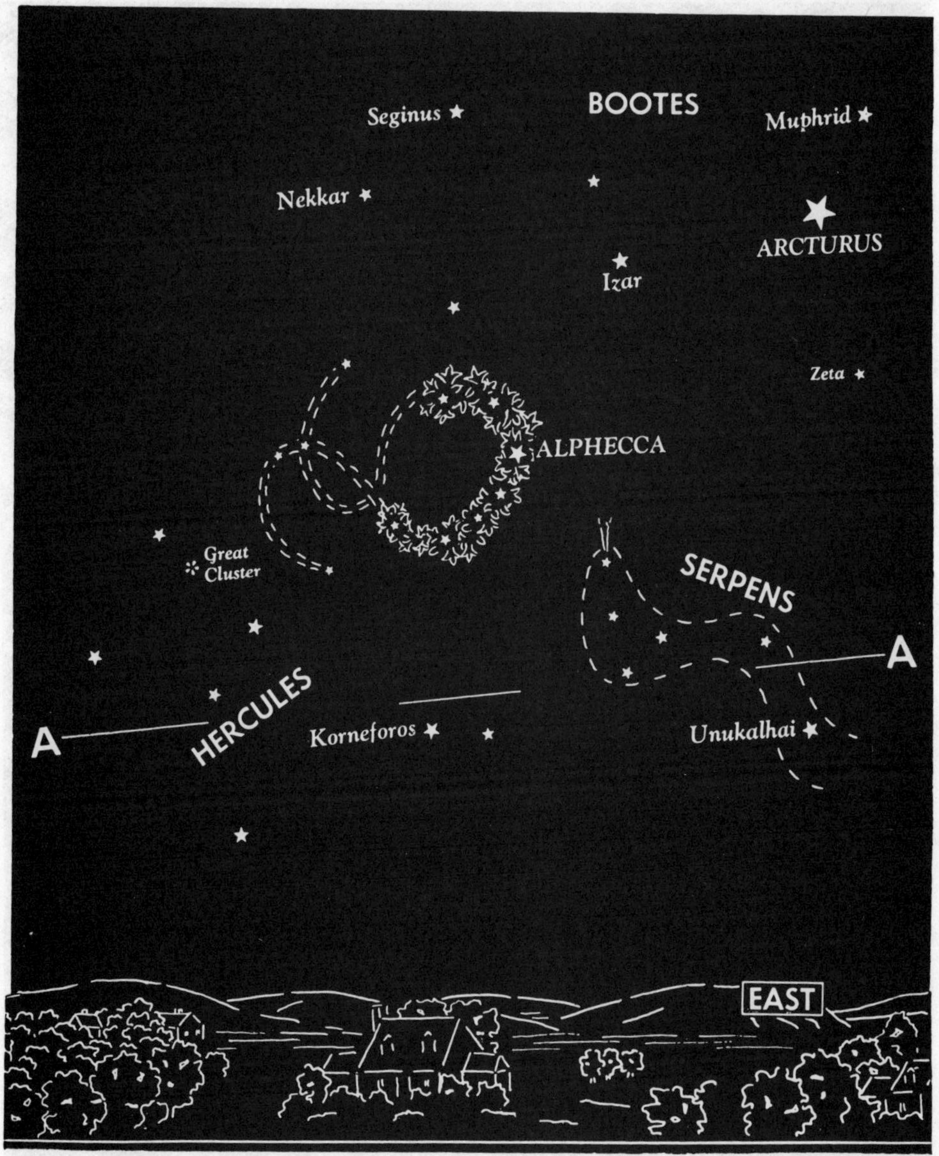


THE NORTHERN CROWN: Ignore the line AA unless it is called for in the instructions. When, however, the line is specified, it means that these stars are not yet so high and you must imagine them lowered until the line rests on the tops of the distant hills in the landscape.

# CHART 64

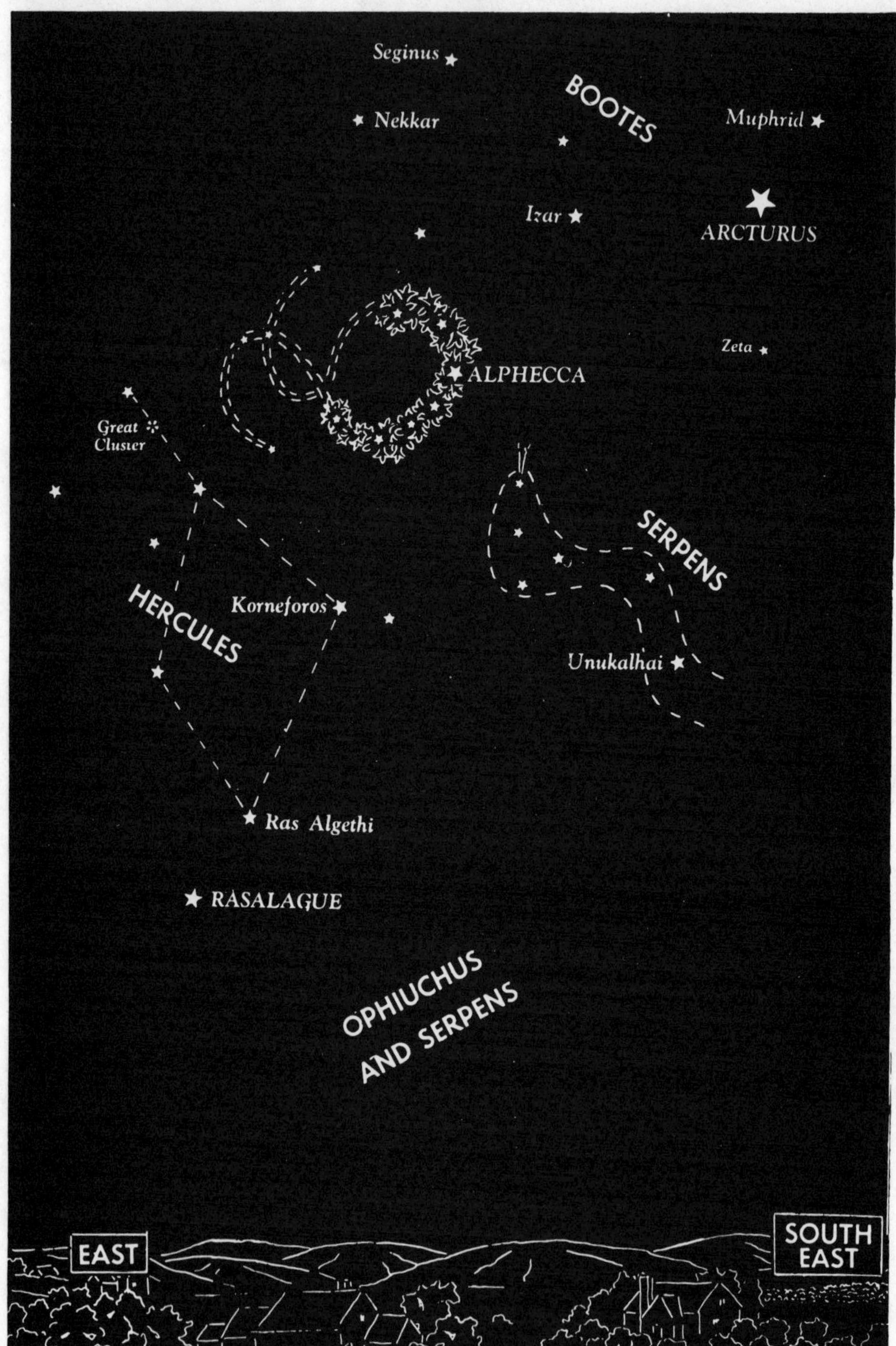


THE NORTHERN CROWN: For Ophiuchus and Serpens at this time, see Chart 73.

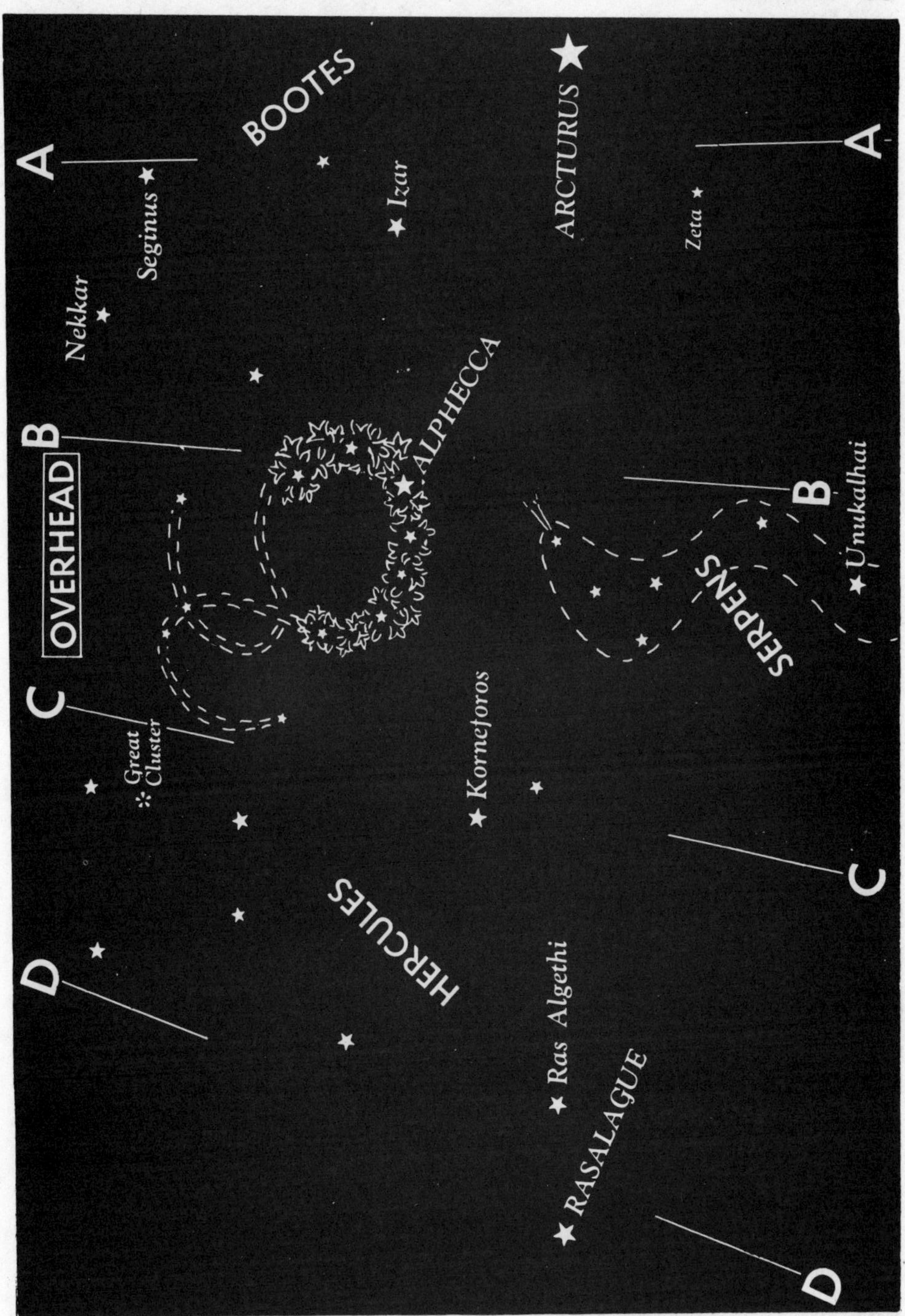


THE NORTHERN CROWN is shown here as it crosses the sky almost overhead. In all cases, when using this picture, face due south, lie back comfortably and raise the book until the word "Overhead" is really overhead. The lines AA etc. should run through your body lengthwise and the right line to use for any particular time will be stipulated in the Calendar and Hour-and-Date Diagram.

# CHART 66

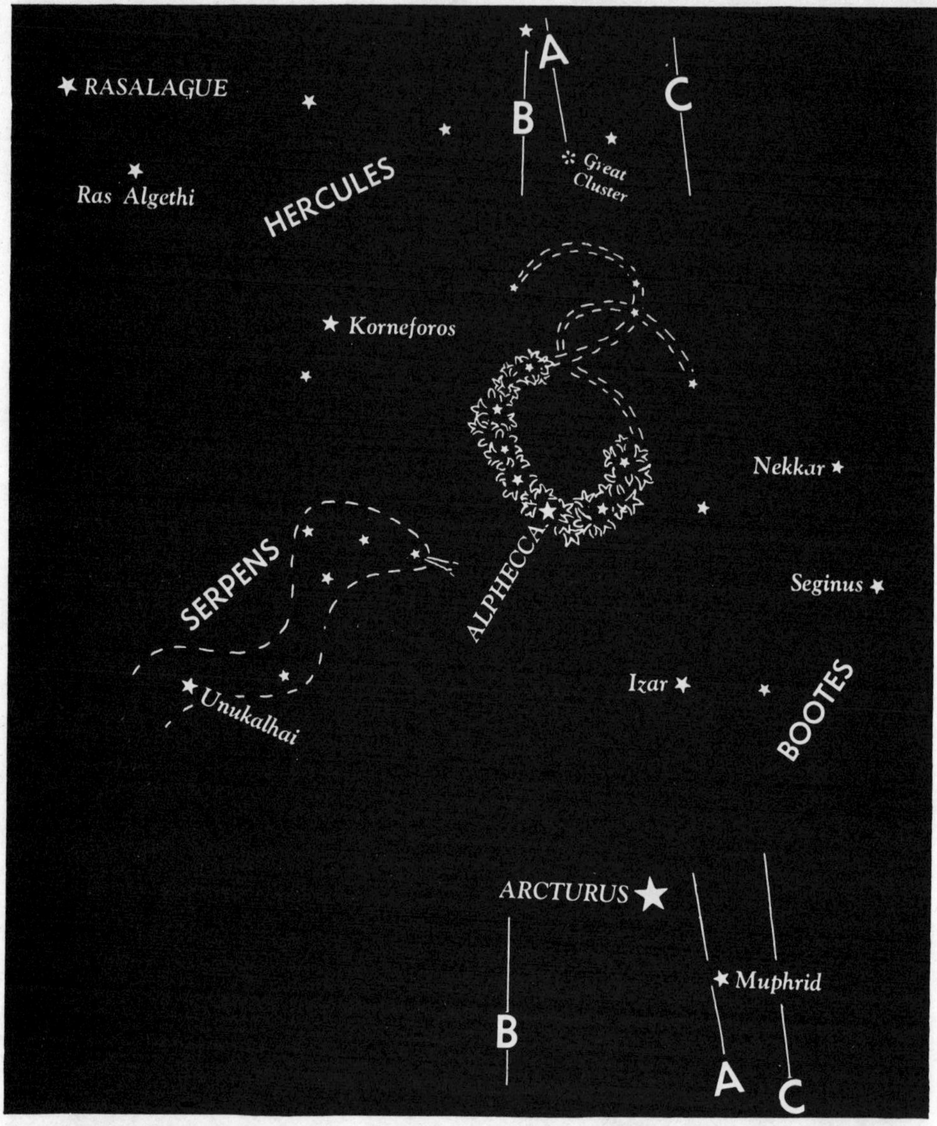


THE NORTHERN CROWN: In the Calendar and the Hour-and-Date Diagram you will find instructions for the use of one of these lines for a particular date and time. In all cases, proceed as follows:

For line AA—face due west; turn the book until the line AA is perpendicular at that compass point; raise the book until the star name Izar is halfway up the sky. Glance around the edge of the book and you will be looking at the groups in the picture.

For line BB—again face west; BB perpendicular; star Alphecca halfway up the sky.

For line CC—face halfway between west and northwest; line CC perpendicular; hold the word "Hercules" halfway up the sky.

# CHART 67

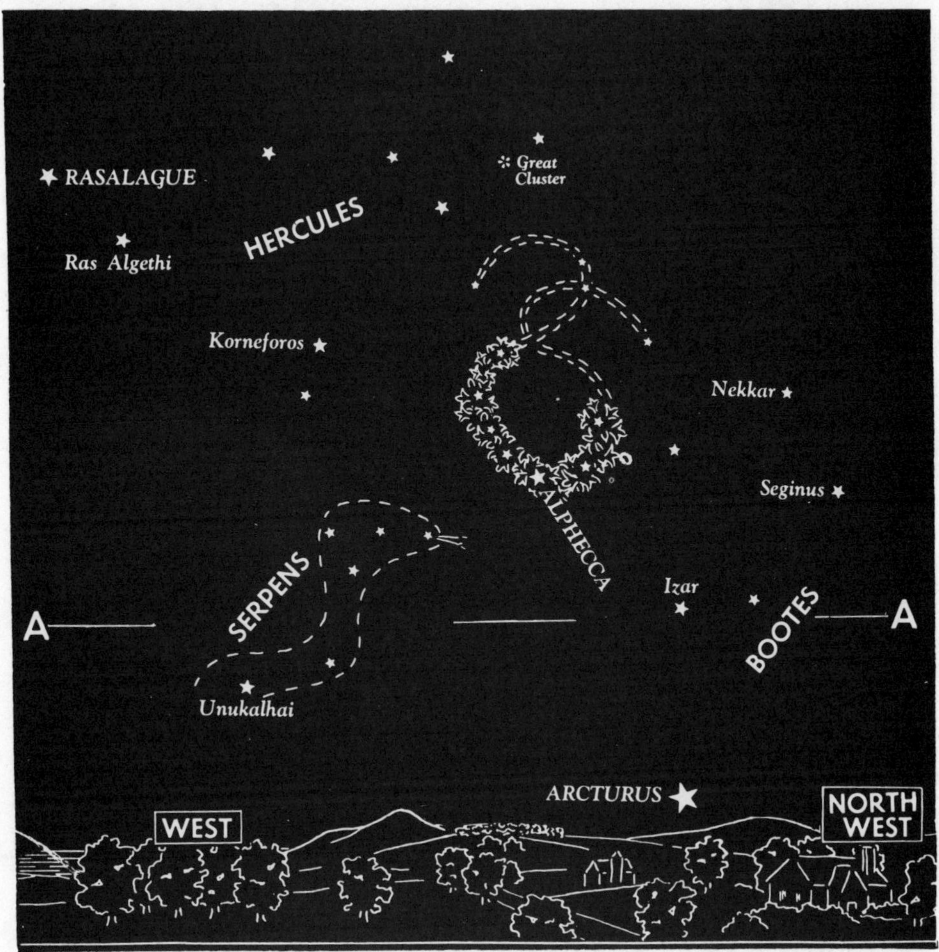


THE NORTHERN CROWN: This chart shows the Northern Crown and its neighbors as they prepare to sink into the horizon haze and as the brilliant star Arcturus bids us farewell. Arcturus soon disappears from the sky and the groups sink lower until the line AA becomes the horizon.

## XXI

## HERCULES AND THE GREAT CLUSTER

THE coming of the constellation of Hercules into the night sky introduces another of those extremely faint and distant, but nevertheless "neighbor," star systems that make a visit to an observatory on nights when the public is admitted a thrilling experience.

The object is the Great Cluster of Hercules, listed in books and catalogues as M13.

To the naked eye, the Great Cluster is close to the limit of ordinary vision but, with a clear, dark night and no street or house lights near, it can be found with a little patience. Binoculars make the job easier, not that such small magnification will reveal any of the amazing details, but a little optical aid at once discloses the difference between the sparkling pin point of a star and the dim haziness of the Cluster.

Dr. Harlow Shapley, in his wonderful book, *Galaxies,* says:

> Astonishment is the lot of every one who sees for the first time, through a competent telescope, the great star cluster in Hercules. And skepticism is registered (or is it, perhaps, respectful awe?) when we offer the information that each glittering point is a star far brighter than our sun, that the whole amazing globular assemblage is so distant that the light now arriving has been en route for more than three hundred centuries.

The "each glittering point" that Dr. Shapley refers to is, of course, one of the stars on the outer, surrounding envelope of the cluster. There is no way of penetrating the much more densely star-populated core, for it is now known that there are over 100,000 stars in this tremendous globe of suns, and it is so vast in the extent of the space it occupies that the light from one of the outer stars, if sent straight through the cluster at 11,000,000 miles a minute, would require some 320 years to reach the fringe of stars on the opposite side. It would require something like 2,500,000 of our suns to equal the total of light emitted by all of the stars in this system.

Yet, to the naked eye, it appears in the sky as a dim little spot which, as Serviss wrote, "would not make a visible speck on the face of the moon."

It seems to be now quite generally agreed that the space-time remoteness of this cluster is about 31,000 years. This reference to it in terms of space-time can perhaps be most graphically explained by a quotation from one of my own favorite authors, Sir James Jeans. In his book, *The Stars in Their Courses* and speaking of the *nearest* known globular cluster, little more than half as far away as the Hercules system, he says:

> We do not see it as it now is or where it now is; we see it where it was and as it was 18,400 years ago—long before man became civilized. We see it by light which started out on its long journey to us while the earth was still covered with primeval forests and overrun with wild beasts, while agriculture was unknown and man lived by the crudest kinds of hunting and fishing. While this light has been traveling through space on its way to us, all the recorded history of mankind has taken place; 600 generations of man have been born, lived their lives and died; empires have risen, decayed and fallen—it has taken all this time for the light from even this nearest of the globular clusters to reach us, traveling through space at the rate of more than eleven million miles every minute.

In that graphic picture, remember, Jeans was speaking of the *nearest* globular star cluster. The Hercules cluster is nearly twice as far away, while the astounding Andromeda Galaxy is twenty times as remote as the Hercules Cluster.

Hercules and its Great Cluster can be seen first by the just-after-dark star-gazer after mid-April. But the enthusiast who is willing to stay up all night to see his favorites in the sky will

*Yerkes Observatory Photo*

M13, THE GREAT CLUSTER IN HERCULES

find it in the same position in the east just before dawn in early December, as shown on the Hour-and-Date Diagram.

This constellation is another of the many in which the traditional mythological figure is confusing to the beginner in these modern days. Oddly enough, primitive men seem to have found no difficulty in picturing the group as forming the figure of a kneeling man, and the old Arabic name of the principal star, Ras Algethi, means "the head of the kneeling one."

This "kneeling one" represented different national conceptions at different times and it was the Greeks who finally pre-empted the idea and declared that "the kneeler" was their great hero, Hercules.

As we see him today, however, Hercules is kneeling "upward" in the sky by doing a headstand on the left shoulder of the giant Ophiuchus.

Because the average beginner will find little of interest in Hercules except the Great Cluster, I have shown the constellation in the charts as forming a kite with a tail. In my own years of star-gazing I have found this to be much the easiest and simplest way to locate the dim and elusive object.

Whenever the Great Cluster is high enough above the horizon to be clearly examined, it will be between two of the brightest stars in the sky—Vega and Arcturus—so that the novice should locate those stars first.

Vega is shown in the Hercules charts and its outstanding brilliance makes it unmistakable. Arcturus is shown with the Northern Crown in Charts 63-67.

With Arcturus identified, your next step is to locate the little Northern Crown and from then on, the Hercules charts will guide you, because they contain both Vega and the Northern Crown and show exactly how the kite is located between them.

There is one difficulty, however, that may require patience on the part of the novice. As the ancient star-gazers conceived the figures of Ophiuchus and Hercules, we find the stars of the heads and shoulders of the two giants seemingly mixed up together in that area of the sky and there is sometimes trouble in deciding which is which. Definite identification of the star Ras Algethi is necessary in order to form the picture of the kite and, as Ras Algethi does not look much more conspicuous than several stars in the neighborhood, this is a preliminary problem but it is quite easily solved and, once solved, will never trouble you again.

In exploring the sky between the Northern Crown and Vega you will soon determine the approximate location of Ras Algethi. The trouble is that he is one of four stars, all fairly close together, and your job is to determine which one he is.

A little inspection will show that one of these four stars is unquestionably brighter than the other three. That will be Rasalague, in the head of Ophiuchus (you had better follow this on Chart 75).

Further inspection will soon show you that two of the near-by stars make almost an equilateral triangle with Rasalague. It is the triangle marked with solid lines in the picture of Ophiuchus. This triangle leaves the fourth star out of the figure entirely, though close to one side of it. That star that is *not* in the triangle is Ras Algethi, in the head of Hercules and the star that forms the first corner of the kite. The rest is easy.

But by all means use opera glasses or binoculars in your search for the Great Cluster if you can.

The star Ras Algethi is the biggest of all the stars visible to the naked eye. For many years, it was thought that Antares, in the Scorpion, held this distinction, but the greater accuracy of modern methods has put Ras Algethi at the top of the list.

This star's diameter is something like 690,000,000 miles. In other words (to use my favorite comparison) if you can imagine the earth shrunk to the size of a baseball, then, on that scale, Ras Algethi would be a ball nearly 4 *miles* in diameter.

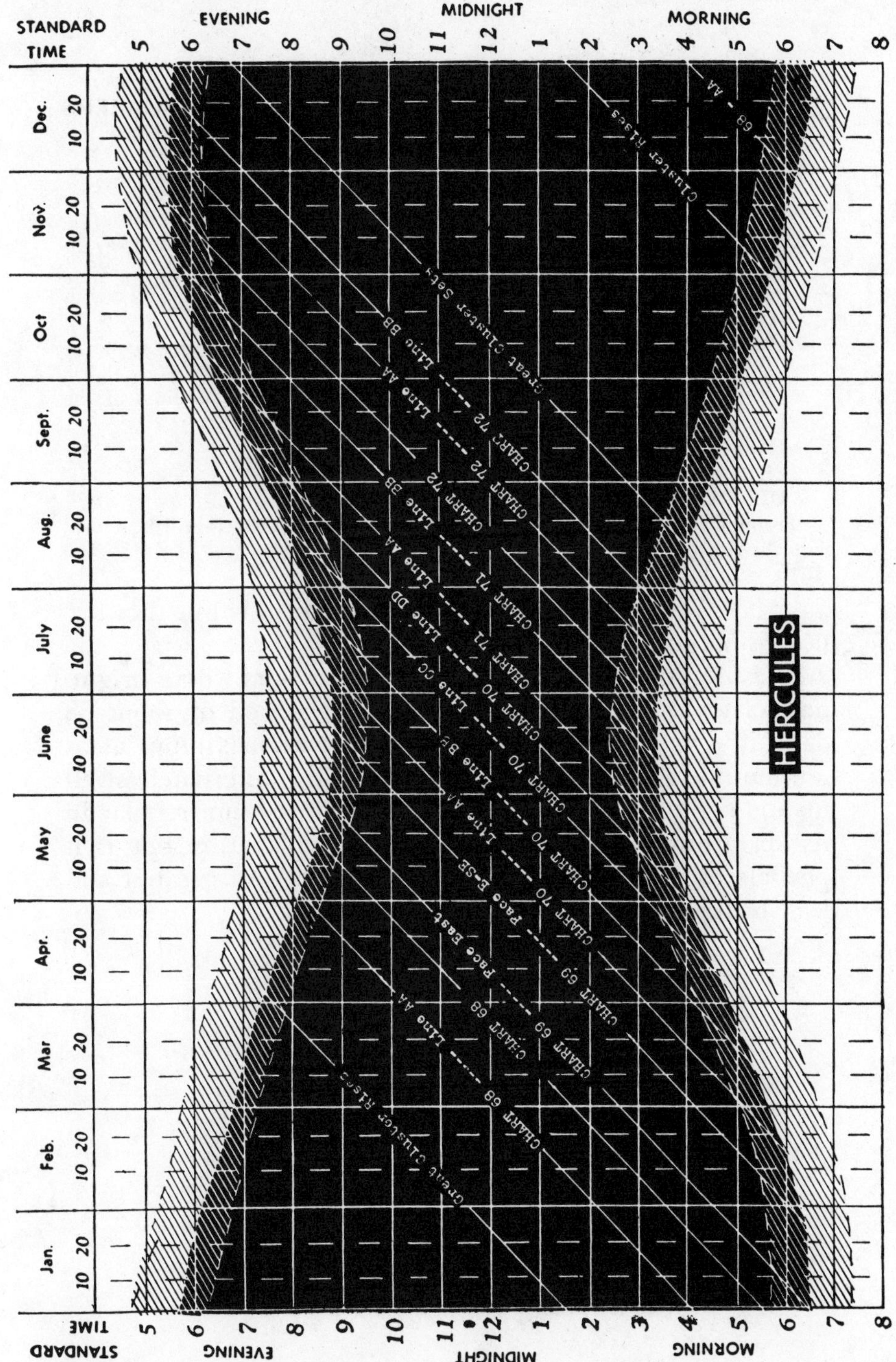


The diagonal line nearest to the hour and date desired shows the correct chart and line to use at that time.

## PRONUNCIATIONS

*HERCULES*—"her-cue-leez." Accent "her."

RAS ALGETHI—"rass al-jee-thee." Accent "jee"; the "th" is soft, as in "theory."

KORNEFOROS—"core-neff-or-oss." Accent "neff"; the "oss" rhymes with "floss."

RASALAGUE—"rass-al-aig-wee." Accent "aig" (see note on this name in the Ophiuchus pronunciations facing Chart 73).

ETA, ZETA and DELTA are not names but are English spellings of the Greek letters assigned to these stars. Pronounce:

ETA—"ate-a." Accent "ate."

ZETA—"zay-ta." Accent "zay."

DELTA—as spelled. Accent first syllable.

Pronunciations of names of other stars shown in the charts will be found with the constellations to which they belong.

There are several stars even larger than this but they are not visible to the naked eye.

Ras Algethi is one of those mysterious stars whose brightness varies irregularly. With an average period of about 88 days, it is nearly 2½ times as brilliant at maximum as at minimum. It is another of those stars which alternately swell up and contract but, unlike the Cepheids, it is not regular in its "breathing" and we have no valid explanation nor is it possible to make any prediction of the times of greatest and least brilliance.

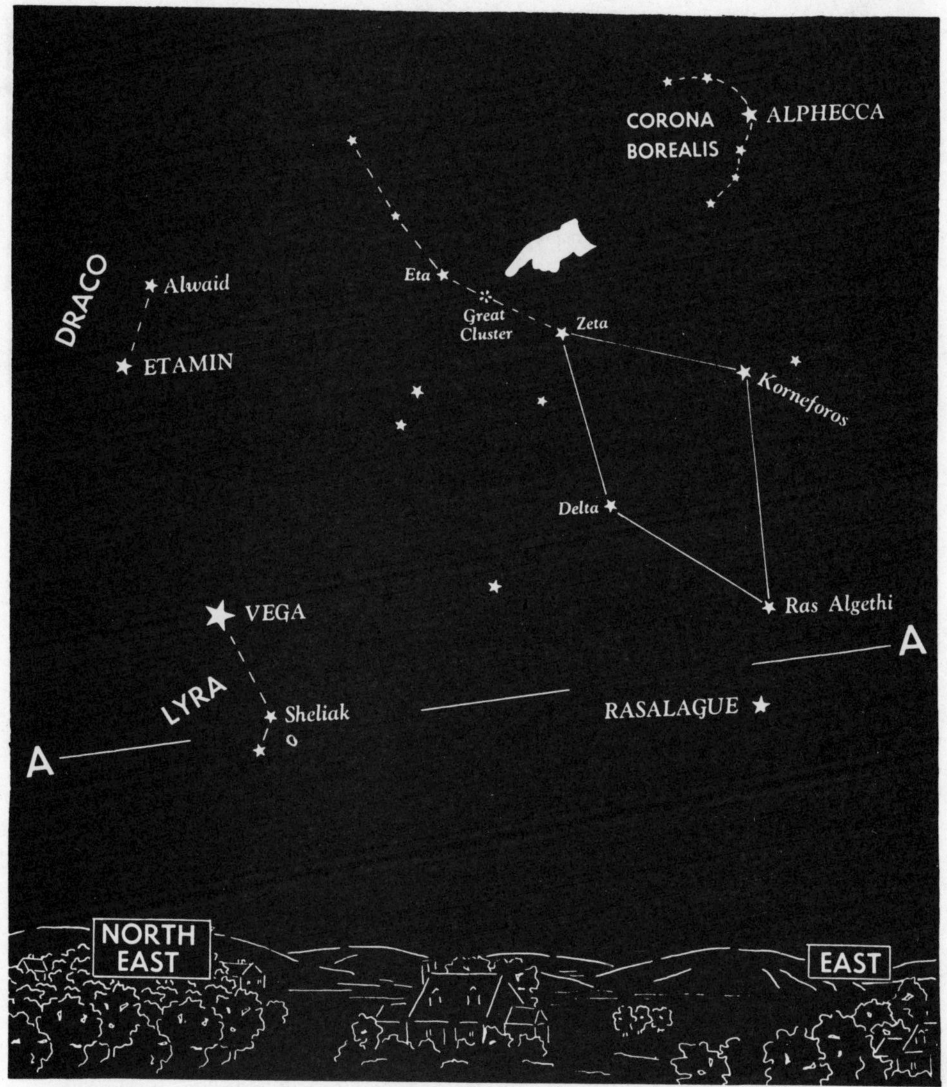


HERCULES: This picture is to be used "as is," ignoring the line AA, when Chart 68 is called for in the Calendar or the Hour-and-Date Diagram. If, however, the line AA is specified, it indicates that these stars are not yet so high and you must imagine them lowered until the line AA rests on the tops of the distant hills in the landscape.

# CHART 69

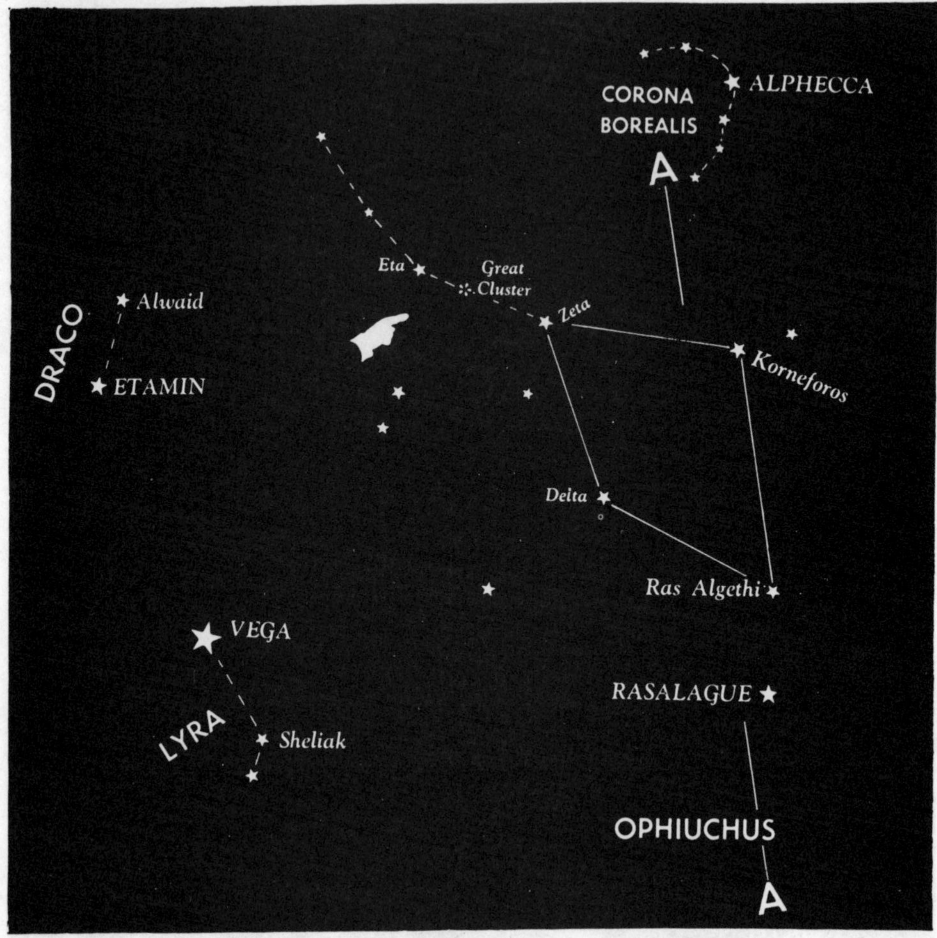


HERCULES: The line AA is the key to this chart. The book is to be turned until the line is vertical but you face different compass directions and raise the book to different heights at different times when using it. The Calendar and the Hour-and-Date Diagram will tell you which facing to use at any particular time. Then:

If you are to face due east with AA vertical, raise the book until the star Korneforos is just halfway up the sky, glance around the edge of the book and you will be looking at Hercules.

If you are to face halfway between east and southeast (abbreviated in the diagram to E-SE), hold AA vertical and raise the book until the star Ras Algethi is halfway up the sky.

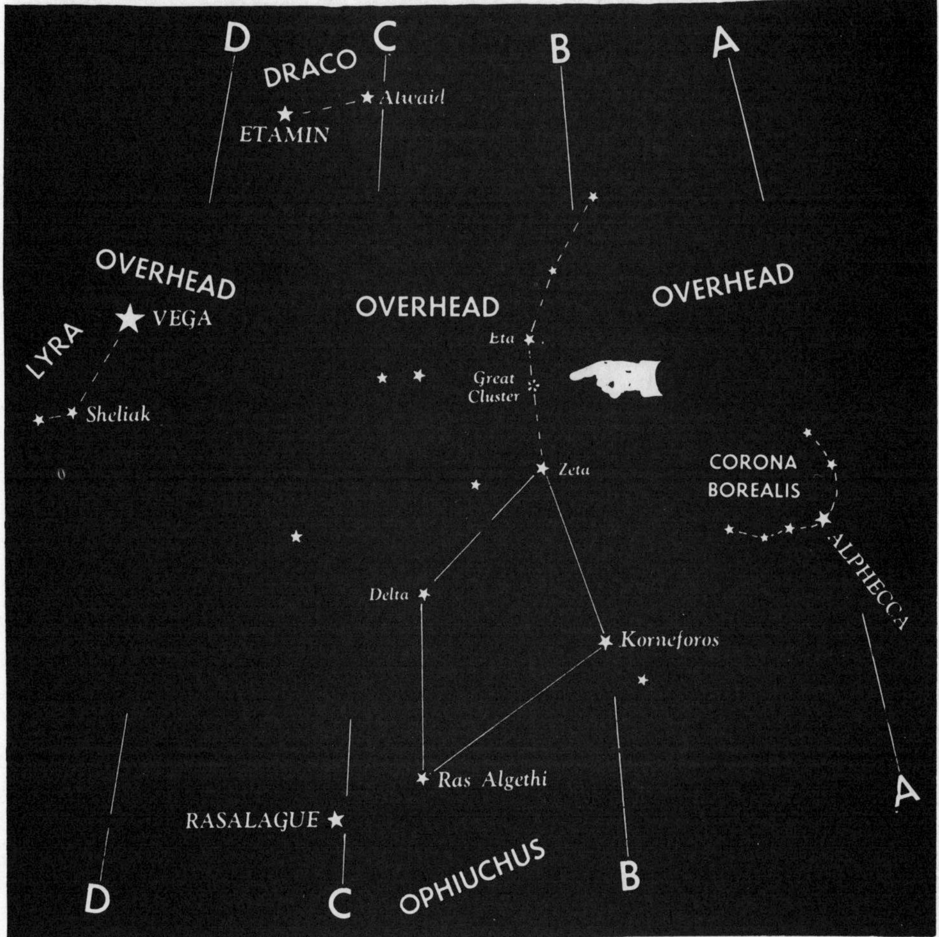


**Hercules:** This picture shows Hercules in his meridian crossing, almost overhead. To use it, face due south, lie back comfortably, hold the book above you and the different lines should be used to bisect your body lengthwise as called for in the Calendar or the Hour-and-Date Diagram. In all cases, be sure the word "Overhead" is overhead.

# CHART 71

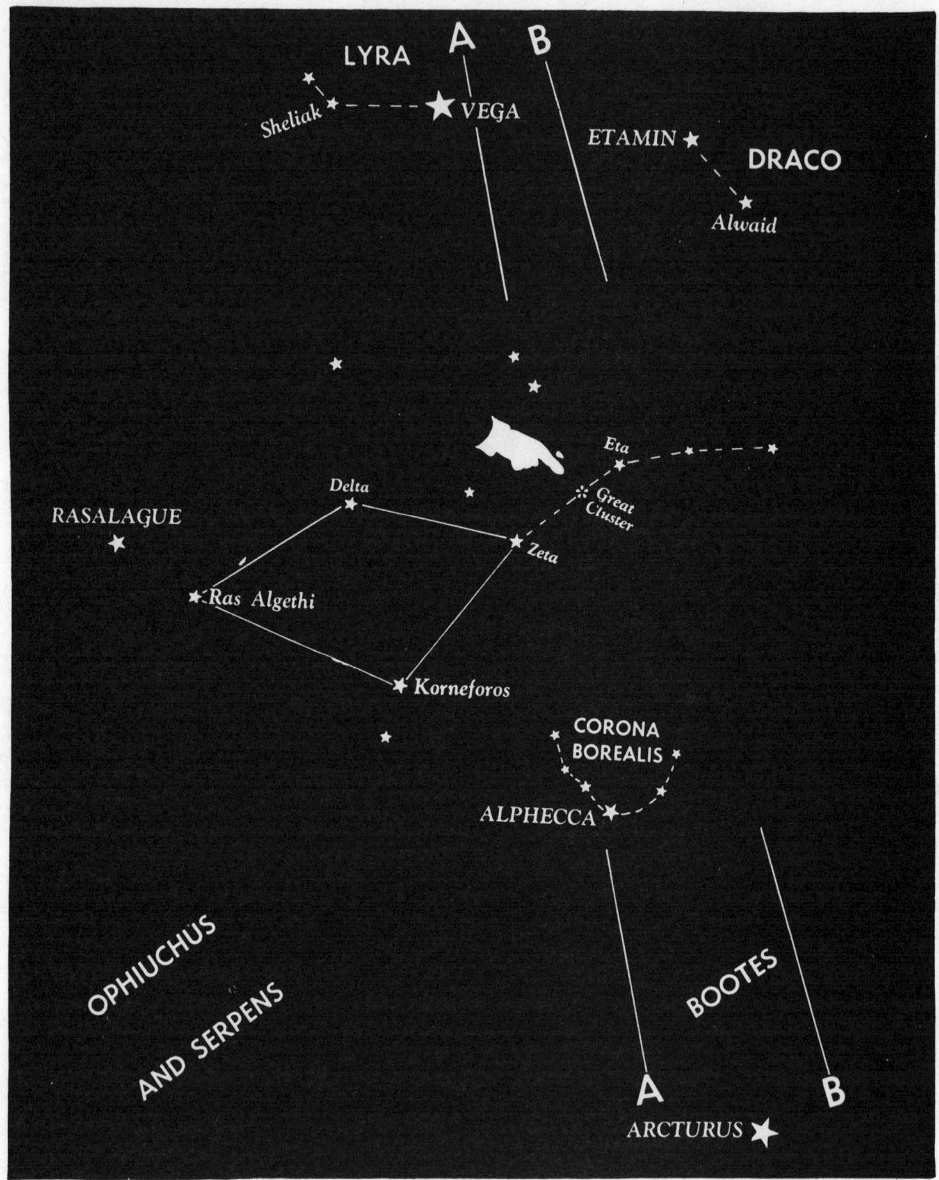


**Hercules:** This chart shows Hercules descending the upper part of the western sky. Line AA or BB will be specified at different times in the Calendar or the Hour-and-Date Diagram. Use as follows:

Line AA—face west; make AA vertical; raise the book to bring Corona Borealis halfway up the sky; glance around the edge of the book and you will be looking at Hercules.

Line BB—face halfway between west and northwest; make BB vertical; raise the book until the Great Cluster is halfway up the sky.

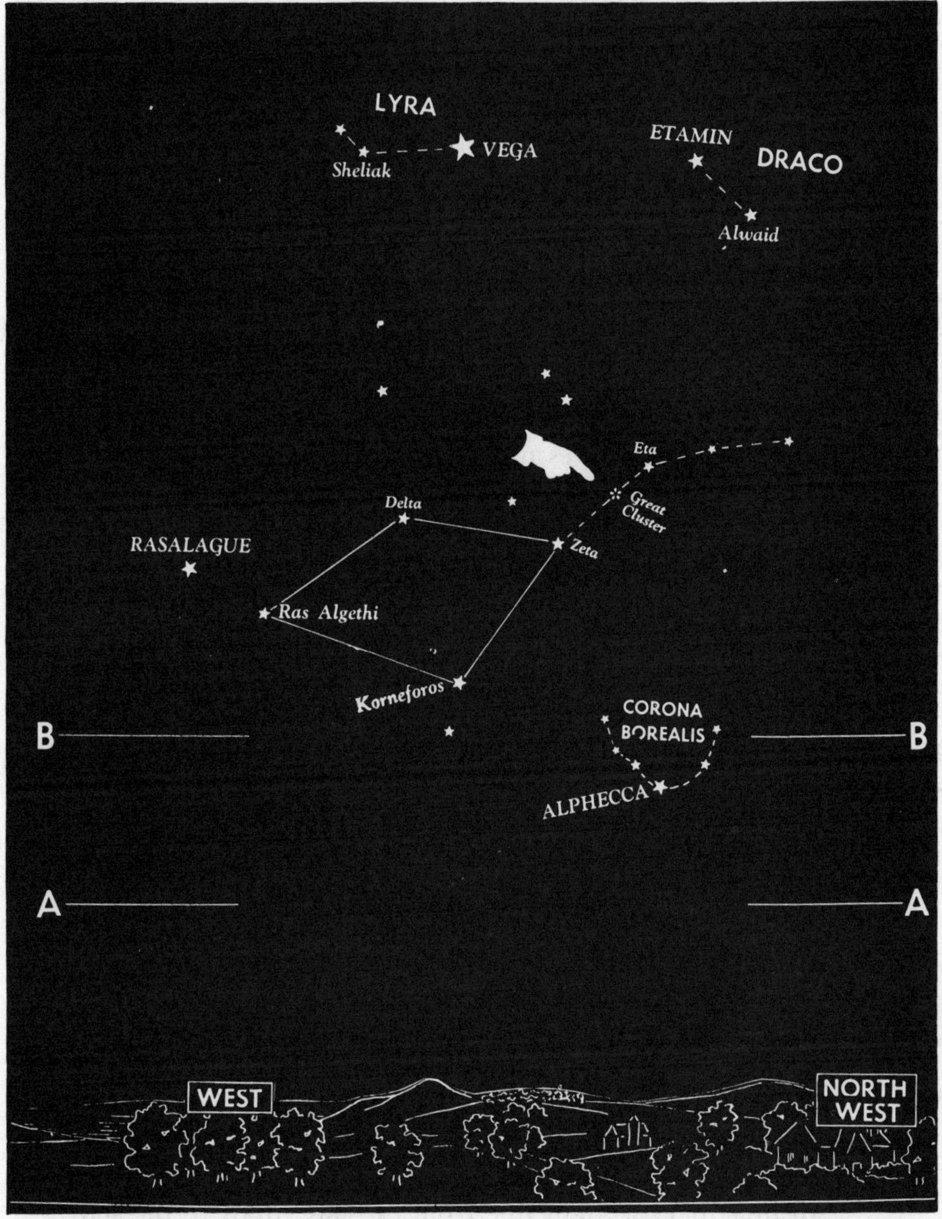


HERCULES: Ignore the lines AA and BB unless one of them is called for in the Calendar or the Hour-and-Date Diagram. If, however, one of these lines is specified, it indicates that the stars are no longer so high and you must imagine them lowered until the specified line rests on the tops of the distant hills in the landscape.

## XXII

# OPHIUCHUS AND HIS SERPENT

Most beginners find it difficult to trace the giant figure of Ophiuchus and the Serpent by the scattered stars that are dotted here and there to mark the various parts of their anatomies.

This is no reason for discouragement, however. The ancient figures themselves are not particularly important; what is important to the star-gazer is to be able to recognize the very large area of the sky which they cover. Then, at your leisure, you can pick out different features, one at a time, until finally you can persuade yourself that you can see what those ancients saw.

My own advice to the novice is not to attempt Ophiuchus and Serpens until he has first become familiar with several surrounding constellations which will help him in his search for this one. Those prior constellations are:

1. Cygnus, with its accompanying bright stars Vega and Altair (Charts 35-39).

2. The Northern Crown and the brilliant star Arcturus (Charts 63-67).

3. The kite which we find in Hercules (Charts 68-72).

4. Scorpius with its blazing star Antares (Charts 78-82).

All of these are easy. With them located, Ophiuchus and Serpens are easy.

The Northern Crown will give you the head and "neck" of the Serpent. The kite in Hercules will give you the head and shoulders of Ophiuchus.

An imaginary straight line from the star Altair to the star Antares will cut across the right shin of the giant, with the bright star Sabik above and the star in the foot below.

A straight line from Antares to the Northern Crown will

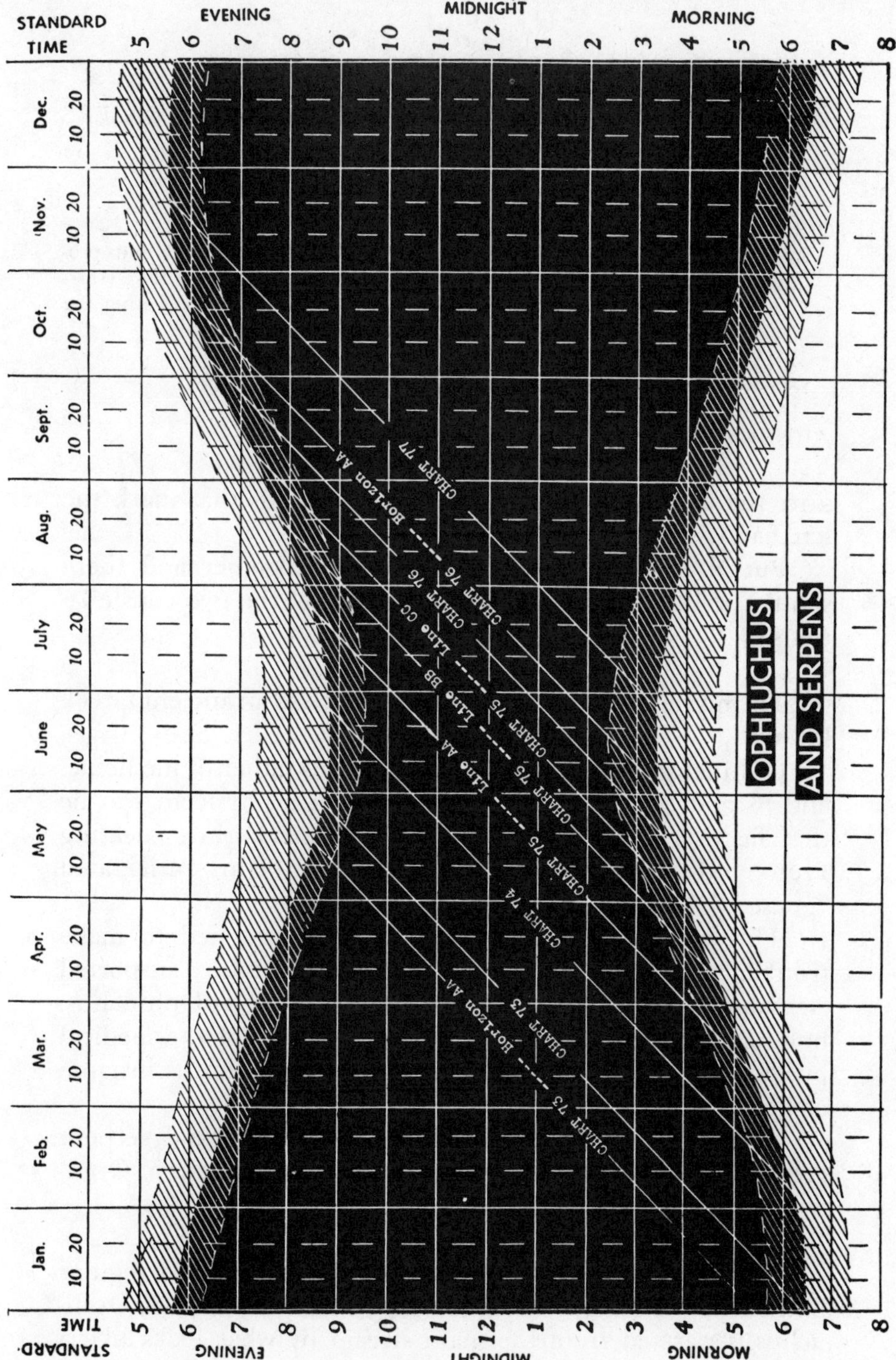


The diagonal line nearest to the hour and date desired shows the correct chart and line to use at that time.

PRONUNCIATIONS

*OPHIUCHUS*—"off-ee-you-kuss." Accent "you."
RASALAGUE—"rass-al-aig-wee." Accent "aig." (You can spell and pronounce this with an "h" in it if you like it better—RASALHAGUE—"rass-al-haig-wee." Many authorities prefer this but I am adopting the spelling given in the *Nautical Almanac* and the *Air Almanac*.)
CEBALRAI—"seb-al-ray-ee." Accent "ray."
SABIK—"say-bick." Accent "say."
MARFIK, ALYA and YED as spelled.
UNUKALHAI—"you-nuck-al-hay-ee." Accent "hay."

skirt the almost-twin stars known as the Yeds that mark the left hand holding the struggling Serpent.

Put all of these anatomical sections together and there should be little difficulty finding the rest of the two constellations.

The mythology of Ophiuchus goes back to an ancient Greek legend.

Ophiuchus is identical with the famous father of medicine, and its god, great Aesculapius. So potent a physician was he that he even succeeded in raising the dead, thus cheating Pluto, god of the nether regions, of some of his anticipated "guests."

This naturally angered Pluto, who threatened to make trouble, so Zeus, to keep peace among the gods, transported Aesculapius to the skies where we see him now as Ophiuchus, holding the Serpent which is still the symbol of the medical profession, made most familiar to us by the caduceus insignia of our Army's Medical Corps.

The legend does not explain how the original serpent grew so big as, apparently, to require all the strength of Ophiuchus to hold him.

The naked eye will discover a long and luminous irregular branch of the Milky Way stretching across the feet of Ophiuchus, separated from the main stream by what looks like a

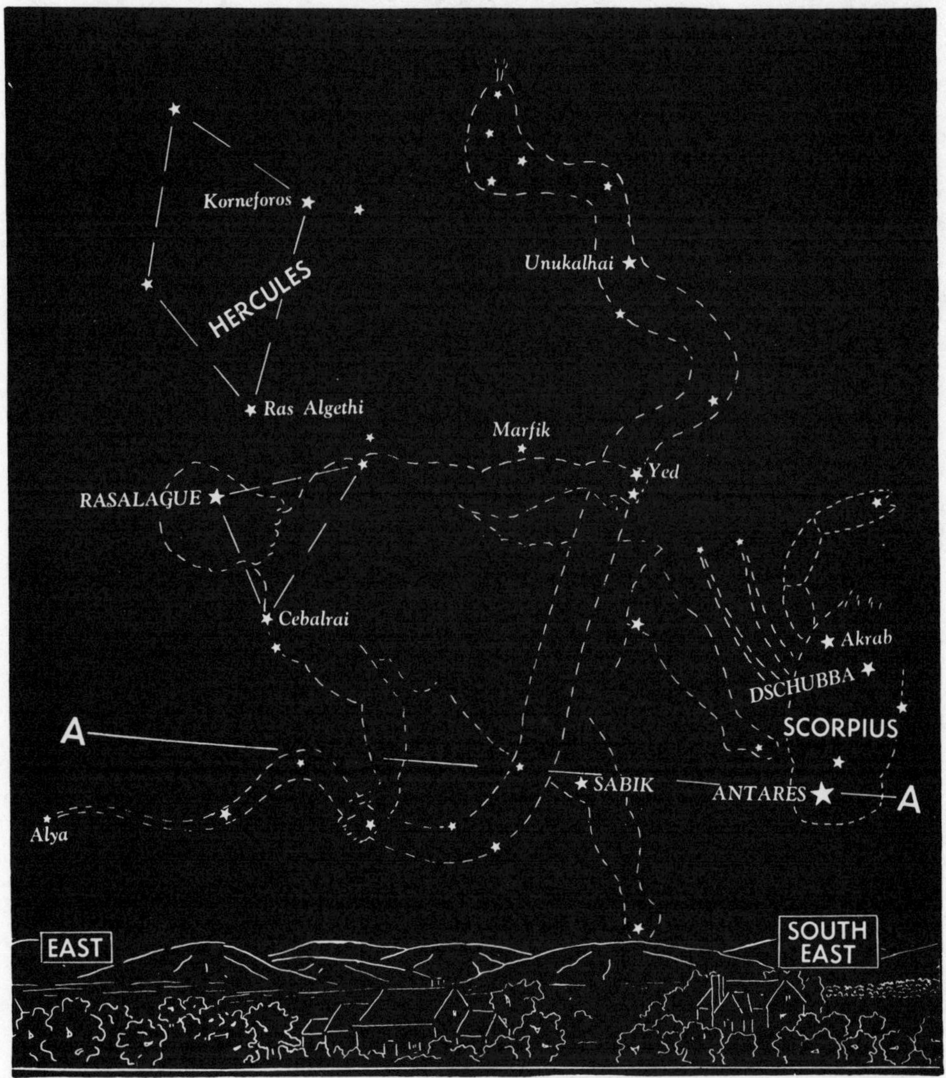


**Ophiuchus and Serpens:** Ignore the line AA unless it is called for in the instructions in the Calendar or the Hour-and-Date Diagram. If, however, the line is specified, it indicates that these stars are not yet so high and you must imagine them lowered until the line rests on the tops of the distant hills in the landscape.

Planets may appear in a part of Ophiuchus. See note with Chart 74.

rift or division. This black streak is, however, a vast cloud of dark, obscuring dust or galactic "smoke" that entirely shuts off our vision and forever hides millions of the stars of the galaxy that lie beyond it in our line of sight.

Professor Russell has estimated that this black cloud is about 400 light-years away from us and, as it shows no illumination of starlight piercing it, the stars on the other side are probably two or three times that distance from us.

Owners of binoculars and telescopes will get many thrills "sweeping" around the luminous areas in this Ophiuchus branch of the Milky Way. The insignificant constellation of Scutum is also well worth attention with a good lens.

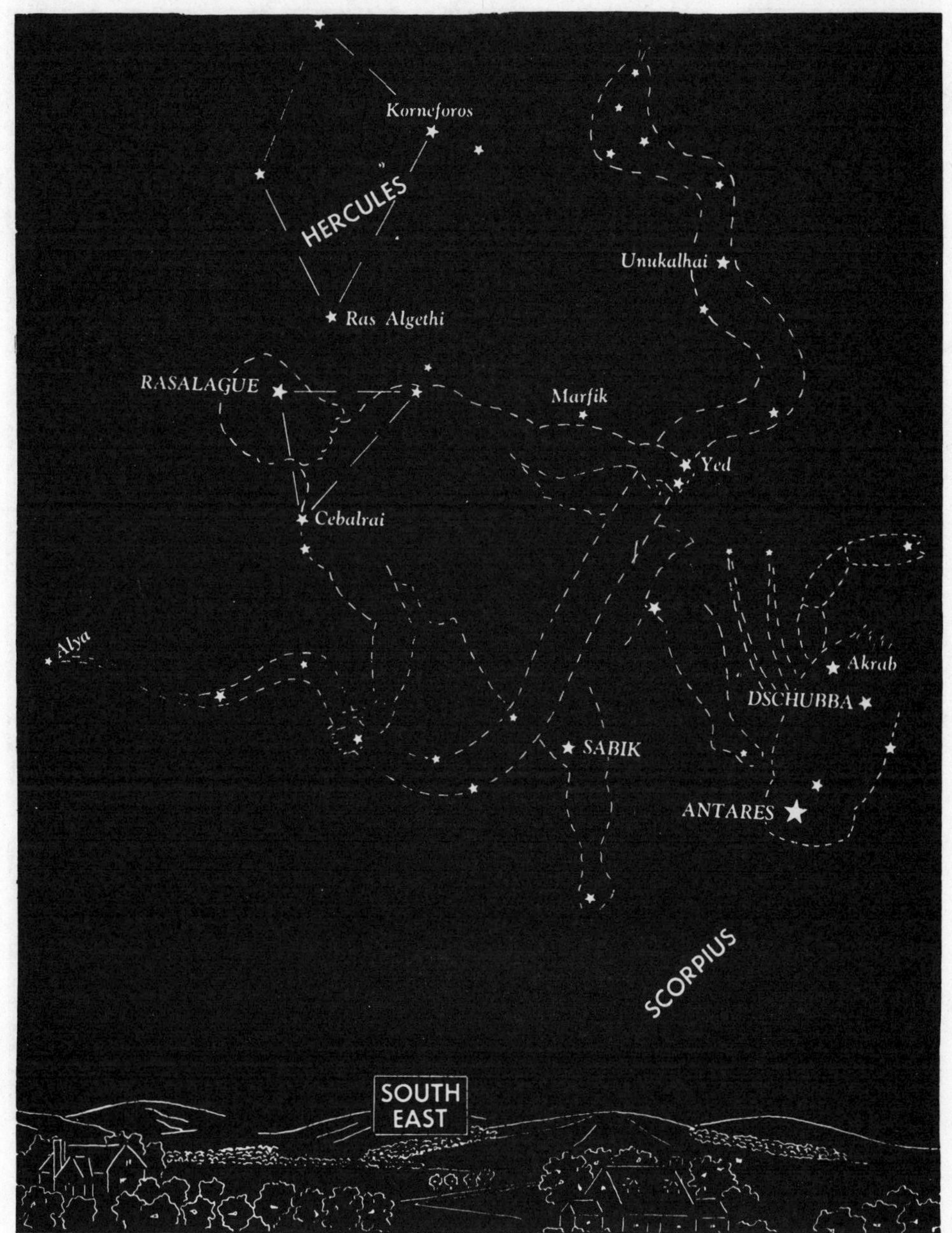


### Planet Warning

Ophiuchus is not included in the ancient list of constellations that form the Zodiac—the pathway followed by the wandering planets—but the Zodiac, in going from Sagittarius to Scorpius, passes across the feet of Ophiuchus and that area is therefore frequently invaded by planets.

If you see a bright "star" here that is not given in our charts, that "star" will be a planet.

# CHART 75

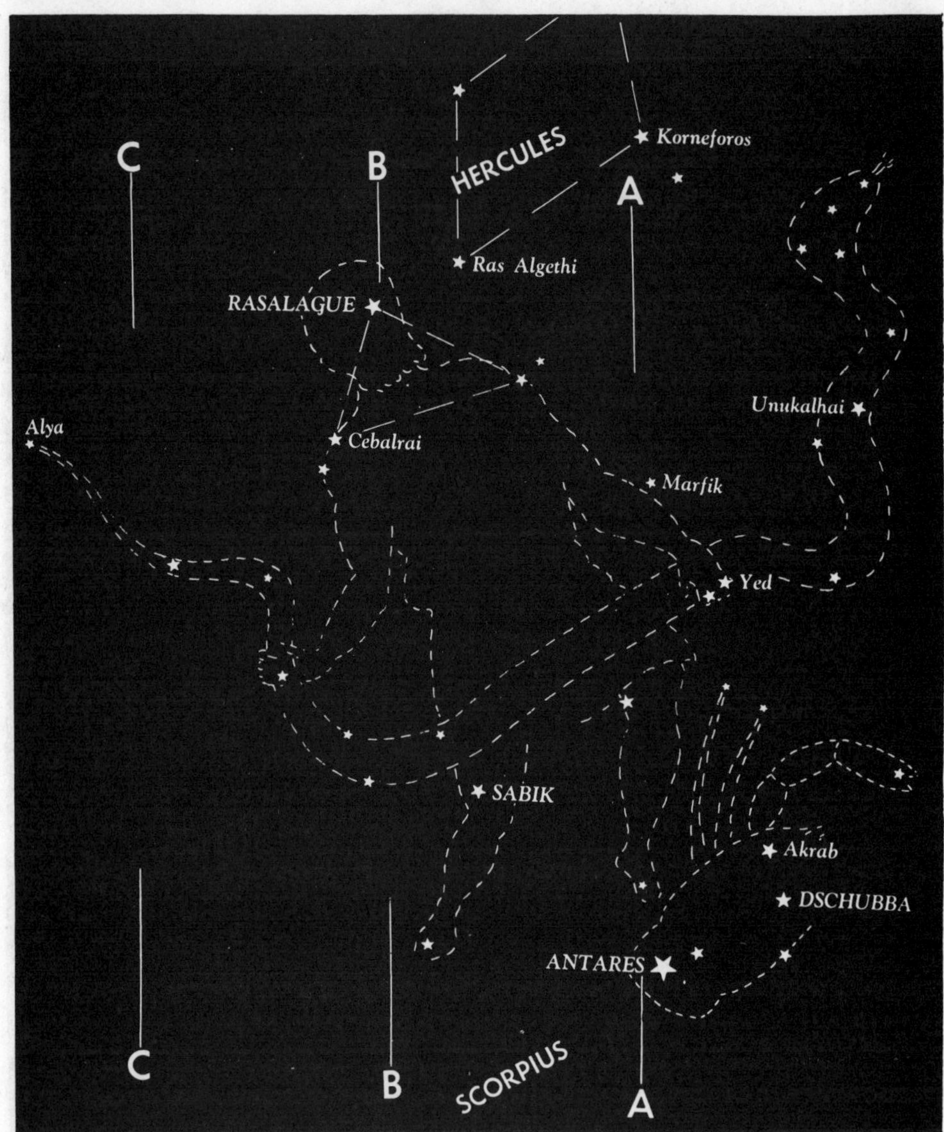


OPHIUCHUS AND SERPENS: This picture shows Ophiuchus passing across the southern meridian —his highest position in the sky. In all cases, face due south and raise the book until the giant's midriff is just halfway up the sky. The lines are to be held perpendicular to the horizon at the south point as directed in the Calendar and the Hour-and-Date Diagram.

Planets may appear in a part of Ophiuchus. See note with Chart 74.

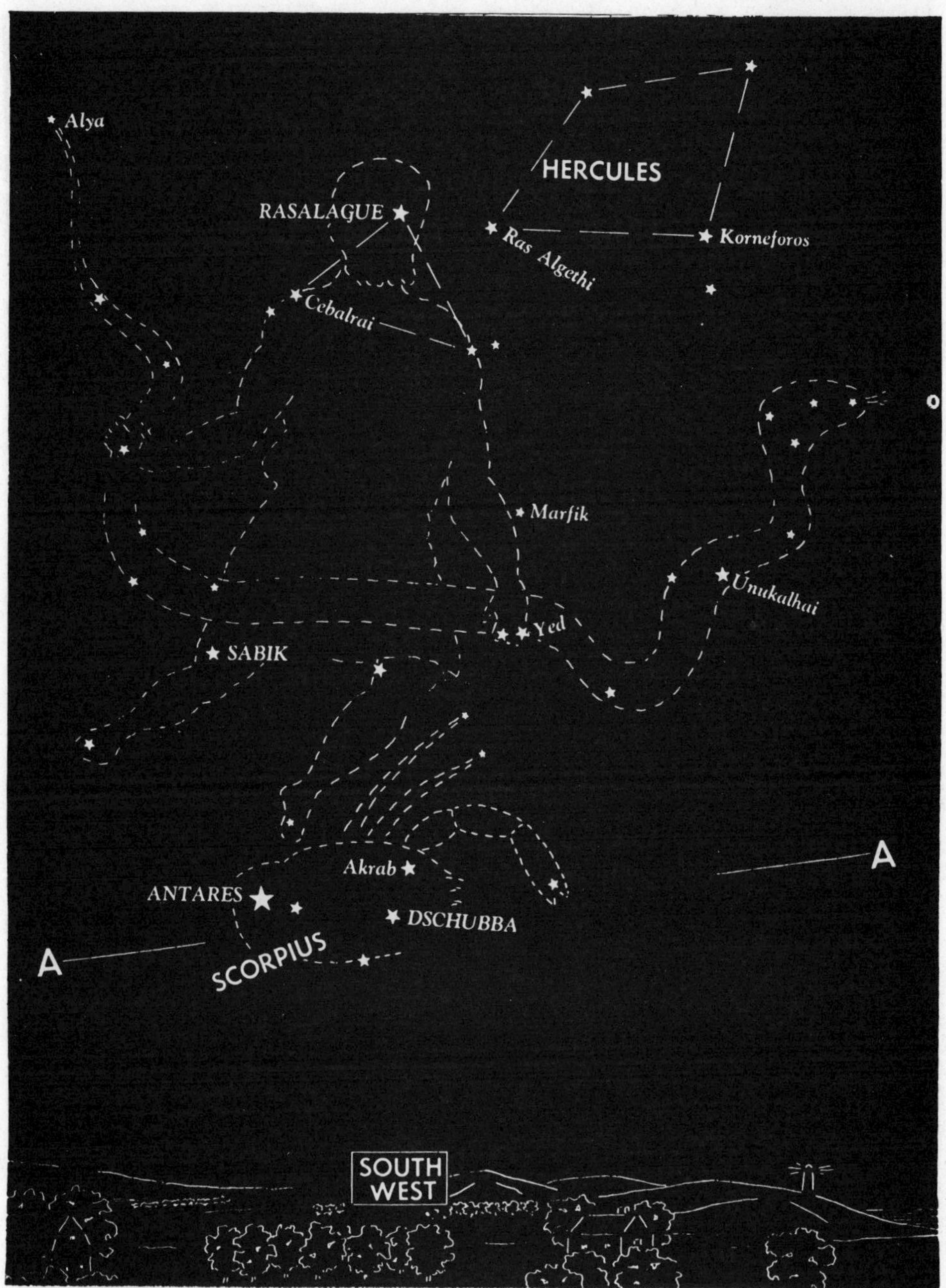


**Ophiuchus and Serpens:** Ignore the line AA unless it is called for in the instructions in the Calendar or the Hour-and-Date Diagram. If, however, the line is specified, it indicates that these stars are no longer so high and you must imagine them lowered until the line rests on the tops of the distant hills in the landscape.

Planets may appear in a part of Ophiuchus. See note with Chart 74.

# CHART 77

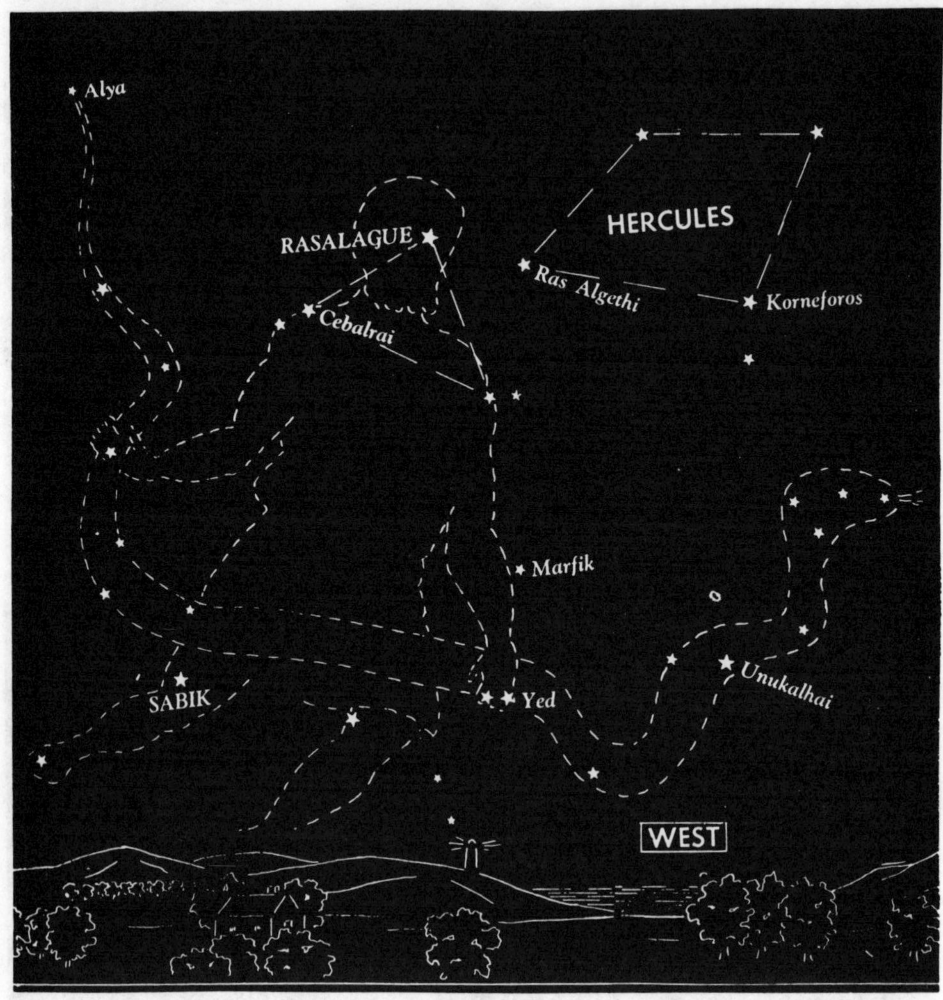


**Ophiuchus and Serpens:** Planets may appear in a part of Ophiuchus. See note with Chart 74.

## XXIII

## SCORPIUS AND HIS NEIGHBORS

THE constellation of Scorpius is so far south that early-evening star-gazers in mid-United States latitudes can see it satisfactorily in its entirety for only about a month—from mid-June to mid-July—and Canadians never can see the lowest curve of the tail.

But its most brilliant and interesting star, Antares, is well north of the tail so that it is visible for the entire summer, even to Canadians.

For far-southerners, Scorpius is a favorite constellation. It has many bright stars, arranged in an unmistakable figure, and it is one of the few groups that readily suggest the mythical form assigned to it by the ancients.

Furthermore, it is situated in a richly bejeweled part of the sky, with Lupus and Centaurus to the right (west) of it and sparkling Sagittarius, with its convincingly shaped Teapot, to the east.

In the charts of Scorpius that follow, only a few of the stars of these adjoining constellations are shown because only those stars can be seen by star-gazers who live much north of the Gulf coast or the Mexican border regions.

In very ancient picture maps of the heavens, Scorpius included the stars of the constellation Libra and his claws were stretched out to the two stars marked Alpha and Beta, the Greek letters now assigned to them. This history is preserved in the old common names which some writers still give these stars.

Alpha is Zuben el Genubi, which is from old Arabic words meaning "the southern claw," and Beta is Zuben es Chamali, meaning "the northern claw." Incidentally, Beta is said to be the only green star visible to the naked eye.

The modern idea, however, based on international agreement, is to make a strict division of the two constellations, and the boundaries accepted today give Libra even the two stars which our charts (based on the old Bayer figure) show in the shortened claws.

We can rid our minds of this confusion if we simply tell ourselves that the Scorpion is shown reaching into Libra to steal two stars to which it no longer has any claim.

The approximate boundaries of these constellations are shown on Chart 80.

Both the Zodiac, pathway of the planets, and the Milky Way pass through Scorpius so that a clear, warm summer night with good binoculars is likely to be a thrilling experience for a confirmed star-gazer. There is beautiful "sweeping" all through the group and a good glass will reveal several galaxies and globular star clusters, smaller brothers of the Andromeda Galaxy and the Great Cluster in Hercules.

The gleaming star Antares in Scorpius is one of the notable objects in our heavens. To the ancients, his distinctive red color suggested the planet Mars and the name Antares means "the rival of Ares," Ares being the Greek name for the God of War. The Chinese in the time of Confucius called the star Ta Who, "the great fire."

Antares is a super-giant star with attributes almost beyond our little earthly comprehension. Until recently, it was believed to be the largest of all visible stars, but later and more accurate methods of determination have shown that Ras Algethi, in Hercules, is actually far larger.

Still Antares is entitled to considerable respect, for its diameter is 330 times the diameter of our sun or about 36,000 times the diameter of the earth. In other words, if you imagine the earth the size of a baseball, you must imagine Antares as a ball nearly two miles in diameter.

Perhaps it is a mistake to refer to Antares as a ball. A ball suggests a solid and there is apparently nothing very solid about Antares. It is, in fact, so extremely tenuous that its

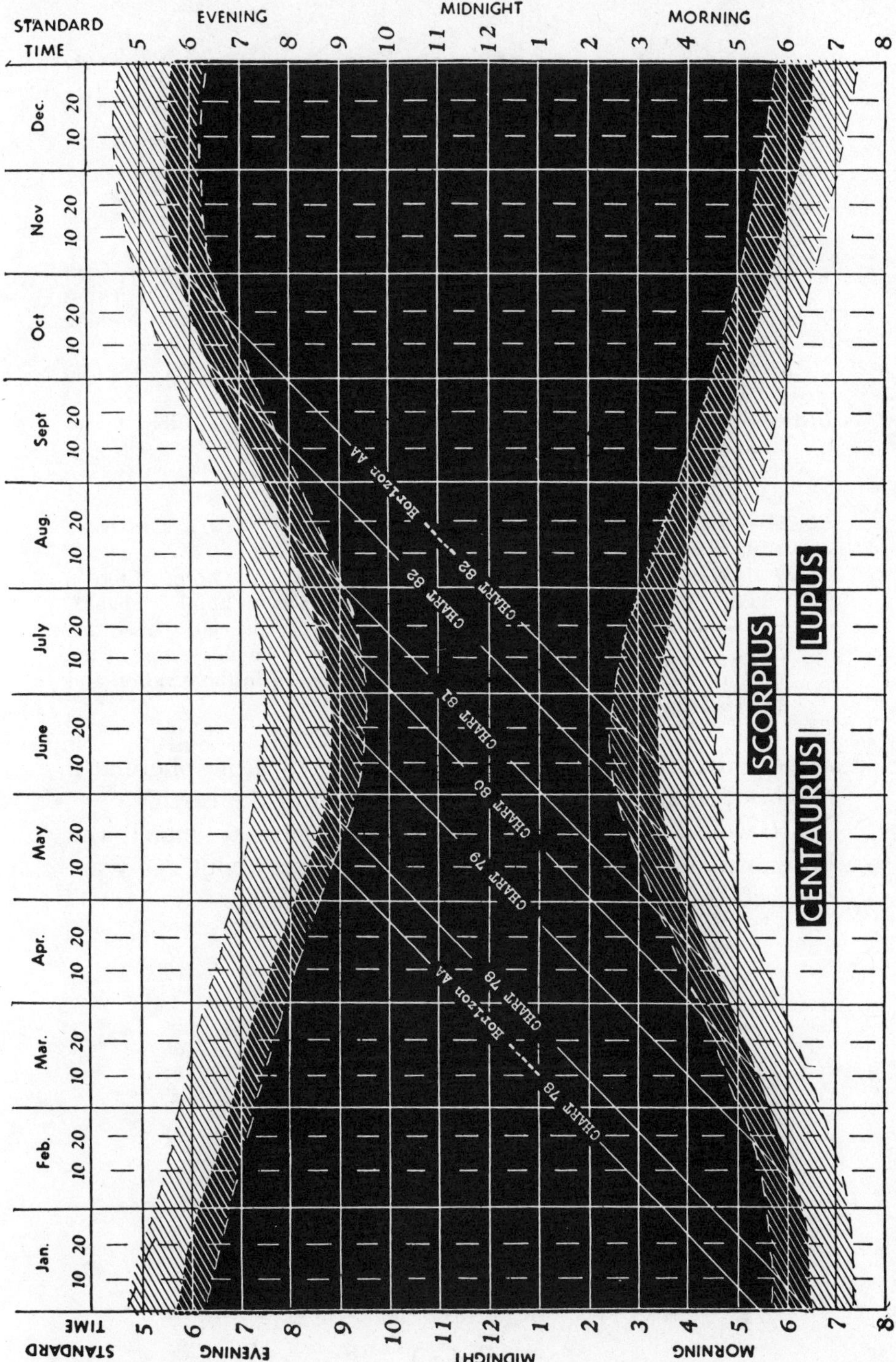


The diagonal line nearest to the hour and date desired shows the correct chart and line to be used at that time.

PRONUNCIATIONS

*SCORPIUS*—"score-pee-us." Accent "score."

ANTARES—"an-tare-eez." Accent "tare."

DSCHUBBA—"jub-a." Accent "jub" (rhymes with "tub," "rub"). Classicists strongly disapprove of this name but it has always been given thus in the government list of navigational stars so I am afraid there is nothing the classicists can do about it.

AKRAB—as spelled. Accent "ak." This star is also known as GRAFFIAS.

SHAULA—"shawl-a." Accent "shawl."

*LIBRA*—"lye-bra." Accent "lye" (rhymes with "try," "cry"). Libra means "the balance" or "weighing scales."

ALPHA—("al-fa"; accent "al") and BETA ("bay-ta"; accent "bay") are not names but are the Greek letters assigned to these stars.

*LUPUS*—"lew-puss." Accent "lew" (rhymes with "new," "few"). This name means "The Wolf."

*CENTAURUS*—"sen-tore-us." Accent "tore" (rhymes with "bore," "store").

THETA—"thay-ta." Accent "thay"; the "th" is soft as in "think," "thank." This is not a name but is a Greek letter assigned to the star. This is one Greek letter, however, that should be remembered, for this is one of the navigational stars for which complete data are given in the *Nautical* and the *Air Almanac.*

average density is comparable to that of our atmosphere at a height of some 21 miles above the surface of the earth.

It would require over 1900 of our suns to match the luminosity of this great star. Its light requires about 250 years to reach the earth.

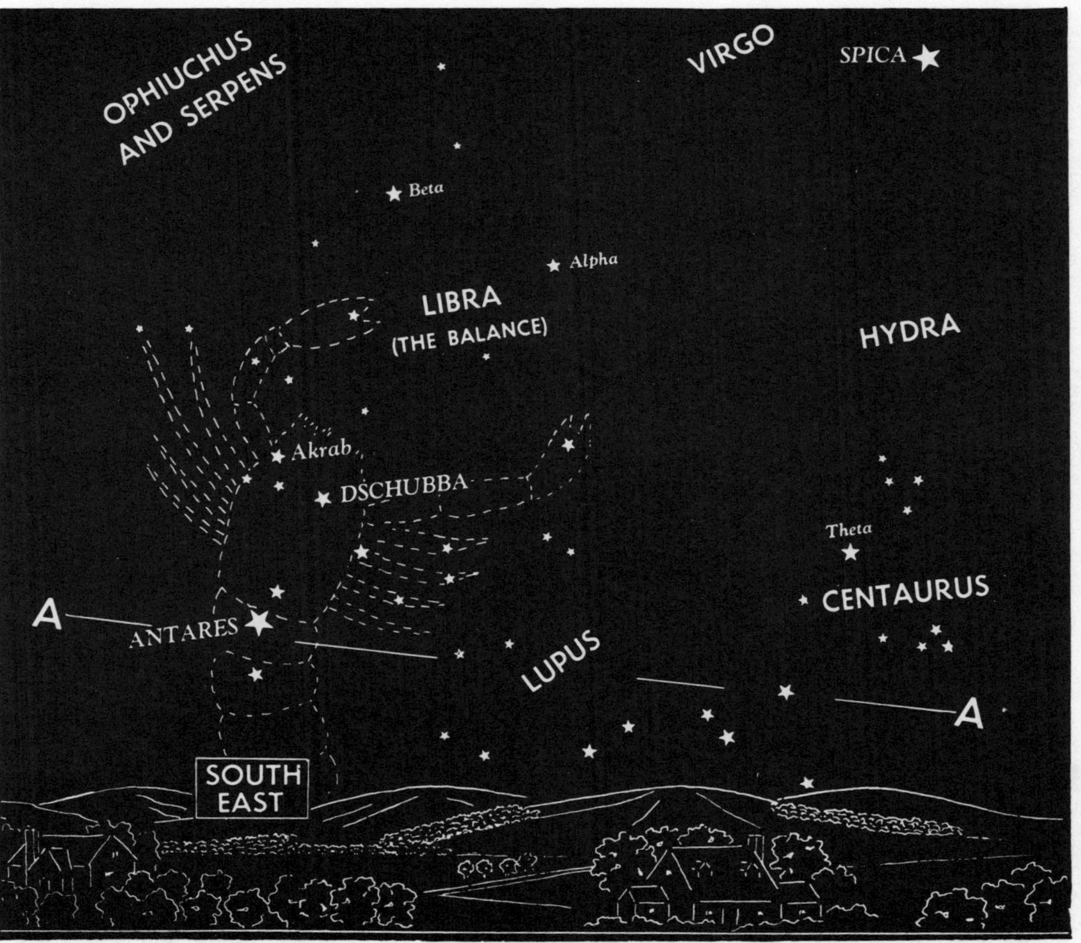


SCORPIUS: Scorpius begins to take form in the sky while his tail and part of his body are still below the horizon, as shown in this chart. The constellation of Libra, however, rises before the Scorpion and is in conspicuous position when Antares is still dimmed by the horizon haze and not yet visible to Canadians. At that time, the line AA will represent the horizon. The Calendar and the Hour-and-Date Diagram will tell you which to use.

The constellations of Scorpius and Libra are in the Zodiac—the pathway followed by the wandering planets. Beware of any strange "stars" among those in this picture. If the "star" is bright and is not shown here, it is a planet.

# CHART 79

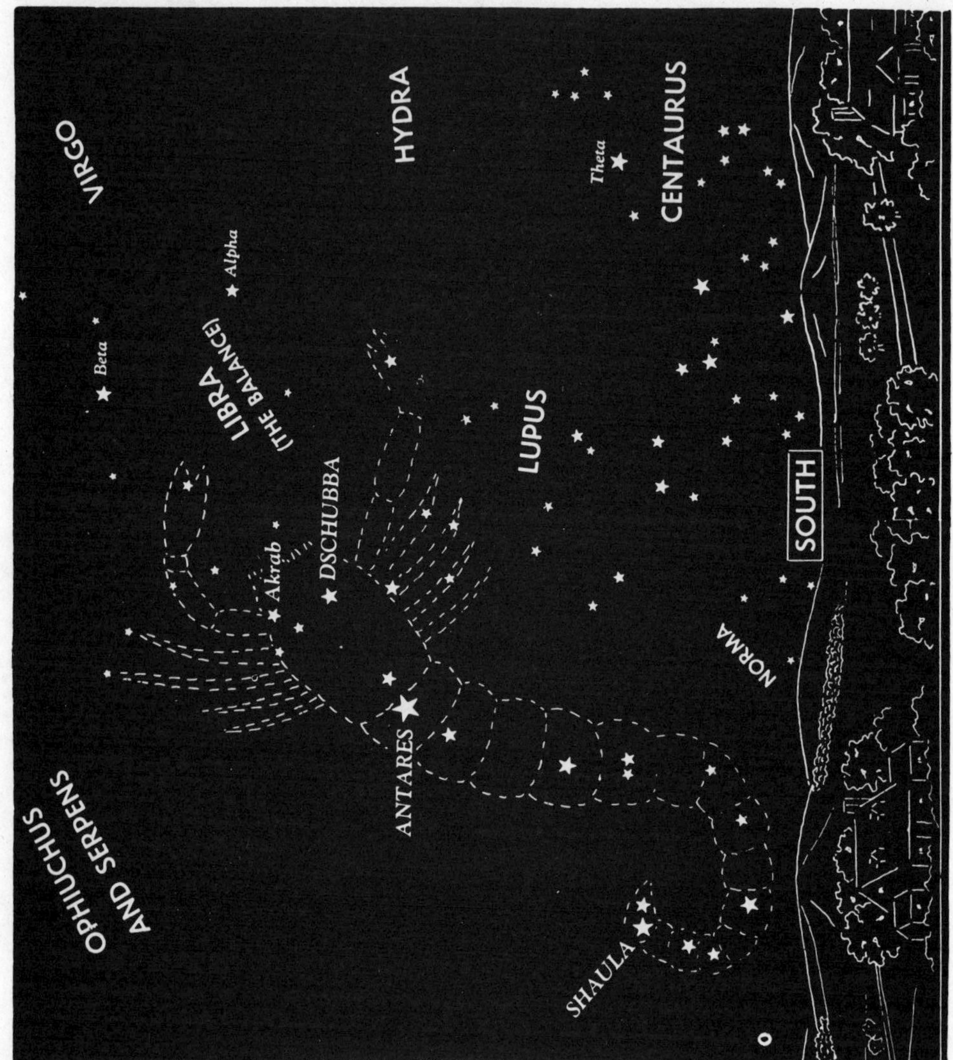


SCORPIUS: The constellations of Scorpius and Libra are in the Zodiac—the pathway followed by the wandering planets. Beware of any strange "stars" among those in this picture. If the "star" is bright and is not shown here, it is a planet.

## CHART 80

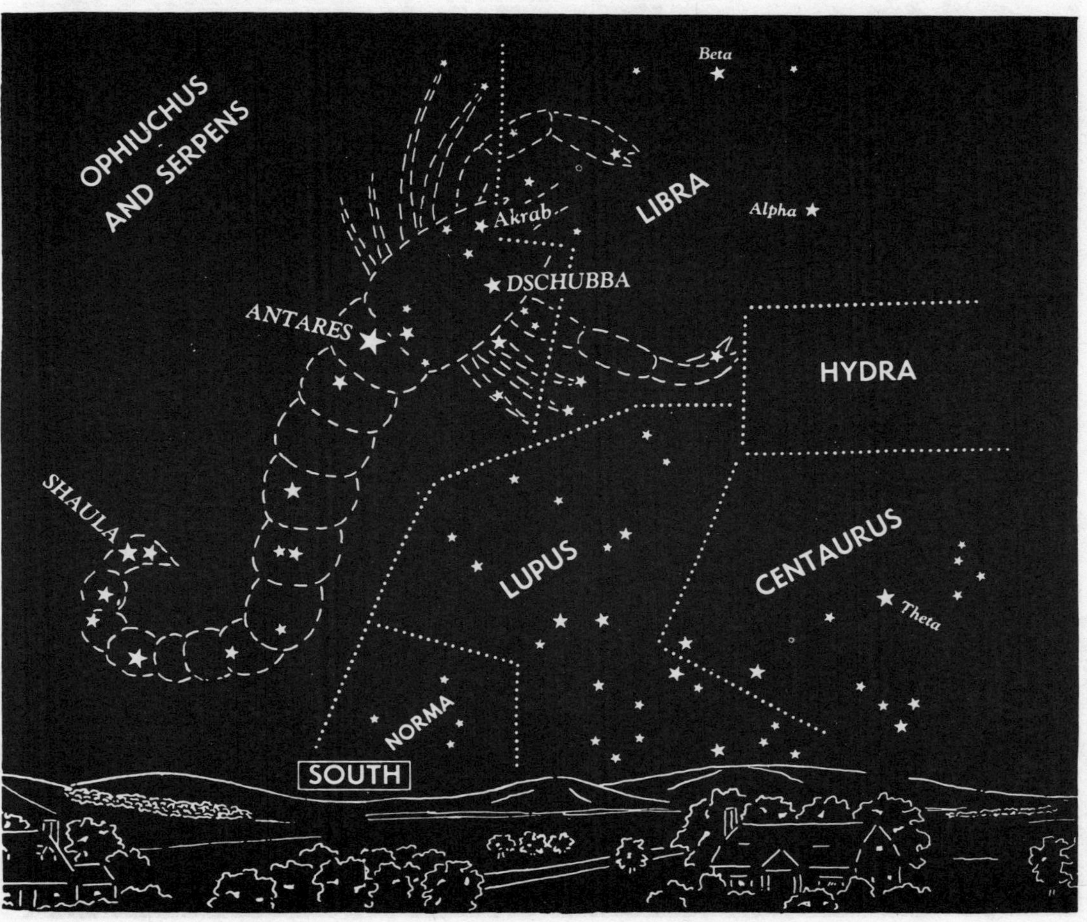


SCORPIUS: In this position, the Scorpion is at its highest point in the sky and gives us the best chance to study the sparkling stars under it. The dotted lines show the approximate boundaries of the various groups for those who like to keep them separated. Far-southerners will, of course, get the best view of these near-horizon stars and Canadians will find them too low for satisfactory observation.

The constellations of Scorpius and Libra are in the Zodiac—the pathway followed by the wandering planets. Beware of any strange "stars" among those in this picture. If the "star" is bright and is not shown here, it is a planet.

# CHART 81

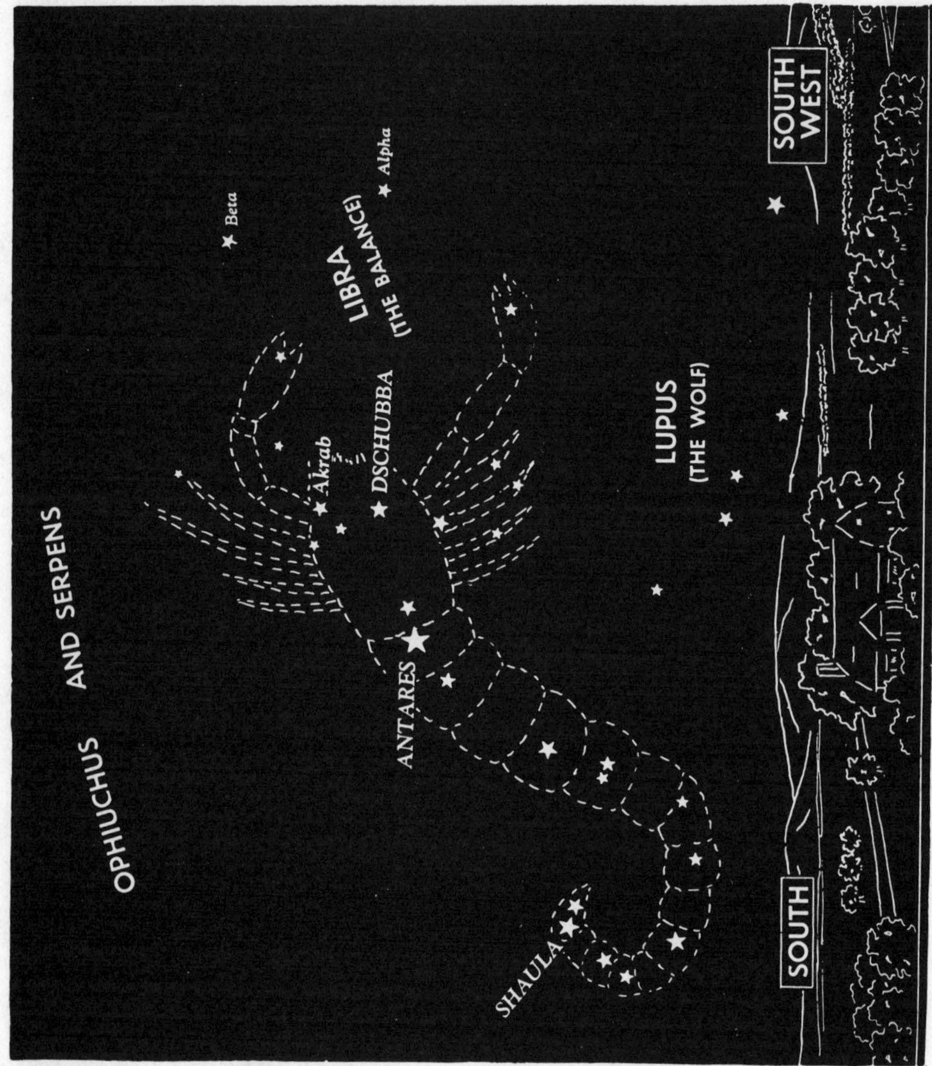


SCORPIUS: The constellations of Scorpius and Libra are in the Zodiac—the pathway followed by the wandering planets. Beware of any strange "stars" among those in this picture. If the "star" is bright and is not shown here, it is a planet.

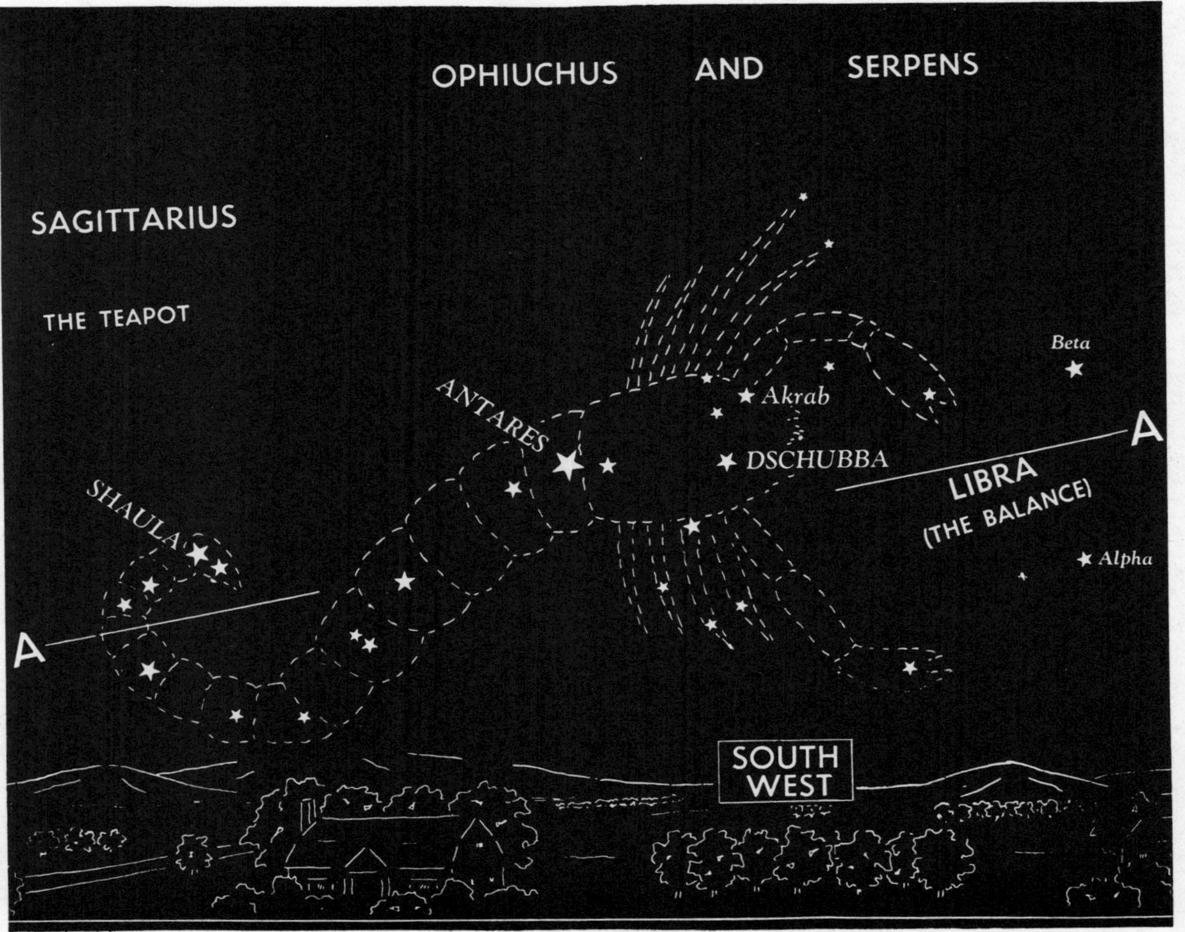


SCORPIUS: If the Calendar or the Hour-and-Date Diagram does not stipulate that the line AA is to be used, Scorpius will be found as in this picture—our last chance to see the figure in its entirety. It will gradually sink until the line AA becomes the horizon and even bright Antares is dimmed by the haze and not visible to Canadians.

The constellations of Scorpius and Libra are in the Zodiac—the pathway followed by the wandering planets. Beware of any strange "stars" among those in this picture. If the "star" is bright and is not shown here, it is a planet.

## XXIV

# SAGITTARIUS AND THE TEAPOT

THE Teapot, in the constellation of Sagittarius, marks a region of the sky which is of the utmost interest to scientists who are trying to solve the mysteries of the universe in which our earth is no more than a microscopic mote of cosmic dust.

Some faint idea of the amazing density of the star and cloud population of this region may be gained from the photograph on the opposite page. This picture, taken by the Yerkes Observatory, shows only a small part of the immense "star cloud" we find in Sagittarius but it is enough to stagger the imagination when we consider that every bright speck in the photograph is the image of a great star, probably bigger and brighter than our sun.

Over the entire area, we see vast clouds, some bright, some dark. This is interstellar dust or "stuff" floating in space throughout our galaxy. The dark areas represent clouds which are between us and the stars beyond and that thus veil much of the light; the bright clouds are illuminated by the light of thousands of stars immersed in them.

With the naked eye, we see this luminous area only as a part of what we call the Milky Way; with good binoculars, we see scintillating groups of the nearer stars, but it requires a long-exposure photograph with a great telescope to register the images shown in the picture.

The modern conception of the great disc-shaped system of several billion stars of which our sun is one is explained in the text and photographs in the chapter on Andromeda where various systems are presented as approximations of what we believe our own galaxy to be.

The outstanding feature of all the galaxies is the swollen, highly luminous central condensation about which all the

*Yerkes Observatory Photograph*

STAR CLOUD IN SAGITTARIUS

outer rim and arms of a system seem to revolve like a great wheel.

Scientists now believe that the crowded area around the Teapot in Sagittarius marks this "hub" or central condensation in our own galactic system. It seems to be the nucleus about which the sun and all the outer stars turn at a rate of speed that apparently requires something like 200,000,000 of our earthly years to make one complete revolution, or one "galactic year."

It is in this region of the sky that the great observatory photographs find an overwhelming percentage of the "globular clusters" like the Great Cluster in Hercules, and these objects are believed to be fairly evenly distributed in a sort of "shell" around the nucleus of our system. Of the 100 or more globular clusters known, fully 90 per cent lie (as seen from the earth) in the direction of Sagittarius and Scorpius.

The bright figure which we visualize as the Teapot (or the Milk Dipper or the Bow and Arrow) is, of course, only a small part of the constellation to which it belongs. The name Sagittarius means "the Archer," and the ancient picture maps of the sky trace among its stars the figure of a centaur—half man, half horse—with the man part holding a bow and arrow aimed at the Scorpion.

The drawings on the opposite page give the three different conceptions and you are, of course, at perfect liberty to make your own choice among them. In our charts on the pages that follow we adopt the Teapot as being the easiest and as including the most stars. The idea of the ancient archer with his bow and arrow is, however, perpetuated in the names of some of the stars whose meanings are given with their pronunciations later in this chapter.

The entire area of the sky covered by Sagittarius, little Scutum, the head of the Scorpion and the feet of Ophiuchus is a rich field for "sweeping" with good binoculars. There are many clusters and nebulae around the Teapot, particularly above its lid. Some of these are visible to the naked eye as

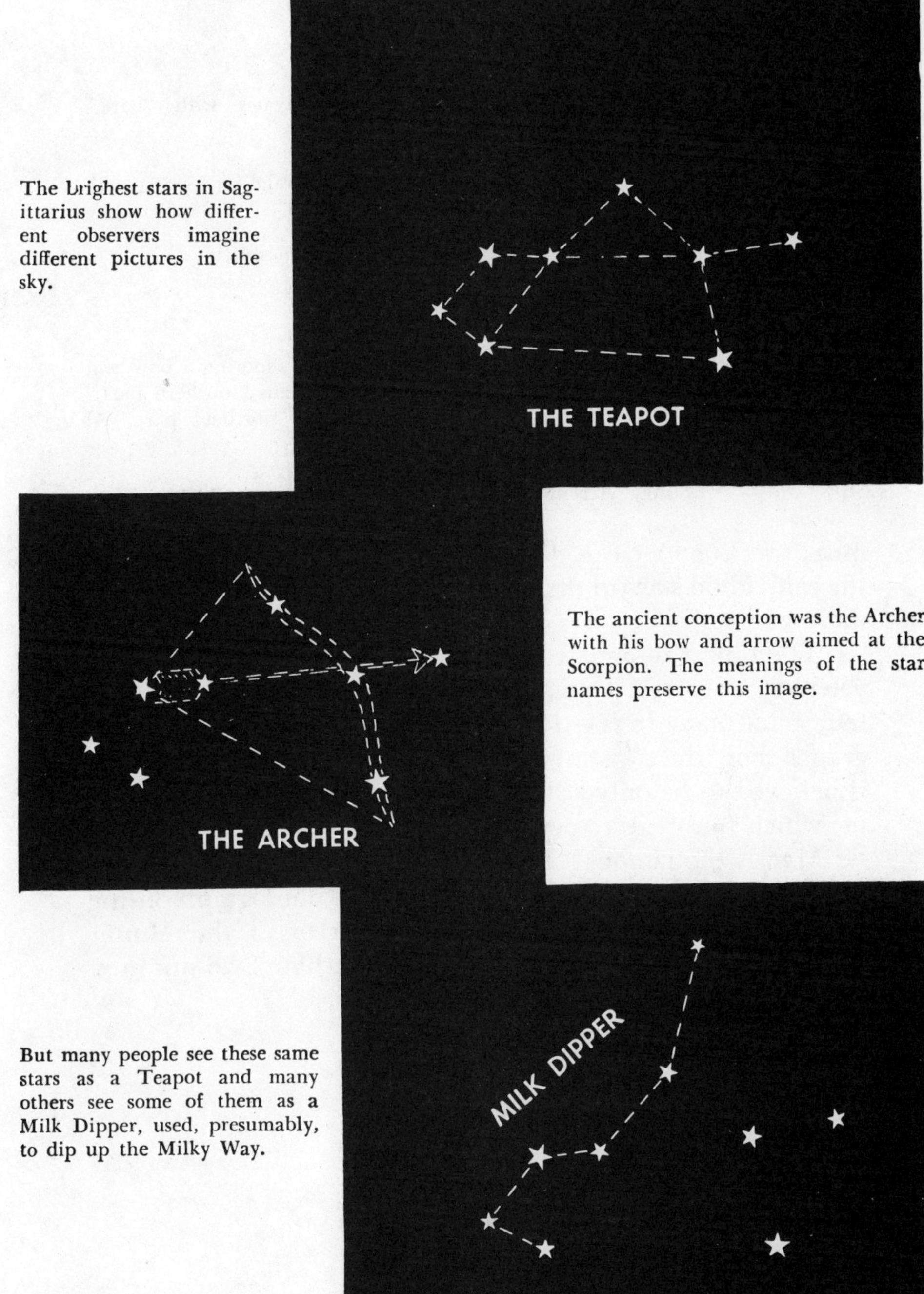


The brighest stars in Sagittarius show how different observers imagine different pictures in the sky.

The ancient conception was the Archer with his bow and arrow aimed at the Scorpion. The meanings of the star names preserve this image.

But many people see these same stars as a Teapot and many others see some of them as a Milk Dipper, used, presumably, to dip up the Milky Way.

PRONUNCIATIONS

*SAGITTARIUS*—"saj-it-tare-ee-us." Accent "tare" (rhymes with "bare," "care").

NUNKI—"nun-kee." Accent "nun."

KAUS AUSTRALIS—"koss oss-trale-iss." Accent "trale" (rhymes with "whale"). The "o's" have the sound of "o" in "lord," "orb" etc.

KAUS MEDIA—"koss mee-dee-a." Accent "mee."

KAUS BOREALIS—"koss bo-ree-ale-iss." Accent "ale." The "bo" rhymes with "go," "so."

AL NASL—"al naze-'l." Accent "naze."

Ancient sky pictures represent Sagittarius as a centaur shooting a bow and arrow. The word "Kaus" means "bow." "Australis" means "southern part," "Media" means "middle part" and "Borealis" means "northern part." Al Nasl means the "point of the arrow."

*SCUTUM*—"skew-tum." Accent "skew." The word means "the Shield."

misty specks on a clear, dark night. Binoculars will not reveal the individual stars in the clusters but will identify the objects more easily.

The object designated as M8 is one of the favorites with veteran star-gazers, particularly with owners of first-class amateur telescopes. It is a loose cluster and observatory photographs show the stars involved in much nebulous matter. M8 is believed to be only a little over 1500 light-years away from us, which makes it a very "close" neighbor.

M20 is the famous "Trifid" Nebula, beyond the reach of binoculars but an impressive object in the photograph on the next page, taken with the 60-inch reflector of the Mount Wilson Observatory with an exposure of 2 hours, 26 minutes

The "Trifid" Nebula in Sagittarius as photographed with the 60-inch reflector at the Mount Wilson Observatory.

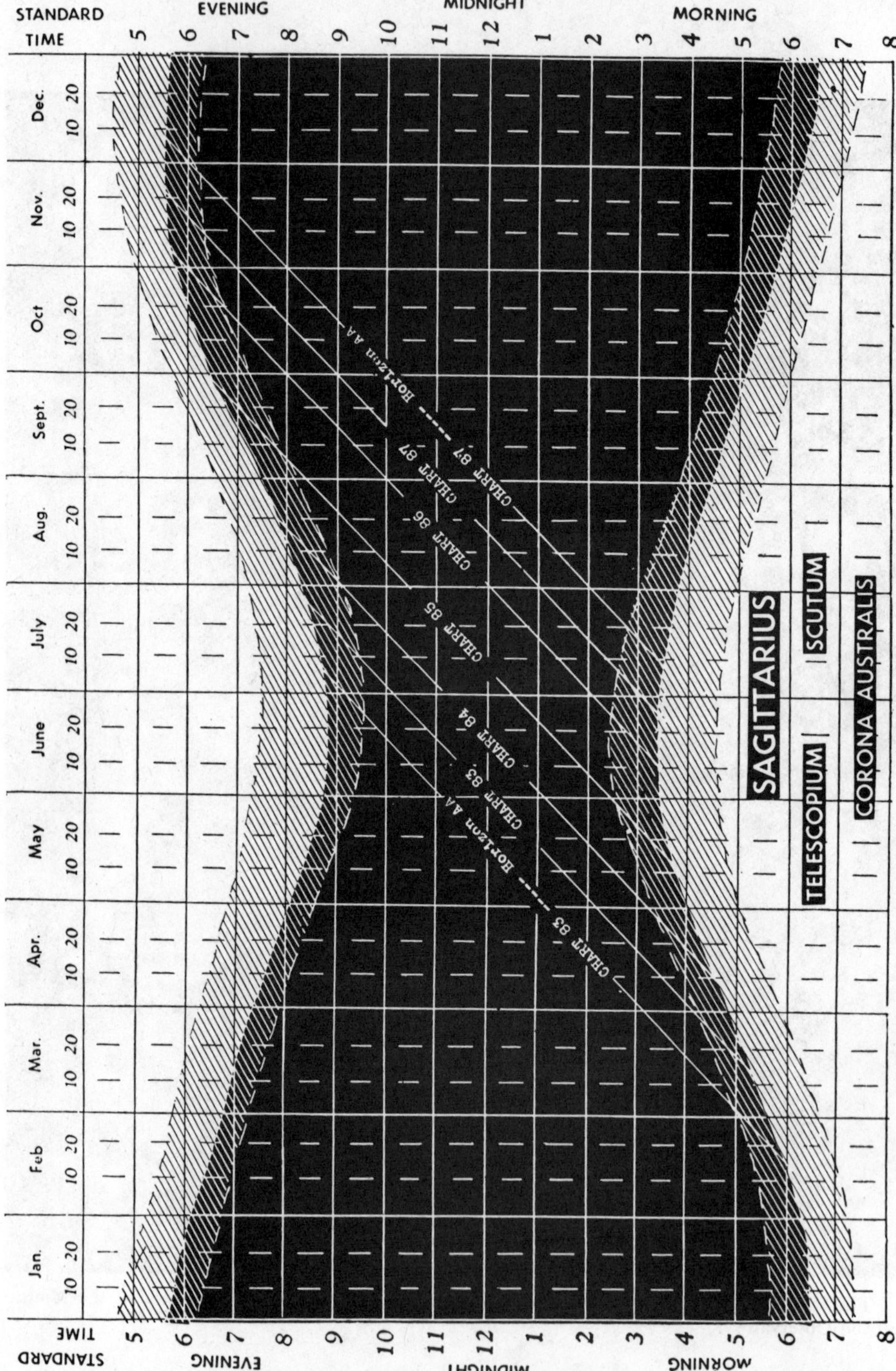


The diagonal line nearest to the hour and date desired shows the correct chart and line to be used at that time.

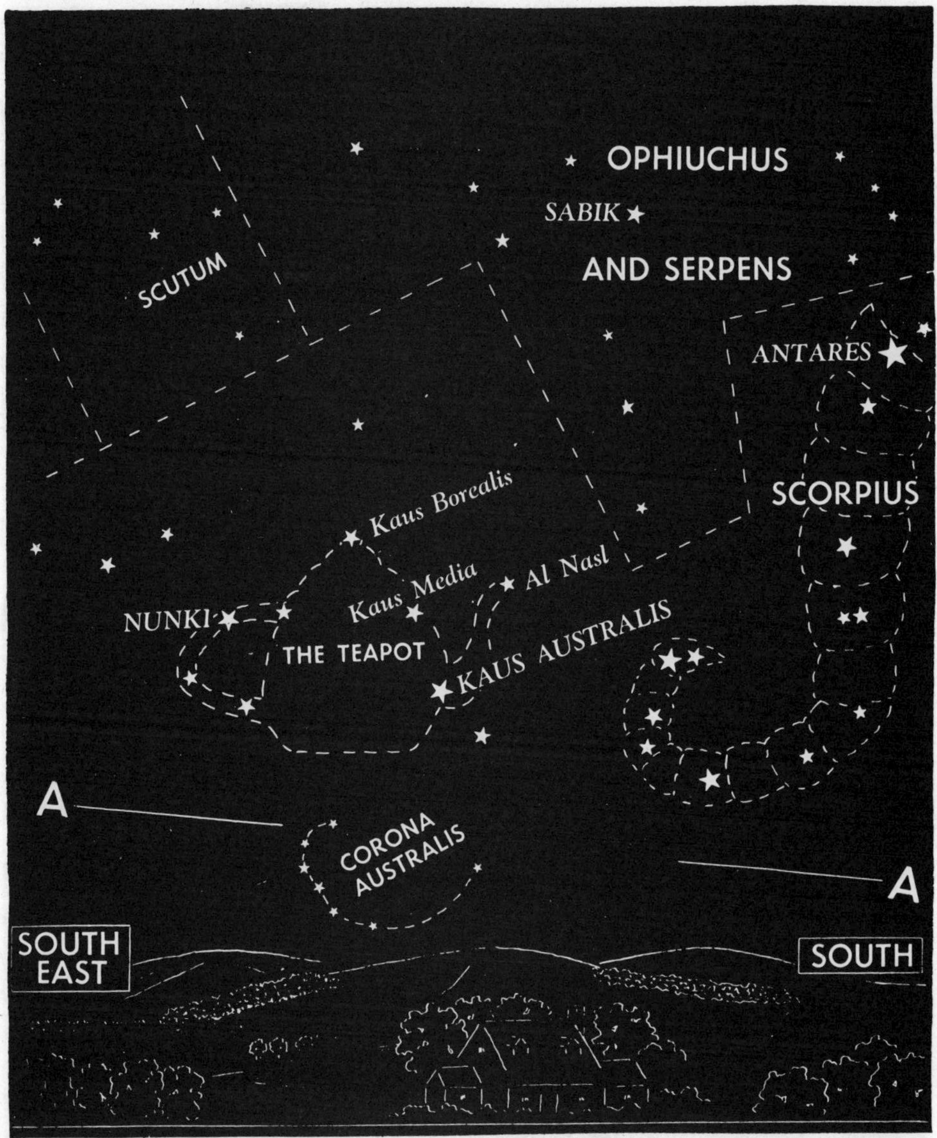


SAGITTARIUS: Whenever Chart 83 is called for in the Calendar or the Hour-and-Date Diagram, this picture is to be used without reference to the line AA. If, however, this line is specified, it means that these stars are not yet so high and you must imagine them all lowered until the line AA rests on the tops of the distant hills in the landscape.

The constellation of Sagittarius is in the Zodiac—the pathway followed by the wandering planets. Beware of any strange "stars" in this area. If the "stars" are bright and are not shown in this picture, they are planets.

# CHART 84

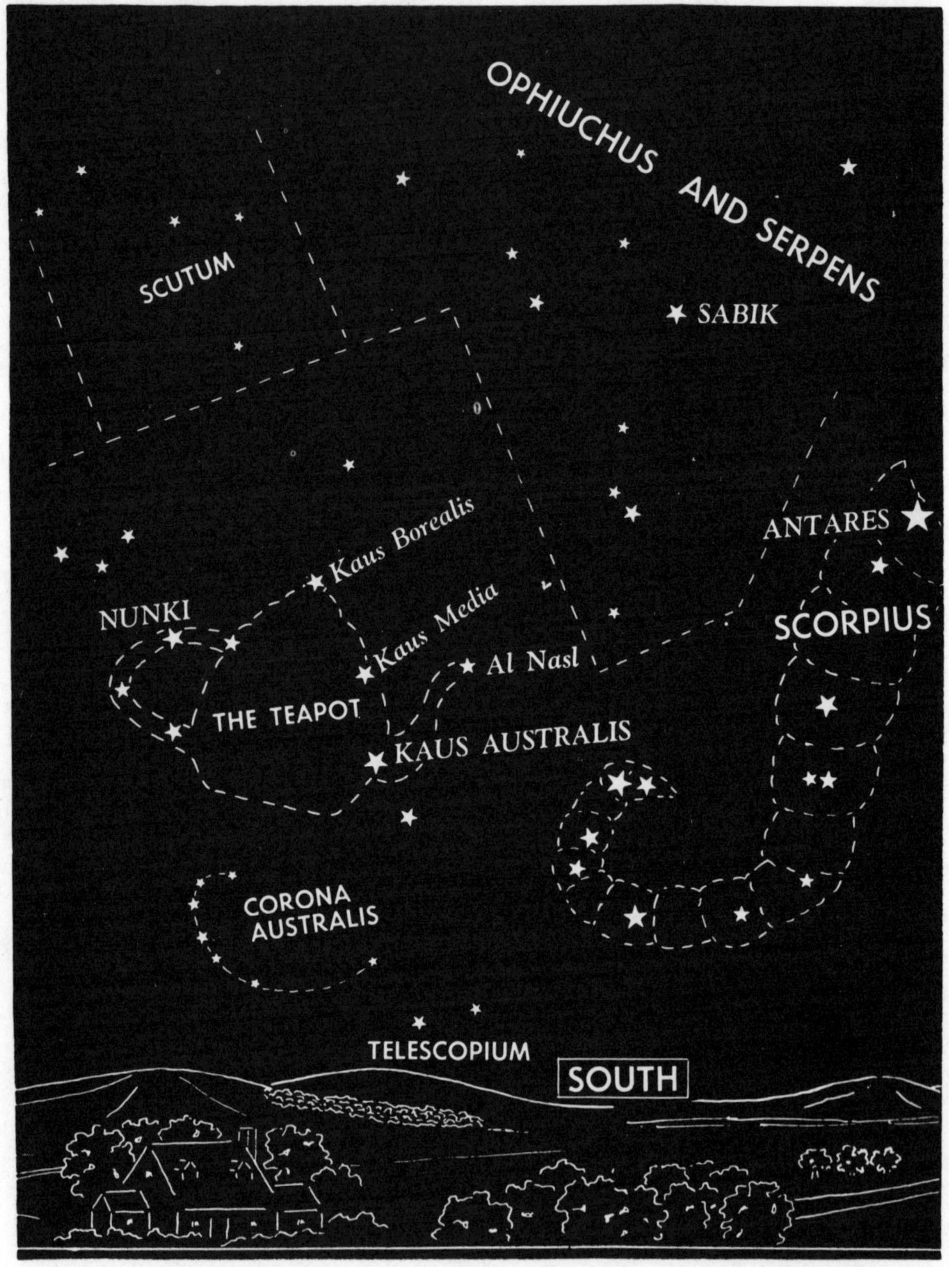


SAGITTARIUS: The constellation of Sagittarius is in the Zodiac—the pathway followed by the wandering planets. Beware of any strange "stars" in this area. If the "stars" are bright and are not shown in this picture, they are planets.

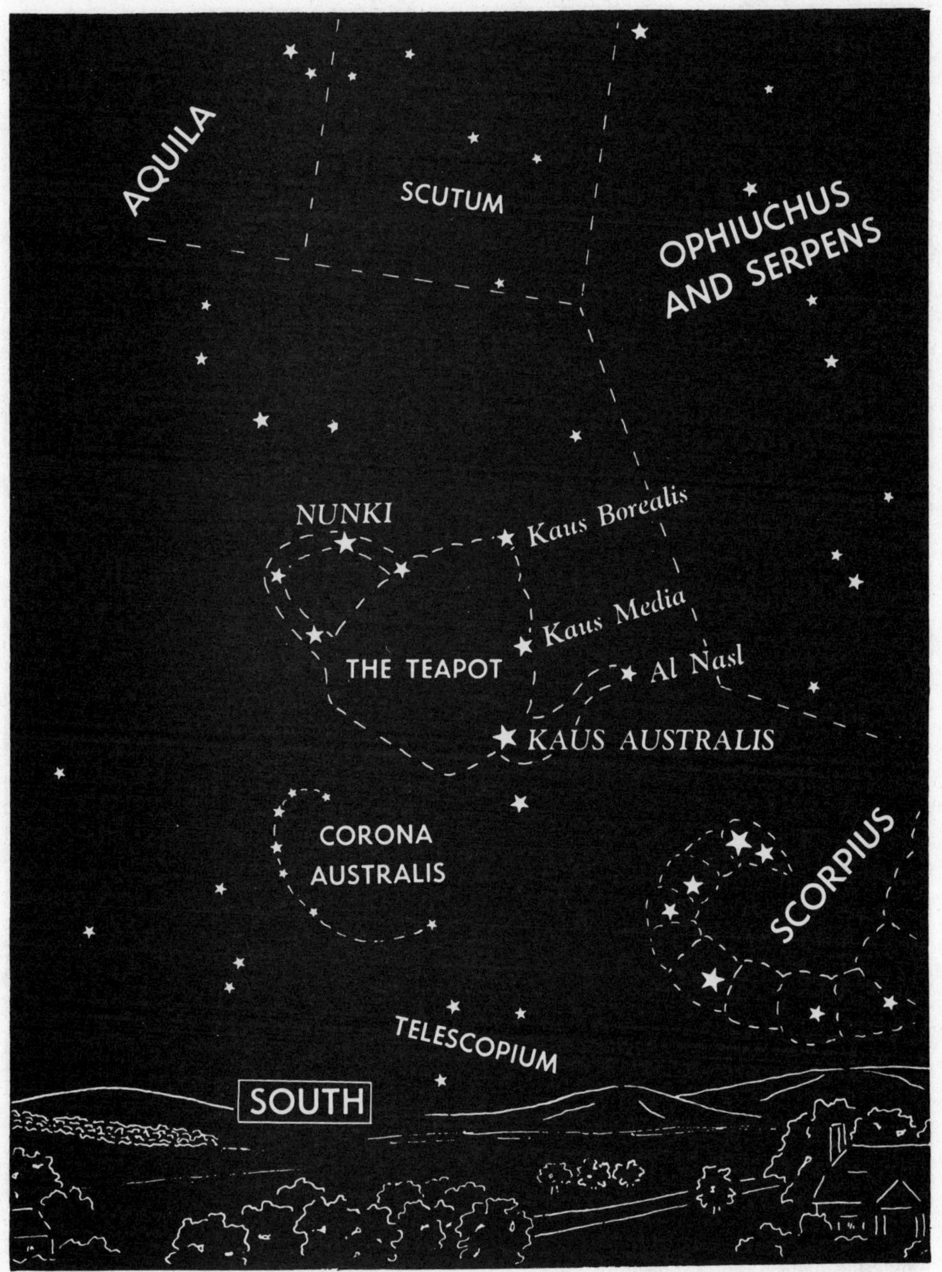


**Sagittarius:** The Constellation of Sagittarius is in the Zodiac—the pathway followed by the wandering planets. Beware of any strange "stars" in this area. If the "stars" are bright and are not shown in this picture, they are planets.

# CHART 86

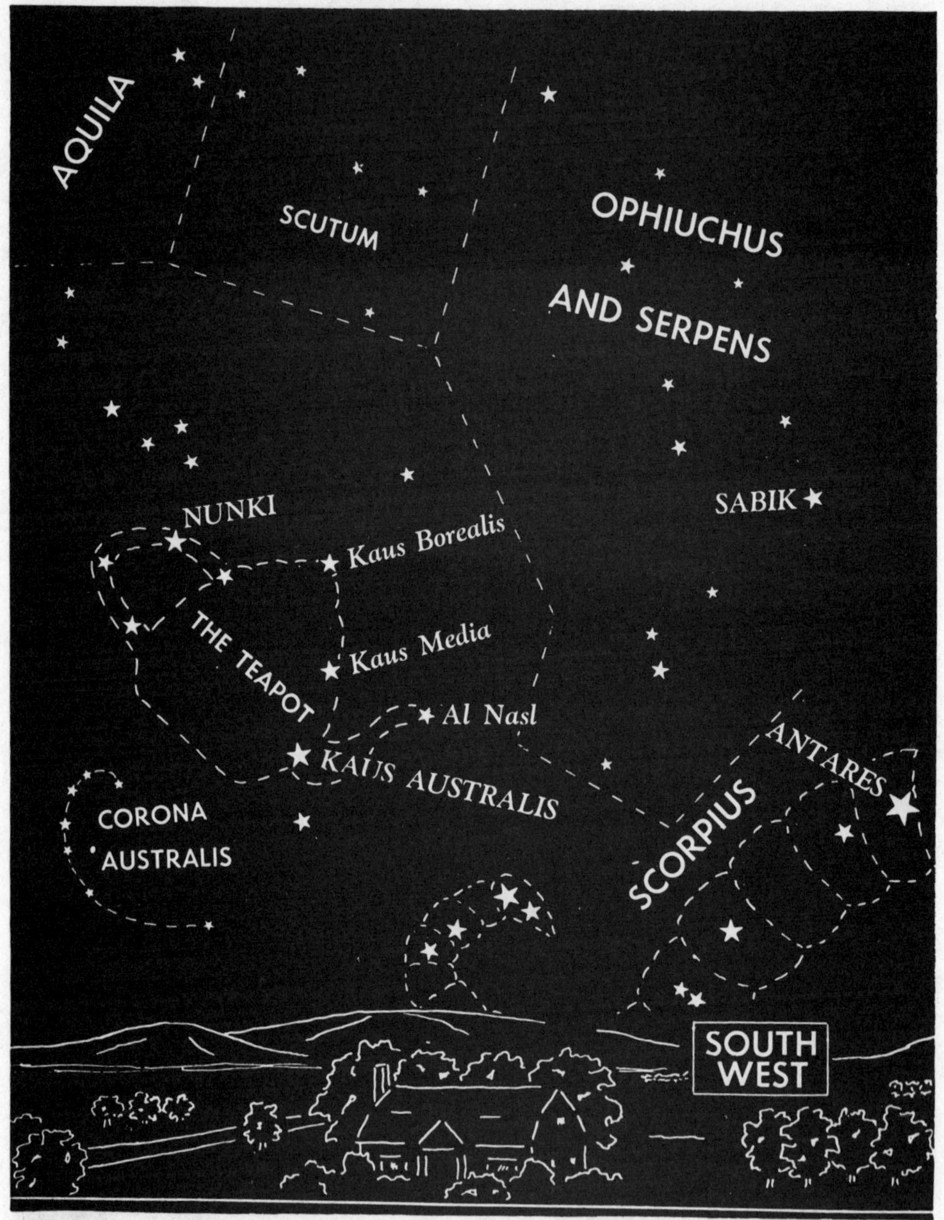


**Sagittarius:** The Constellation of Sagittarius is in the Zodiac—the pathway followed by the wandering planets. Beware of any strange "stars" in this area. If the "stars" are bright and are not shown in this picture, they are planets.

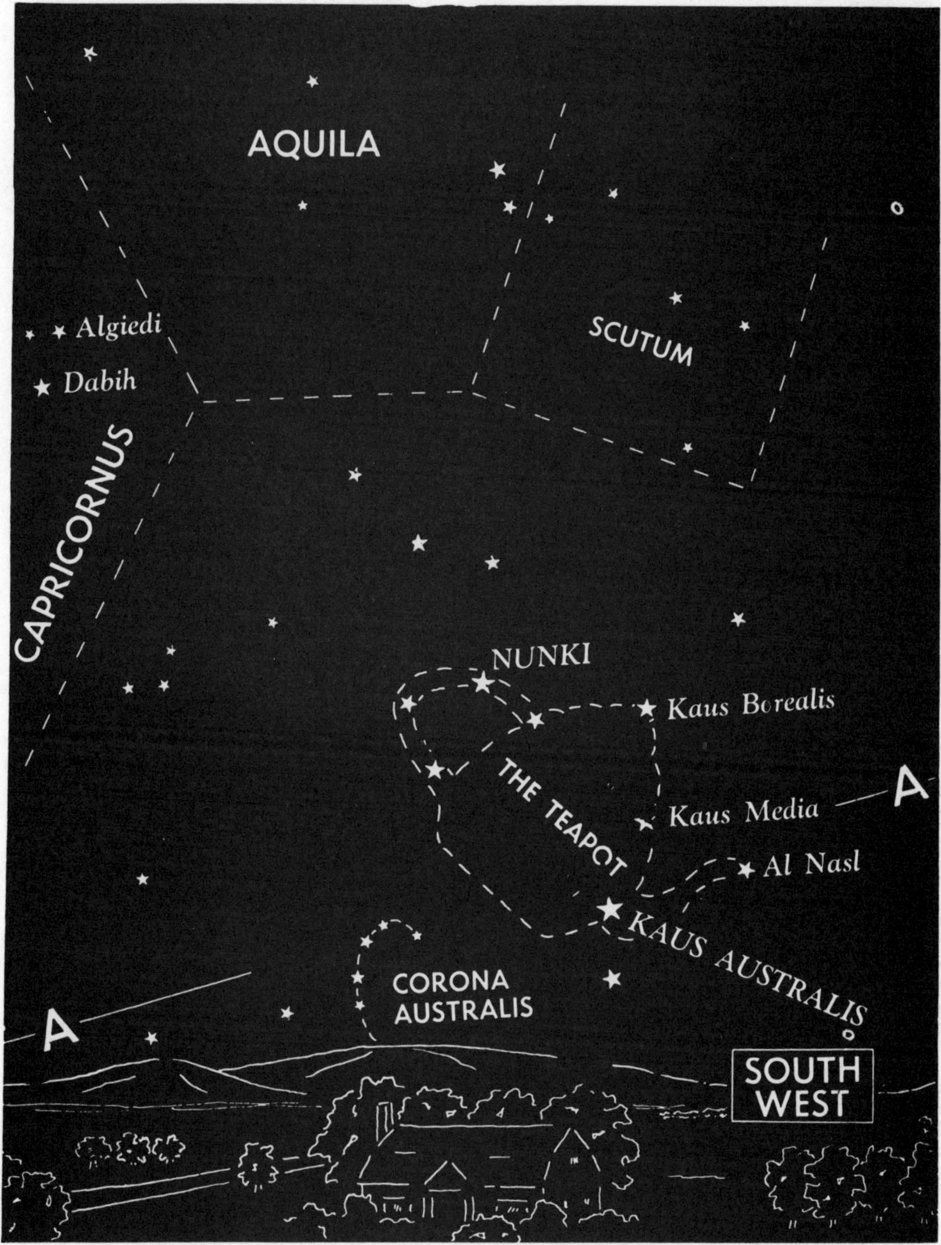


SAGITTARIUS: The picture is to be used "as is," ignoring line AA, whenever Chart 87 is called for in the Calendar or the Hour-and-Date Diagram. When, however, line AA is stipulated, it means that these stars are no longer so high and you must imagine them lowered until line AA rests on the tops of the distant hills in the landscape.

The constellation of Sagittarius is in the Zodiac—the pathway followed by the wandering planets. Beware of any strange "stars" in this area. If the "stars" are bright and are not shown in this picture, they are planets.

# GROUPS
*for*
# ADVANCED STAR-GAZERS

## PISCES, THE FISHES

THE lines AA, BB, CC, etc. on Chart 88 are always to be turned to the vertical and the particular line to use at any time will be specified.

Instructions for each line follow:

AA—face halfway between east and northeast. The word "Pisces" on the map will be the horizon and stars below it will not be seen.

BB—face east; the horizon is just above the star Al Rischa.

CC—face east; Al Rischa is now above the horizon; Alpheratz is halfway up the sky.

DD—face halfway between east and southeast; the "northern fish" (the little stars in Pisces near Mirach) is halfway up the sky.

EE—face halfway between east and southeast; hold the word "Pisces" halfway up the sky.

FF—face southeast; Al Rischa is almost halfway up the sky.

GG—face halfway between southeast and south; Al Rischa is now a little more than halfway up the sky.

HH—face south; the area from Mirach to Almach is overhead.

JJ—face halfway between west and southwest; the left corner of the Great Square is halfway up the sky.

KK—face halfway between west and southwest; Al Rischa is halfway up the sky.

LL—face west; Mirach is halfway up the sky.

MM—face halfway between west and northwest; the Great Square is setting; the group of Pisces stars near Aquarius has set.

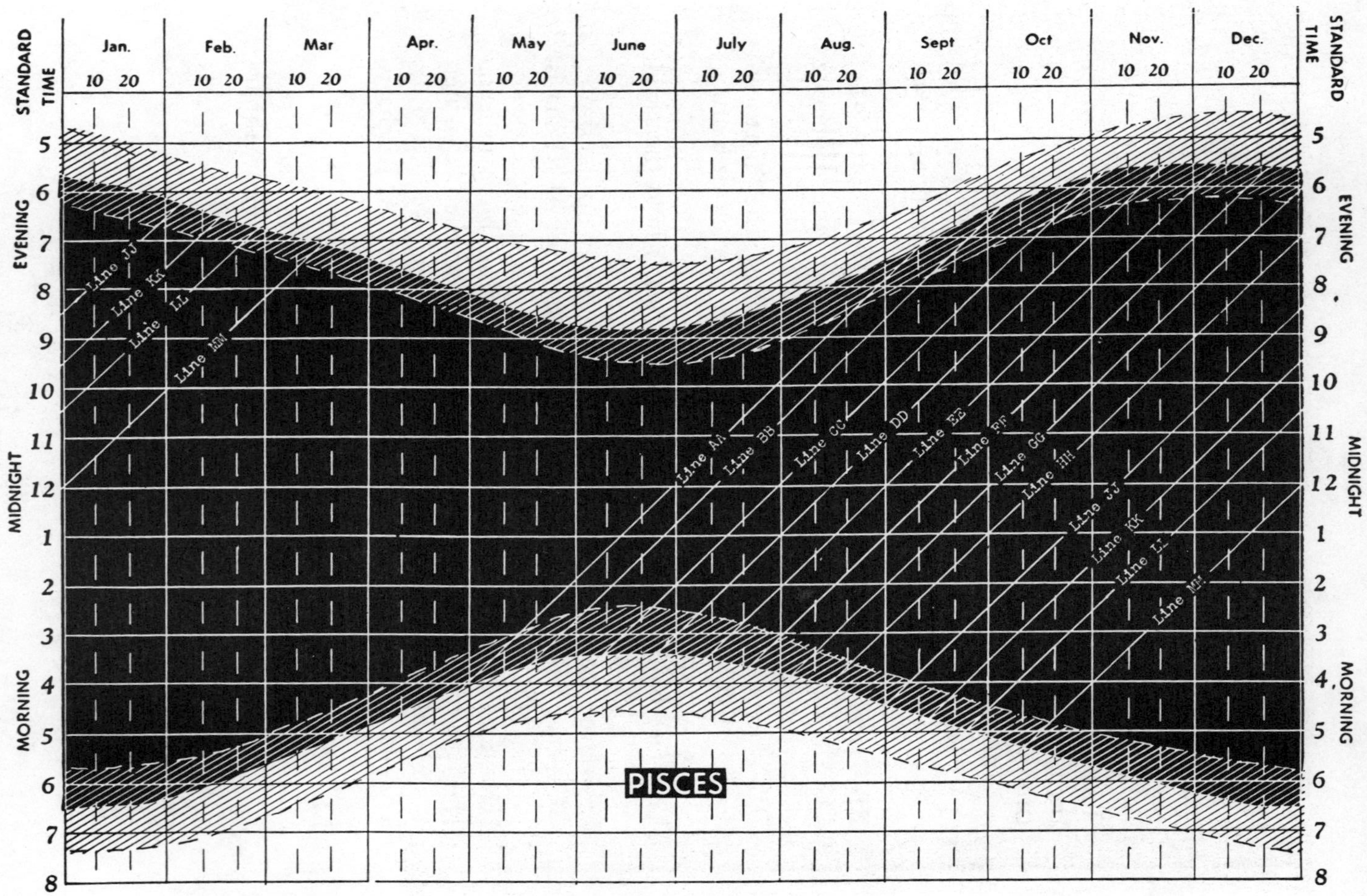
STANDARD TIME
EVENING
MIDNIGHT
MORNING
5 6 7 8 9 10 11 12 1 2 3 4 5 6 7 8
Jan. 10 20
Feb. 10 20
Mar 10 20
Apr. 10 20
May 10 20
June 10 20
July 10 20
Aug. 10 20
Sept 10 20
Oct 10 20
Nov. 10 20
Dec. 10 20
Line AA
Line BB
Line CC
Line DD
Line EE
Line FF
Line GG
Line HH
Line JJ
Line KK
Line LL
Line MM
PISCES

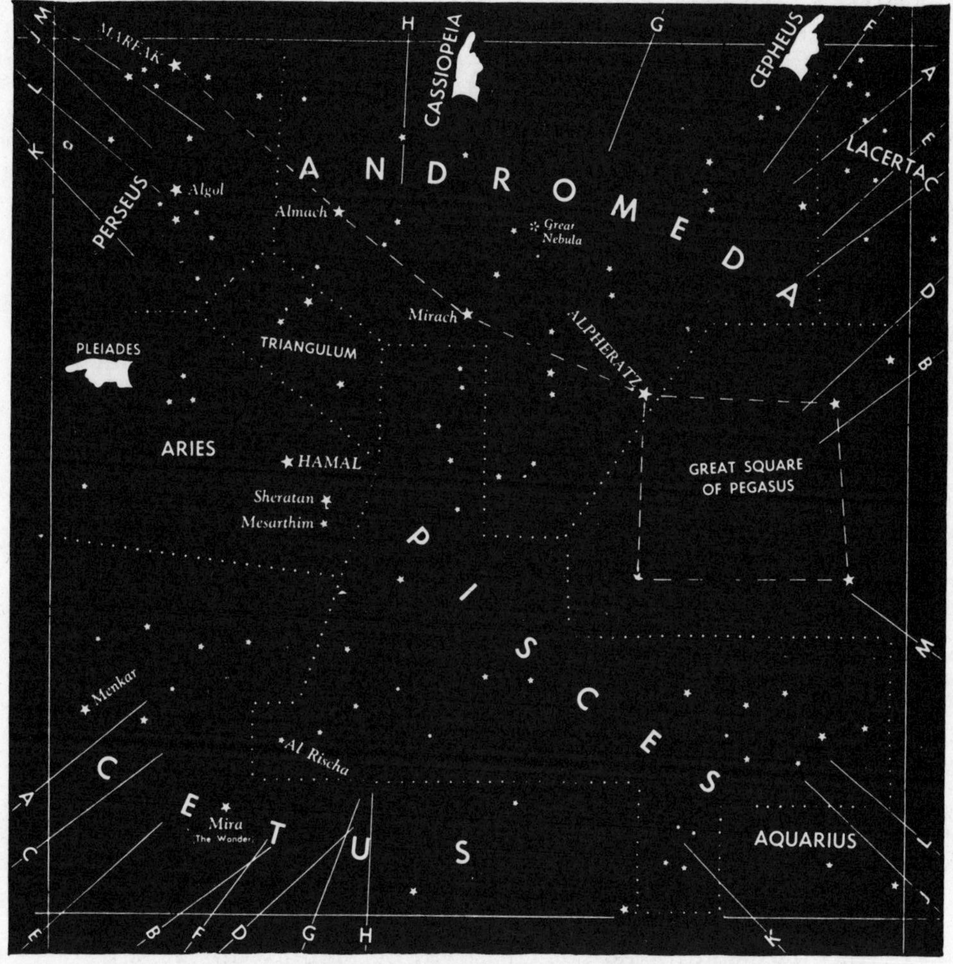


NOTE: Pisces is in the Zodiac. Beware of wandering planets.

## CETUS AND ITS NEIGHBORS

CETUS (pronounced "see-tuss; accent "see") is of interest to the experienced star-gazer almost exclusively because it contains one of the most famous irregular stars.

This star is Mira (pronounced "my-ra"; accent "my"), known for centuries as "The Wonder." Most of the time, Mira is too faint to be seen even with binoculars. Then, about every eleven months, it grows brighter, stays at an unpredictable maximum for a few weeks and then fades to invisibility again.

CETUS is supposed to represent the Sea Monster from whom Perseus saved the beautiful Andromeda—the story told in connection with Chart 3.

The various lines, AA, BB, CC, etc., on the map are to be turned vertical when specified in the Calendar.

Instructions for each line follow:

AA—face halfway between east and southeast; the circled A will be the horizon.

BB—face halfway between east and southeast; the circled B will be the horizon.

CC—face southeast; the circled C will be the horizon.

DD—face southeast; the circled D will be the horizon.

EE—face south; the circled E will be halfway up the sky.

FF—face south; the star Mira will be halfway up the sky even though it may be invisible.

GG—face south; Mira will be halfway up the sky.

HH—face southwest; Al Rischa will be halfway up the sky.

JJ—face southwest; Menkar will be halfway up the sky.

KK—face halfway between west and southwest; the circled A will be on the horizon.

# CHART 89

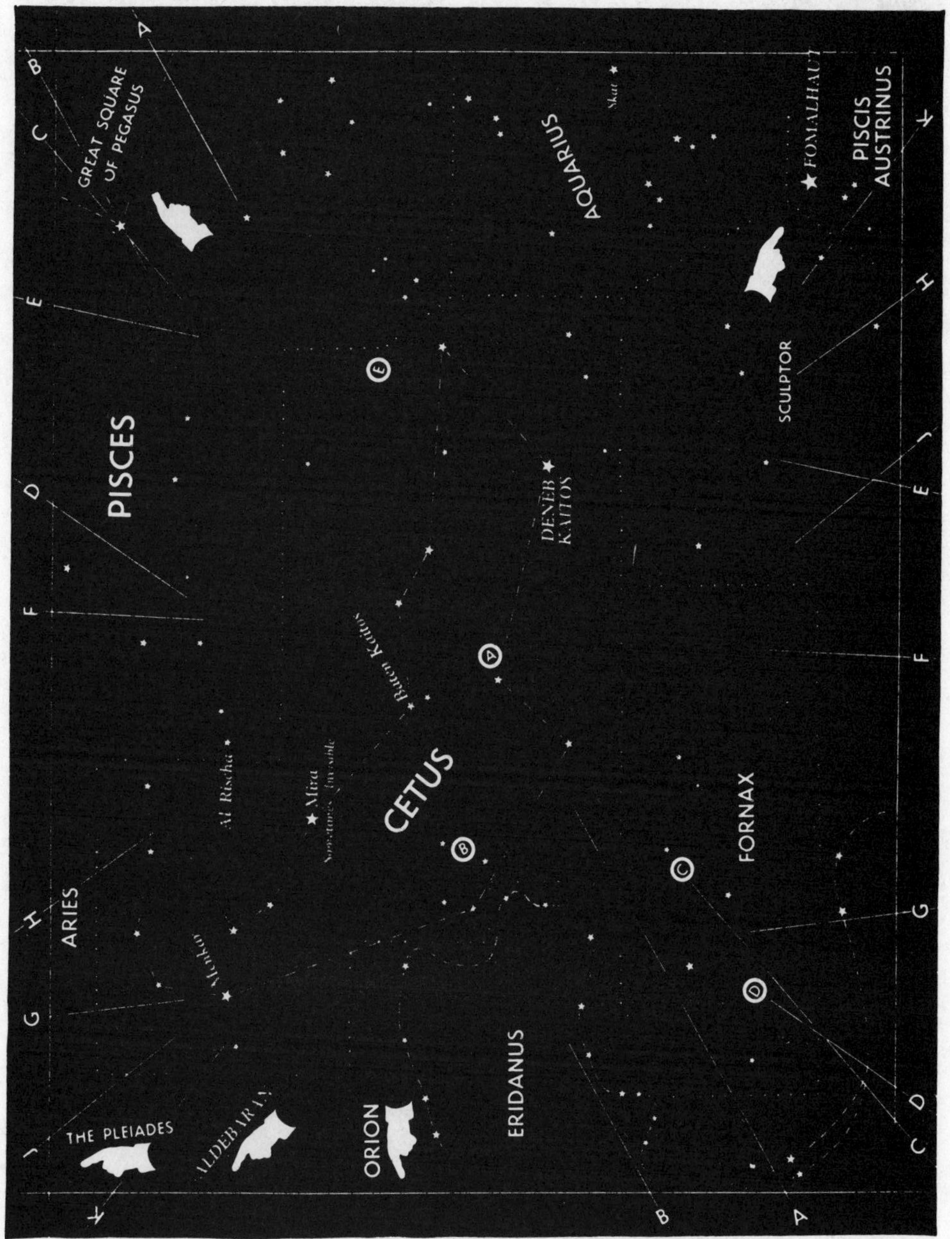


The Hour-and-Date Diagram for Cetus will be found on the next page.

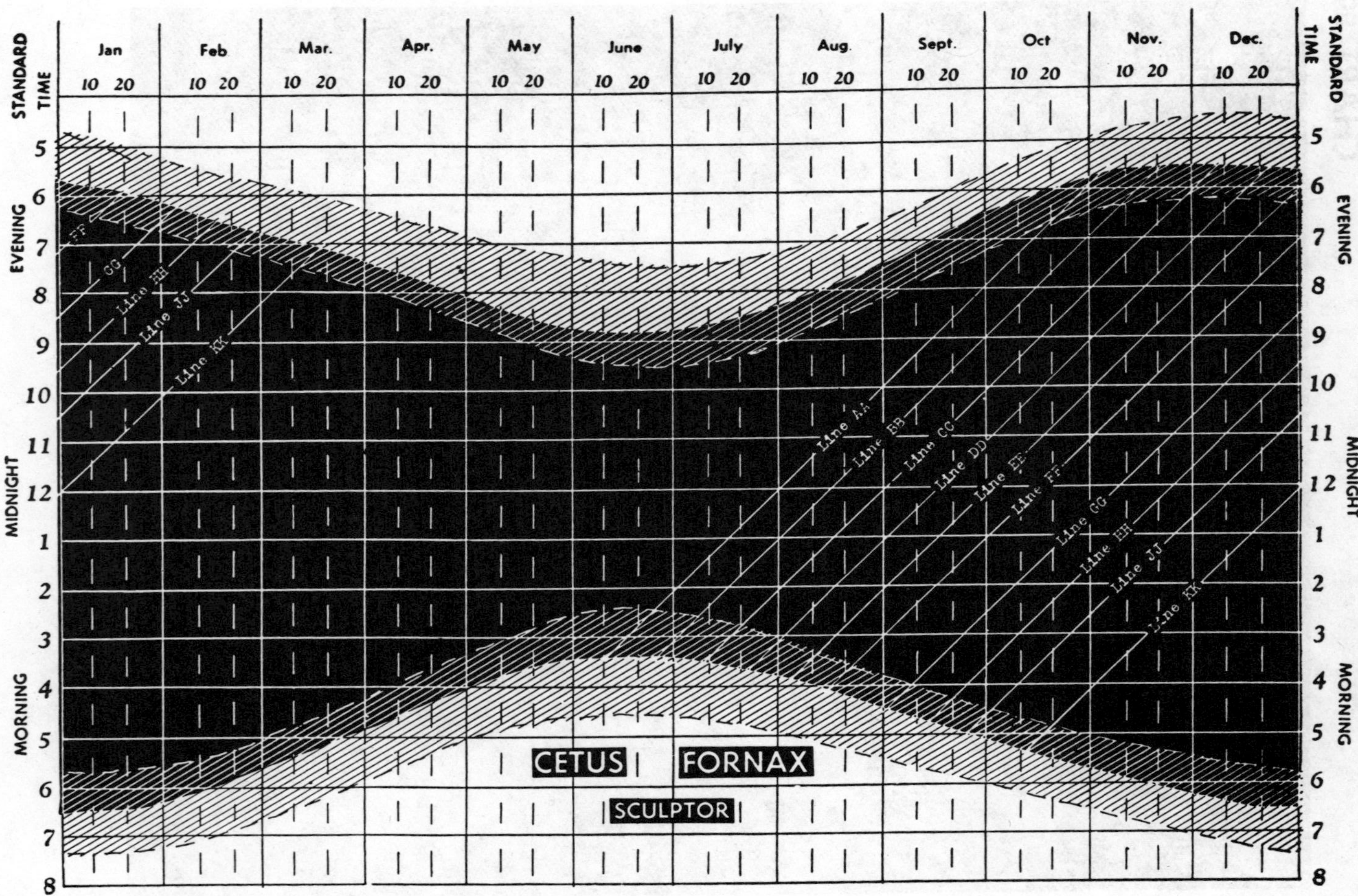
STANDARD TIME
Jan 10 20
Feb 10 20
Mar. 10 20
Apr. 10 20
May 10 20
June 10 20
July 10 20
Aug. 10 20
Sept. 10 20
Oct 10 20
Nov. 10 20
Dec. 10 20
EVENING
MIDNIGHT
MORNING
5 6 7 8 9 10 11 12 1 2 3 4 5 6 7 8
Line AA
Line BB
Line CC
Line DD
Line EE
Line FF
Line GG
Line HH
Line JJ
Line KK
CETUS
FORNAX
SCULPTOR

## ERIDANUS AND ITS NEIGHBORS

The lines AA, BB, CC, etc. are to be turned vertical at the times specified in the Calendar.

Instructions for using each line follow:

AA—face halfway between east and southeast; the circled A marks the horizon at this time.

BB—face southeast; the circled B is the horizon.

CC—face halfway between south and southeast; the circled C is the horizon.

DD—face halfway between south and southeast; the circled D is the horizon; top curve of Eridanus is almost halfway up the sky.

EE—face south; top curve of Eridanus now a little more than halfway up the sky.

FF—face halfway between south and southwest; the top curve of Eridanus is halfway up the sky.

GG—face southwest; Fornax is now on the horizon.

HH—face southwest; the star Betelgeuse is a little more than halfway up the sky.

JJ—face halfway between west and southwest; the star Zaurack is now in the haze over the horizon.

### PRONUNCIATIONS

*ERIDANUS* (pronounced "err-rid-dan-us"; accent "rid") means "the River."

CURSA—"curse-a." Accent "curse."

ZAURACK—"zore-ack." Accent "zore."

ACAMAR—"ake-am-ar." Accent "ake" (rhymes with "make").

ACHERNAR—this star is seen only by far-southerners and is not shown on this map but is on the map of Phoenix and Grus, Chart 96. It is pronounced "ake-er-nar."

*COLUMBA*—(accent "lum") means "the Dove."

*CAELUM*—"see-lum." Accent "see." This word means "the Graving Tool" and refers to the tools used by stone-carvers.

*LEPUS*—"lee-puss." Accent "lee." This word means "the Hare."

ARNEB—as spelled. Accent "ar."

NIHAL—"nye-al." Accent "nye" (rhymes with "rye").

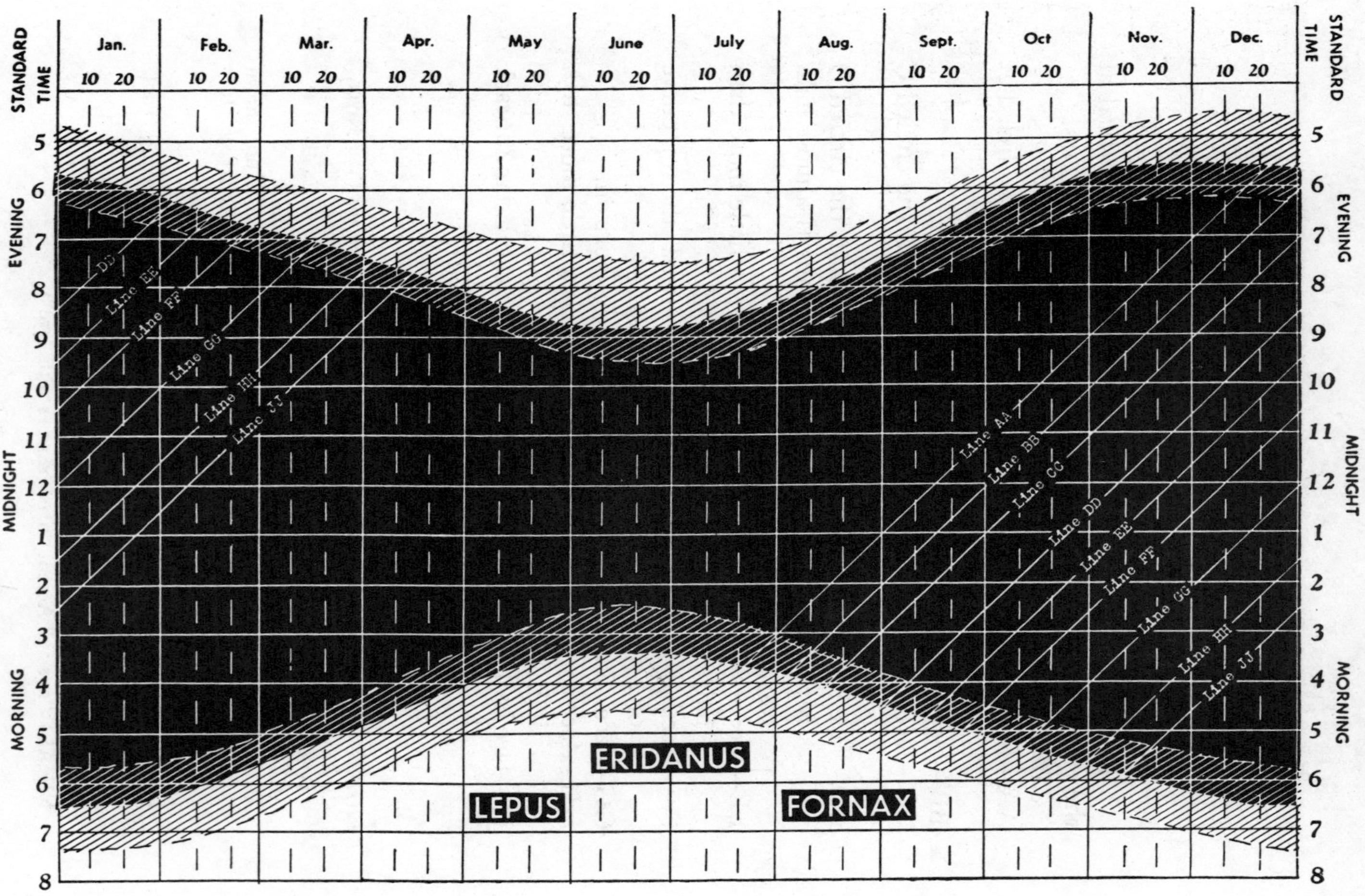
STANDARD TIME
Jan. 10 20
Feb. 10 20
Mar. 10 20
Apr. 10 20
May 10 20
June 10 20
July 10 20
Aug. 10 20
Sept. 10 20
Oct 10 20
Nov. 10 20
Dec. 10 20
EVENING
MIDNIGHT
MORNING
5 6 7 8 9 10 11 12 1 2 3 4 5 6 7 8
Line AA
Line BB
Line CC
Line DD
Line EE
Line FF
Line GG
Line HH
Line JJ
ERIDANUS
LEPUS
FORNAX

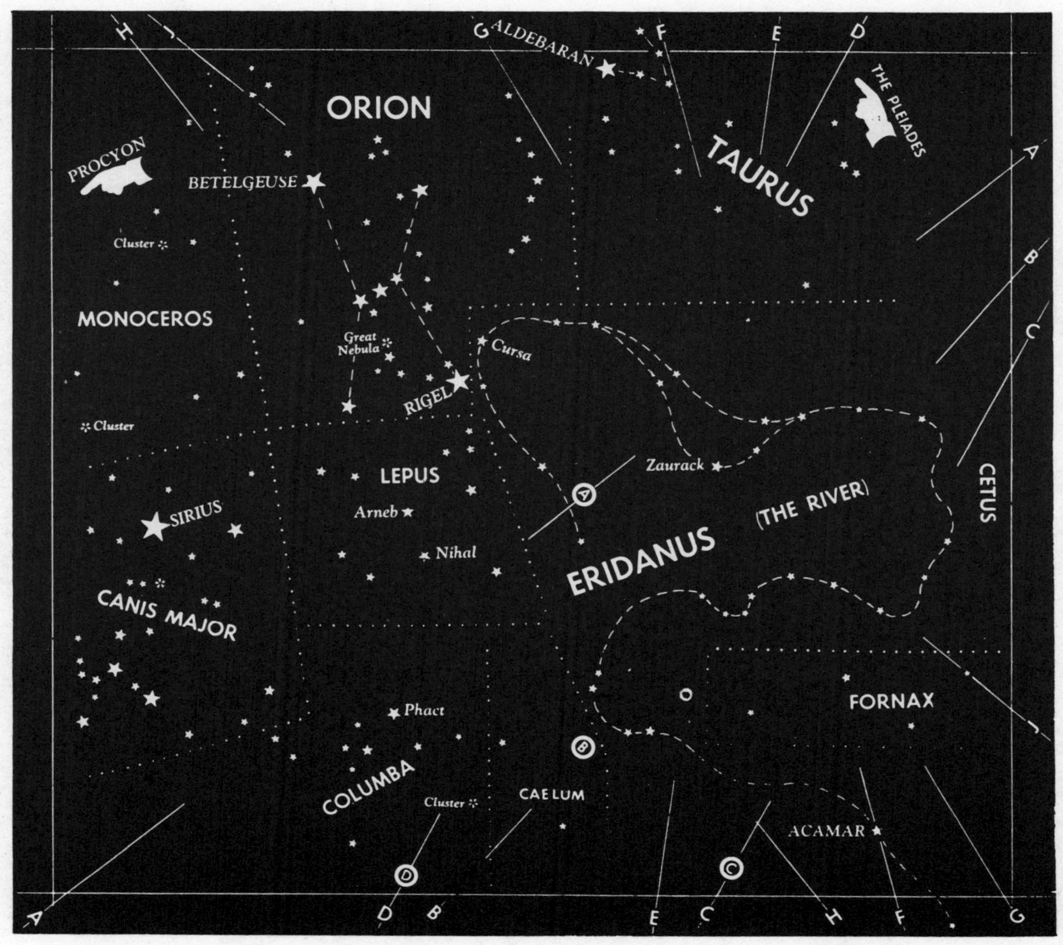

ORION
ALDEBARAN
TAURUS
THE PLEIADES
PROCYON
BETELGEUSE
Cluster
MONOCEROS
Great Nebula
Cursa
RIGEL
Cluster
LEPUS
Zaurack
Arneb
SIRIUS
Nihal
(THE RIVER)
ERIDANUS
CETUS
CANIS MAJOR
Phact
FORNAX
COLUMBA
Cluster
CAELUM
ACAMAR


# CHART 90

## LITTLE GROUPS AROUND CYGNUS—VULPECULA, LACERTA, EQUULEUS, DELPHINUS, SAGITTA

AA—face halfway between east and northeast; the circled A will be the horizon.

BB—face halfway between east and northeast; the star Vega will be halfway up the sky.

CC—face halfway between east and northeast; the upper arm of the Northern Cross will be halfway up the sky.

DD—face east; the Great Square will be on the horizon.

EE—face east; the lowest corners of Vulpecula and Cygnus will be halfway up the sky.

FF—face between east and southeast; Vega overhead.

GG—face southeast; Scheat will be halfway up the sky.

HH—face south; Cygnus will be overhead.

JJ—face south; Cygnus and Lacerta will be overhead.

KK—face between west and southwest; Lacerta will be overhead.

LL—face west; Vulpecula will be halfway up the sky.

MM—face west; center of Northern Cross half-way up the sky.

NN—face halfway between west and northwest; the bottom corner of the map will be on the horizon.

OO—face between west and northwest; Sagitta on horizon.

PP—face northwest; the circled letter P will be on the horizon.

This map of Cygnus shows the little star known as 61 Cygni. This was the first star whose distance was ascertained by the surveyor's method of triangulation. The distance is 10.4 light-years. These seems much evidence that there may be an actual planet involved in the system.

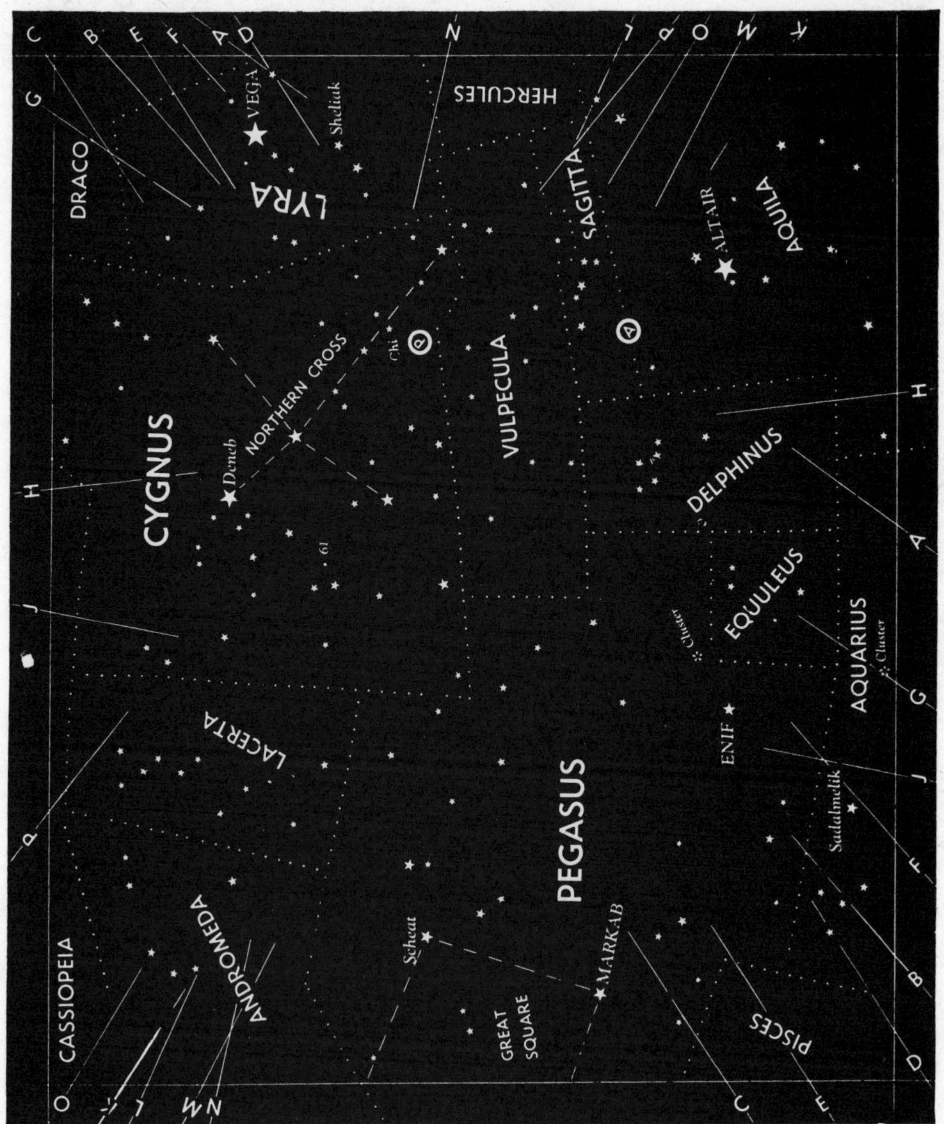


The Hour-and-Date Diagram for this map will be found on the next page.

## PRONUNCIATIONS

*VULPECULA*—"pronounced "vul-peck-you-la." Accent "peck." The word means "Fox."

*SAGITTA*—pronounced "saj-it-ta." Accent "it." The "saj" rhymes with "Madge." Means "the Arrow."

*DELPHINUS*—pronounced "del-fine-us." Accent "fine." Means "the Dolphin."

*EQUULEUS*—pronounced "ee-kwool-ee-us." Accent "kwool." Means "the Colt."

*LACERTA*—pronounced "la-sur-ta." Accent "sur." Means "the Lizard."

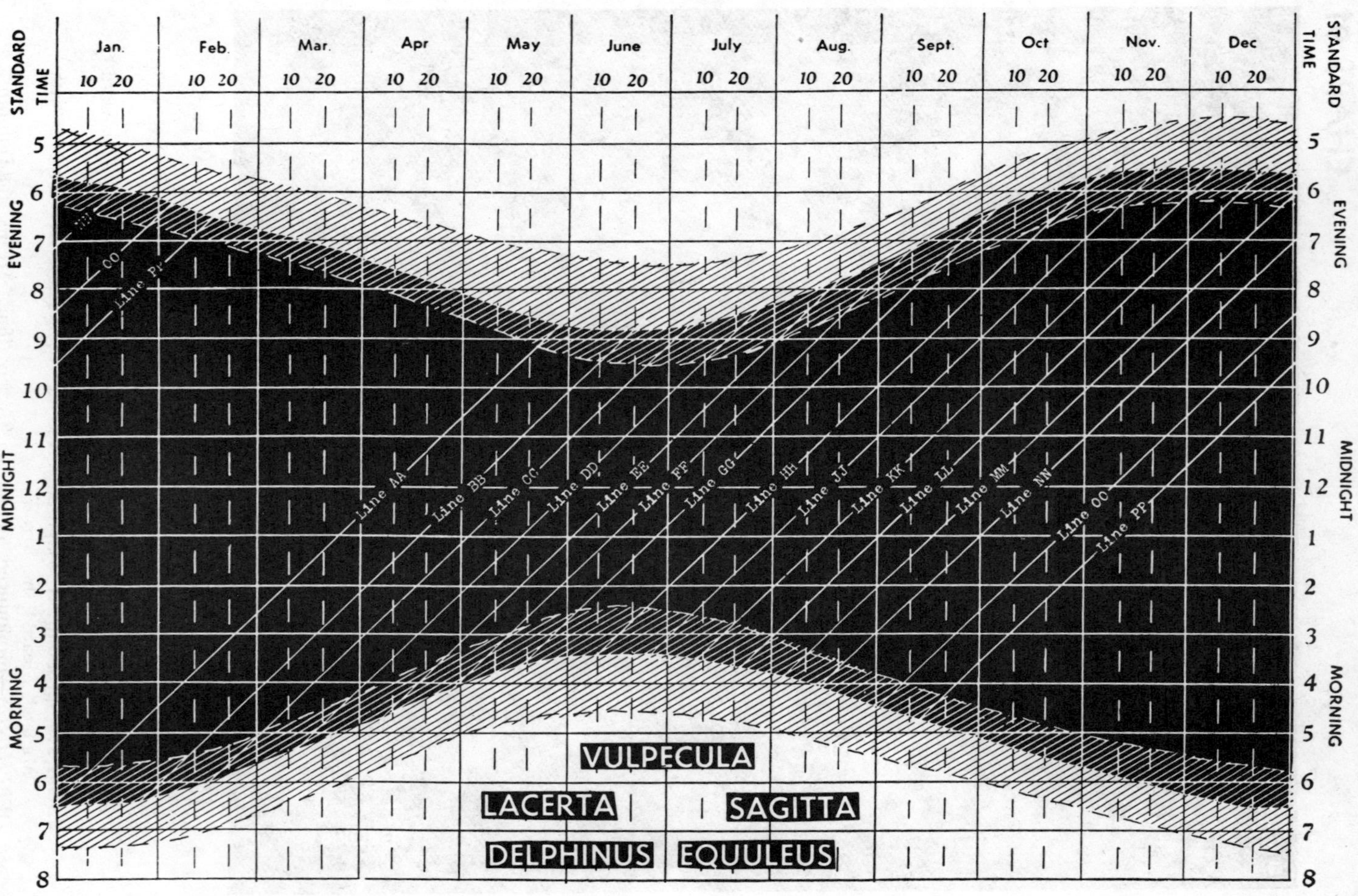
STANDARD TIME
Jan. 10 20
Feb. 10 20
Mar. 10 20
Apr 10 20
May 10 20
June 10 20
July 10 20
Aug. 10 20
Sept. 10 20
Oct 10 20
Nov. 10 20
Dec 10 20
EVENING
MIDNIGHT
MORNING
5 6 7 8 9 10 11 12 1 2 3 4 5 6 7 8
Line AA
Line BB
Line CC
Line DD
Line EE
Line FF
Line GG
Line HH
Line JJ
Line KK
Line LL
Line MM
Line NN
Line OO
Line PP
VULPECULA
LACERTA
SAGITTA
DELPHINUS
EQUULEUS

## CANCER, LYNX AND LEO MINOR

Cancer, Gemini and Leo are in the Zodiac; beware of planets. Cancer means "the Crab." Praesepe (pronounced "pree-see-pee"; accent "see") is a loose cluster visible to the naked eye in clear weather. Acubens is pronounced "ack-you-bens"; accent "ack."

The lines on the map—AA, BB, CC, etc.—are to be held vertical at the times specified in the Calendar.

Instructions for the use of the lines follow:

AA—face northeast; only the upper part of Lynx is above the horizon.

BB—face northeast; about one-half of the map is above the horizon.

CC—face halfway between east and northeast; the hand pointing at Capella is halfway up the sky.

DD—face halfway between east and northeast; Hydra and the blade of the Sickle are on the horizon.

EE—face east; Castor and Pollux are now halfway up the sky.

FF—face east; Cancer is halfway up the sky.

GG—face halfway between east and southeast; the Sickle is now halfway up the sky.

HH—face south; Lynx is overhead for Canadians, Cancer for far-southerners.

JJ—face south; Lynx still overhead for Canadians and Cancer for southerners but they have moved westward.

KK—face halfway between west and southwest; Procyon and Alhena are nearly halfway up the sky.

LL—face west; the top edge of Cancer is halfway up the sky.

MM—face west; the Sickle is halfway up the sky.

NN—face halfway between west and northwest; Castor and Pollux barely above the horizon.

OO—face halfway between west and northwest; horizon cuts through the middle of Cancer.

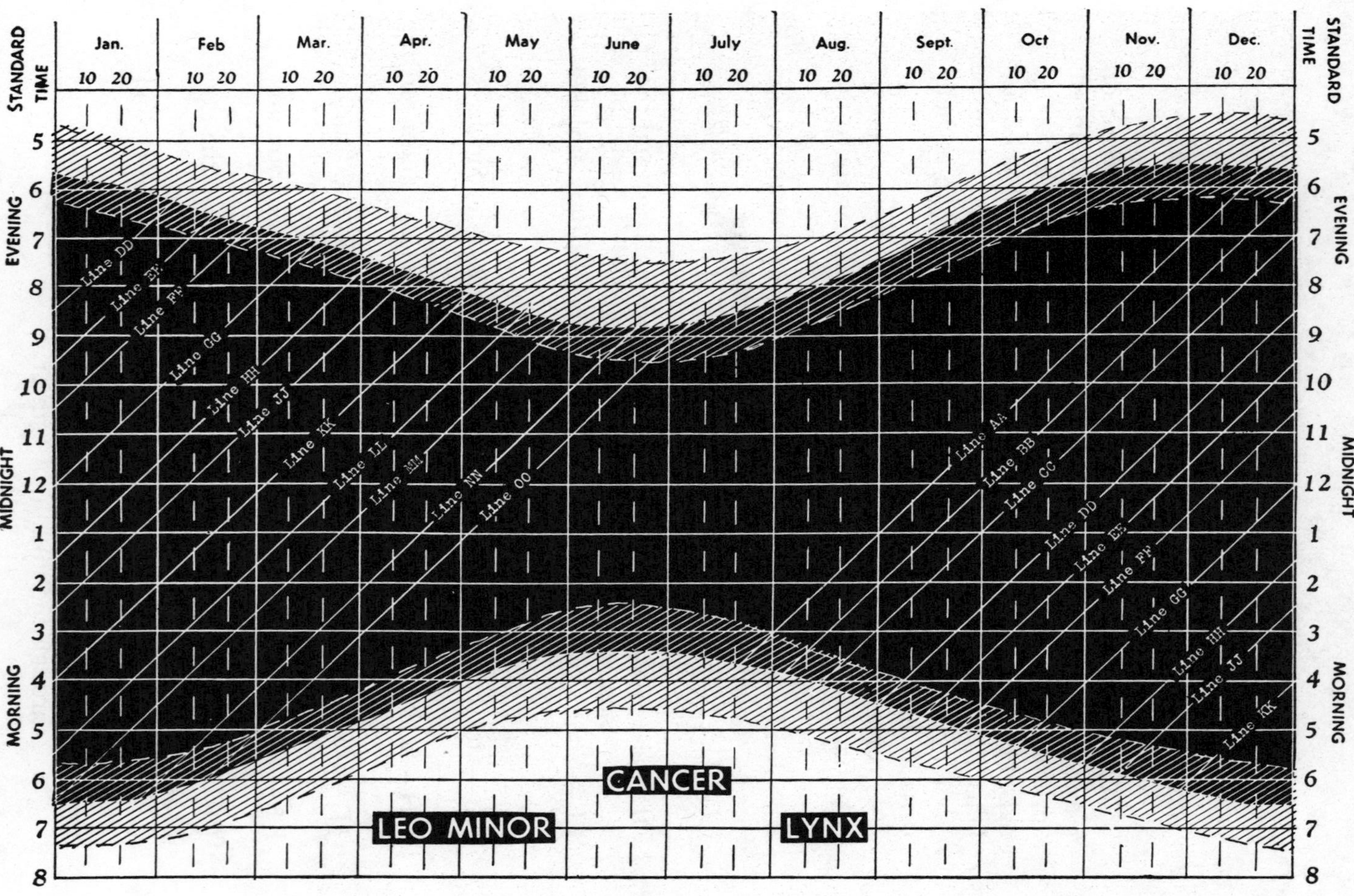

STANDARD TIME
Jan. Feb Mar. Apr. May June July Aug. Sept. Oct Nov. Dec.
10 20
5 6 7 8 9 10 11 12 1 2 3 4 5 6 7 8
EVENING
MIDNIGHT
MORNING
Line AA
Line BB
Line CC
Line DD
Line EE
Line FF
Line GG
Line HH
Line JJ
Line KK
Line LL
Line MM
Line NN
Line OO
CANCER
LEO MINOR
LYNX

# CHART 92

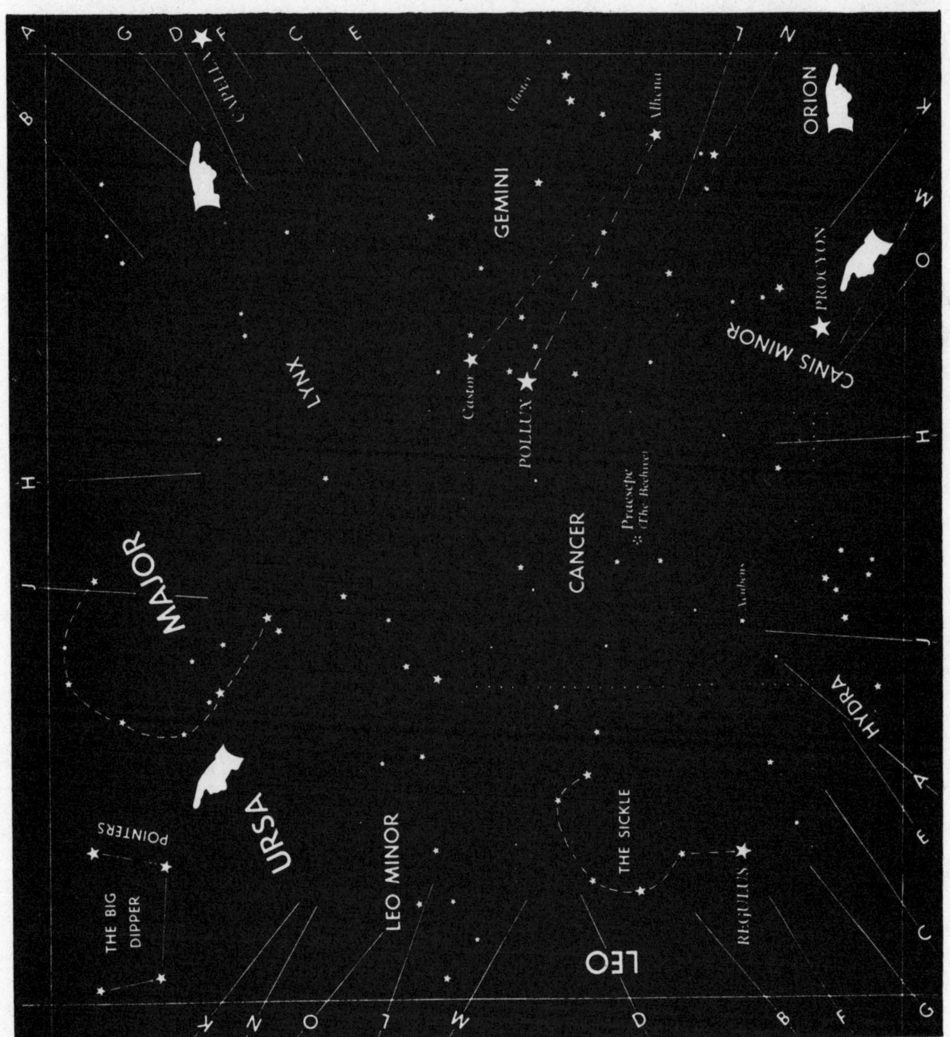

ORION
PROCYON
CANIS MINOR
GEMINI
Alhena
Castor
POLLUX
CAPELLA
LYNX
CANCER
Praesepe
(The Beehive)
Acubens
HYDRA
THE SICKLE
REGULUS
LEO
LEO MINOR
URSA MAJOR
POINTERS
THE BIG DIPPER

## MONOCEROS AND ITS CLUSTERS

The name is pronounced "mone-oss-err-oss"; accent "oss." Means "Unicorn." There is little in this constellation for the naked-eye observer. Binoculars will reveal two attractive star clusters and brilliant areas of the Milky Way. The cluster near the line from Betelgeuse to Procyon is known technically as NGC 2244. The cluster near the line from Sirius to Procyon is M50—a favorite with amateurs.

The lines AA, BB, CC, etc. are to be held vertical at the times specified in the Calendar.

Instructions for the use of each line follow:

AA—face east; the star Procyon will be just clear of the horizon haze.

BB—face halfway between east and southeast; the stars of Puppis are just under the horizon.

CC—face southeast; the horizon runs just over Pyxis; the star Betelgeuse is halfway up the sky.

DD—face southeast; the bottom of the map will then be on the horizon.

EE—face south; the lower part of Monoceros is halfway up the sky.

FF—face south; the lower part of Monoceros is halfway up the sky.

GG—face southwest; the top of Monoceros is halfway up the sky.

HH—face halfway between west and southwest; Lepus is on the horizon.

JJ—face halfway between west and southwest; the horizon cuts across just above Sirius; Sirius is now visible only to very-far-southerners.

# CHART 93

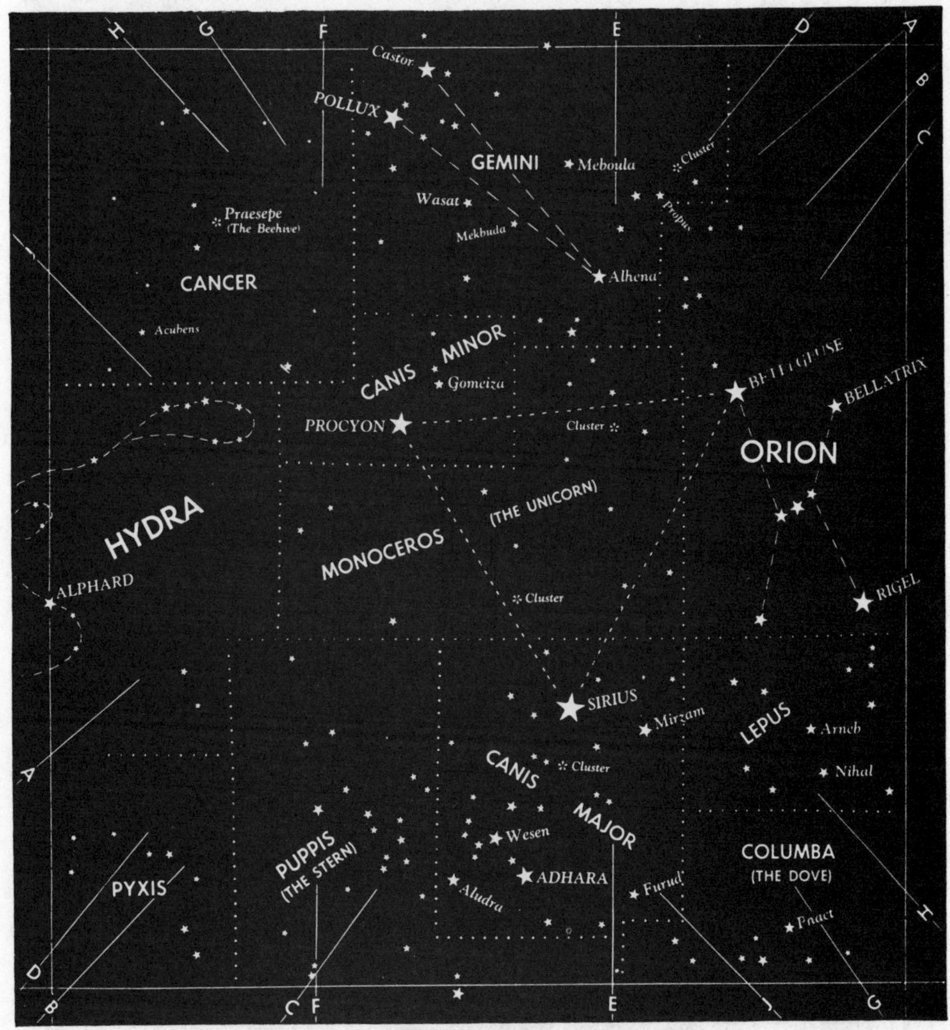


The Hour-and-Date Diagram for this Chart will be found on the next page.

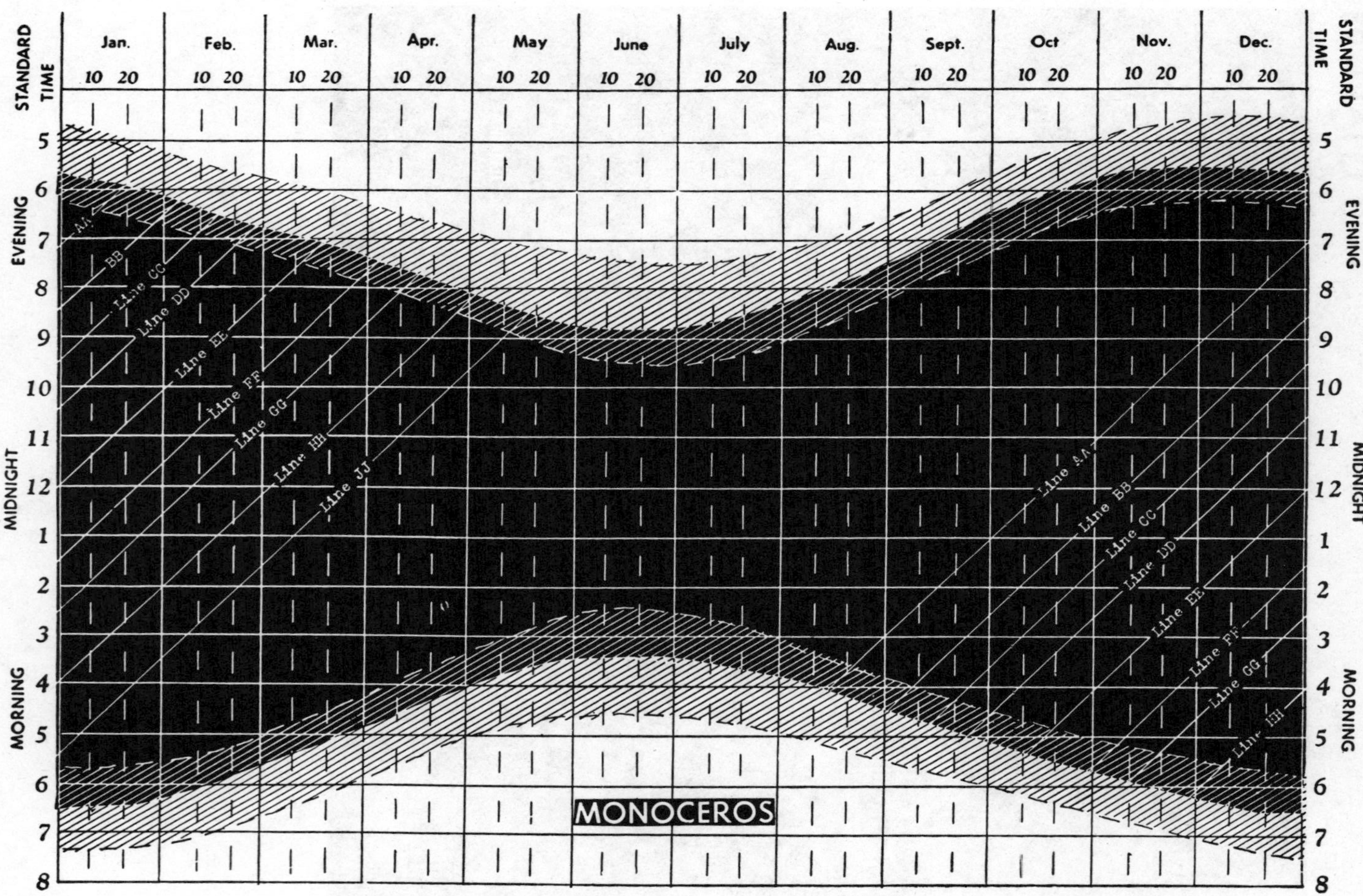

STANDARD TIME
Jan. 10 20
Feb. 10 20
Mar. 10 20
Apr. 10 20
May 10 20
June 10 20
July 10 20
Aug. 10 20
Sept. 10 20
Oct 10 20
Nov. 10 20
Dec. 10 20
EVENING
MIDNIGHT
MORNING
5 6 7 8 9 10 11 12 1 2 3 4 5 6 7 8
Line AA
Line BB
Line CC
Line DD
Line EE
Line FF
Line GG
Line HH
Line JJ
MONOCEROS

## HYDRA AND HIS NEIGHBORS

The lines AA, BB, CC, etc. are to be held vertical at the times specified in the Calendar. Hold the map according to these instructions:

AA—face east; only the head shows; the stars Zosma in Leo and Alphard in Hydra are barely above the horizon.

BB—face east; Sextans is now resting on the horizon.

CC—face southeast; Crater is resting on the horizon.

DD—face southeast; Corvus is on the horizon.

EE—face halfway between south and southeast; the top of Sextans and the twist in Hydra's neck are halfway up the sky.

FF—face south; Sextans is halfway up the sky.

GG—face southwest; Sextans is halfway up the sky.

HH—face southwest; Regulus is halfway up the sky.

JJ—face southwest; the letter "G" in the word "Virgo" is halfway up the sky; the Hydra's head is due west.

KK—face southwest; Vindemiatrix is halfway up the sky.

NOTE: Hydra is a southern constellation; therefore remember that these heights are for observers in mid-United States. For Canadians, the stars will always be a little lower than indicated; for far-southerners, a little higher.

### PRONUNCIATIONS

*HYDRA, CORVUS, CRATER* and *SEXTANS* are pronounced as spelled.

ALPHARD is accented on the first syllable.

ALCHIBA—"al-kee-ba." Accent "kee."

GIENA—"jee-na." Accent "jee."

ALGORES—"al-go-rays." Accent "go." This star is also known as ALGORAB.

ALKES—"al-kez." Accent "al."

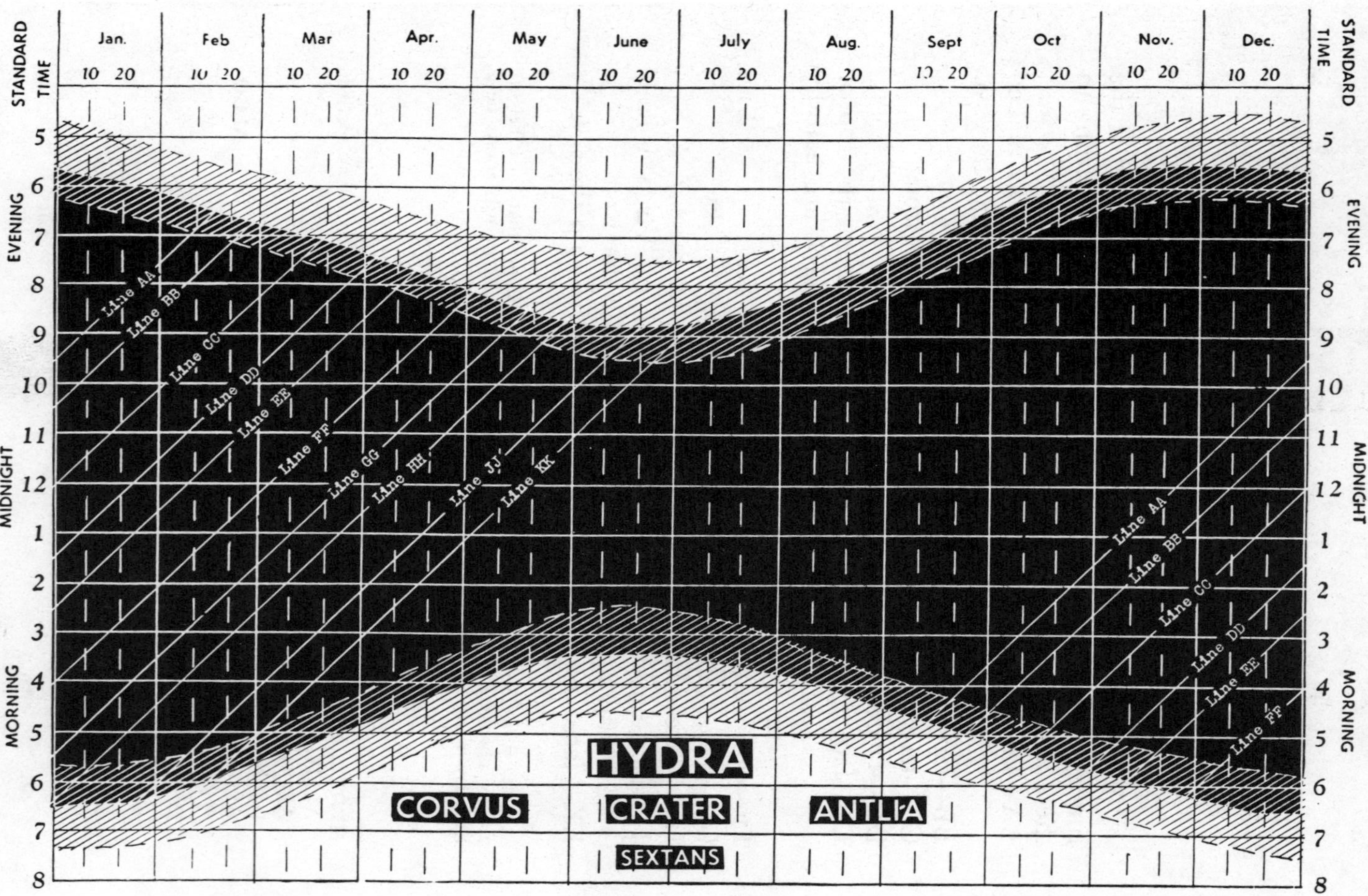

STANDARD TIME
Jan. Feb Mar Apr. May June July Aug. Sept Oct Nov. Dec.
10 20
EVENING
MIDNIGHT
MORNING
5 6 7 8 9 10 11 12 1 2 3 4 5 6 7 8
Line AA
Line BB
Line CC
Line DD
Line EE
Line FF
Line GG
Line HH
Line JJ
Line KK
HYDRA
CORVUS
CRATER
ANTLIA
SEXTANS

# CHART 94

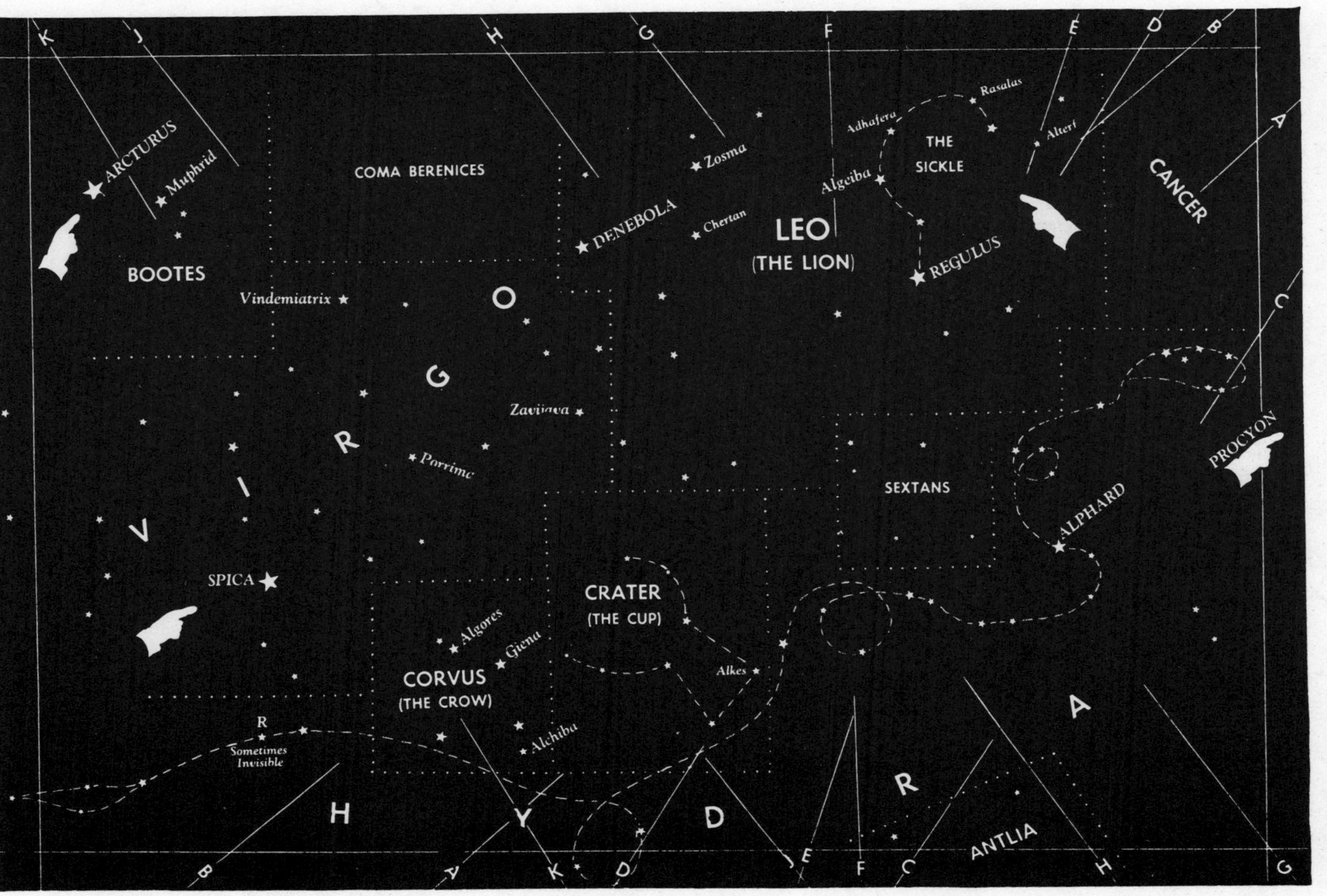

ARCTURUS
Muphrid
BOOTES
COMA BERENICES
Zosma
DENEBOLA
Chertan
Adhafera
Rasalas
Algeiba
THE
SICKLE
Alterf
LEO
(THE LION)
REGULUS
CANCER
Vindemiatrix
V I R G O
Zaviiava
Porrima
PROCYON
SEXTANS
ALPHARD
SPICA
CRATER
(THE CUP)
Algores
Giena
CORVUS
(THE CROW)
Alkes
Alchiba
R
Sometimes
Invisible
H Y D R A
ANTLIA

## CANES VENATICI AND COMA BERENICES

*CANES VENATICI*—means "Hunting Dogs." Pronounced "kane-neez ven-at-tiss-sy." Accent "kane" and "at."

COR CAROLI—pronounced "kore carol-eye."

*COMA BERENICES*—means "Berenice's Hair." Pronounced "ko-ma berry-nye-seez. Accent "ko" and "nye."

The lines AA, BB, CC, etc. will be specified at various times in the Calendar. They are always to be turned vertical in accordance with the instructions which follow:

AA—face northeast; the circled A will be on the horizon.

BB—face halfway between east and northeast; the bottom border of Ursa Major will be halfway up the sky.

CC—face halfway between east and northeast; the star Cor Caroli will be halfway up the sky.

DD—face east; the top of the map will be overhead.

EE—face south; Canes Venatici will be overhead.

FF—face south; Canes Venatici will be overhead.

GG—face south; Canes Venatici will be overhead.

HH—face west; the letter E in Boötes will be overhead; bottom of Coma Berenices will be halfway up the sky.

JJ—face west; Coma Berenices will be halfway up the sky.

KK—face halfway between west and northwest; the handle of the Big Dipper will be halfway up the sky.

LL—face halfway between west and northwest; the star Seginus in Boötes will be halfway up the sky.

MM—face halfway between west and northwest; Coma Berenices will be on the horizon.

# CHART 95

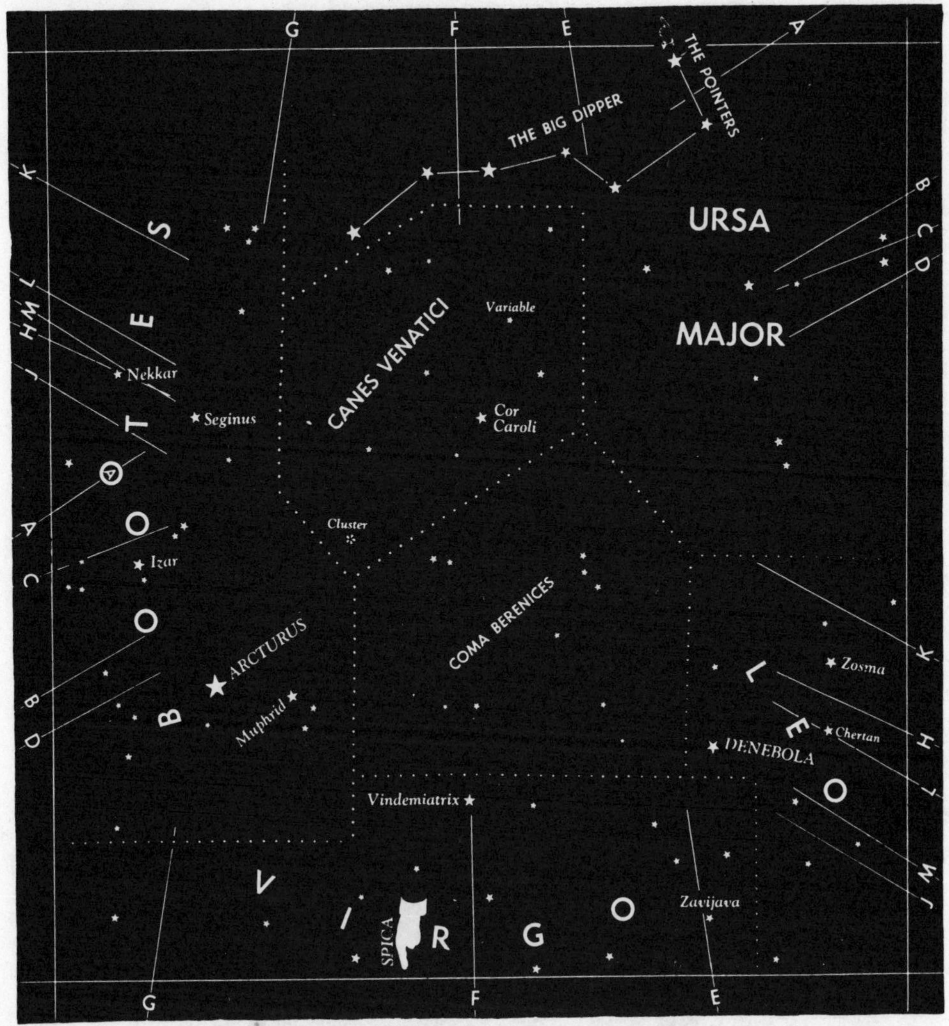


The Hour-and-Date Diagram for this Chart will be found on the next page.

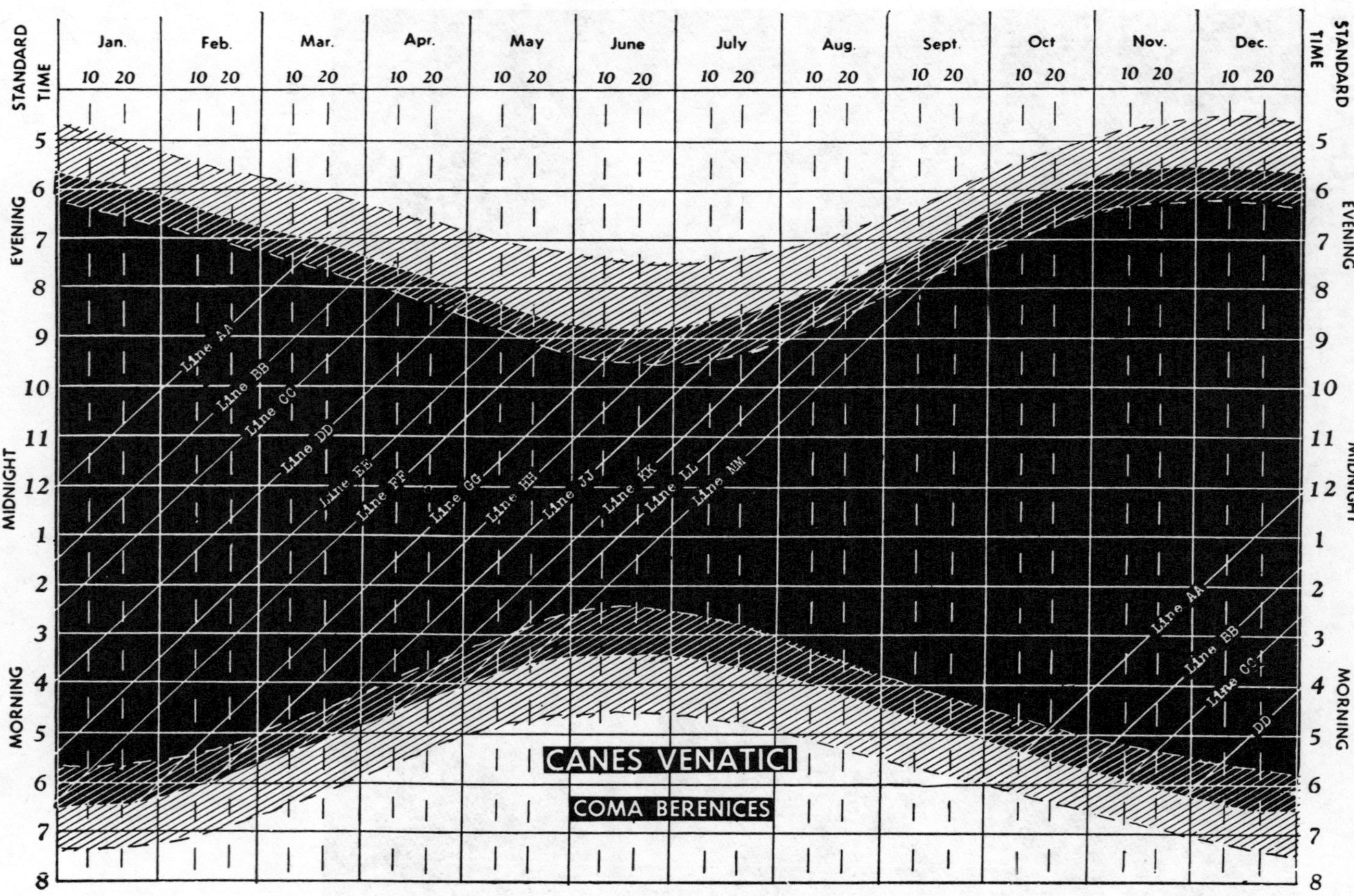
STANDARD TIME
Jan. 10 20
Feb. 10 20
Mar. 10 20
Apr. 10 20
May 10 20
June 10 20
July 10 20
Aug. 10 20
Sept. 10 20
Oct 10 20
Nov. 10 20
Dec. 10 20
EVENING
MIDNIGHT
MORNING
5 6 7 8 9 10 11 12 1 2 3 4 5 6 7 8
Line AA
Line BB
Line CC
Line DD
Line EE
Line FF
Line GG
Line HH
Line JJ
Line KK
Line LL
Line MM
CANES VENATICI
COMA BERENICES

# PHOENIX AND GRUS

The lines AA, BB, CC, etc. are to be turned to the vertical whenever they are specified in the Calendar.

The lines must be used according to the instructions that follow:

AA—face halfway between south and southeast; the circled A indicates the horizon at this time.
BB—face south; the circled B is the horizon.
CC—face south; the word "Grus" is the horizon.
DD—face south; the "X" in "Phoenix" is the horizon.
EE—face south; again the "X" in "Phoenix" is the horizon.
FF—face south; the circled F is the horizon.

Phoenix and Grus never rise far enough above the southern horizon to be good for Canadians and they are seen only briefly and none too well by star-gazers in the middle belt across the United States.

Far-southerners, however, have quite clear views of them and of the faint and quite inconsequential constellations Horologium (the Clock) and Microscopium (the Microscope).

## PRONUNCIATIONS

*PHOENIX* is pronounced "fee-nicks." Accent "fee."
*GRUS* is pronounced to rhyme with "fuss," "muss."

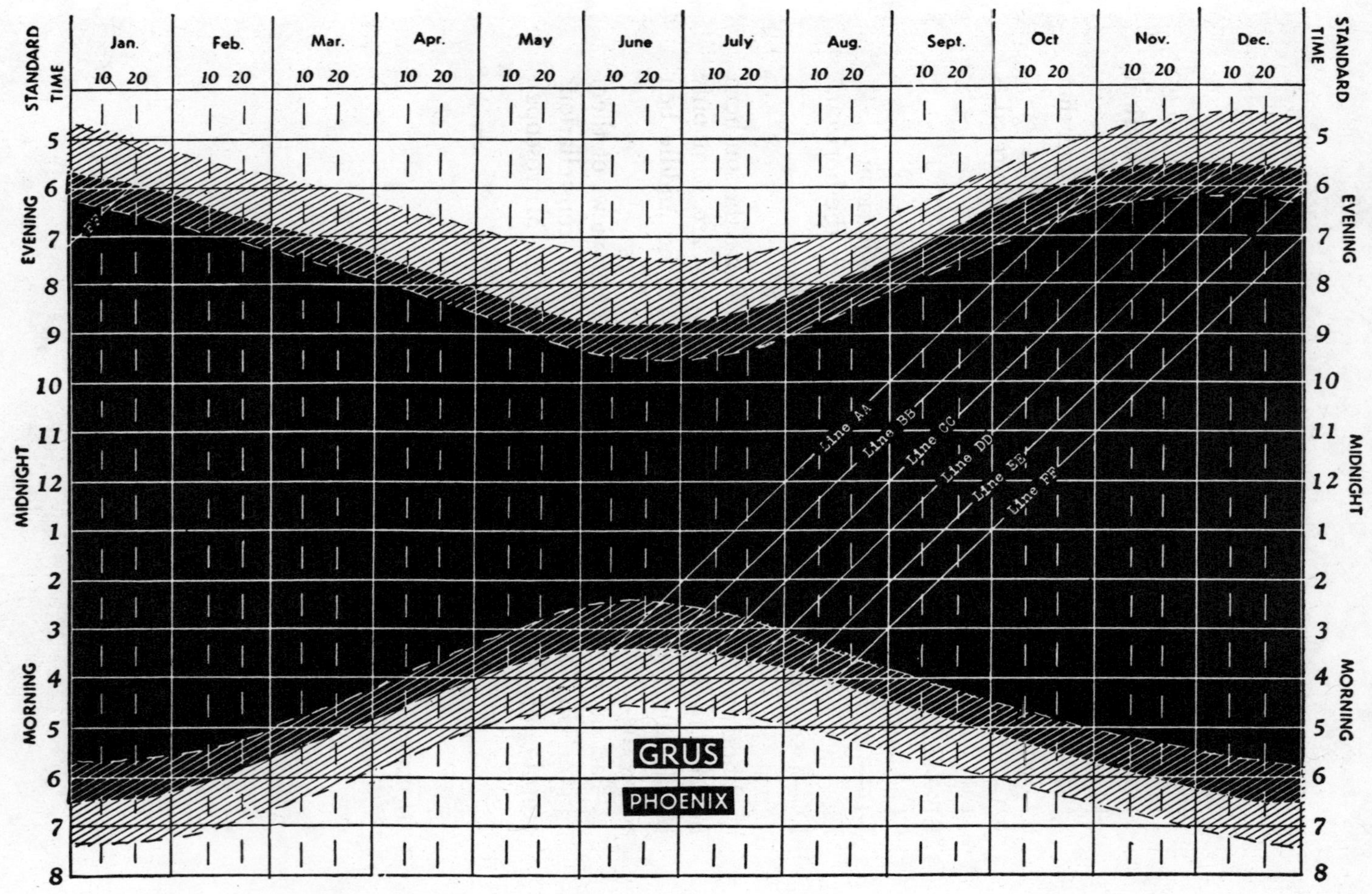
STANDARD TIME
Jan. 10 20
Feb. 10 20
Mar. 10 20
Apr. 10 20
May 10 20
June 10 20
July 10 20
Aug. 10 20
Sept. 10 20
Oct 10 20
Nov. 10 20
Dec. 10 20
EVENING
MIDNIGHT
MORNING
5 6 7 8 9 10 11 12 1 2 3 4 5 6 7 8
Line AA
Line BB
Line CC
Line DD
Line EE
Line FF
GRUS
PHOENIX

# CHART 96

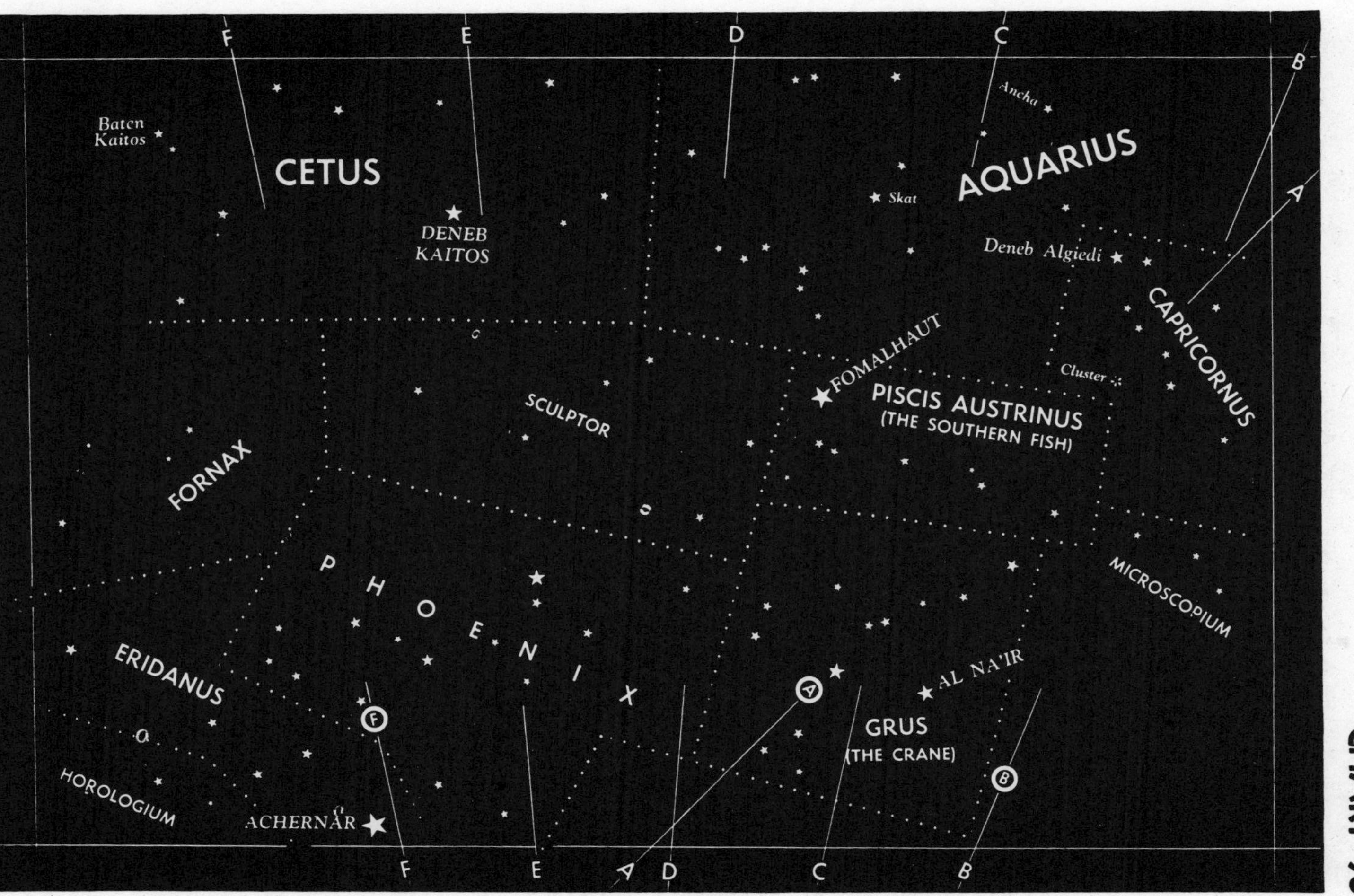

Baten
Kaitos
CETUS
DENEB
KAITOS
AQUARIUS
Ancha
Skat
Deneb Algiedi
CAPRICORNUS
Cluster
FOMALHAUT
PISCIS AUSTRINUS
(THE SOUTHERN FISH)
SCULPTOR
FORNAX
MICROSCOPIUM
PHOENIX
ERIDANUS
HOROLOGIUM
ACHERNAR
AL NA'IR
GRUS
(THE CRANE)
A
B
C
D
E
F

# INDEX

The following abbreviations are used in this Index—Chapt. (chapter); Cht. (chart); Pron. (pronunciation); Sect. (section); Diag. (diagram); H-D (Hour-and-date diagram); Phot. (photograph); Def. (definition).

In the case of charts, the number *is the chart number,* not the page number.

## INDEX

## INDEX

ALPHA DRACONIS

ALCYONE (CENTER POINT SUNS ORBIT) [Pole Star] △
BRIGHTEST STAR PLEIADES

PLEIADES / ATLANTIDES — 7 SISTERS — ATLAS / ATLANTIS
(OCCULT / ESOTERIC)

MAIA
ELECTRA ASTEROPE MEROPE
TAYGETA CELAENO ALCYONE

POLARIS – FAR END URSA MINOR'S TAIL

URSA MAJOR (7 STARS) (PLEIADES?) (SIRIUS)

PLEIADES / GREAT BEAR / SIRUS

SIRIUS (DOG STAR)

*ORION — GREAT NEBULA NIMROD